COLLEGE
READING
AND
STUDY
SKILLS

COLLEGE READING AND STUDY SKILLS

Robert D. Postman
Barbara Keckler
Peter Schneckner

MERCY COLLEGE
Dobbs Ferry, N.Y.

Macmillan Publishing Company
New York
Collier Macmillan Publishers
London

Macmillan Publishing Company
866 Third Avenue, New York, New York 10022
Collier Macmillan Canada, Inc.

Library of Congress Cataloging in Publication Data
Postman, Robert D.
  College reading and study skills.

  Includes index.
  1. Study, Method of. 2. Reading (Higher education)
I. Keckler, Barbara. II. Schneckner, Peter. III. Title.
LB2395.P67 1985   428.4'07'11   83-11269
ISBN 0-02-396170-8

Printing: 1 2 3 4 5 6 7 8   Year: 5 6 7 8 9 0 1 2 3

ISBN 0-02-396170-8 NB2I

ACKNOWLEDGMENTS

Grateful acknowledgment is made to the following for permission to reprint previously published material:

Academic Press, Inc.: Excerpts from *Invitation to Psychology* by Houston, Bee, and Hatfield. Copyright © 1979 by Academic Press, Inc. Used with permission.

Amsco School Publications, Inc.: Excerpt reprinted from *Review Text in American History* by Irving Gordon. Copyright © 1981 by Irving Gordon. Excerpt reprinted from *Basic Principles of American Government* by Sanford and Green. Copyright © 1977 by Sanford and Green. Used with permission of Amsco School Publications, Inc.

Thomas Elliott Berry: Adapted from *Journalism Today* by Thomas Elliott Berry. Copyright © 1958 by Chilton Co. Reprinted by permission of the author.

Brandt & Brandt Literary Agents, Inc.: Excerpt from "The Devil and Daniel Webster" by Stephen Vincent Benet, from *The Selected Works of Stephen Vincent Benet*. Copyright, 1936, by the Curtis Publishing Company. Copyright renewed © 1964 by Thomas C. Benet, Stephanie B. Mahin, and Rachel B. Lewis. Reprinted by permission of Brandt & Brandt Literary Agents, Inc.

Cambridge Book Company: Excerpt from *Interpretation of Reading Materials in the Natural Sciences* by John T. Walsh. Copyright © 1973 by Cambridge Book Company. Reprinted by permission of the publisher.

The Conservationist: "Snake Bit!" by Milan Fiske, from *The Conservationist*, Vol. 36, No. 1, July –August 1981. Reprinted by permission of the publisher.

Frank Marshall Davis: "The Four Glimpses of Night" by Frank Marshall Davis, from *American Negro Poetry*, ed. by Arna Bontemps (Farrar, Straus & Giroux, Inc.). "Four Glimpses of Night" by Frank Marshall Davis, from *The Poetry of Black America*, ed. by Arnold Adoff (Harper & Row). Reprinted by permission of Frank Marshall Davis.

Doubleday & Company, Inc.: Excerpt from *Judas Kiss* by Victoria Holt. Copyright © 1981 by Victoria Holt. Reprinted by permission of Doubleday & Company, Inc.

Dover Publications, Inc.: Excerpts from *The Game of Logic*, 1897, by C. L. Dodgson. Reprinted by permission of Dover Publications, Inc.

Farrar, Straus & Giroux, Inc.: Excerpt from "Salvation" from *The Big Sea* by Langston Hughes. Copyright 1940 by Langston Hughes. Copyright renewed © 1968 by Arna Bontemps and George Houston Bass. Reprinted by permission of Hill and Wang (a division of Farrar, Straus & Giroux, Inc.).

Harcourt Brace Jovanovich, Inc.: Excerpt from *The Mainstream of Civilization*, Third Edition, by Joseph Strayer and Hans Gatzke, copyright © 1979 by Harcourt Brace Jovanovich, Inc. Reprinted and reproduced by permission of the publisher. Excerpt from p. 56 of *Warriner's English Grammar and Composition*, Heritage Edition, 1973, by John Warriner and Francis Griffith. Reprinted by permission of the publisher.

Harper & Row, Publishers, Inc.: Excerpt from Chapter 1, "Backdrop of Poverty," in *Spanish Harlem: An Anatomy of Poverty* by Patricia Cayo Sexton. Copyright © 1965 by Patricia Cayo Sexton. "Avoiding Immobilization" from *Your Erroneous Zones* by Wayne W. Dyer (Funk & Wagnalls). Copyright © 1976 by Wayne W. Dyer. Reprinted by permission of Harper & Row, Publishers, Inc.

Harvard University Press: "The Lightning Is a Yellow Fork" by Emily Dickinson. Reprinted by permission of the publishers and Trustees of Amherst College from *The Poems of Emily Dickinson*, edited by Thomas H. Johnson, Cambridge Mass.: The Belknap Press of Harvard University Press, Copyright 1951, © 1955, 1979 by the President and Fellows of Harvard College.

D. C. Heath and Company: Excerpt from *The American Profile*, Second Edition, by Morton Borden and Otis L. Graham, Jr. Copyright © 1978 by D. C. Heath and Company. Reprinted by permission of the publisher.

Holt, Rinehart and Winston, Publishers: "Nothing Gold Can Stay" and "Two Tramps in Mud Time" by Robert Frost, from *The Poetry of Robert Frost*, edited by Edward Connery Lathem. Copyright 1923, © 1969 by Holt, Rinehart and Winston. Copyright 1936, 1951 by Robert Frost. Copyright © 1964 by Lesley Frost Ballantine. "The Ballad of William Sycamore" by Stephen Vincent Benet, from *Ballads and Poems* by Stephen Vincent Benet. Copyright 1931 by Stephen Vincent Benet. Copyright © 1959 by Rosemary Carr Benet. Reprinted by permission of Holt, Rinehart and Winston, Publishers. Excerpt adapted from *The Theatre—An Introduction* by Oscar G. Brockett. Copyright © 1964 by Holt, Rinehart and Winston, Inc. Reprinted by permission of Holt, Rinehart and Winston, CBS College Publishing.

Houghton Mifflin Company: Excerpts from *Economics: Macroeconomic Principles and Issues* by James Cicarelli. Copyright © 1978 by Houghton Mifflin Company. Used with permission.

Kendall/Hunt Publishing Company: Excerpts from *Between Two Worlds: An Introduction to Geography* by Robert Harper and Theodore Schmudde. Copyright © 1978 by Houghton Mifflin Company. Reprinted by permission of Kendall/Hunt Publishing Company.

Alfred A. Knopf, Inc.: Excerpt from "The Open Boat" by Stephen Crane, from *The Open Boat and Other Tales* by Stephen Crane (public domain).

Macmillan Publishing Company: Excerpt from *Healthy Personality*, Fourth Edition, by Sidney M. Jourard and Theodore Landsman. Copyright © 1980 by Macmillan Publishing Company, Inc. Excerpt from *Marketing* by Joel R. Evans and Barry Berman. Copyright © 1982, 1983 by Macmillan Publishing Company. Excerpt from *Introduction to Logic* by Irving M. Copi. Copyright © 1968, 1972, 1978, 1982 by Irving M. Copi. Excerpt from *Sexuality: The Human Experience* by William H. Gotwald, Jr. and Gale Holtz Golden. Copyright © 1981 by William H. Gotwald, Jr. and Gale Holtz Golden. Excerpt from *Biology: The Science of Life* by Joan E. Rahn. Copyright © 1974, 1980 by Joan E. Rahn. Excerpt from *Biology*, Second Edition, by Joan E. Rahn. Copyright © 1980 by Joan E. Rahn. Excerpts from *Fundamentals of Mathematics* by William M. Setek, Jr. Copyright © 1976, 1979 by William M. Setek, Jr. Excerpt from *Macmillan School Dictionary*. Copyright © 1981 by Macmillan Publishing Co., Inc. Reprinted with permission of Macmillan Publishing Company.

Newsweek, Inc.: "Genes That Move to Fight Disease" by Sharon Begley and Mary Hager, from *Newsweek* (9/22/81). Copyright 1981 by Newsweek, Inc. All rights reserved. Reprinted by permission.

New York Times Company: "Elect Tarzan Mayor" by Christopher Nyerges, from *The New York Times* (7/23/79). © 1979 by The New York Times Company.

Random House, Inc.: Excerpt from *The Arrogance of Power* by William Fulbright.

Copyright © 1966 by William Fulbright. Excerpts from *Psychology Today: An Introduction*, Fourth Edition, by J. Braun and Daryn Linder. Copyright © 1975 by Random House, Inc. Excerpts from *Business Today*, Second Edition, by David Rachman and Michael Mescon. Copyright © 1976, 1979, 1982 by Random House, Inc. Reprinted by permission of Random House, Inc.

Scott, Foresman and Company: Map and excerpt from *Living World History*, 5th edition, by T. Walter Wallbank and Arnold Schrier. Copyright © 1982 Scott, Foresman and Company. Illustrations and excerpt from *Biology: Human Perspectives* by Charles Kingsley Levy. Copyright © 1979 Scott, Foresman and Company. Reprinted by permission.

Charles Scribner's Sons: Excerpt from "Circus at Dawn," in *From Death to Morning* by Thomas Wolfe. Copyright 1935 Charles Scribner's Sons; copyright renewed 1963 Paul Gitlin. Reprinted with the permission of Charles Scribner's Sons.

Viking Penguin, Inc.: Excerpt from *One Flew Over the Cuckoo's Nest* by Ken Kesey. Copyright © 1962 by Ken Kesey. Excerpt from "Flight" from *The Long Valley* by John Steinbeck. Copyright 1938 by John Steinbeck. Copyright renewed 1966 by John Steinbeck. Reprinted by permission of Viking Penguin, Inc.

Estate of Thomas Wolfe: Excerpt from *The Lost Boy* by Thomas Wolfe, (New York: Harper & Row, 1937). Reprinted by permission of Paul Gitlin, Administrator.

World Book, Inc.: "Diatom" from *The World Book Encyclopedia*. © 1983 World Book, Inc. Reprinted by permission of the publisher.

Worth Publishers, Inc.: Excerpts from *Biology*, Third Edition, by Helena Curtis. Excerpts from *Sociology*, Second Edition by Ian Robertson. Reprinted by permission of Worth Publishers, Inc.

PREFACE

Reading is the most efficient way to process information. This book will help a student become the best reader he or she can be.

This book teaches the reading skills needed for college and teaches how to read rapidly and critically. It shows how to approach readings in the different content areas and how to take notes, prepare for examinations, and remember what has been read.

Reading is just as important a college subject as English or mathematics. In fact, reading may be the single most important factor for success in college. Even the very best student has a lot to learn about reading college-level material. We are beginning to realize that many of the problems that students encounter in college are due to a lack of appropriate reading instruction. This book responds to that need by showing how to build on the ability to read to learn the whole range of reading, studying, and analytical techniques necessary to pursue college study.

The chapters in this book can be seen in four parts. Chapters 1–9 develop basic vocabulary and reading technique. Chapters 10–14 give suggestions for reading the different content areas. Chapters 15–18 discuss critical reading and present techniques for identifying biased writing. The remaining chapters focus on note taking, study skills, and use of the library. This text can be adapted to a range of ability levels.

Each chapter begins with an explanation, along with a series of exercises or short readings. The instructor will usually review the explanation and work on most of the exercises and activities in class with the students. Some exercises and activities will be assigned for homework. Each chapter ends with a project that asks the student to apply what has been learned, usually to a longer reading. The project is usually assigned at the completion of each chapter as a homework assignment and discussed in class.

The longer readings in the text have been carefully selected. These readings have been chosen from some of the most popular college texts and range in length from 1400 words to 10,000 words. The shorter readings have also been carefully selected, and all readings represent the material that students will encounter in college.

The instructor's manual that accompanies this text contains objectives, suggestions for teaching, additional projects, and test questions and answers for each chapter. The manual also has the answers for *all* exercises, activities, and projects in the text. There are also charts and graphs to help students increase reading speed.

Preliminary versions of this text were used by scores of instructors and thousands of students at Mercy College. We owe them special thanks. Many others at Mercy College were most helpful, most notably the department secretary, Mrs. Laura Pascacello. Eben Ludlow at Macmillan, our editor, is the complete professional and was helpful throughout the development of this text. Ron Harris of Macmillan brought his special editing talents and his encyclopedic knowledge to bear on this text. This book is much more than it could have been without him.

We are most grateful to our spouses and children, Liz, Chad, Blaire, and Ryan; Richard, Kristen, and Kara; Jane, Christie, and Thomas. It is they who sustained us.

This book is dedicated to the students who use it. The skills and concepts discussed herein will lead them to successful and rewarding college careers.

R. D. P.
B. K.
P. S.

CONTENTS

Chapter One   UNDERSTANDING VOCABULARY   1

Use the Sentence to Gain Meaning—Context Clues   1
　　Activity I   2
Use the Textbook Print Aids   3
　　Activity II   3
Analyze the Word to Identify the Meaning   5
　　Exercise I   5
Using a Dictionary to Learn Vocabulary   7
　　Exercise II   7
Project   9
　　Reading: "Transportation"   10

Chapter Two   PREVIEWING   17

Previewing a Chapter in a Textbook   17
　　Activity I   18
Previewing an Essay   22
　　Activity II   23
Previewing a Novel and a Short Story   25
Previewing a Play   26
Previewing a Poem   26
Project   27
　　Reading: "Memory"   28

Chapter Three   SENTENCE MEANING   51

Key Words and Important Modifiers   51
Sentence Meaning Review   52
　　Activity I   52
Linking Words   53
　　Exercise I   54
　　Exercise II   55
Project   55
　　Reading: "Various Kinds of Meaning"   56

Chapter Four   IN SEARCH OF A TOPIC   61

　　Exercise I   61
　　Exercise II   62
Project   64
　　Reading: "Denial"   65

Chapter Five   MAIN IDEA   71

Stated Main Idea   71
　　Exercise I   71
Unstated Main Idea   72
　　Exercise II   73
Project   76
　　Reading: "Education"   77

Chapter Six   DETAILS ... DETAILS   **87**

Clues to Help Find Important Details   87
  Exercise I   *88*
  Exercise II   *89*
  Exercise III   *89*
Project   90
  Reading: "Industrialism"   *91*

Chapter Seven   PARAGRAPH TYPES AND PATTERNS   **95**

Author's Purpose   95
Paragraph Types   95
Patterns of Paragraph Development   98
  Exercise I   *100*
Project   104
  Readings   *105*

Chapter Eight   SKIMMING AND SCANNING   **107**

Skimming   107
Skimming an Article or Chapter   107
  Activity I   *108*
Scanning   109
  Activity II   *109*
  Activity III   *110*
  Activity IV   *111*
Project   113
  Reading: "Retailing"   *114*

Chapter Nine   THE ART OF READING RAPIDLY   **133**

  Activity I   *134*
  Activity II   *135*
  Activity III   *136*
Summary   137
  Activity IV   *137*
Procedure for Estimating the Number of Words in a Sentence   140
  Activity V   *141*
Project   141
  Reading I: "Birth Defects"   *143*
  Reading II: "Some Basic Needs in Humans"   *150*
  Reading III: "The Big Bear of Arkansas"   *155*

Chapter Ten   STEPS IN TEXTBOOK STUDY   **163**

Knowing Your Textbook   163
  Activity I   *163*
An Effective Textbook Study Technique   164
Checklist: Textbook Study   165
  Activity II   *165*
Project   169
  Reading: "Consumer Demographics"   *170*

Chapter Eleven NOTE TAKING IN THE TEXTBOOK 185

Activity I 186
Activity II 187
Project 190
Reading: "Social Structure in Vertebrate Societies" 190

Chapter Twelve READING MATHEMATICS 195

Mathematical Symbols 195
Exercise I 195
Arithmetic 196
Exercise II 196
Solving Word Problems 197
Activity I 198
Equations 199
The RATS Method 199
Activity II 200
Projects 201

Chapter Thirteen READING SCIENCE 205

Scientific Terms 205
Scientific Symbols 206
Charts and Diagrams 206
Steps for Reading Science 206
Activity I 207
Project 209
Reading: "Plant Hormones" 210

Chapter Fourteen READING HISTORY 219

Activity I 220
Time Line 223
Projects 223
Reading I "The Great Stalemate, 1914–1916" 224
Reading II: "Mohammed and the Rise of the Arab Empire" 227

Chapter Fifteen FIGURATIVE LANGUAGE 237

Simile and Metaphor 237
Personification and Hyperbole 237
Activity I 238
Activity II 239
Activity III 240
Activity IV 242
Project 242
Reading I: "Sounds" 244
Reading II: "The Tide Rises, The Tide Falls" 246
Reading III: "The Last Leaf" 247
Reading IV: "The Tell-Tale Heart" 249

Chapter Sixteen READING CRITICALLY: DEDUCTIVE REASONING 253

Exercise I 254
Invalid Reasoning 255
Exercise II 256
Project 257

Chapter Seventeen   READING CRITICALLY: INDUCTIVE REASONING   **259**

Fallacious Inductive Arguments   260
   Exercise I   *261*
Project   262

Chapter Eighteen   READING CRITICALLY: PROPAGANDA   **265**

   Activity I   *267*
Project   269

Chapter Nineteen   TAKING LECTURE NOTES   **271**

Organize Yourself and Your Notebook   271
Be an Efficient Listener   272
   Activity I   *272*
   Activity II   *272*
Notebook Pages   274
   Activity III   *275*
Project   277
   Reading: "Theories of Psychosexual Development"   *279*

Chapter Twenty   EXAMS   **287**

Studying   287
An Intense Review Schedule   288
Examinations   289
   Activity I   *292*
Project   293
   Reading: "The American Class System"   *296*

Chapter Twenty-One   MEMORY TECHNIQUES   **305**

Understand What You Want to Remember   305
Make a Concerted Effort to Remember   305
   Activity I   *306*
Organize Information to Be Memorized   306
   Activity II   *306*
Mnemonic Devices   307
   Activity III   *308*
Memory Techniques—Summary   308
Project   309
   Reading: "Some Disorders of the Respiratory System"   *309*

Chapter Twenty-Two   AIDS TO READING IN THE LIBRARY   **315**

The Reader's Guide to Periodical Literature   *315*
   Activity I   *316*
The Book Review Digest   *317*
   Activity II   *317*
Psychological Abstracts   *318*
   Activity III   *318*
The New York Times Index   *319*
Projects   320

INDEX   **321**

One

UNDERSTANDING VOCABULARY

Learning new vocabulary from college texts is an important part of reading. These words are usually more difficult than the words you commonly use. In addition, most of the important ideas and concepts discussed in introductory or survey courses are actually new vocabulary words. You must master new vocabulary words before reading on.

Use the following three strategies to learn and understand new vocabulary terms.

USE THE SENTENCE TO GAIN MEANING—CONTEXT CLUES

Look at the way a term or word is used in a phrase or a sentence. Is this a different use or meaning for you? Is this a new word for you? If so, predict the meaning from its use in the sentence. This technique is called using context clues for gaining word meaning.

Example A. Defining the important vocabulary term in a sentence.

Intelligence is sometimes defined as the ability to learn new information in a different or unique situation.

The sentence defines intelligence for us.

Example B. Synonyms are used in phrases and sentences to define the term.

Sleep may be the most ubiquitous or pervasive characteristic common to humans which controls our physiology.

We can tell that *ubiquitous* means "pervasive."

Example C. Examples help to clarify terms.

When writing a feature article, the journalist's whole tone becomes personal. The feature story writer concentrates on the human interest angle and treats it subjectively. For example, the seasonal story, the unusual, or a dramatic situation are common angles for feature stories.[1]

After feature articles have been described, examples of features are given.

Example D. Explanation through comparison and contrast.

News is said to be slanted when the facts of a story are so arranged as to lead the reader to a desired conclusion. . . . News is said to be colored when some facts are stressed and others are made inconspicuous or omitted. . . . In other words, news is slanted when the writer has attempted to influence the reader by the arrangement of facts alone and news is colored when the writer attempts to influence the reader by arrangement of facts and by choice of words.[2]

After slanted and colored news are defined, further explanation is given through comparison.

ACTIVITY I

Read the following selection, taken from the drama textbok *The Theatre: An Introduction* by Oscar Brockett. Vocabulary words are given at the end of the selection. Write a definition for each word based on the way the word is used in the sentence.

The auditorium was the first part of the theatre to assume a permanent form. Stadiumlike seating was provided by setting stones into the hillside. This auditorium was semicircular and curved around the orchestra (which was circular). The theatre was very large—it seated about 14,000 persons—and the orchestra was approximately sixty-five feet in diameter. The auditorium and the orchestra remained relatively unchanged, and there is little disagreement today about their features.

The stage house (or *skene*) was late in developing as a part of the theatre. It was the last part to be constructed in stone, and it was remodeled many times after that. For all of these reasons, it is difficult to get a clear impression of the scenic background of plays in the fifth century [B.C.].

The skene (which was unknown in the sixth century) was originally constructed as a place where actors might dress and retire to change roles. Gradually this house came to be used as a background for the action of the play, and its usefulness for scenic purposes was exploited. In the late fifth century the skene was a long building which, with its projecting side wings (called *paraskene*), formed a rectangular background for the orchestra on the side away from the spectators. It was not joined to the auditorium, and the space on each side between the paraskene and the auditorium provided entrances into the orchestra. . . .

The appearance of the skene is much debated. Most of the plays are set before temples or palaces, but some take place outside of caves or tents, or in wooded landscapes. There is much controversy over the extent to which the stage may have been altered to meet these differing demands. . . .

Another effect frequently demanded in Greek plays is the appearance of gods. These characters may descend to the orchestra level or be lifted up from the orchestra to the roof of the stage house. For this purpose, a cranelike device called the *machina* was used. The overuse of gods to resolve difficult dramatic situations led to the expression *deus ex machina* to describe any contrived ending. The eccyclema and the machina are the only two machines which can definitely be ascribed to the fifth century, and these were not used extensively.[3]

Listed below are the important vocabulary words from the reading selection. Space is provided after each word for you to write your definition of the word according to its use in the sentence. After you have written the meanings, check them in your college dictionary. Do they match?

auditorium   Your definition: _____

_____

Dictionary definition: _____

_____

orchestra   Your definition: _____

_____

Dictionary definition: _____

_____

skene   Your definition: _____

_____

Dictionary definition: _____

_____

paraskene   Your definition: _____

_____

Dictionary definition: _____

_____

machina   Your definition: _____

_____

Dictionary definition: _____

_____

deus ex machina   Your definition: _____

_____

Dictionary definition: _____

_____

USE THE TEXTBOOK PRINT AIDS

Textbooks often use headings and highlighted (italic or boldface) words to mark important terms. Margin notes or footnotes can indicate important vocabulary. Write these words in your notebook.

ACTIVITY II

Read the following article from a psychology textbook. After you have read the article, write a brief definition of the words listed at the end.

Dollard and Miller's Psychodynamic Behavior Theory[4]

The most ambitious attempt at assimilation was made during the 1940s at Yale University by John Dollard and Neal Miller. Their approach is called *psychodynamic behavior theory* by some psychologists because it represents an effort to deal with the psychodynamic phenomena identified by Freud. . . .

Dollard and Miller (1950) used the term *drives*, roughly equivalent to Freud's *instincts*, to refer to the motivational basis for behavior. Like instincts, drives are states of arousal that require some satisfaction or reduction. Dollard and Miller introduced the term *response* to refer to any act or thought related to the satisfaction or reduction of a drive. Hunger, then, is a drive that is reduced by the response of eating. They used the term *cue* to refer to any feature of the environment that indicates that a particular drive can be satisfied or reduced then and there. If someone is hungry, a sign advertising a restaurant is a cue that is useful in guiding that person's behavior toward the reduction of hunger. Dollard and Miller used the term *reinforcement* to describe the strengthening of the tendency to emit a given response once it has successfully reduced or satisfied a drive. The reinforced response can thus be expected to reappear when the drive is aroused again.

These terms used by Dollard and Miller do not translate directly into Freud's concepts, but in combination they can be used to explain some of the same phenomena that Freud identified. Take, for example, displaced aggression. According to Freud the child, born with an aggressive instinct, searches for a way to release aggressive energy. But, being afraid of attacking a parent, who is often the real object of anger, the child displaces the aggression by fighting with a younger sibling or talking back to a teacher. Dollard and Miller would explain this displacement phenomenon in a somewhat different manner. According to their **frustration-aggression hypothesis,** the aggressive drive is aroused by the thwarting of progress toward some important goal. The child is therefore motivated to commit aggression against the frustrating agent. If, however, the frustrating agent is a powerful figure against whom it is dangerous to express aggression, such as a mother or father, the child will displace the aggression onto other people whose cue value is similar to that of the real target—perhaps a sibling or teacher (Dollard et al., 1939).

Freudian theory explains behavior as a response to internal stimuli—aggressive drives, for example—while behaviorist theory explains it in terms of external stimuli—the frustration of a goal-oriented response. Moreover, Dollard and Miller's theory has social applications that Freud's psychoanalytic theory does not. They believe that displacement can and will be learned even by large segments of a population if the response to the new target in some way satisfies or reduces the drive that underlies the response. Thus, in times of economic depression or political unrest, when the real target for the anger and aggression of the populace is unknown or too powerful to attack directly, aggression is displaced toward "outsiders" or a minority group. If this aggression is reinforced—if it satisfactorily reduces the aggressive drive—it will be continued. This kind of scapegoating becomes a learned and almost institutionalized response, as was the case with the anti-Semitism of Nazi Germany and the anticommunism of the McCarthy era in the United States during the 1950s.

drives _____

_____

instincts _____

_____

response _____

_____

cue _____

_____

reinforcement _____

_____

frustration-aggression hypothesis _____

_____

ANALYZE THE WORD TO IDENTIFY THE MEANING

Often it is helpful to look at word parts when identifying the meaning of an unknown word. Many words contain a root or base. The base has an essential meaning for many of the words in our language. Prefixes are added at the beginning of a root word and suffixes are added at the end. These prefixes and suffixes alter the essential meaning. The new meaning of the word can often be identified by combining the meaning of the root word with the prefix and suffix.

Consider the word *telegraph*. The root word for this word is *graph*. This common root word comes from the Greek word *graphein*, which means "to write." What is the prefix in *telegraph*? The common prefix *tele* means "far" or "far off." We can identify the meaning of the word *telegraph* as "writing from far off."

In a similar way, *graphologist* contains the root *graph* and the suffix *ologist*. The suffix *ology* means "study of" and the suffix *ist* means "performer of." A graphologist is a person who studies writing, specifically handwriting.

Read the following common root words and their meanings:

Root	Common Forms	Meaning	Examples
capere	cap, cept, ceive	take, seize	capture, concept, receive
legein	leg, lex, log, ology	say, words, study	Lexicon, monologue, sociology
specere	spec, spect, spic, spy	see, look	spectacle, suspicious, spy
faerce	fac, fact, fic, feat	make, do	deficient, factory, fictitious
scribere	scrib, script, scrip, scriv	write	scribe, subscribe, scribble
tangere	tang, tact, ting	touch	tactile, tangent
portare	port	carry	portage, transport
graphos	graph	drawn or written	photograph, autograph, paragraph

EXERCISE I

Listed below are common prefixes. For each a brief meaning is given. This meaning is followed by an example of the word with the prefix. In the space at the right of the page, write a brief definition for the example. The first is done for you.

Prefix	Meaning	Example	Definition
mono	one	monolingual	*Speaking one language*
bi	two	bicycle	
deci	ten	decade	
multi	many	multilingual	
super	above	supernatural	
hyper	excessive	hypertense	
omni	all	omnipotent	
mort	death	mortified	
tele	far	telephone	
inter	between	intertwine	
trans	across	transcontinental	
trac, tract	pull	traction	
derm	skin	dermatologist	
therm	heat	thermonuclear	
pseudo	false	pseudopod	
ante	before	anteroom	
anti	against	antiviral	
cred	believe	credibility	
bibl	book	bibliography	
neo	new	Neo-Nazi	
theo	god	theologist	
in, im, ir, il, non	not	incomplete	
		irreverent	
		nonstop	
fore	before	forearm	
intra	within	intravenous	

Listed below are common suffixes. For each a brief meaning is given. This is followed by examples of words with the suffix. In the space at the right of the page, write a brief definition of one example. The first one is done for you.

Suffix	Meaning	Example	Definition
er, or, ist, ian, ar, eer, ster	performer of	reader, sailor, physicist, librarian, engineer, huckster	*Someone who reads, sails,...*

Suffix	Meaning	Example	Definition
ee, ite, ive	one who receives	testee, Denverite, captive	_____
ity, ness, ship	condition of	surety, loneliness, kinship	_____
ful, ous	full of	helpful, victorious	_____
ile, al, ic, ish, like, ive, ly, ative	relating to	infantile, comical, cryptic, ticklish, talkative	_____
able, ible	capable of being	returnable, sensible	_____
ate, ify, ize	to make or do	subjugate, specify, finalize	_____

USING A DICTIONARY TO LEARN VOCABULARY

When meanings are not evident from usage in a sentence or from analysis of the structure or parts of the word, a dictionary is the source you should turn to, to find the definition.

Different kinds of dictionaries can be used to identify unknown words. The glossary included at the end of many college texts is a handy specialized dictionary you can use for your subjects. The glossary will include terms from the text that are technical or unique to the subject. Sometimes, technical terms must be looked up in even more specialized dictionaries found in the reference section of the library. Scientific dictionaries, dictionaries of literary terms, and biographical dictionaries are examples of these highly specialized reference sources.

Most of the time a standard desk dictionary such as *The American College Dictionary* or *Webster's New Collegiate Dictionary* can be used to identify common vocabulary terms. Successful college students learn to keep their dictionary handy and to use it often. When checking any dictionary entry, it is important to read through all of the meanings or entries listed because words have many meanings and you need to find the meaning appropriate for the subject or context you are studying. For example, the word *base* can have different meanings in different subjects or disciplines.

EXERCISE II

Listed below are several different subject areas. Write the different definitions for the word *base* in each of the subjects listed. A page from a standard desk dictionary[5] appears for help. Consult a specialized dictionary in the reference section of the library for additional help.

barrage / base²

bar·rage (bə räzh′) *n.* **1.** a heavy amount of fire from artillery or other guns: *The barrage from the enemy mortars kept the men pinned down in the trenches.* **2.** any large or overwhelming amount: *The reporters met the President with a barrage of questions.* —*v.t.,* **bar·raged, bar·rag·ing.** to attack or confront with a barrage: *The movie star was barraged with requests for her autograph.*

Bar·ran·quil·la (bär′räng kē′yä) *n.* the chief seaport of Colombia, in the northern part of the country. Pop. (1969 est.), 816,700.

bar·rel (bar′əl) *n.* **1.** a large wooden container shaped like a cylinder, having bulging sides and round, flat ends. Barrels are usually made up of boards bound together by metal hoops. **2.** any container resembling this: *a trash barrel.* **3.** the amount that a barrel can hold: *The family packed four barrels of dishes when they moved.* **4.** any of various measures of weight or quantity. The standard U.S. barrel for liquids holds 31½ gallons. **5.** the tube-shaped part of a gun through which the bullet or shell is shot. **6.** any part shaped like a cylinder or tube: *the barrel of a fountain pen.* **7.** *Informal.* a large quantity: *a barrel of fun, a barrel of money.* —*v.,* **bar·reled, bar·rel·ing;** *also, British,* **bar·relled, bar·rel·ling.** —*v.t.* to put or pack in barrels. —*v.i. Informal.* to move rapidly: *Steve barreled in through the front door when he heard the phone ringing.*

barrel organ, another term for **hand organ.**

bar·ren (bar′ən) *adj.* **1.** having little or no plant life; not productive: *barren soil.* **2.** not able to produce offspring: *a barren woman, a barren fruit tree.* **3.** not leading to any results or gain: *The barren talks with the union failed to prevent a strike.* **4.** without interest, charm, or hopefulness; empty; dreary: *The future seemed barren for the old woman until her stolen money was recovered.* —*n. also,* **barrens.** an area of barren land. —**bar′ren·ness,** *n.*

bar·rette (bə ret′) *n.* a clasp or clip, often in the shape of a bar, for holding the hair in place.

bar·ri·cade (bar′ə kād′) *n.* **1.** a hastily made barrier for defense: *The rebels built barricades against the approaching army.* **2.** any barrier that blocks passage: *The police barricades kept the crowds back.* —*v.t.,* **bar·ri·cad·ed, bar·ri·cad·ing.** to block; obstruct: *Fallen trees barricaded the road.*

Bar·rie, Sir James M. (bar′ē) 1860–1937, Scottish playwright and novelist.

bar·ri·er (bar′ē ər) *n.* **1.** something that blocks the way: *A mountain barrier sealed off the valley.* **2.** something that restricts or hinders: *The country's lack of industry was a barrier to economic growth.* **3.** something that divides or keeps apart: *The difference in language was a barrier between the people of the two nations.*

barrier reef, a coral reef that is parallel to the shoreline, usually acting as a breakwater.

bar·ring (bär′ing) *prep.* with the exception of; except for: *Barring delays, we will arrive on Wednesday.*

bar·ris·ter (bar′is tər) *n.* in Great Britain, a lawyer who argues cases in court.

bar·room (bär′rōōm′, bär′room′) *n.* a room or place having a bar where alcoholic drinks are sold.

bar·row¹ (bar′ō) *n.* **1.** see **wheelbarrow.** [Old English *bearwe* wheelbarrow.]

bar·row² (bar′ō) *n.* a mound of earth or stones marking an ancient grave. [Old English *beorg* hill, mound.]

Bar·row, Point (bar′ō) a small Alaskan peninsula that is the northernmost point of the United States.

bar sinister, a diagonal stripe on a coat of arms, falsely supposed to indicate illegitimate birth.

Bart., Baronet.

bar·tend·er (bär′ten′dər) *n.* a person who makes and serves alcoholic drinks at a bar.

bar·ter (bär′tər) *v.t.* to trade (goods for other goods) without using money: *The early settlers bartered seed for animal skins with the Indians.* —*v.i.* to barter goods. —*n.* **1.** the act or practice of bartering: *Among these tribes trade is carried on by barter.* **2.** something bartered.

Bar·thol·o·mew, Saint (bär thol′ə myōō′) one of the twelve apostles.

Bart·lett pear (bärt′lit) a large, yellow, juicy pear. [From Enoch *Bartlett,* a merchant who popularized it in the United States.]

Bar·tók, Be·la (bär′tok; bā′lə) 1881–1945, Hungarian composer and pianist.

Bar·ton, Clara (bärt′ən) 1821–1912, the founder of the American Red Cross.

ba·sal (bā′səl) *adj.* of or at the base; forming the base; fundamental; basic.

basal metabolism, the amount of energy used up by an animal or plant when it is completely at rest. Basal metabolism is measured by the rate of oxygen used up and heat given off.

ba·salt (bə sôlt′) *n.* a dark, usually fine-grained volcanic rock.

bas·cule bridge (bas′kyōōl) a drawbridge hinged at the bank so that it may be raised to allow ships to pass under it.

Bascule bridge

base¹ (bās) *n. pl.,* **bas·es.** **1.** the part on which a thing rests or stands: *The base of the statue was a marble block.* **2.** the underlying part that supports something; foundation: *That political party has a broad base among the working people.* **3.** the lowest part; bottom: *The base of the mountain is surrounded by thick jungle.* **4.** the chief or essential part of a thing; main element: *This paint has an oil base.* **5.** a military area and facilities where supplies are kept or from which operations are started: *an air force base, a missile base.* **6.** any center or starting point of activity: *the base of a mountain climbing expedition.* **7.** a station, goal, or safety area in certain games. **8.** any of the four corners of a baseball diamond. **9.** *Chemistry.* a compound that reacts with an acid to form a salt. A base has bitter taste in a water solution and turns red litmus paper blue. **10.** *Mathematics.* **a.** the number in a numerical system that marks the point in counting when a new digit is added at the left and counting begins again. Simple arithmetic is usually done in the decimal system, whose base is 10. According to this system, the numeral 40 represents 4 times the base of 10. Computers use the binary system, whose base is 2. According to this system, the numeral 10 represents 1 times the base of 2. **b.** a line or plane in a geometrical figure on which it is thought to rest: *the base of a triangle.* —*v.t.,* **based, bas·ing.** **1.** to place on a basis or foundation: *to base a house on concrete. Alice always tries to base her opinions on the facts. This movie is based on a popular novel.* **2.** to locate; station: *These troops have been based in Europe for two years.* [Latin *basis* foundation, pedestal, from Greek *basis* step, pedestal.]

off base. *Informal.* not accurate; mistaken: *Your guess was really off base.*

base² (bās) *adj.,* **bas·er, bas·est.** **1.** having or showing a lack of decency or bravery; morally low; dishonorable: *Abandoning his men during the battle was a base act.* **2.** menial; degrading: *base labor.* **3.** low in value in comparison to something else: *Iron is a base metal.* [Old French *bas* low, from Late Latin *bassus* low, short.] —**base′ly,** *adv.* —**base′ness,** *n.*

Base

chemistry _____

_____

math _____

_____

geometry _____

_____

music _____

_____

sports _____

_____

sculpture _____

_____

painting _____

_____

PROJECT

The following selection, taken from a business marketing textbook, has many vocabulary words that are printed in italic type. Skim the selection and list the important vocabulary words below. Some are done for you. Next, reread the selection to find the meanings for the vocabulary terms. If you cannot identify the meaning from its use in a sentence, use the parts of the word to help discover its meaning or use a standard desk dictionary. Write the definition of each term.

Term	Definition
ton mile	_____
transportation modes	_____
railroads	_____
piggyback services	_____
transit privileges	_____
diversion in transit	_____
pool car	_____
rail deregulation	_____
merging	_____
motor trucks	_____
intercity-waterway transportation	_____
_____	_____
_____	_____
_____	_____
_____	_____
_____	_____
_____	_____

Term	Definition
_____	_____
_____	_____
_____	_____
_____	_____
_____	_____
_____	_____
_____	_____
_____	_____
_____	_____
_____	_____
_____	_____
_____	_____
_____	_____

TRANSPORTATION[6]

Table 14–1 presents the proportion of _ton miles_ (the movement of one ton of freight over the distance of one mile) shipped via each of the five major transportation modes: railroads, motor trucks, waterways, pipelines, and airways.

Since 1950 the share of ton miles shipped via pipelines has more than doubled. During the same period the relative importance of railroads has declined substantially, despite their continuing leadership in ton miles. Waterway shipments have retained a stable share for the last thirty years, and motor trucks have increased their share of ton miles by 50 per cent during this period. Despite the growth of airlines, freight deliveries through the airways remain at less than 1 per cent of all shipments.

Figure 14–5 ranks the transportation modes on the basis of six operating statistics. In the figure a ranking of 1 represents the highest performance among

Transportation modes may be rated on the basis of speed, availability, dependability, capability, frequency, and cost.

Table 14–1 CARRIER PROPORTIONS OF U.S. INTERCITY FREIGHT (IN TON MILES)* 1950–1979

Carrier	% of Total					
	1979	1975	1970	1965	1960	
Railroads	35.7	36.4	40.8	43.5	44.1	56.2
Motor trucks	24.3	23.4	21.0	23.1	21.7	16.3
Inland waterways†	16.4	16.5	16.2	16.0	16.8	15.4
Pipelines (oil)	23.4	23.5	21.8	17.3	17.4	12.1
Airways (domestic)	0.2	0.2	0.2	0.1	—	—
	100.0	100.0	100.0	100.0	100.0	100.0

*A ton mile is the movement of 1 ton (2,000 lb) of freight for the distance of one mile.
†Includes rivers, canals, and domestic traffic on Great Lakes.
SOURCES: Interstate Commerce Commission, Civil Aeronautics Board, and Association of American Railroads.

Figure 14–5:
Relative Operating Characteristics of Five Basic Transportation Modes

Operating Characteristics[1]	Railroads	Motor Trucks	Waterways	Pipelines	Airlines
Speed[2]	3	2	4	5	1
Availability[3]	2	1	4	5	3
Dependability[4]	3	2	4	1	5
Capability[5]	2	3	1	5	4
Frequency[6]	4	2	5	1	3
Cost per ton mile[7]	3	4	2	1	5

[1] 1 = high rank; 5 = lowest rank
[2] Speed = Door-to-door delivery time
[3] Availability = Number of geographic points served
[4] Dependability = Ability to meet schedules on time
[5] Capability = Ability to handle various products
[6] Frequency = Scheduled shipments per day
[7] Cost per ton mile = Illustrative costs per ton mile are pipeline, $.27; waterways, $.30; railroad, $1.43; motor truck, $7.70; and airways, $21.88.
SOURCE: Adapted from Donald J. Bowersox, *Logistical Management,* Second Edition (New York: Macmillan, 1978), p. 120. (Copyright © 1978, Donald J. Bowersox); reprinted by permission.

the five modes; 5 is the lowest performance. Airways have the best rating for speed. Pipelines are superior in dependability (time schedules met), frequency (shipments per day), and cost per ton mile. Waterways are able to handle the most different products. Motor trucks have the highest availability in terms of number of geographic points served. Figure 14–6 lists the typical goods shipped by each type of transportation.

Each transportation mode and such transportation services as parcel post are studied in the following pages.

Railroads

Railroads usually carry heavy, bulky items that are low in value in relation to their weight over long distances. Railroads ship items whose weight is too heavy for trucks.

Railroads transport over long distances items that are low in value in relation to weight.

Despite their dominant position in ton miles shipped, railroads have been beset by a variety of problems in recent years. Fixed costs are high because of investments in facilities. There are railroad car shortages during high demand months for agricultural goods. Some tracks and railroad cars are in serious need of repair. Trucks are faster, more flexible, and are packed more easily.[12]

The railroads are relying on three solutions to improve their outlook: new shipping techniques, deregulation, and mergers.

Figure 14–6:
Typical Products Handled by Five Basic Transportation Modes

Railroads	Motor Trucks	Waterways	Pipelines	Airways
Iron	Clothing	Fuel oil	Petroleum	Flowers
Steel scrap	Paper goods	Cement	Coal	Auto parts
Coal	Computers	Coal	Chemicals	Fashions
Sand	Books	Metallic ore	Natural gas	Technical instruments
Steel	Fabricated	Chemicals		High-value industrial
Lumber	metalwork	Iron ore		parts
Automobiles		Coal		
Chemicals		Grains		
Minerals		Minerals		
Autos		Nonperishable goods		

SOURCE: Adapted from James L. Heskett, Robert Ivie, and J. Nicholas Glaskowsky, *Business Logistics,* Second Edition (New York: Ronald Press, 1973).

[12] See Edward Schumacher, "Modern Rail Freight Leaving New York Behind," *New York Times* (July 8, 1980), p. B4.

New railroad shipping techniques include *piggyback services, transit privileges, diversion in transit,* and *pool cars.*

To maintain and generate business, railroads have developed several new shipping techniques. *Piggyback services* enable truck trailers to be placed directly on railroad flat cars. Under this system, products are first loaded on trucks at the seller's shipping dock, then the truck trailers are moved on to railroad flat cars, transported to a rail station near customers, and moved to a final destination by truck tractors. Piggyback service is available between 1,400 cities in the United States and Canada. Either railroad or privately owned equipment is used.[13] With piggyback service, door-to-door delivery is provided at lower freight costs than if trucks are used alone; and, goods are handled less.

Transit privileges allow shippers to unload and further process goods at a point between origin and final destination, then reload the goods, and continue the trip without further charge. *Diversion in transit* allows shippers to load goods and send them in the general direction of their final destination. As customer orders are received, the shipper diverts the goods to a specific final destination. A small fee is charged for this service. *Pool car* shipments enable two or more firms to combine their goods, so that the lowest shipping rates (based on full carloads) are received. Railroads now encourage pool cars.

Railroad deregulation allows competitive prices and routes to be abandoned. The *merging* of railroad lines enables longer runs and shifts traffic to the best routes.

On October 14, 1980 President Jimmy Carter signed a *rail deregulation* bill. This gave railroads more freedom to raise freight rates (without Interstate Commerce Commission control) and broader authority to sign long term contracts with major shippers, and let railroads more easily abandon routes and branch lines.[14]

The *merging* of railroad lines should enable firms to be more profitable. They would be able to make longer runs, and rates could be cut because duplicate equipment purchases would be eliminated. Traffic loads would be shifted to the best-maintained, most heavily traveled routes.[15]

Mergers must be approved by both the Interstate Commerce Commission and the Justice Department. Five proposed rail mergers have sought this approval: Union Pacific/Missouri Pacific, Norfolk & Western/Southern, Chessie System/Seaboard Coast Line, Burlington North/St. Louis-San Francisco Railway, and Southern Pacific/Santa Fe.[16]

Motor Trucks

Motor trucks handle small shipments over short distances. They are flexible.

Motor trucks predominatly transport small shipments over short distances. Motor carriers handle about 80 per cent of the country's shipments of less than 500 or 1,000 pounds.[17] Seventy per cent of all trucks are used for local deliveries and 50 per cent of total truck miles are local.

The government data shown in Table 14–1 understate the importance of trucking. These statistics exclude truck shipments handled by privately owned trucks as well as intracity freight. One source estimates that trucks haul more than one half of the nation's freight.[18]

Trucks are more flexible than rail because they can pick up packages at the factory or warehouse and deliver them to the customer's door. For example, General Motors moves half its total shipments by trucks, which carry parts from one plant right to the assembly area of another.[19] In addition, trucks are faster than rail for short distances.

[13]George L. Stern, "Surface Transportation: Middle-of-the road Solution," *Harvard Business Review*, Vol. 53 (November-December 1975), p. 82.

[14]John D. Williams, "Rail-Rate Increases Due for Early Arrival Thanks to New Law," *Wall Street Journal* (October 14, 1980), p. 1, p. 20.

[15]John D. Williams, "N.&W. and Southern Roads Propose $2 Billion Merger, Response to Big Consolidation Announced This Year," *Wall Street Journal* (June 3, 1980), p. 3, and "Why Santa Fe Wants the Southern Pacific," *Business Week* (June 2, 1980), pp. 29–30.

[16]See "Back to Railroading for a New Era," *Business Week* (July 14, 1980), pp. 64, 68, 69.

[17]Walter F. Friedman, "Physical Distribution: The Concept of Shared Services," *Harvard Business Review*, Vol. 53 (March-April 1975), p. 25.

[18]"Getting Ready: Businessmen Brace for a Trucking Strike, But There's a Limit to What They Can Do," *Wall Street Journal* (March 29, 1979), p. 46.

[19]Ibid.

Figure 14–7:
What the Interstate Trucking De-regulation Law Does

The trucking deregulation law, signed by President Jimmy Carter on July 1, 1980, makes it easier for truckers to operate. Among its components are

1. The Interstate Commerce Commission (ICC) will ease restrictions on allowing truckers to enter new markets and expand their business.
2. The new rules will remove many of the limits previously imposed on truckers—involving what they carry, the areas they serve, and how they get to and from those areas.
3. The ICC must generally process applications for new operating rights in 180 days.
4. Although truckers will still have to file rate changes with the ICC, under the new law approval will be given much faster and rate changes of as much as 10 per cent can be made automatically for the first two years.

This law affects approximately 17,000 trucking companies that do business across state lines.

SOURCE: "Trucking Bill Passed by House," *New York Times* (June 20, 1980), p. D1; "Trucking Rules Are Eased as ICC Cuts Regulation," *Wall Street Journal* (July 3, 1980), p. 6; "What Trucking Bill Does," *New York Times* (July 2, 1980), p. D5; and John D. Williams, "Trucking Industry Will See Big Changes with the Expected Easing of ICC's Grip," *Wall Street Journal* (June 27, 1980), p. 5.

On July 1, 1980, President Jimmy Carter signed legislation deregulating the $41 billion interstate trucking industry.[20] See Figure 14–7 for an explanation of the implications of trucking deregulation.

Waterways

Intercity-waterway transportation moves low-value, high-bulk freight throughout in-coast waters at extremely low rates.

Intercity-waterway transportation involves the movement of goods on barges via inland rivers and on tankers and general merchandise freighters through the Great Lakes, in-coastal shipping, and the St. Lawrence Seaway. Waterways are used primarily for transporting low-value, high-bulk freight (such as coal, iron ore, gravel, grain, and cement). Although this transportation is slow, and may be closed by ice during the winter, the rates are extremely low.

Various improvements in vessel design have recently occurred. For example, nine "supervessels" are now operating on the Great Lakes. These supervessels can each carry 61,000 gross tons of iron-bearing rock in one trip. The conveyor system is twice as efficient as the one on older boats. One supervessel can annually deliver three and one-half million gross tons of rock along a route from Lake Superior to Gary, Indiana. This is enough to keep Gary's blast furnaces operating for 160 days.[21]

Pipelines

Pipelines minimize handling and labor costs through continuous movement without interruptions or inventories.

Within *pipelines*, there is continuous movement and there are no interruptions, inventories (except those held by a carrier), and intervening storage locations. Thus, handling and labor costs are minimized. Even though pipelines are very reliable, only certain commodities can be moved through them. In the past, emphasis was on gas and petroleum-based products. Recently, pipelines have been modified to accept coal and wood chips, which are transported in a semiliquid state. Nonetheless, lack of flexibility limits the potential of pipelines.

Some pipelines are enormous in size. For example, the Alaska Natural Gas Transportation System (ANGTS) will eventually cover 4,800 miles and deliver 2.4 billion cubic feet of natural gas per day to the lower 48 states.[22] It has been estimated that this pipeline will cost $10 billion to construct.

[20]"Carter Signs Bill for Deregulation of Truck Lines," *New York Times* (July 2, 1980), pp. D1, D5.
[21]Seth Cropsey, "King of the Ore Boats," *Fortune* (March 10, 1980), pp. 104–106.
[22]"McMillian: A Tough Pipeliner Vs. the Producers," *Business Week* (March 31, 1980), pp. 62, 65.

Airways

Airways are fast, expensive, and used for high-value products, perishable goods, and emergency goods.

Airways are the fastest, most expensive form of transportation. As a result, high-value products, perishable goods, and emergency goods dominate air shipments. Even though air transit is costly, it may lower other costs, such as the need for outlying or even regional warehouses. The costs of packing, unpacking, and preparing goods for transportation are lower than for other modes.

Airfreight has been deregulated since late 1977. As a result, some airlines have stepped up cargo operations, but others have curtailed them. Many carriers now employ wide-bodied jets that can handle large containers. In addition, modern communications and sorting equipment have been added to airfreight operations. Firms specializing in air shipments, such as Emery Air Freight and Federal Express, have done well by emphasizing fast, guaranteed service at reasonable prices.

One large air carrier (TWA) discontinued cargo flights but continues to offer cargo service on passenger planes.[23] TWA may face problems with this strategy, because most businesses prefer to make air shipments in the evening, at the end of the day's operations. Evening flights also ensure that delivery is made by the opening of business the next day. In contrast, most passenger flights are during the day.

Transportation Services

Three types of *transportation service companies* ship moderate-sized packages: government parcel post, private parcel, and express.

Transportation service companies handle the shipments of moderate-sized packages. Some pick up packages from the shipping firm's office and deliver direct to the addressee. Others require packages to be brought to a service company outlet. The three major kinds of service companies are government parcel post, private parcel, and express.

Government parcel post operates out of post offices and utilizes rates based on postal zones, of which there are eight. Parcel post can be insured or sent COD (collect on delivery). Special handling is available to expedite shipments. Express mail is available for next day service from a post office to an addressee.

Private parcel services specialize in small-package delivery, usually less than 50-pound shipments. Most services ship from manufacturers, wholesalers, distributors, and retailers to their customers within a several-state area. The largest private firm is United Parcel Post (UPS), a multibillion dollar, national company.

Express companies, such as Federal Express, Emery Air Freight, Burlington Northern Air Freight, and Purolator Carrier Corporation, generally provide guaranteed nationwide delivery of small packages for the morning after pickup. The average express delivery is 10 pounds.

Coordination of Transportation

Because a single shipment may involve a combination of transportation modes, coordination is necessary. Two major innovations that improve a firm's ability to coordinate shipments are containerization and freight forwarding.

With *containerization*, items are sealed and placed on trains, trucks, ships, or planes.

Under *containerization*, goods are placed into study containers that can be placed on trains, trucks, ships, or planes. These marked containers are sealed until delivered, thereby reducing damage and pilferage. Their progress and destination are frequently validated. The containers are mobile warehouses that can be moved from manufacturing plants to receiving docks, where they remain until the contents are needed.

---

[23]William M. Conley, "TWA Will Terminate Cargo Jet Business But Keep the Service on Passenger Planes," *Wall Street Journal* (November 6, 1978), p. 7.

Freight forwarders accumulate shipments from several companies and arrange for delivery.

Freight forwarders consolidate small shipments (usually less than 500 pounds each) from several companies. They pick up merchandise at the shipper's place of business and arrange for delivery at the buyer's door. Freight forwarders prosper because less than carload (lcl) rates are sharply higher than carload (cl) rates. Freight forwarders also provide traffic management services, such as selecting the best transportation mode at the most reasonable rate.

Legal Status of Transportation Firms

Transportation firms are categorized as common, contract, exempt, or private carriers. *Common carriers* must provide service between designated points on a fixed schedule. They are not permitted to change operating schedules or rates without permission, and they cannot refuse to transport the goods of any shipper unless the carrier's rules are violated. Common carriers must obtain franchises from the appropriate regulatory agency. The main agencies are

Common carriers are franchised by the government and must provide service for all shippers.

Interstate Commerce Commission (ICC) for railroads, motor trucks, and inland waterway carriers;

Civil Aeronautics Board (CAB) and Federal Aviation Agency (FAA) for air carriers;

Federal Maritime Commission (FMC) for ocean-going water carriers;

Federal Power Commission (FPC) for pipelines.

All railroads and petroleum pipelines and some air, motor truck, and water transporters are common carriers.

Contract carriers provide one or a few shippers with transportation services as defined by contract. Although contract carriers must obtain certificates in order to operate, they are not required to maintain fixed routes or schedules, and rates may be negotiated. Many motor-truck, inland-waterway, and airfreight transporters are contract carriers.

Contract carriers provide transportation services as specified by contract.

Exempt carriers have no economic regulations, only safety requirements. Exempt carriers are specified by law. Some commodities moved by water, such as coal, and most agricultural goods are exempt from economic restrictions.

Exempt carriers are specified by law.

Private carriers are shippers who possess their own transportation facilities. They are subject to safety rules. Private carriers are common in the trucking industry. . . .

Private carriers possess their own transportation facilities.

NOTES

1. Adapted from **Thomas Elliott Berry,** *Journalism Today* (Radnor, Pa.: Chilton Books, 1966), pp. 110–111, 120–121.
2. **Berry,** pp. 78–79.
3. Adapted from **Oscar Brockett,** *The Theatre: An Introduction* (New York: Holt, Rinehart & Winston, 1964), pp. 58–60.
4. **J. J. Braun** and **Darwyn Linder,** *Psychology Today: An Introduction,* 4th ed. (New York: Random House, 1979), pp. 426–427.
5. *Macmillan School Dictionary* (New York: Macmillan, 1977), p. 80.
6. **Joel R. Evans** and **Barry Berman,** *Marketing* (New York: Macmillan, 1982), pp. 388–395.

Two

PREVIEWING

Before you take the plunge—STOP! Think and preview before you read. Previewing is the thinking process that precedes reading. Previewing helps you organize material so that you will

1. Understand what you are reading.
2. Remember details.

Previewing is one of those reading skills that can literally make the difference between understanding and not understanding what you read. Do not be tempted to skip previewing because it seems to be time-consuming. In the end, you will save twice the time you spend previewing.

In the following you will be shown how to preview textbooks, essays, novels, short stories, and plays. If you only master and use this technique, this book will have been a worthwhile investment.

PREVIEWING A CHAPTER IN A TEXTBOOK

The first thing for you to do when previewing is to pay attention to the organizational aids provided by the author. Headings, introductions, illustrations, tables, charts, questions, and chapter summaries are examples of these aids.

The introductory portion of the chapter will acquaint you with material covered in the chapter. You should read this portion carefully as a part of your preview.

Headings and subheadings in boldface and italics are also important parts of your preview. Headings give clues to the topics that will be discussed in succeeding paragraphs. You should turn headings into questions. For example, a heading in the following section is "Criticisms of Marketing." You should turn this heading into the question, "What are criticisms of marketing?" and then read on to answer the question. Some texts do not have headings or subheadings. In these cases, read the first and last sentence of each paragraph.

Be sure to include tables, illustrations, and charts in your preview. The author often uses these visual aids to summarize information from the text. From time to time you must refer to these aids to understand the text.

The summary of a chapter, when available, presents the contents of a chapter in condensed form. The author may also present the main points and conclusions in the summary. As you read the summary, try to recall all the important information from the introduction, headings, and graphic aids.

You should always preview a chapter before reading it carefully.

ACTIVITY I

The following pages contain excerpts from a textbook chapter. Follow the steps below as you preview the material. Then answer the questions on p. 22.

1. Read all headings and subheadings.
2. Read all typographical aids such as italics and boldface.
3. Review graphs, tables, charts, and illustrations.
4. Read the first and last sentences of each paragraph.
5. Read the questions at the end of the chapter.
6. Read the summary or chapter review.

THE FOUR Ps OF MARKETING[1]

Product

A manufacturer obviously must decide what products will best attract consumers in its target market. In recent years, for example, Xerox has been making steadily larger and more expensive copying machines. A smaller competitor, Savin, realized there was no point in trying to challenge Xerox head-on, so it entered the field instead with a line of more compact, less expensive desktop copiers that found a segment of the market waiting for them. Around the same time Xerox's dominance of the upper range of the copier market came under attack by Kodak, which after a decade of research introduced its own line of high-priced, high-quality copying machines.

Product lines must be constantly re-evaluated in light of changing conditions. Items may be added or dropped as the market dictates. The Gerber baby-food company, faced with a declining birth rate, has diversified into the insurance field and other areas, backing up the effort with a carefully targeted advertising campaign. Howard Johnson's, Stouffer's, and other restaurant chains have made profitable inroads into the frozen-food market, aided by the public's familiarity with their names.

Other product-related decisions involve such factors as brand names, packaging, and guarantees—all multiplying the number of choices a market manager has to consider in determining what to offer the consumer.

Price

Once the basic decisions on the product line have been made, the market manager must decide how the company should price its products. Will a policy based on low prices maximize profits? Supermarkets have used this tactic to encourage people to buy their own brand merchandise rather than nationally advertised products. . . .

Promotion

Very often the key decision a market manager must make is how the manufacturer should inform prospective customers about its products. This involves promotion, which includes the four kinds of selling previously mentioned. Some managers, like those at Fuller Brush, may decide to emphasize direct

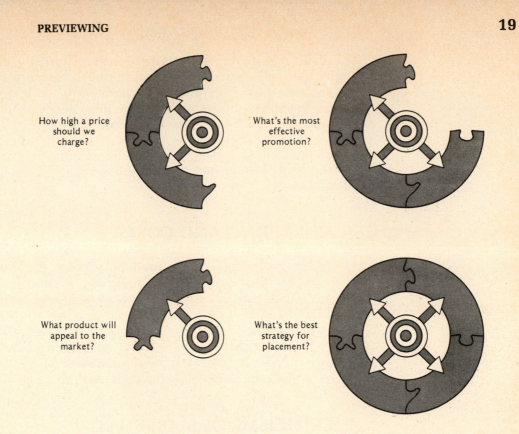

How high a price should we charge?

What's the most effective promotion?

What product will appeal to the market?

What's the best strategy for placement?

selling and spend most of their promotion dollars in training and paying salespeople. Others, like producers of soap and headache remedies, promote their products through advertising, primarily on television. Firms like department stores also spend heavily on advertising, but they choose newspapers as the most effective medium. The alternatives are many, the choice of which may determine the success of a marketing effort. . . .

Placement

The fourth element of the marketing mix is placement (or distribution): how the manufacturer gets its products to the cutomers. Some firms, like Tupperware with its party plans, sell directly to the consumer. Manhattan Shirt Company and other apparel companies sell to retailers who then resell to consumers. Westinghouse and other appliance industries sell to wholesalers in major areas of the country. Some firms use several channels. Sears distributes its products through stores and a catalog. Pepperidge Farm not only sells baked goods through retail grocery stores, but also offers a special gift line to consumers through a mail-order division. . . .

MARKETING-MIX DECISIONS CAN BE HARD TO MAKE

Finding the right combination of product, price, promotion, and placement has become an increasingly complex task for most businesses. Marketing directors have found that even the most subtle changes—in the shape or color of packaging, for instance, or the way the product is displayed in a store, or the location of the store itself—can have a decisive impact on a product's success, quite apart from its actual quality. In effect, you may have built a better mousetrap, but unless you package it well, set up good distribution, target your advertising appropriately, and offer a good warranty, the world won't necessarily take any notice. Indeed, it has become more common to reverse the process—as did the Squibb Corporation when it developed a new product called Bubble-Yum. It was created to meet the demands of customers who were dissatisfied with existing bubblegums: they were too hard and lost their flavor too quickly. The company also had to price its new gum within the reach of bubblegum customers, place it in the stores where they usually bought gum, and stress in its advertising that Bubble-Yum had the qualities that rival brands lacked.

MARKETING AND COSTS

Today, marketing activities probably account for about half the price of the consumer's average purchase. There are, of course, tremendous variations in marketing costs among products. Standard Oil of New Jersey estimated at one time that $1 of natural gas purchased by a family in New York City cost only 4 cents at the wellhead in Texas; transportation and other marketing costs made up the balance of 96 cents. However, as Figure 4 illustrates, of every dollar spent by a shopper for a steak at the supermarket, 63 cents went to the rancher and meat packer as a cost of productions; the remainder involves marketing costs.

CRITICISMS OF MARKETING

Confronted with statistics such as the ones just presented, many people feel that marketing costs too much. They believe that at least some prices could be lowered if marketing were reduced or eliminated. In fact, however, many products might cost even more without marketing. Marketing functions like storage, transportation, and selling increase the demand for goods to the point where mass production becomes feasible. If products like color television or pocketsized computers were not advertised, demand might never reach the levels that make mass production possible. The small quantities of goods produced would thus cost much more.

Another charge leveled against marketing is that it encourages people to buy products they don't really need. Does our economy really "need" dozens of different brands of underarm deodorants, each packaged and promoted at great expense? Do we "need" cars with elaborate chrome trim and stereo systems? Marketing professionals answer these questions by redefining "need" to in-

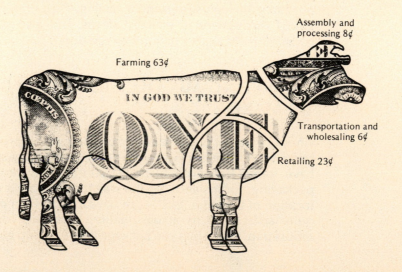

Assembly and processing 8¢

Farming 63¢

Transportation and wholesaling 6¢

Retailing 23¢

IN GOD WE TRUST

clude more than basic necessities. They claim that the objective of our present economic system is to supply not only basic goods and services, but also products that make living more enjoyable and satisfy our egos. It is true that many of the products marketed are not essential. But that millions of Americans voluntarily purchase them suggests that they are filling real needs. And those who feel that no legitimate want is satisfied by a product can simply choose not to buy it.

In short, there are a number of arguments to suggest that the costs of marketing are well worth incurring. This point will become clearer as we look at the various aspects of marketing in more detail in the chapters that follow.

CHAPTER REVIEW

Marketing is the process of moving goods and services from the producer to the consumer. It consists of eight specific functions: buying, selling, storing, transporting, financing, risk bearing, securing information, and standardization and grading.

Marketing has changed drastically over the past hundred years. Originally most firms were production-oriented, with marketing restricted primarily to taking orders and shipping goods. Then came sales-oriented marketing, which emphasized selling. Since World War II, however, most large firms have adopted the total marketing concept, a consumer-oriented marketing approach.

The marketing manager tries to develop the marketing program that will be best suited to the target market. A firm has four elements to work with in setting up its marketing program. These are product, promotion, price, and placement. They are sometimes called the four Ps of marketing. The particular combination of the four Ps that the marketing manager chooses is called the marketing mix.

It is important to distinguish between the different kinds of markets, or groups of customers, at which a marketing program must be directed. Two major categories are the consumer market, which can be subdivided into markets for convenience goods, shopping goods, and specialty goods; and the business market which buys industrial and commercial goods.

KEYWORD REVIEW

marketing ** total marketing concept
market research ** speculative production
time utility ** place utility
borrowing to carry inventory
market ** target market
market segmentation ** consumer market
convenience goods ** shopping goods
specialty goods ** business market
industrial goods ** commercial goods
marketing mix

REVIEW QUESTIONS

1. What are the "four Ps of marketing"?
2. List four different ways a product can be promoted.
3. Give an example of each of the three different kinds of goods consumers buy.
4. Why may the same product be classified as a consumer good or a business-goods item?

Answer these questions based on your preview of the preceding pages.

1. What are two major criticisms leveled against marketing? _____

_____

_____

2. What accounts for the major portion of each dollar spent on steak? _____

_____

_____

3. What accounts for the smallest portion of each dollar spent on steak? _____

_____

_____

4. What are the four steps in the marketing process? _____

_____

_____

_____

_____

5. What is the latest trend in marketing? _____

_____

_____

6. What kind of program does the marketing manager try to develop? _____

_____

_____

7. How many different kinds of markets are there? _____

_____

_____

PREVIEWING AN ESSAY

You will often encounter essays in books of readings or in other material handed out or assigned by the instructor. Follow the four steps given below to preview an essay.

1. Read the title and the author's name. The title is a particularly useful guide when previewing an essay. If the author's name is familiar, it may prepare you for a particular writing style or point of view.
2. The author of an essay will usually make clear the purpose of the essay in the opening paragraphs. You should always read the first, and possibly the second, paragraph as a part of your preview.
3. The first sentences of subsequent paragraphs are important. Read each and

note how they relate to the author's stated purpose in the opening paragraphs.

4. The last paragraph usually contains a summary. This paragraph should be read carefully.

ACTIVITY II

Preview the following essay using the four steps noted above. The material you should read when previewing this essay has been marked for you.

Once your preview is complete, answer the questions following the essay.

IMMOBILIZATION[2]

Wayne W. Dyer

As you consider your potential for choosing happiness, keep in mind the word immobilization as the indicator of negative emotions in your life. You might believe that anger, hostility, shyness, and other similar feelings are worth having at times, and so you want to hang on to them. Your guide should be the extent to which you are in any way immobilized by the feeling.

Immobilization can range from total inaction to mild indecision and hesitancy. Does your anger keep you from saying, feeling, or doing something? If so, then you are immobilized. Does your shyness prevent you from meeting people you want to know? If so, you are immobilized and missing out on experiences that are rightfully yours. Is your hate and jealousy helping you to grow an ulcer or to raise your blood pressure? Does it keep you from working effectively on the job? Are you unable to sleep or make love because of a negative present-moment feeling? These are all signs of immobilization. Immobilization: A state, however mild or serious, in which you are not functioning at the level that you would like to. If feelings lead to such a state, you need to look no further for a reason to get rid of them.

Here is a brief checklist of some instances in which you may be immobilized. They range from minor to major states of immobility.

You are immobilized when . . .
You can't talk lovingly to your spouse and children though you want to.
You can't work on a project that interests you.
You don't make love and would like to.
You sit in the house all day and brood.
You don't play golf, tennis, or other enjoyable activities, because of a leftover gnawing feeling.
You can't introduce yourself to someone who appeals to you.
You avoid talking to someone when you realize that a simple gesture would improve your relationship.
You can't sleep because something is bothering you.
Your anger keeps you from thinking clearly.
You say something abusive to someone that you love.
Your face is twitching, or you are so nervous that you don't function the way you would prefer.

Immobilization cuts a wide swath. Virtually all negative emotions result in some degree of self-immobility, and this alone is a solid reason for eliminating them entirely from your life. Perhaps you are thinking of occasions when a negative emotion has a payoff, such as yelling at a young child in an angry voice to emphasize that you do not want him to play in the street. If the angry voice is simply a device for emphasis and it works, then you've adopted a healthy strategy. However, if you yell at others not to make a point, but because you are internally upset, then you've immobilized yourself, and it's time to begin working at new choices that will help you to reach your goal of keeping your child out of the street without experiencing feelings that are hurtful to you.

Answer the following questions based on your preview of the essay.

1. What is the author's general thesis? _____

_____

_____

_____

2. What, in the author's view, is the key to happiness? _____

_____

_____

_____

3. What does the author feel results from negative emotions? _____

_____

_____

_____

4. If you are immobilized by negative emotion, what does the author suggest that you

do? _____

_____

_____

_____

_____

PREVIEWING A NOVEL AND A SHORT STORY

Both the novel and short story require a similar previewing technique. This technique involves a four-step questioning guide, which is given below. Read lightly through the story until you can answer these questions. When you have all four answers, your preview will be complete and you can begin reading.

1. Who?
     Who is the main character?
     With what other characters is this main character involved?
2. Where? When?
     In what time and place is the story set?
3. What?
     In general, what is the story about?
     What is the author's point of view in the story?
4. What are the author's tone and style?

Tone refers to the author's feelings or attitudes about the subject or characters in the story. The tone of a selection may be serious or amused. An optimistic tone indicates that the author is looking forward to something better, whereas a pessimistic tone conveys a sense of foreboding. Satire mocks the subject or characters, whereas an ironic tone indicates a contrast between what is said and what is meant.

Style refers to the way the author uses language. The style may be formal, characterized by long, complicated sentences and strict adherence to the rules of grammar. The style may be informal, characterized by "everyday" language and the standard grammar of spoken English. The style may be terse, with short, concise sentences, or flowery, with longer sentences that are very descriptive.

Let us think for a moment about the tone and style of the following passage taken from Thomas Wolfe's "The Lost Boy."

And out of the enchanted wood, that thicket of man's memory, Eugene knew that the dark eye and quiet face of his friend and brother—poor child, life's stranger, and life's exile, lost like all of us, a cipher in blind mazes, long ago—the lost boy was gone forever, and would not return.[3]

A certain feeling is communicated by the author. The words "poor child" and "life's stranger" certainly evoke a sense of sorrow and pity. A serious, nostalgic tone is further reflected through the words "lost boy gone forever." The author expresses a sad yearning for what is gone and will never come again. "Lost like all of us, a cipher in blind mazes"—here the author conveys a pessimistic view of life. We are lost in a world we cannot comprehend. By analyzing the emotions expressed in this passage the reader can conclude that the tone is serious, nostalgic, and pessimistic.

Style

The style of this excerpt is basically informal. Poetic style can be detected in the final lines, where Eugene communicates a sense of loneliness by the dramatic use of metaphor.

The descriptions of tone and style above give just a few of the different feelings, attitudes, and uses of language that influence a literary work. Preview enough of the story to understand the author's tone and style and you will enjoy and understand the work when you read.

PREVIEWING A PLAY

A play, a short story, and a novel have a lot in common. The format of a play is the most obvious difference. A play gives sketchy descriptions of the characters. However, we are able to read every word that each character speaks along with descriptions of how the character acts.

With this difference in mind, you can use the four steps above to preview a play. Browse through the list of characters and the stage directions to get a feeling for the setting of a play and its characters. Sample the dialogue to get a taste of the author's point of view, tone, and style.

PREVIEWING A POEM

Poetry is considered by many to be the most powerful form of writing. It is particularly important to experience a poem by reading it aloud. A poem read aloud will enable you to hear many of the "sounds" of the writing. Reading aloud will also allow you to feel, to sense, what is happening.

It is important to feel a poem, to live it. So all the formal rules for previewing other forms of writing are replaced here by a single suggestion. Read the poem aloud once and then you can read it silently and analytically. After you have read the poem aloud, use these questions as your guide:

1. What feelings does the poem create through visual images and sounds?
2. What thoughts does the poem evoke (pleasant or unpleasant)?

Nothing Gold Can Stay[4]

Nature's first green is gold,
Her hardest hue to hold.
Her early leaf's a flower;
But only so an hour,
Then leaf subsides to leaf.
So Eden sank to grief.
So dawn goes down to day.
Nothing gold can stay.

PROJECT

Preview the following selection on memory. Use the techniques recommended in this chapter. Remember to pay particular attention to topic headings. Each lettered topic heading should be turned into a question. Use this page to write the headings in question form.

A   *What is memory?*

B   *How do memory and attention work together?*

C   _____

D   _____

E   _____

F   _____

G   _____

H   _____

I   _____

J   _____

K   _____

L   _____

M   _____

N   _____

O   _____

P   _____

Q   _____

R   _____

S   _____

T   _____

MEMORY[5]

We have at our disposal a seemingly limitless quantity of facts about our past (Where did you go to kindergarten? Who was your second-grade teacher? Who was your best friend when you were twelve?). We can also recall innumerable facts about our environment (Who is President of the United States? What does a red traffic light mean?). Most of us remember our telephone number, social security number, address, birth date, and thousands of other such facts.

Memory also includes information from each of the senses. For example, visual memories enable us to recognize pictures, places we have visited, and the faces of people we have met. With our memory for sounds, we can recall the melody of a song (Hum "The Star-Spangled Banner") and the tone of people's voices. We can also recognize odors (How does the air smell after it rains?) and tactile sensations (How does velvet feel?). The capacity of memory seems almost infinite, and it is dificult to imagine leading a normal life without this ability to call upon past experience.

Memory is a crucial part of the learning process, for without it, experiences would be lost as soon as they became part of the past. Each experience would be completely novel. There would be no means of using past experiences to shape our behavior, and the same information would have to be learned again and again.

In a sense, memory and learning are two sides of the same coin. We could not learn without memory, and conversely, memory would have no content if we were not learning from the environment. Memory gives learning some permanence and also influences the ways in which we learn. Past learning experiences, retained as memories, alter our perspectives in new learning situations. For example, the memory of having failed an exam because class notes were ignored will probably result in an intensive effort to learn those notes for the next exam. At the same time, new learning often modifies our memories of the past. A teacher who is disliked for his strictness may be recalled with more kindness if new experiences prove that his advice was correct. Learning and memory continually interact in this way, each providing fuel and direction for the other.

[A] WHAT IS MEMORY?

Memory is the retention of experience, the foundation of a person's knowledge about the world. It is memory that allows us to greet a new day knowing more than we did on the previous one. The central mystery of memory is how experience is encoded, or registered, by the brain. Numerous analogies have been proposed to account for this phenomenon.

Following Richard Caton's discovery of electrical brain activity in 1875, it was suggested that memories are represented by unique patterns of electrical activity in the brain. Almost a century later, E. Roy John (1967) summarized a number of experiments which indicated that consistent changes in the patterns of electrical brain activity do take place as an animal learns to perform and remember some task. It has also been shown, however, that learned behavior can occur in the absence of these changes, and that these changes can even occur without the appropriate behavior being displayed (Chow, Dement, and John, 1957; Schuckman and Battersby, 1965). In addition, experiments in which strips of tantalum wire were implanted in the brains of monkeys (under the assumption that unique patterns of electrical activity would be short-circuited by the wire) indicated that memories for specific tasks were not disrupted by this procedure (Sperry, Miner, and Myers, 1955). Thus, memory does not appear to be based on obvious changes in the electrical activity of the brain.

The associationist school of thought . . . has hypothesized that memory, like learning, is represented by the associations formed (presumably in the brain) between stimuli and responses: the stronger an association, the more likely we are to remember a particular sequence of movements (such as swinging a tennis racket) or a certain perceptual experience (such as the image of someone's face). Associationists concentrated on studying the conditions that strengthen or weaken memory processes. They described the organization of memory in various ways: as analogous to a large set of "storage bins," each holding separate memories, or to a telephone switchboard in which dialing a certain number (the stimulus) activates a particular line (the association link), which results in the ringing of a specific phone (the response).

The switchboard analogy was based on what associationists called a "connectionist theory" of learning, which held that the strengthening of a stimulus-response link occurs within a limited and special set of connections in the brain. The connectionist theory does not appear to be correct. If memory were based on specific connections in the brain, then it should be possible to find certain brain areas, damage to which would lead to the loss of specific memories. In a lifetime of research devoted to examining the relationships among memory, learning, and the brain, an eminent physiological psychologist, Karl S. Lashley, was unable to identify areas for specific memories in animal subjects. . . . In fact, surveying the results of his extensive experiments, Lashley (1950) said that he was tempted to conclude that learning was impossible! And yet learning and memory do occur, at least as defined by the research of experimental psychologists and by the everyday experiences of anybody who pauses to think about it.

While the specific nature of memory encoding by the brain remains a mystery, two explanations for the process seem most likely: changes in the anatomical structure and changes in the chemistry of brain cells. Neuroscientists and physiological psychologists are currently exploring these two possibilities. Though they are still unable to explain the physiological bases of memory, psychologists who study cognition (the process of knowing) have made substantial progress in defining the nature of memory processes as they are reflected in behavior.

Cognitive psychologists became convinced that many facets of human memory cannot be understood by analyzing stimulus-response associations (why, for example, are some memories inaccessible at one time but accessible at another?). After all, instead of automatically responding to a particular "stimulus," humans tend to evaluate their options, to think about them, and then to select the best one. An experiment (Carmichael, Hogan, and Walter, 1932) demonstrated how "thought" can bias a person's memory for visual material (see Figure 5.1). In this experiment, the way people reproduced figures shown to them was determined to a large degree by how the figures were described: a figure consisting of two circles connected by a short, straight line was reproduced quite differently depending on whether it was labeled "eyeglasses" or "dumbbell."

So the cognitive psychologists discarded the concepts of stimulus and response and replaced them with those of knowledge and mental activity. They also portrayed humans as active organizers of information, rather than as passive recipients of the stimuli that produce automatic responses. This approach focuses on the activities that occur in a person's mind between the time it is presented with information and the time it recalls or responds to it.

Researchers who study memory usually focus on three closely related but separable processes: attention, memory storage, and memory retrieval. Attention refers to the ability to deal with limited amounts of information from the

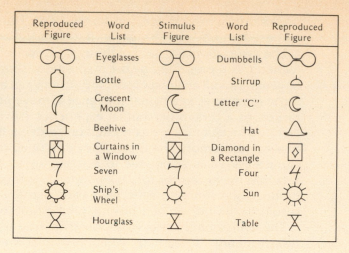

Figure 5.1
Carmichael, Hogan, and Walter designed an experiment to study the influence of set on perception. Subjects were shown the line patterns in the middle column of this figure, and these stimuli were described as drawings of various objects. Later, when the subjects were asked to reproduce from memory the patterns they had seen, they made the drawings shown in the right and left columns. You can see how the naming of the patterns influenced their drawings. (After Carmichael, Hogan, and Walter, 1932.)

environment at any one time; storage refers to the process by which certain information is retained; and retrieval refers to the means used to gain access to the stored information. These three components of memory are easily recognized in everyday life. Everyone has had the frustrating experience of learning a particular fact—a name, place, or date—and then being unable to produce that fact when it is needed. For example, information that has been memorized for an exam may stubbornly refuse to appear when it is required, but then become available when the exam is over. In this situation, the grade on the exam reflects a failure of the retrieval process, but the grade does not serve as an accurate measure of what has been attended to and stored in memory. While memory is a function of all three components, each phase of the memory process can be described and studied individually.

[B] MEMORY AND ATTENTION

Storing information in memory and retrieving it at a later time depend a great deal on **attention,** the ability to focus on certain information from the environment while ignoring other information.

Attention is a crucial concept for understanding why only some information enters into memory storage. Our senses are constantly being bombarded by the environment—sights, sounds, odors, tactile sensations are all present simultaneously. But there are limitations on the amount of information that can be attended to at one time. While listening to music, for example, a person may be unaware of the discomfort of a tight pair of shoes. If the irritation were to grow more intense, however, it would probably become difficult to concentrate on the music. Likewise, if you were instructed to count and remember the number of vowels from a passage in this book, you would probably recall very little of the meaning conveyed in that passage. Conversely, when you read for content, you are unlikely to notice the number of vowels in the passage.

Past experiences can also influence which environmental information we attend to. We are likely to be more attentive to information about driving safety if we remember a previous automobile accident. The present also influences memory, though: when information is retrieved from memory, it is often because we are devoting attention to a situation—such as an exam or a problem-solving task—that demands the information. One of the goals of psychologists who study memory is to determine how attention operates to select what information gets stored in and summoned from memory.

[C] Sensory Gating

The brain monitors incoming sensory information to some extent, directing attention to one type of sensory input while putting a damper on information that is less important. For example, while attending to a visual stimulus the brain reduces the volume of information coming from other sensory channels. Thus, when examining a painting, a person usually is less aware of the surrounding sounds and odors. This selective turning to one kind of input while reducing others is called **sensory gating.** It cuts down extraneous "noise" in the environment, permitting attention to be focused in one place. Sensory gating does not completely eliminate information from the damped-down senses, however. If a strange sound—or an unexpected silence—is detected, attention will probably shift from what is being seen to what is being heard. This indicates that information in the tuned-down sensory systems is still processed to some extent, thus enabling us to know when to shift our attention.

[D] Selective Attention

A more complex form of information selection can occur within a *single* sensory channel. When we carry on a conversation at a crowded cocktail party, for example, our ears receive a great deal of extraneous information. In addition to hearing the person we are speaking with, we may also hear the din of other conversations, the clink of glasses, the sounds of music. Despite the confusion of sounds, we somehow manage to follow our partner's conversation, the message being attended to. . . . It may seem that this is accomplished by completely ignoring all other sounds, but in fact, research indicates that the sounds seemingly not attended to are given an elementary form of attention. In the same way that sensory gating does not completely eliminate information from the other senses, **selective attention** permits some processing of information within the same sensory channel that is not at the focus of attention.

Psychologists have studied this "cocktail party phenomenon" of hearing. One researcher (Cherry, 1953) used a **dichotic listening** technique, in which a subject wearing a set of earphones heard two different messages played simultaneously one in each ear. The subject was instructed to "shadow" the message coming into one ear. To shadow a message is to repeat it aloud as it is received; the subject's voice, like a shadow, trails along immediately behind the recorded message. Later, the subject was asked to recognize or recall material from the nonshadowed message, the one coming into the other ear. If the nonshadowed message had been completely ignored, the subject would have been unable to remember anything about it. This was not the case. Under most conditions, people detected the broad characteristics of the nonshadowed message. They could report whether a voice was present and whether it changed midway from male to female, but they generally did not remember the content of the message or the language in which it was spoken. They did not even notice the difference between speech and nonsense sounds. However, people did hear their names in the unattended channel, as well as information that was relevant to the shadowed message.

One researcher postulated that selective attention is based on our analysis of the physical aspects of information coming in through different sensory channels (Broadbent, 1958). When we attend to something we hear in one ear at the expense of information coming into the other ear (as in the shadowing experiments), we have become attuned to the difference in the location of the two messages (right and left); this physical difference guides our attention to one of them and allows it to be maintained there while the other message is filtered out. . . . Some experiments have shown that a person's attention can flip back and forth between separate channels to follow the meaning of a message

(Triesman, 1960). When a subject followed a message in one ear and the message jumped to the other ear, the subject's attention also jumped to follow the message. This happened despite instructions to stay with the original channel no matter what. . . . That the sound was a message—that is to say, it had *meaning*—seems to have been an important factor in selective attention. Attention may first operate on the basis of the physical characteristics of the message (where it comes from, what the voice quality is), but this can yield to the meaning or content of a message when enough information has been gathered to make sense of it (Triesman, 1964).

[E] MEMORY STORAGE

Once an item of information has been attended to, it must be stored or retained if it is to have any future usefulness. **Memory storage** refers to the ability to retain the lessons of experience for later application. This storage ability cannot be observed directly; instead, psychologists make inferences about storage by examining the performance of subjects on memory retrieval tasks.

Memory storage ability seems to take three forms. **Sensory storage** refers to the momentary persistence of sensory information after the stimulation has ceased; we can store a great deal of information in this memory system, but only for an instant. **Short-term memory** is the memory of events that have just taken place; this storage system holds only a small amount of information, but can keep it available for several seconds. **Long-term memory** stores information indefinitely, to be used over and over again; its capacity is thought to be limitless.

[F] Sensory Storage

When the pattern of letters and numbers in Figure 5.2 is presented very briefly, most people are able to remember between five and nine of the twelve items. People who try this task usually believe, immediately after the presentation, that they will recall more than eight or nine, but by the time they have reported six or so, the other items seem to have evaporated from their memory. Are the subjects correct in saying that they remembered more items before they began to report them? In 1960 George Sperling devised a technique to answer this question. He flashed an array like the one in Figure 5.2 to subjects and followed it by sounding a high, medium, or low tone to indicate which line they should report. Under these conditions, the subjects displayed almost perfect recall, indicating that immediately after the presentation of a stimulus, all the symbols *are* available in memory. During the span of time it took to report about six symbols, however, the remaining symbols seem to have been lost from memory.

Sensory storage appears to be **modality specific**—that is, the storage occurs within the sensory system that received the information, not at some central location. Additional information coming in the same sensory path immediately disrupts the storage. If, shortly after the array in Figure 5.2 is presented, a second visual stimulus—say a set of X's—is flashed, people's memory for the initial array may be lost. However, if the second stimulus is a sound or an odor, it does not interfere with memory for the visual array. Moreover, memory for the visual array is even better if the stimulus is made brighter during presentation or if the presentation is preceded and followed by darkness.

Sensory storage is not limited to the visual system. As another example, if several of a person's finger joints are touched simultaneously by air jets, it is difficult for that person to report more than three touch locations correctly. However, if the finger joints are classified into three sets—upper, middle, and lower (analogous to Sperling's three tones)—memory is significantly improved,

Figure 5.2
When exposed to this array of unrelated items for a brief period, people typically recall no more than nine of them. But if subjects are signaled immediately after the exposure to recall just one of the lines, they can always recall all four items correctly. This evidence suggests that people "read" the information from some sort of complete sensory image of the stimulus, which fades in the time it takes to say the names of a few of the letters and numbers in the image.

indicating that most of the pressure information was stored for at least a moment.

The "shadowing" study discussed earlier (Cherry, 1953) provides an example of sensory storage in the auditory system. The shadowed material, remember, had to be stored long enough to be repeated aloud. However, when subjects who performed this task were questioned about the shadowed, and therefore attended to, message, they were usually able to repeat only the last three or four words of the message. Apparently, the process of shadowing the incoming message actually interfered with instating it into memory. Even though the information was processed in sensory storage (going into the ear and out of the mouth, as it were), this did not ensure that it would become a part of permanent memory.

What sensory storage seems to be able to provide is a second or so during which information that warrants further processing can be selected. Usually we are not aware of the existence of this very brief memory, but special circumstances can make us aware of it. For instance, in today's movies the action seems smooth and realistic because the time lapse between frames is extremely small. The time lapse is within the limits of sensory information storage, so that successive images blend together smoothly, giving the illusion of continuous motion. When movies made early in this century are shown with a modern projector, however, the action seems jerky and unnatural. The reason for the jerkiness is that too much time is left between frames, which permits the sensory image of one frame to begin to fade from sensory storage before the next frame appears.

[G] Short-Term Memory

If memory ability were limited to sensory storage, where images fade within about a second, we would have a fragile foundation for storing experiences. However, information does remain in memory long enough to be useful. After we look up a telephone number in the local directory, we can certainly remember it longer than a second—otherwise we would be unable to dial it. However, most of us probably dial quickly, knowing that we will not remember the number very long without some special effort. Often, we must repeat or rehearse the number—either aloud or mentally—several times before it is dialed. If we get distracted for a few seconds and rehearsal stops, we will probably be forced to consult the directory again. This example illustrates two basic features of **short-term memory** (STM). First, the information entering short-term memory is lost within seconds unless the individual regards it as important enough to renew it by **rehearsal,** or repetition. Second, because only a limited amount of information can be rehearsed at one time, the capacity of short-term memory is quite limited.

The rehearsal process seems to require some kind of speech—either overt, as in repeating the telephone number aloud, or implicit, as in rehearsing the number mentally. Rehearsal seems to maintain information in short-term memory in the following way: the subject says the information either aloud or silently, hears what is being said, and then re-stores this information. This cycle is repeated until it is time to use the information. In the rehearsal, items are maintained in memory acoustically—that is, the *sounds* of the items are repeated and stored. Although rehearsal can also be visual, acoustic rehearsal (especially implicit) seems to be faster (Weber and Castleman, 1970). Yet it is easily disrupted by either external distractions—for instance, the sounds of someone talking—or internal events—such as thinking about one's own telephone number while trying to remember the new number.

How long does an item stay in short-term memory without rehearsal? Various experiments have yielded figures under twenty seconds. When subjects are given a short series of letters—say CPQ—to remember and then are asked to count backwards by threes from say, 270 (267 . . . 264 . . . 261, and so on), they are likely to forget the letters within about fifteen seconds. The backward counting is an interfering task, a device used by psychologists to keep subjects from rehearsing the letters. If the subjects could secretly rehearse CPQ while appearing to take a deep breath between counts, their memory for CPQ would probably last longer than fifteen seconds. The duration varies from situation to situation, depending on the information to be remembered, the type of interfering task, and the amount of rehearsal allowed (Peterson and Peterson, 1959).

What is the capacity of short-term memory? In other words, how much information will it hold? In 1956, George Miller published a paper entitled "The Magical Number Seven, Plus or Minus Two: Some Limits on Our Capacity for Processing Information." In 1956, Miller summarized the results of many experiments, all indicating that a majority of humans can hold between five and nine items in memory. Although the magical number has never been pinned down precisely, everyone agrees that it is near the range specified by Miller. If anything, his estimate may have been a bit too high.

Miller was puzzled by the ability of humans, despite their limited short-term memory capacity, to process large amounts of information. He concluded that we expand our relatively small capacity by chunking information. If we could process only seven letters at a time, our thoughts would be limited indeed. Instead, however, we can arrange letters into words (chunk them) and then group words into familiar phrases (larger chunks), which permits us to hold about seven phrases in memory. By chunking phrases into sentences, we can further expand the capacity of short-term memory.

The process of chunking actually makes use of already established memory stores to categorize or encode new information. For example, the number "1492" is easier to recall than the number "2568" if we remember the year that Columbus landed in America. By using this "old" information, we reduce our memory load to one date instead of four numbers. In this fashion, we could conceivably recall a string of twenty-eight numbers if the numbers could be chunked into seven familiar dates.

Information can also be chunked by using a rule that organizes it. Consider the following number sequence: 149162536496481100121. While the sequence contains twenty-one numbers, it can be recalled as only one chunk of information. All we need do is to remember to square, in succession, the numbers 1 through 11 ($1^2 = 1$; $2^2 = 4$; $3^2 = 9$; $4^2 = 16$, and so on). In this way, chunking

Figure 5.3A

Study this arrangement of chess pieces for five seconds. Then turn to the empty chessboard on the next page and try to reproduce the arrangement. The amount you are able to recall correctly represents approximately seven of the chunks you have developed for processing information about chess games.

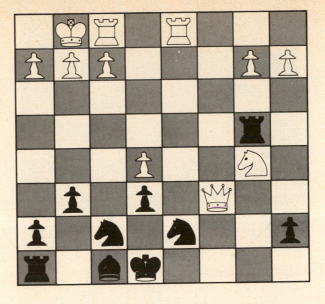

allows us to bypass the seven-item "bottleneck" that seems to characterize short-term memory.

Chunks need not be verbal; in fact, some of the most useful ones are visual. Study the chessboard shown in Figure 5.3A for about five seconds, then turn the page and see how many pieces you can draw correctly on the empty board there (Figure 5.3B). If you are unfamiliar with the game of chess, you will probably be limited to the "magical" range of about seven pieces. You may well recall even fewer than seven pieces, because the position of each piece requires several chunks of information: what the piece looks like and the row and column of its location. It may surprise you to know that excellent chessplayers are able to reproduce the entire board after a five-second exposure. At one time, this kind of performance led people to believe that master chess players had unusually good memories. However, experiments have shown that this amazing memory is lost if the pieces are arranged in a random pattern that is unlikely to occur in games between good players. In such cases, the masters' memory range is no greater than anyone else's. Thus, the masters' superiority has something to do with recognizing familiar visual configurations or chunks, and is not a sign of unusual intelligence or memory capacity.

Research on chess masters suggests that they can identify 25,000 to 100,000 visual chunks. Although this sounds like an astronomical number, it seems plausible when we consider that the educated speaker of English has a vocabulary that is about the same size. When we realize that the chess master probably starts playing the game in early childhood and is likely to devote more time to the game than anything else, the large number of chunks does not seem so unreasonable.

[H] Long-Term Memory

A few pages back we discussed the process of looking up a telephone number and holding it in short-term memory. The number remains available only as long as we repeat it to ourselves, and if we are distracted for several seconds we are likely to forget it. If this were the entire capacity of our memory, we would be forced to spend our day continuously repeating our own telephone number, and we would never be able to learn anyone else's number. Obviously, there is more to memory than this short-term "holding pattern."

Figure 5.3B
Turn to Figure 5.3A on the preceding page, if you have not already looked at it, and study it for five seconds. Then try to reproduce the arrangement shown there on this empty chessboard. Your success in doing so will depend heavily on your experience with the game of chess.

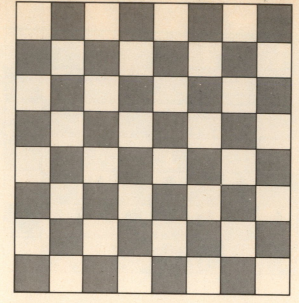

Long-term memory (LTM) can be considered the repository of our permanent knowledge. The amount of information in long-term memory is almost beyond comprehension. There are some theorists (for example, Penfield, 1959) who suggest that every fact that enters this long-term storage remains there in some form throughout a person's life.

How information is transferred from short-term to long-term memory is not completely understood. It is generally believed that the transfer depends on the amount of time the information has remained in the rehearsal cycle: the longer the time, the more likely the transfer. Once information begins to enter long-term storage, still more time is needed for consolidation processes to firmly fix it there. According to this consolidation theory, unless the initial physiological change, or memory trace, caused by the new information has time to become stable and firm, new information coming in may interfere with or obliterate it. The longer the consolidation processes operate, the more durable the memory. Although we cannot observe these transfer and consolidation processes directly, there is increasing evidence to support their existence. . . .

Free-Recall Experiments. Bennet Murdock (1962) reported a series of memory experiments that seem to indicate the effects of rehearsal and consolidation time on short- and long-term memory. Subjects listened to a list of twenty words presented at a rate of one per second. At the end of the list the subjects were given a minute and a half to recall as many words as they could. After a short break, a new list of twenty words was read, followed by another recall test. The results of the experiment, averaged over several subjects and many trials, are summarized in Figure 5.4A, a **serial position curve,** which shows the percentage of words recalled at each of the twenty positions on the list. It indicates that memory was excellent for the last few words on the list; these are thought to have been stored in short-term memory and still were being rehearsed when the subject was asked to recall them. Memory was next best for items at the beginning of the list; these items are believed to have been stored in long-term memory because there was more time for the rehearsal and consolidation process to operate. Memory was weakest for items in the middle of the list.

Figure 5.4B shows that when more time was allowed between items, making longer rehearsal and consolidation possible, long-term memory for these items improved, while short-term memory for items on the later part of the list was not affected. However, when subjects were asked to count backward by threes as soon as the last word was presented, the upturn at the end of the curve was

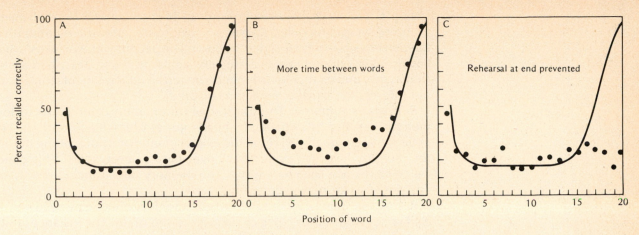

Figure 5.4

The results of a series of experiments by Murdock (A and B) and by Postman and Phillips (C) that elegantly demonstrate the separate contributions of short-term memory (STM) and long-term memory (LTM) to the serial position curve. The black dots show the percentage of correct recalls as a function of the position of the word in the list. The colored line in A represents the idealized form of the data there and is repeated in B and C for purposes of comparison. Note that in B, LTM's contribution has been enhanced by the allowance of more rehearsal and organization time between words, but STM's contribution is unaffected. In C, the contribution of STM has been completely eliminated by the prevention of rehearsal, but LTM's contribution is unchanged.

destroyed, as shown in Figure 5.4C; short-term memory was eliminated by preventing rehearsal, but long-term memory of items from the beginning of the list remained the same.

Anterograde Amnesia. The most striking studies of transfer and consolidation processes have involved epileptics who had undergone certain kinds of brain surgery to prevent seizures. These patients obtained relief from their epilepsy, but they sometimes suffered an unfortunate side effect: they could no longer transfer information from short-term to long-term memory; that is, they could no longer learn from and retain new experiences. This condition is called **anterograde amnesia** because the patient's memory for events that occurred *before* brain surgery remains unaffected.

Brenda Milner (1962) analyzed a number of such cases of anterograde amnesia. According to Milner, it is damage to the part of the brain called the hippocampus that is responsible for the disruption of memory, but this does not cause any other impairments in intellectual functioning. She described a twenty-seven-year-old man who had undergone radical brain surgery to prevent severe seizures. When Milner interviewed him two years after the operation, he still reported his age to be twenty-seven. He retained little memory of the operation, and kept repeating, "It is as though I am just waking up from a dream; it seems as though it has just happened." He had little, if any, memory of events since the operation; he did slightly better on an IQ test than he had done before the surgery, and his memory for events before the operation was completely intact. Because he could not memorize new information he faced enormous problems in his day-to-day life. For instance, when his family moved to a new house, he was unable to learn his address and kept returning to his old house. He would reread magazines without finding their contents familiar. He would forget where household articles were kept. It appeared that he could retain items in short-term memory, but the moment he became distracted and shifted his attention, the memories would be lost.

Anterograde amnesia can also be caused by certain diseases of the brain. For example, severe chronic alcoholism can lead to general brain damage and a group of symptoms called Korsakov's Syndrome (after the nineteenth-century Russian physician who first described it). The patient with Korsakov's Syndrome has problems of memory that are very similar to those described by Milner— that is, new information is no longer transferred to permanent storage, although old information usually remains available.

Retrograde Amnesia. The transfer of information from short- to long-term memory can also be impaired by head injuries (Russell and Nathan, 1946). The patient may be unable to recall the events immediately preceding the injury, or the memory loss may extend back over days or even years. This condition is called **retrograde amnesia** because the memory deficit includes only the past, and memory for new events is normal.

Retrograde amnesia, though most commonly produced by head injuries, may also result from other types of damage to the brain. For instance, the patient undergoing electroconvulsive shock therapy usually experiences memory loss, as may the victim of carbon monoxide poisoning. The extent of the memory loss appears to be related to the severity of the damage to the brain. One explanation of retrograde amnesia suggests that the consolidation period is disrupted by the brain injury, so the new memory does not get firmly recorded. Thus, the victim of an automobile accident may remember nothing of the events that immediately preceded the crash because a head injury disrupted the consolidation of those events into permanent memory. Recent memories immediately preceding an injury appear to be more fragile than older ones.

Recovery from retrograde amnesia may occur in a few minutes or over a period of years, depending on the severity of the injury. Memory return is usually gradual. With recovery, the span of time covered by the retrograde amnesia begins to lessen. Usually, memories of the distant past are the first to reappear; sometimes, memory of events that occurred immediately before the injury happened never is recovered.

Drug Facilitation. Although brain injuries can impair the transfer of information to long-term memory, certain drugs can increase transfer and consolidation. For instance, Breen and McGaugh (1961) reported that low doses of the neural stimulant strychnine sulfate, injected into rats just after a learning trial, result in better memory of the task at some later date when the drug is no longer present in the animal's system.

In another study, of rats learning to perform a maze-running task, Breen and McGaugh used the neural stimulant pictrotoxin. Rats receiving the highest doses after their trials made significantly fewer errors in future trials than rats given lower dosages, and all the rats given the drug performed better than a control group that was given saline injections. The researchers concluded that pictrotoxin facilitates memory by enhancing the consolidation process. According to this view, the rat that receives this neural stimulant after a trial remembers more of what was learned on the trial because the stimulant produces greater than normal consolidation activity.

[I] MEMORY RETRIEVAL

Retrieving stored information is in some ways the key property of memory. Individuals can retrieve a vast number of facts when presented with a specified topic (How much do you know about cars? What does your bedroom look like?) and can recall relevant information in a very short time. The speed and efficiency of retrieval from human memory are astounding. Consider how this is reflected in our reading ability: the average person can follow and comprehend from 300 to 600 words per minute—five to ten words per second!

[J] Recognition and Recall

Retrieval takes two basic forms: recognition and recall. In recognition, we are presented with something and asked if we have seen or heard it before. We can look at a face or an object and know almost immediately whether it is familiar. The process seems to occur automatically and is usually accurate. In **recall,** we are asked to retrieve specific pieces of information, usually on the basis of certain cues, and this often requires an active search of our memory stores (What is your mother's family name?).

Recognition is easier than recall. If we pass someone on the street whom we knew in elementary school, we may recognize the face but be unable to recall the name. In recognition, we need only decide if the person, object, experience, sound, or word before us is the one we are seeking. An experiment (Haber and Standing, 1969) showed that recognition for visual memories seems to be practically limitless. Subjects were shown 2,560 photographs of various scenes, each shown for ten seconds. On a subsequent day, the subjects were able to recognize between 85 and 95 percent of these pictures!

Recall is often a quite difficult type of retrieval. In this method we must recover information on the basis of cues that are sometimes quite sparse. When recall does occur, it generally tends to be accurate. The most common recall failure is the inability to retrieve anything, as when people stumble in speaking, trying to find the word they want, or fail to remember a name they thought they knew. False recalls are rare. When they do occur, it is usually possible to explain them in terms of strong, familiar associations. For example, parents sometimes call one of their children by another's name, an error that is especially easy for us to understand in large families.

[K] Relearning

Sometimes, memory is so poor that information cannot be recalled or even recognized with certainty. Nevertheless, we may be able to **relearn** the information in less time than the original learning required. Even though the information is no longer accessible, it apparently leaves a trace that can facilitate new storage and retrieval.

This subtle trace can be revealed by means of the **relearning score,** or **savings score,** a measurement devised by Hermann Ebbinghaus in 1885 (see Figure 5.5). Using himself as a subject, Ebbinghaus recorded the number of repetitions needed to learn a list of unrelated items accurately. Then he waited some time (presumably without thinking about the list) and relearned the list, again recording the number of repetitions needed for him to be able to repeat it accurately from memory. The difference in the number of trials between the

Figure 5.5
Relearning. The savings score (time saved in relearning a set of nonsense syllables) as a function of time since the first learning. (After Ebbinghaus, 1885).

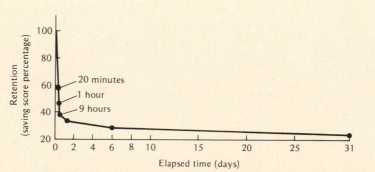

original and the second learning session he called the savings score. The results showed that the shorter the time period between the first and second sessions, the fewer the trials needed for relearning and the higher the savings score.

[L] Remembering as Reconstructing

Most of us can readily recite the alphabet or the days of the week. But how fast can we say the alphabet backwards? How rapidly can we give the days of the week in alphabetical order? The fact that our retrieval system breaks down when faced with these requests indicates something very important about how memory is organized and how the retrieval system operates. Items are stored in memory in a very specific, sometimes even rigid, fashion. Large groups of items tend to be structured in the way that they are most frequently practiced or the context in which they most frequently occur. Thus, retrieval is most efficient when the memory search strategy parallels the original memory storage strategy.

If you live in a college dormitory, you are probably familiar with the names and faces of the other students who share that living space. Still, if you were spending your summer vacation traveling in Europe and spotted one of those familiar faces in a London pub, you might well have some difficulties matching the face with a name. But should your former dorm-mate approach you and say, "We shared a bathroom in our freshman year," this information could help to focus your memory. Once you have placed the face in its **context,** or setting, it becomes easier to retrieve the missing name. You can begin by reconstructing the scene where the face was familiar. Where did you live in your freshman year? What did the bathroom look like? Whom did you see at the time you took your morning shower? By reconstructing the scene, you direct your attention to the right "area" of your memory.

Retrieval can be viewed as a problem-solving task in which the correct answer comes from asking the correct question (Lindsay and Norman, 1972). Suppose you were asked to recall what you were wearing exactly one month ago. Your initial reaction to such a question probably would be that it is impossible to answer. However, you probably could answer it if you broke it down into smaller subproblems—for instance, "What day of the week was it? What classes do I have on that day? What was the weather like?" By solving each of these subproblems, you probably could reconstruct the day in question, eventually hitting upon the cue that would lead directly to your memory of what you wore that day. In this example, successful retrieval depends not on attacking the problem directly, but rather on actively searching memory stores and narrowing down the alternatives until the correct memory is pinpointed. You can test your retrieval by trying one of the problems in Figure 5.6.

Figure 5.6
Retrieval problems that demonstrate the reconstructive nature of memory. If, at first glance, any of these questions seems impossible to answer, try anyway. You may be surprised at what you can recall if you put your mind to it. (After Lindsay and Norman, 1972.)

In the rooms you live in, how many windows are there?

What were you doing on Monday afternoon in the third week of September two years ago?

Can pigeons fly airplanes?

[M] Confabulation

Motivation affects retrieval, as it does most human activities. A person offered a thousand dollars to remember the name of his first-grade teacher is more likely to come up with it than is the person who is offered a dime. But under conditions of high motivation, we often commit a memory error called **confabulation:** If unable to retrieve a certain item from memory, we may manufacture something else that seems appropriate. For some time, psychologists were impressed by the apparent ability of people in deep states of hypnosis to give detailed reports of events that occurred during childhood. The hypnotist would ask the subject to describe, for instance, his sixth birthday. Typically, the subject, if in a deep trance, would give a lengthy and quite impressive account of a birthday party complete with cake, candles, presents, and guests. He would seem absolutely convinced that the report was accurate, but objective evidence usually contradicted him. It could almost always be shown that the subject had confabulated—that he had combined several birthday parties and invented missing details; even under further questioning, the subject could not distinguish the true parts of the story from the imaginary parts.

[N] State-Dependent Memory

Successful retrieval can sometimes depend on the state an individual was in when the memory was originally stored. Consider the plight of Charlie Chaplin in his movie *City Lights*. Chaplin plays the role of a tramp befriended by an alcoholic millionaire who invites him to live in his mansion. Unfortunately, on the rare occasions when the millionarie is sober, he has no memory of who Chaplin is, and throws him out of the mansion. But as soon as the millionaire gets drunk agan, Chaplin once more becomes an honored guest.

Although Chaplin's friend depicts an extreme form of state-dependent memory, a number of drugs, including alcohol, have been shown to be capable of producing various degrees of memory **dissociation**—that is, a separation between the storage and retrieval processes. What happens is that information learned while one is under the influence of certain drugs may not be retrieved well without the drug, but may be retrieved much better when the drug condition is restored.

In one study of dissociation, Donald Overton (1964) trained rats to run a maze while they were under the influence of the drug sodium pentobarbital (a barbiturate drug sometimes used in sleeping pills). Later, half the rats were drugged again and tested for memory of the maze, while the other half were tested in a nondrug state. The group tested in the drug state remembered the maze much better than the group tested in the nondrug state. In one experiment the dissociation was so extreme that Overton was able to teach the rats one solution in the drug state and the opposite solution in the nondrug state, with no interference between the two states.

State-dependent memory has also been demonstrated in people under the influence of alcohol and marijuana, although the results are far from clearcut. One study (Goodwin, Crane, and Guze, 1969) showed that memory loss was greater for subjects going from the alcohol to the nonalcohol state than for those going from nonalcohol to alcohol. In the same way, subjects who learned while under the influence of marijuana and were tested while drug-free, showed greater memory loss than subjects who learned while drug-free and were tested while under the influence of marijuana (Darley et al., 1973). These findings suggest that some commonly used drugs may alter the storage of new information but may have a lesser effect on the retrieval of previously stored information.

[O] Imagery

We have already seen how remarkable our capacity for visual memory is. Research has shown that people can remember verbal materials better if they hook them to a visual image of some kind (Bower and Clark, 1969; Paivio, 1971). Many popular **mnemonic,** or memory-assisting, devices rely on visual imagery. . . . For example, to recall the French word for snail—*escargot*—we may think of a giant snail carrying a cargo of S's on its back, leaving us with an image of "S-cargo." Other mnemonic devices are discussed in the accompanying special feature.

Imagery is most helpful to verbal memory when the items to be remembered are concrete rather than abstract. For example, compare the word combinations "steamship–canary" and "dissonance–republic." The first pair of words, both concrete nouns, immediately suggests specific images, while the second pair, both abstract nouns, either suggests no images at all or suggests images that are not uniquely tied to the words to be remembered. For instance, the word "republic" may suggest an image of the American flag, but later, when this image is recalled, the word "democracy" rather than "republic" may come to mind.

Memory for visual images is further improved if we can weave the images into some sort of scene. Examine, for a moment, the two parts of Figure 5.7. An experiment (Horowitz, Lampel, and Takanashi, 1969) showed that the top part—the rabbit *in* the cart—was remembered much better than the bottom part—the rabbit and the cart.

Why imagery is such a powerful tool of memory is not completely understood. It may not be because images are inherently memorable but because imagery is processed in the nonlinguistic systems of the brain. According to this line of reasoning, we are more likely to remember words plus images than words alone for the same reason that it is better to have two reminder notes for ourselves—one at home and one in our pockets—than to have only one. The two kinds of "notes"—verbal and visual—make it twice as likely that we will remember the message.

A very small percentage of the human population possesses a unique ability known as **eidetic imagery.** While most of us maintain visual images that are more or less vague, people with eidetic imagery can visualize a scene with almost photographic clarity. Research with children indicates that only about 5 percent have this ability, and this figure drops even lower after adolescence (Haber, 1969). Though the eidetic child can describe in detail many of the elements of a complex picture, this ability does not seem to aid long-term memory processes. For instance, if an eidetic child is asked to describe a picture while in the act of viewing it, the eidetic image is not formed. It seems that verbal processes interfere with the formation of an eidetic image, and that the eidetic child is no more skilled than other children in storing verbal information.

Some recent research done with subjects who were totally blind from birth indicates that imagery can be used as a memory-improving device even in people who have never had visual experience. In one experiment (Jonides, Kahn, and Rozin, 1975), both sighted and congenitally blind adults showed improved memory when they were given word pairs such as "locomotive-dishtowel" and told to imagine a relationship between the words of each pair—for example, the locomotive wrapped in the dishtowel. . . . The fact that the imagery instructions improved the memory of blind subjects as well as sighted ones indicates that the imagery effect does not rely on vision. The researchers were puzzled as to how to explain this imagery effectiveness; attempts to relate it to other sensory channels, such as hearing or touch, were unsuccessful.

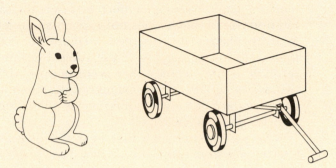

[P] FORGETTING

We have concentrated until now on successes of the memory system—information gets in, is stored, and is retrieved. When something goes wrong with the process of memory retrieval, forgetting occurs.

There are three major explanations of forgetting: decay, interference, and motivated forgetting. Though these explanations conflict with one another at several important points, they are not entirely incompatible. A comprehensive account of forgetting will probably include all of them.

[Q] Decay of Memory Traces

Perhaps the oldest theory of forgetting states that memories wear away, or **decay**, with the passage of time. Decay theory presumes that when a new fact is learned or a new experience occurs, a physiological change or memory trace is formed in the brain. With time, the trace decays and may disappear altogether—the information is forgotten. The only way to increase the strength of the memory trace is to make use of, or practice, the stored information. Decay theory appears to account for the transience of the more fragile sensory and short-term memory stores, but the application of decay theory to long-term memory is open to question.

The notion that memories "fade" with time has a certain poetic appeal and may well fit in with some of our subjective experiences. For instance, our memory of a movie seen last week is probably stronger and more detailed than of a movie seen last year. However, there are many long-term memory phenomena that cannot be explained by decay theory. Motor skills tend to be remembered over long periods of time without practice; for example, an adult who has not ridden a bicycle for twenty years usually has little trouble demonstrating the skill for a child. A senile person who cannot remember what happened yesterday may readily recall childhood experiences. Also, research has demonstrated that people forget substantially less if they sleep for several hours after learning something than if they stay awake (see Figure 5.8). These facts are difficult to explain if we assume that memories simply decay with the passage of time.

[R] Interference

Another explanation of forgetting attributes it to **interference**—other material blocks out the memory. This explanation would say that the apparent "decay" of our memory of last year's movie is caused by interference from all the events, including movies we had seen. Had we seen no other movies, perhaps the memory would have faded much less over the same period of time. Although interference probably does not explain all forgetting, it does account for the experimental results presented in Figure 5.8. People who learned something, then went to sleep and were not subject to interference, were better able to recall what they learned than were people who continued their waking activities; the subjects who remained awake remembered only about 10 percent of the material after eight hours; those who slept recalled about 60 percent (Jenkins and Dallenbach, 1924).

We have already seen that near the beginning of the storage process, interference from extraneous material can prevent new information from pass-

Figure 5.8
Two subjects were given lits of nonsense syllables to learn (BIK, QAJ, NIC, for example) and were tested after various periods of time. When the subjects were allowed to sleep during the time interval between learning and recall, they remembered much more than they did if they had stayed awake. (After Jenkins and Dallenbach, 1924.)

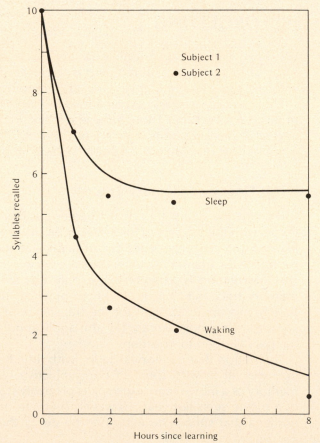

TABLE 5.1 LISTS OF ADJECTIVES USED IN TESTING LONG-TERM MEMORY

List A	List B	List C
happy	gay	58
big	large	22
hard	solid	18
funny	humorous	19
thin	slender	33
calming	soothing	71
neat	tidy	45

ing into long-term memory. Suppose we are asked to memorize list A of the adjectives shown in Table 5.1 and then asked to memorize list B.

If in the future we are asked to recall list A, we will probably find that we have forgotten some of the list A words. We may hesitate, recall some of the list A items, and add some words from list B. When material memorized later (list B) interferes with remembering material memorized earlier (list A), psychologists say that **retroactive interference** has taken place. "Retro" means backward, indicating that the interference has moved backward from list B to list A. Suppose we are asked to recall items from list B but mistakenly include some of the words from list A. This is called **proactive interference**—"pro" means forward, with the interference moving forward from list A to list B.

Now suppose that after we memorize list A, we are given list C instead of list B to learn. It is likely that list C will interfere very little with our memory of list A. Some researchers did experiments with this type of material (McGeoch, 1942). Their results indicated that the greater the similarity between the materials to be memorized, the greater the interference during recall. Because lists A and B contain very similar material, list B creates more interference with list A than does list C. Similarly, if list B were translated into French, this would reduce its interference with list A, because it would be easier to distinguish between the two lists.

These findings can be applied to your own study habits to minimize the effects of interference. For example, it may be wise not to study highly similar subjects—such as math and physics, or psychology and sociology—close together in time. By separating the study of similar kinds of material, you give yourself time to consolidate new information and reduce both proactive and retroactive interference between the subjects. Sleep provides the best protection from interference, for when you sleep you are not absorbing new information that can interfere with the material you have studied already. Students rarely have time to nap between studying subjects, though, so a more practical suggestion is to study dissimilar material—like chemistry and anthropology—in the same study session.

[S] Motivated Forgetting

The failure to retrieve an item from memory is not always caused by decay or interference. Sometimes, forgetting occurs without any actual memory loss. This kind of forgetting is a matter of **suppression** or **repression,** a conscious or unconscious decision to "forget" unpleasant or disturbing memories. Although the material has not disappeared from storage, the person has arranged things so that the retrieval mechanism bypasses the path to the repressed memory. However, indications that the apparently forgotten material is still available usually show up in the person's behavior—he or she may pause or fumble for words when discussing events related to the critical memory, and there may be other signs of anxiety, such as sweating or blushing.

[T] AN OVERVIEW OF MEMORY PROCESSES

Let us conclude this chapter by briefly reviewing the memory processes we have been discussing. Figure 5.9 shows how those processes fit together. The box represents the individual, and the elements within the box—attention, consolidation, memory, remembering, and forgetting—are not directly observable, but are inferred from performance. Outside the box are elements that can be manipulated, controlled, and measured in memory experiments: sensory information, rehearsal, and performance. Though the processes of storage and retrieval are presented within separate brackets, there is some overlap in the areas covered by these brackets. This indicates that although storage and retrieval are discussed as distinct processes, there is not always a clear boundary between them.

The model illustrates the relationships among a series of memory processes. For example:

1. A large amount of *sensory information,* represented by the arrows, is impinging on the "organism." Only a limited amount of that information actually enters the memory system. The single arrow that breaks through the box represents that small amount of information that actually receives our attention. At the same time, the information already stored in memory directs our attention to important, novel, or relevant sensory information from the external environment.

2. *Rehearsal* is portrayed as a "looping" process that bridges the gap between instatement and storage of information in memory. The rehearsal loop is necessary if information is to be transferred from short-term to long-term storage. Although rehearsal takes place within the individual, the model shows the rehearsal loop partially outside the organism because it can be observed and controlled externally.

3. *Consolidation* is a "reverbatory" process that we assume occurs in the brain when permanent memories are established. It is portrayed as cyclical, connecting the attention and storage processes. The longer the consolidation cycle, the more durable the stored memory will be.

4. *Memory* refers to the three forms of storage—sensory, short-term, long-term. It includes all categories of stored information: visual, verbal, auditory, tactile, and so on.

5. *Remembering and forgetting* are both aspects of the process of retrieving information from storage. The solid line to remembering indicates that an item may be successfully retrieved from storage; the broken line to forgetting illustrates that retrieval may be partially or completely unsuccessful. When forgetting takes place, the organism is likely to scan memory storage again in search of a new pathway to the lost information.

6. *Performance* is portrayed by an arrow extending out from the box, for performance is behavior that is observable. It is determined both by what is

Figure 5.9
Memory processes.

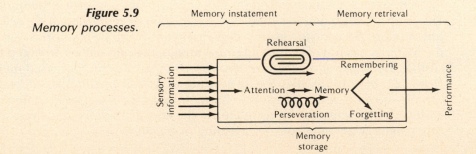

remembered and by what is forgotten. Performance is also influenced by such factors as motivation, emotional state, and drug use.

SUMMARY

1. Memory is the capacity to retain information. The study of memory cannot be clearly separated from the study of learning. Learning provides the substance, or content, of memory. In turn, memory of past experiences and their consequences provides the basis for learning in future situations of a similar nature. One of the main questions addressed in memory research is how new information is encoded, or registered, by the brain.
   A. As yet, the physiological bases of memory remain a mystery. Researchers are investigating possible anatomical or chemical changes that may occur in brain cells when specific memories are encoded.
   B. Cognitive psychologists believe that humans actively organize their experiences and information. Their cognitive approach to memory research emphasizes the mental activities that occur between the presentation of information and its later recall or recognition.
   C. Most researchers have focused on three related yet distinct memory processes: attention, memory storage, and memory retrieval.
      1. **Attention** is the ability to focus on specific information from the environment.
      2. **Memory storage** refers to the process of information retention.
      3. **Memory retrieval** refers to the methods by which access to the stored information is achieved.
2. Attention plays a critical role in determining which information will enter into our memory storage. Our senses are continually bombarded with information, but we are limited in the amount of information we can attend to at any one time. Past experience may influence which information we attend to.
   A. **Sensory gating** is a process that directs attention to information coming in through one sensory channel, while decreasing the attention paid to information coming in through other sensory channels.
   B. **Selective attention** is a somewhat more complex phenomenon that occurs within a *single* sensory channel. It allows us to attend to some information coming in on a channel, while muting the extraneous information that comes in on that channel at the same time. In both sensory gating and selective attention, some processing of information does occur in the channel that is not the primary focus of attention.
3. There seem to be three forms of memory storage: sensory storage, short-term memory, and long-term memory.
   A. **Sensory storage** describes our ability to retain a great deal of sensory information for an instant (less than one second) after the stimulus is no longer present. This type of memory storage seems to be **modality specific,** meaning that the sensory system that receives the information is the same one that stores it. When additional information comes in on the same sensory path, it disrupts the storage of the earlier information. If, however, the first stimulus is received by one sensory system (say, vision) and the second stimulus is received by another (say, hearing or smell), the original (visual) memory is not disrupted. The purpose of sensory storage seems to be to provide a brief moment during which certain information is selected for further processing.
   B. Memory for events for a short while after they have occurred is called **short-term memory.** This type of storage system retains a small amount of information for several seconds. Short-term memory (STM) has two

basic characteristics. First, information entering STM is lost within seconds unless it is *rehearsed,* or repeated. Second, the amount of information that can be stored in STM is very limited. George Miller summarized experiments indicating that most people can hold between five and nine items in STM. Information can, however, be chunked to form larger units, thereby increasing the amount of information that can be stored.

C. **Long-term memory** (LTM) refers to the storage of our permanent knowledge; its capacity is thought to be boundless. The actual process by which information is transferred from short-term to long-term memory is not completely understood. It is generally believed, however, that the longer a piece of information has been rehearsed, the more likely the transfer. When information first enters long-term storage, a certain amount of additional time is necessary to stabilize or consolidate the memory trace (initial physiological change) produced by the new information.

1. Experiments using a free-recall technique have yielded data that formed what is known as the **serial position curve.** Items from the end of a list were remembered best (thought to be stored in STM); items at the beginning of a list (thought to be stored in LTM) were less well remembered; and items from the middle of a list were not well remembered at all.

2. The transfer of new information into LTM can be impaired by certain types of brain injuries. Some epileptics who had undergone brain surgery to prevent severe seizures developed **anterograde amnesia:** they could not retain new experiences, although their memory for events prior to surgery remained intact.

3. Another type of memory disturbance known as **retrograde amnesia** may be brought on by head injuries. In this type of amnesia, the patient may not remember events that occurred before the injury; memory for new events, however, often occurs normally.

4. The transfer of information to LTM and its consolidation can be enhanced by certain drugs.

4. The two basic methods of information retrieval are **recognition** and **recall** of material. In recognition, we need only decide if a stimulus is one we have encountered before. Recall, however, involves being able to recover and actually produce information, often on the basis of sparse cues.

A. There are times when memory is so severely impaired that information cannot be recalled or even recognized. However, a subtle trace of the information seems to be retained, since we are able to **relearn** information in less time than the original learning required. The difference in the number of trials it takes to learn a list perfectly between the original and subsequent learning sessions is called the savings score.

B. Retrieval occurs most efficiently when the strategies for memory search coincide with the strategies for memory storage. Also, by placing objects or people in **context,** we can more easily retrieve the information about them that we want.

C. Motivation can affect memory retrieval; we remember things more easily if we have a reason to do so. When motivation is very high, however, a memory error called **confabulation** may occur. Confabulation involves inventing information that seems appropriate, to fill in a memory gap.

D. The retrieval of information may depend on the state an individual was in when the memory was stored. Several drugs, including alcohol, can produce memory **dissociation,** a separation between the storage and retrieval processes.

E. Research suggests that memory for verbal materials can be improved by associating the verbal stimulus with a visual image. Many **mnemonic** devices rely on visual imagery. Most people produce visual images that are somewhat vague. A few people, however, possess an ability known as **eidetic imagery,** which enables them to visualize a scene with almost the same detail and clarity found in a photograph.

5. **Forgetting** reflects a failure of the memory retrieval system. There are three major explanations of forgetting: decay, interference, and motivated forgetting. A comprehensive account of forgetting will probably include all three.

    A. Perhaps the oldest theory of forgetting states that memories **decay,** or wear away, with the passage of time; the only way to retain a memory trace is to use or practice the stored information. This theory does not adequately explain the presence of many long-term memory phenomena, such as knowing how to ride a bicycle after not having practiced for many years.

    B. Another theory states that forgetting occurs as a result of **interference—** when other material blocks out the memory.

        1. When material memorized later (list B) interferes with remembering material memorized earlier (list A), this is called **retroactive interference.**

        2. When material memorized earlier (list A) interferes with remembering material memorized later (list B), this is called **proactive interference.**

        3. Other research suggests that the greater the similarity of materials to be memorized, the greater the interference during recall.

    C. Failure to retrieve an item from memory may occur without being caused by decay or interference. In these cases, ''forgetting'' is due to **suppression** or **repression,** a conscious or unconscious decision to ''forget'' certain disturbing memories.

RECOMMENDED READINGS

Baddeley, Alan D. *The Psychology of Memory.* New York: Basic Books, 1976. An excellent, comprehensive textbook on memory.

Klatzky, Roberta. *Human Memory: Structure and Processes.* San Francisco: Freeman, 1975. An introduction to memory from a cognitive perspective.

Meyer, Bonnie A. F. *The Organization of Prose and Its Effects on Memory.* New York: Oxford American Elsevier, 1975. An intriguing discussion of how the organization of language influences our memory for written works.

Norman, Donald. *Memory and Attention: An Introduction to Human Information Processing.* 2nd ed. New York: Wiley, 1976. An up-to-date analysis of the processes of memory and attention.

NOTES

1. **David J. Rachman** and **Michael M. Mescon,** *Business Today* (New York: Random House, 1979), pp. 204–208.
2. **Wayne W. Dyer,** ''Immobilization,'' from *Your Erroneous Zones* (New York: Funk & Wagnalls, 1976), pp. 21–22.
3. **Thomas Wolfe,** ''The Lost Boy,'' from *The Hills Beyond* (New York: Harper & Row, 1937), p. 42.
4. **Robert Frost,** ''Nothing Gold Can Stay,'' *The Poetry of Robert Frost,* edited by Edward Latham (New York: Holt, Rinehart & Winston, 1969), p. 222.
5. **J. J. Braun** and **Darwyn Linder,** *Psychology Today: An Introduction,* 4th ed. (New York: Random House, 1979), pp. 101–123.

Three

SENTENCE MEANING

Sentences are the building blocks of paragraphs. We can best understand paragraphs by understanding sentences. This chapter will give you the "keys" to unlock the meaning of a sentence.

Every sentence contains key words that are basic to the meaning of that sentence. Key words show the flow of ideas and unlock sentence meaning. As you read, you should look for key words that:

1. Identify who or what the sentence is about (subject—person or thing).
2. Tell what the person is doing (verb—action) or tell what the sentence is saying (verb—state of being).
3. Identify who or what is receiving the action or what is being said about the subject (complement).

Look at the four sentences below. The sentences are followed by a chart showing the key words in each sentence.

A. The frightened person clutched the bag.
B. Ms. Jones is our family lawyer.
C. Mary and John returned home after the game.
D. The intruder crept slowly and slipped out through the window.

Listed below are the key words. These key words are absolutely necessary to grasp the basic meaning of the sentence.

Subject	Verb	Complement	
A. person	clutched	bag	action verb
B. Ms. Jones	is	lawyer	state-of-being verb
C. Mary and John	returned	home	compound subject
D. intruder	crept and slipped	—	compound verb

KEY WORDS AND IMPORTANT MODIFIERS

You know from your own reading that many sentences are not as short and simple as those above. Sentences often contain descriptive words and phrases. In these sentences, the descriptive words and phrases often answer the questions: Who? What? When? Where? and Why? It will be easier if you learn to recognize the key words and the words and phrases that modify these key words.

Look at the two sentences below. The key words in each sentence are the same. Note, though, that the descriptive words and phrases give each sentence its own special meaning.

1. The experienced player shot the ball into the basket for the final victory point.
2. The rookie player shot the ball, missing the basket and a final victory point.

Authors convey the different meanings by using the appropriate modifiers as well as the key words.

SENTENCE MEANING REVIEW

Let us review the important components of a sentence which lead us to sentence meaning. The components of subject, verb, and complement are the fundamentals of writing a sentence, and they must also be the fundamentals of reading a sentence.

1. All sentences, whether long or short, simple or complex, must contain a complete thought.
2. The meaning of a sentence is conveyed primarily through key words. These key words are the subject, verb, and complement. The complement is considered a key word, although a complement is not necessary for sentence formation. (See sentence D in the preceding section.)
3. To gain a complete understanding of a sentence we must consider the words that modify the key words.
4. The subject is the word that tells who or what the sentence is about. In the sentences below, the subject is italicized.

John digs.   The *clock* ticks.
Florida is a state.   The *picnic* was a success.

5. A verb denotes an action or conveys a state of being. The sentences below show action verbs. These verbs tell us what the subject is "doing."

John digs.   The clock ticks.

The sentences below use two state-of-being verbs. These verbs direct our attention to the complement to find out more about the subject. With this type of verb we should ask, "What does the complement tell me about the subject?"

Florida is a state.
The picnic was a success.

ACTIVITY I

Read each sentence in the paragraph that follows. Use the chart to list the key words and modifiers found in each sentence.

(1) Did you ever wonder about the pyramids of Egypt? (2) How could an ancient race, even with 100,000 workers, build such enormous monuments? (3) Almost every visitor makes a trip out into the desert to see the massive tombs. (4) They appear majestic from a distance. (5) The Great Pyramid of Khufu is one of the wonders of the ancient world. (6) It was once encased with blocks of polished limestone. (7) However, weather and thievery have combined to destroy its original casing. (8) The pyramids look weather-beaten. (9) Still they are impressive sights.[1]

	Subject	Verb	Complement	Important Modifiers
1.				
2.				
3.				
4.				
5.				
6.				
7.				
8.				
9.				

LINKING WORDS

Some sentences may have more than one set of key words. These sentences are usually long and laden with an unusual number of descriptive words and phrases. If you are able to identify the key words quickly, the meaning of the sentence will become clear.

Key words in long, complicated sentences are usually connected by words known as linking words. These linking words have an impact on the meaning of the sentence and signal the writer's thought patterns. As an efficient reader, you should become familiar with these words and use them as important signposts.

Below is a list of the most common linking words and the thought patterns they signal.

Thought Pattern	Linking Words
1. Time pattern	Before, after, since, while, soon, later, next, when, until . . .
2. Cause and effect	Because, therefore, consequently, thus, unless, although, if, for this reason, as a result . . .
3. Spatial	Over, under, above, around, beside, between, next to . . .
4. Emphasis	Moreover, furthermore, most important, finally . . .
5. Comparison	Like, as similarly, both, all
6. Contrast	But, on the other hand, however, nevertheless, unlike, despite
7. Example	For example, for instance, to illustrate
8. Conclusion	Therefore, thus, so . . .

EXERCISE I

Circle all the linking words in each passage. Beneath each passage write each linking word and the thought pattern it conveys. Some passages may include several thought patterns.

1. Because of the inclement weather, the strategic air attacks were postponed.

_____
(Linking word)   (Thought pattern)

2. When buying used products, the condition, rather than their age, should be of primary concern to the buyer.

_____
(Linking word)   (Thought pattern)

3. Despite Beethoven's deafness, he produced great classical works of music.

_____
(Linking word)   (Thought pattern)

4. Like people, nations begin their lives accepting challenges, then rise to a peak performance, and eventually decline and fall.

_____
(Linking word)   (Thought pattern)

_____
(Linking word)   (Thought pattern)

_____
(Linking word)   (Thought pattern)

5. The fish in the Great Lakes region are still plentiful but not of a desirable kind. These fish are not quality food. Furthermore, the level of oxygen has fallen to a dangerous low. All types of life found in the lakes are in danger of extinction. This tremendous body of water could someday become nothing but a noxious mass of decayed organic matter.

_____
(Linking word)   (Thought pattern)

_____
(Linking word)   (Thought pattern)

_____
(Linking word)   (Thought pattern)

6. The physical events of puberty, and the meaning of those events in our culture, help shape a whole series of new social and emotional tasks for the adolescent. Erikson sees the major dilemma of this period as being identity versus role confusion. Thus he emphasizes not only the sexual awakening itself, but also the identity crisis that accompanies it. The younger child may have achieved a reasonable sense of self. He knows his own gender, and has acquired some of the basic sex role behaviors. He also knows some of his own intellectual and physical skills. But in adolescence, many of the old patterns and systems break down as a result of physical and social changes.[2]

_____
(Linking word)   (Thought pattern)

_____
(Linking word)   (Thought pattern)

_____

(Linking word)   (Thought pattern)

_____

(Linking word)   (Thought pattern)

_____

(Linking word)   (Thought pattern)

EXERCISE II

Circle all linking words in the following passage. Above each word, write the thought pattern it conveys.

Underline all key words (or key phrases) in the following passage.

Quickly reading words or pages means little if you do not grasp some meaning from what you read. The most important part of reading is comprehension. However, good reading does not require perfect comprehension, which is identical to memorization, and is seldom essential. How much you understand is measured by how well you comprehend the main ideas and basic facts expressed in the reading. In some reading, it is more important to get a fairly thorough knowledge of these facts than in others. Therefore, comprehension should be flexible and adjusted not only to the type of material read but also to the purpose of reading. Unless memorization is the goal, one hundred percent comprehension is seldom needed. Adequate comprehension can be achieved by reading alone. Here, you need to use a balanced study approach that will make use of other techniques to understand and remember the material.

PROJECT

Read the selection titled "Various Kinds of Meaning." Underline key words and important modifiers found in the lettered paragraphs. Use the word box set up for each lettered paragraph to jot down any difficult vocabulary words.

A.

|_____|

B.

|_____|

C.

|_____|

D.

E.

F.

G.

VARIOUS KINDS OF MEANING[3]

[A] Since a definition states the *meaning* of a term, it is important for us to have clearly in mind the different senses of the word "meaning." This topic was discussed in Chapter 2 and we need not repeat what was said there. However, a certain further distinction must be drawn in connection with what was there called descriptive or literal meaning, especially in connection with *general terms* or *class terms* applicable to more than a single object. A general term such as "planet" is applicable in the same sense equally to Mercury, Venus, Earth, Mars, and so on. In a perfectly acceptable sense, these various objects to which the term "planet" is applied are meant by the word; the collection of them constitutes its meaning. Thus if I assert that all planets have elliptical orbits, part of what I may intend to assert is that Mars has an elliptical orbit, and another part that Venus has an elliptical orbit, and so on. In one sense the meaning of a term consists of the class of objects to which the term may be applied. This sense of "meaning," its referential sense, has traditionally been called *extensional* or *denotative* meaning. A general or class term *denotes* the objects to which it may correctly be applied, and the collection or class of these objects constitutes the extension or denotation of the term.

[B] However, the foregoing is not the only sense of the word "meaning." To understand a term is to know how to apply it correctly, but for this it is not necessary to know all of the objects to which it may be correctly applied. It is required only that we have a criterion for deciding of any given object whether it falls within the extension of that term or not. All objects in the extension of a given term have some common attributes or characteristics which lead us to use the same term to denote them. We explain next, in a preliminary way, the terms "intension" and "connotation," whose alternative senses will be distinguished in the following paragraphs. The collection of attributes shared by all and only those objects in a term's extension is called the *intension* or *connotation* of that term. General or class terms have both an *intension* or *connotative* meaning and an extensional or denotative one. Thus, the intension or connotation of the term "skyscraper" consists of the attributes common and peculiar to all buildings over a certain height, while the extension or denotation of that term is the class containing the Empire State Building, the World Trade Center, the Wrigley Tower, and so on.

[C] The word "connotation" has other uses, in which it refers to the total significance of a word, emotive as well as descriptive, and sometimes to its emotive meaning alone. Thus one may deny that a person is "human." Here the word "human" is used expressively, to communicate a certain attitude or feeling. This expressive function is sometimes equated with, sometimes included in, the "connotation" of a term. But logicians use the word in a narrower sense. In our usage, connotation and intension are part of the informative significance of a term.

[D] Even with this restriction, various senses of "connotation" have yet to be distinguished. There are three different senses of the term "connotation," which have been called the *subjective,* the *objective,* and the *conventional.* The subjective connotation of a word for a speaker is the set of all the attributes that particular speaker believes to be possessed by the objects comprising that word's extension. It is clear that the subjective connotation of a term may vary from one individual to another. I have met New Yorkers for whom the word "skyscraper" had a subjective connotation which included the attribute of being located in New York City. The notion of subjective connotation is inconvenient for purposes of definition because it varies not merely from individual to individual but even from time to time for the same individual, as new beliefs are acquired or old ones abandoned. We are more interested in the public meanings of words than in their private interpretations; so, having mentioned subjective connotations, we shall eliminate them from further consideration.

[E] The objective connotation or objective intension of a term is the total set of characteristics common to all the objects that make up that term's extension. It does not vary at all from interpreter to interpreter, for if all planets do have the attribute of moving in elliptical orbits, for example, this will be part of the objective connotation of the word "planet" whether any user of the term knows it or not. But the concept of objective connotation is inconvenient for reasons of its own. Even in those rare cases where the complete extension of a term is known, it would require omniscience to know all the attributes shared by the objects in that extension. And since no one has that omniscience, the objective connotation of a term is not the public meaning in whose explanation we are interested.

[F] Since we do communicate with each other and understand the terms we use, the intensional or connotative meanings involved are neither subjective nor objective in the senses just explained. Those who attach the same meaning to a term use the same criterion for deciding of any object whether it is part of the term's extension. Thus we have agreed to use *the attribute of being a closed plane curve, all points of which are equidistant from a point within called the center* as our criterion for deciding of any figure whether it is to be called a "circle" or not. This agreement establishes a convention, and so this meaning of a term is known as its conventional connotation or conventional intension. The conventional connotation of a term is its most important aspect for purposes of definition and communication, since it is both public and can be known by people who are not omniscient. For the sake of brevity we shall use the words "connotation" and "intension" to mean "conventional connotation" or "conventional intension" unless otherwise specified.

[G] The extension or denotation of a term has been explained to be the collection of all those objects to which the term applies. There are no troublesome different senses of extension comparable to those found in the case of intension. However, the notion of extension is not without interest. For one thing, the extension of a term has been alleged to change from time to time in a way that the intension does not. The extension of the term "person" has been said to change almost continually as people die and babies are born. This varying extension does not belong to the term "person" conceived as denoting *all* persons, the dead as well as the yet unborn, but rather to the term "living person." But the term "living person" has the sense of "person living now," in which the word "now" refers to the fleeting present. Thus the intension of the term "living person" is different at different times. Any term with a changing extension has a changing intension also. So, in spite of the apparent difference, one is as constant as the other; when the intension of a term is fixed, the extension is fixed also.

It is worth mentioning in this connection that extension is determined by intension, but not the other way around. Thus the term "equilateral triangle" has for its intension or connotation the attribute of being a plane figure enclosed by three straight line segments of equal length. It has as its extension the class of all those objects and only those objects which have this attribute. The term "equiangular triangle" has a different intension, connoting the attribute of being a plane figure enclosed by three straight line segments which intersect each other to form equal angles. But the extension of the term "equiangular triangle" is exactly the same as the extension of the term "equilateral triangle." Thus terms may have different intensions but the same extension, although terms with different extensions cannot possibly have the same intension.

Consider the following sequence of terms, each of whose intensions is included within the intension of the terms following it: "person," "living person," "living person over twenty years old," "living person over twenty years old having red hair." The intension of each of these terms (except the first, of course) is greater than the intensions of those preceding it in the sequence; the terms are arranged, we may say, in order of *increasing intension*. But if we turn to the extensions of those terms, we find the reverse to be the case. The extension of the term "person" is greater than that of "living person" and so on. In other words, the terms are arranged in order of *decreasing extension*. Consideration of such sequences has led some logicians to formulate a "law of inverse variation," asserting that if a series of terms is arranged in order of increasing intension, their extensions will be in decreasing order; or, in other words, that extension and intension vary inversely with each other. This alleged law may have a certain suggestive value, but it cannot be accepted without qualification. That is shown by the following sequence of terms: "living person," "living person with a spinal column," "living person with a spinal column less than one thousand years old," "living person with a spinal column less than one thousand years old who has not read all the books in the Library of Congress." Here the terms are clearly in order of increasing intension, but the extension of each of them is the same, not decreasing at all. The law has been revised to accommodate such cases. In its amended version it asserts that if terms are arranged in order of increasing intension, their extensions will be in nonincreasing order; that is, if the extensions vary at all, they will vary inversely with the intensions.

Finally, we turn to those terms which, although perfectly meaningful, do not denote any things at all. We use such terms whenever we (correctly) deny the existence of things of a certain kind. When we say that there are no unicorns, we assert that the term "unicorn" does not denote, that it has an "empty" extension or denotation. Such terms show that "meaning" pertains more to intension than to extension. For although the term "unicorn" has an empty extension, this is not to say that the term "unicorn" is meaningless. It does not denote any thing because there are no unicorns; but if the term "unicorn" were meaningless, so also would be the statement "There are no unicorns." But far from being meaningless, the statement is in fact true.

Our distinction between intension and extension, and the recognition that extensions may be empty can be used to resolve the ambiguity of some occurrences of the term "meaning." Thus we can refute the following fallacy of equivocation:

> *The word "God" is not meaningless and therefore has a meaning. But by definition the word "God" means a supremely good and omnipotent being. Therefore, that supremely good and omnipotent being, God, must exist.*

The equivocation here is on the words "meaning" and "meaningless." The word "God" is not meaningless, and so there is an intension or connotation which is its meaning in one sense. But it does not follow simply from the fact that a term has connotation that it denotes anything. The distinction between intension and extension is an old one, but it is still valuable and important.[7]

NOTES

1. **John Warriner** and **Francis Griffith,** *Warriner's English Grammar and Composition,* 4th course (New York: Harcourt, 1973), p. 56.
2. **Houston, Bee, Hatfield,** and **Rimm,** *Invitation to Psychology* (New York: Academic Press, 1979), p. 409.
3. **Irving Copi,** *Introduction to Logic,* 6th ed. (New York: Macmillan, 1982), pp. 154–158.

[7]The useful distinction between intension and extension was introduced and emphasized by St. Anselm of Canterbury (1033–1109), who is best known for his ''ontological argument,'' to which the preceding fallacious argument has little if any resemblance. See Jan Pinborg, *Logik und Semantik im Mittelalter. Ein Überblick mit einem Nachwort von Helmut Kohlenberger* (Stuttgart-Bad Cannstatt: Friedrich Frommann Verlag, 1972), and Wolfgang L. Gombocz, ''Logik und Existenz im Mittelalter,'' *Philosophische Rundschau,* Hett 3/4, 1977.

Four

IN SEARCH OF A TOPIC

A paragraph is a group of related sentences that express a main idea. The elements of topic, main idea, and details interact to unify and connect ideas within a paragraph. Topic is the first of these elements. The topic is what the whole paragraph is about. The topic is precise. That is, the topic is neither too general or broad nor too specific or narrow.

A precise topic is established by asking: What is the whole paragraph about? You should answer this question with a single word or phrase.

Look at the excerpt below. It will illustrate how to arrive at a precise topic.

> The most important concept in all nature is energy. It represents a fundamental entity common to all forms of matter in all parts of the physical world. Closely associated with energy is work. To a layman, work is a word used to describe the expenditure of one's physical or mental energy. In science, work is a quantity that is the product of force times the distance through which the force acts. In other words, work is done when force moves an object. Work and energy are related because energy is the ability to do work.[1]

Energy		
Work	The paragraph would have to contain more information	Too general
Physical or mental energy	This is a detail which describes work	Too specific
Work and energy	These words include all the details in the paragraph	Precise!

The precise topic is work and energy.

EXERCISE I

Read the following paragraphs. Analyze each paragraph and think about a precise topic for each. State whether the given topics are (1) too general, (2) too specific, (3) precise.

> Plant leaves come in various shapes. Among the most distinctive leaf shapes are the fanlike tooth-edged foliage of the *Fatsia japonica* and the deeply lobed leaves of the ubiquitous *Philodendron selloum*. But among the most popular of contemporary plants are the *Dracaena marginata*, whose long sword-shaped leaves are edged with a reddish tinge.[2]

What is the whole paragraph about?

Plants _____

Tooth-edged foliage _____

Plant leaf shapes _____

Contemporary plants _____

> Plant leaves come in various shapes, but sometimes a plant is distinguished by the arrangement of its leaves on the stem rather than by their shape; the oval leaflets of the *Brassais actinophylla* radiate out from one point on the stem, whereas the leaves of the *Pleomele reflexa* break out from the center of the head in a rosettelike effect.[3]

What is the whole paragraph about?

Plants _____

Leaf arrangement
and plant shapes _____

Oval leaves _____

Leaf shapes _____

Now let us analyze the content of each paragraph. Both paragraphs contain similar information. Readers who tend to generalize information could easily arrive at the same topic for each paragraph. Generally speaking, both paragraphs discuss plants. In order to be precise, however, the word *plants* should be modified. Each paragraph contains its own pertinent information about plants. This information is necessary to make the topic precise. Look below at the topics that might be considered for each paragraph. An explanation of each is given.

TOPIC ANALYSIS

First Paragraph		Second Paragraph
TOPIC		TOPIC
Plants	*Too general* More information is needed to substantiate this topic.	Plants
Tooth-edged foliage	*Too specific* These are only details. Only a specific point made in each paragraph.	Oval leaves
Contemporary plants		Leaf shapes
Plant leaf shapes	*Precise* Includes details and is neither too specific nor too general.	Leaf arrangements and plant shape

EXERCISE II

Analyze the following paragraphs and label the given topics as too general, too specific, or precise.

1.   When we think about memory on an intuitive level, it often seems as though our memories just fade away with the passage of time. It is as though some physical or chemical trace of an experience decays or degenerates as time progresses. The decay interpretation of memory is an old one and it is perhaps the most widely believed by the general public. But the idea that memories fade with the passage of time has not been supported by experimental research. Somewhat surprisingly, there is no direct evidence to support the decay interpretation. Although the idea is a simple one, it has not led to fruitful experimentation and must, at present, be taken as nothing more than an interesting possibility.[4]

Topics

1. Memory _____

2. Decay theory of memory _____

3. Memory on an intuitive level _____

4. An old interpretation _____

2.   The task of classifying emotions, once a popular academic pastime, has fallen on hard times. There are just too many shades and variations among emotions to allow clear-cut, satisfactory definitions of them all. Modern psychology therefore limits identifying a few major emotions and classifying most emotions as either pleasant or unpleasant. (If you think about it, there just don't seem to be many neutral emotions.) In addition to the pleasant–unpleasant distinction, modern psychology also tends to view emotions along a dimension from weak to strong.[5]

Topic

1. Emotions _____

2. A few major emotions _____

3. Classifying and
   identifying emotions _____

Read and analyze each paragraph. Write a precise topic for each.

3.   Special pricing possibilities are involved when manufacturers introduce a new product. The most popular approach is called skimming. The manufacturer charges a high price during the introductory stage, later reducing it when the product is no longer a novelty and competition enters the market. Companies that adopt a skimming policy try to recover their development costs as quickly as possible through high initial prices. Typical examples of skimming involved the first color TV sets and penicillin. Skimming is also widely used in the movie industry. A new picture often premieres in a "showcase" theater for a dollar or two above what will be charged when it reaches neighborhood theaters.[6]

What is the whole paragraph about?

Precise topic _____

4. The distinctions between positive and normative economics are fundamental. For one thing, a normative economic statement implies a desired outcome or state of affairs; a positive economic statement need not. When the President's Council of Economic Advisors predicts a rise in unemployment, it is merely asserting what it thinks will happen, not what it thinks should happen. On the other hand, anyone who maintains that the rate of inflation ought to be reduced of necessity must believe that such a reduction would be a good thing.[7]

What is the whole paragraph about?

Precise topic _____

5. Blows to the head are a common cause of brain damage. The symptoms vary widely, depending on the severity and the location of the blow. You have probably heard the term "punch-drunk" applied to prizefighters. Their speech is slow and slurred, and their physical movements may be awkward. They are showing the cumulative effects of many contusions, or bruises to brain tissue caused by the repeated battering they have received in the ring.[8]

What is the whole paragraph about?

Precise topic _____

6. Economic models are supposed to provide insights into the operation of the real world (in the same way a laboratory-built prototype of a new model automobile provides information about the operating characteristics of yet-to-be-built production-line cars). But not all models do this. The effectiveness of a specific economic model is related to its predictive value. This is determined by comparing the theoretical predictions of the model with appropriate empirical evidence. If there is little or no significant difference between theory and fact, the model is considered an accurate representation of reality. If there is sizable disparity between the real world and the theory, the model must be modified until it gives a better approximation of reality, or scrapped in favor of an entirely new approach. This is the essence of positive economics.[9]

What is the whole paragraph about?

Precise topic _____

PROJECT

Additional readings from a college text can be found on the following pages. Read the lettered paragraphs found on these pages and write a topic for each. Remember to write topics as short titles or phrases. Write the topics below.

Paragraphs	Topics
A	_____
	_____

Paragraphs	Topics
	_____
B	_____
	_____
C	_____
	_____
D	_____
	_____
E	_____
	_____
F	_____
	_____
G	_____
	_____
H	_____
	_____
I	_____
	_____
J	_____
	_____
K	_____
	_____
L	_____
	_____
M	_____
	_____

Denial[10]

[A] Repression is really an instance of refusing to see or hear aspects of inner reality, the real self. But one can defend one's self-structure by refusing to see or hear aspects of outer reality if such perception would result in threat to the self-structure. The psychoanalysts coined the term *denial* to describe this tendency to ignore aspects of outer reality that induced anxiety and losses in self-esteem. Experimental psychologists use the term *perceptual defense* to describe the same phenomena. Sullivan spoke of "selective inattention" in this connection.

[B] Humans tend to ignore or reconstruct reality when it is painful. It is such a stubborn tendency that Freud spoke of it as one of the "principles" of mental functioning—the pleasure principle in contrast with the reality principle. When there are two possible meanings that might be assigned to some perception, one pleasant but untrue and the other true but painful, we must actually fight the pleasure principle in order to arrive at accurate cognition. Thus, we do not hear derogatory remarks uttered by someone about us, even though our hearing is quite adequate to notice whispered praise. We do not see the blemishes in our loved ones if our self-esteem rests on the premise that we have made a wise choice of a perfect mate. In extreme forms, among persons with weak egos, we may actually see something quite clearly but then deny we saw it and believe the denial. For some persons the death of a loved one is so catastrophic, calling as it does for much reorganization of behavior and the self-structure, that they will not believe the person is dead.

Psychic Contactlessness

[C] The term *psychic contactlessness,* coined by Wilhelm Reich, refers to an inability, or a refusal, to communicate with or get emotionally involved with another person. If one has been deeply hurt in relationships with people, one may protect oneself against further hurt and losses in self-esteem by walling the self off from people. One is *among* people without being really *with* them. Avoidance of close contact and emotional involvement with others serves many defensive functions, not the least of which is the fact that others will never come to know you. Because others are never given the opportunity to observe someone's real self, the contactless person can entertain all manner of grandiose fantasies about the self; these are never known or criticized by others.

Depersonalizing Others

[D] If individuals do not allow themselves to think of others as human beings with feelings and hopes, they protect themselves in many ways. They may be afraid to become personally involved, and so they stubbornly refuse to pay attention to the other person as a feeling, sensitive human being. Instead, other people are seen only as the embodiment of their social role; they are workers, or wives, or doctors, not persons. The act of depersonalizing others may thus protect persons against guilt feelings they might experience if they knew they were hurting others. Or if they suffer from an inability to love, they might protect themselves against such a disquieting insight through depersonalizing others. Physicians, nurses, and dentists often depersonalize their patients or clients, adopting a "bedside manner" or a "chair-side manner," when dealing with them. The adoption of such contrived patterns of interaction permits them to treat their patient without being disturbed by the latter's suffering. Further, it permits them to hide their true feelings of like or dislike behind a professional mask. Depersonalizing makes it possible for acts of extreme violence to be performed. The Nazis were able to slaughter millions of Jews because they had convinced themselves Jews were not human beings.

Sublimation

[E] A rare defense mechanism in that it calls out positive results is called sublimation. In its narrowest sense, it refers to the substitution of a socially acceptable activity for erotic, sexual strivings that cannot be directly satisfied because of social standards. In a broader sense, it may also be interpreted to mean substitution of a socially acceptable behavior for *any* drive or motivation that is not socially acceptable, including hostility and aggression.

[F] For a person who, for religious or other reasons, can either not marry or chooses not to marry and to live a celibate, sexless life, throwing one's energy into volunteer leadership in the community or into an absorbing job is a good, socially desirable alternative. Sometimes this sublimation may be temporary, as in the case of a teenager who may keep physically active to the point of exhaustion in order to avoid encounters with the opposite sex, or it can also be a permanent lifestyle as in the case of some corporate executives who are "married to their jobs." In any event, sublimation is often seen as an entirely desirable defense pattern.

EVALUATING DEFENSE MECHANISMS

[G] Although a healthy personality characteristically is free of frequent use of the defense mechanisms, they are in actuality a normal occurrence. Defense mechanisms have survived as concepts from earliest days of Freudian psychoanalysis and still are useful as illuminators of some forms of behavior. There seems to be some evidence concerning the relative value of various defense mechanisms. For example, in a study by Barenbaum of people who had lost young sons or husbands in the Yom Kippur war in Israel, denial was one of the most often used defense mechanisms by the bereaved parents or wives. In another study by Jacobowitz, the brighter preadolescent children, facing problems in moral transgressions, would most likely use projection and displacement, whereas the less academically talented peers would use denial. And the value of some of the mechanisms may be seen in a third study by Viney and Manton, who found that university students who used some of the defense mechanisms had reduced anxiety, indicating the therapeutic purpose of the mechanisms.

DEFENSE OF THE PUBLIC SELF

[H] Persons' various public selves are important to them. They can feel assured others will like them only when they believe that other people see them as the kind of persons that they can like. And, as Willie Loman pointed out in *Death of a Salesman,* it is important to be well liked. Consequently, it is not enough simply to construct public selves; a person usually feels obliged to defend them.

[I] The most general means of defending the public self is by means of selective suppression of behavior that is inconsistent with the public self, replacing authentic with false self-disclosure. A mother may have heard reports about her son's behavior that conflict with her concept of him. She confronts him with the report, and he denies it flatly. He does not want her to believe that he behaves in such a way. Secrecy is more common than lying as a means of defending our public selves. We can do almost anything without fear (though not necessarily without guilt) if no one discovers what we have done. The secret activities may be incredibly disparate with the public selves of the individual. People at conventions sometimes display behavior markedly different from their usual hometown behavior and are quite disconcerted if their family and neighbors hear reports of their conduct.

[J] A really intelligent person can construct public selves with ingenuity and finesse—sometimes fantastically diverse and contradictory selves. The more diverse they are, however, the greater the difficulty in maintaining them; persons who hold contrasting concepts of the individual may meet this person simultaneously, and then the individual is at a loss to know how to behave.

PERSISTENCE OF THE SELF-IDEAL

[K] Once a self-ideal has been constructed, the person finds it difficult to change it. Why is this so, especially when the conscience is inhumane and impossibly strict? Consider an individual with incredibly high standards of performance; this person never attains them and believes he or she is a failure. If only the person's self-ideal could be altered, he or she could experience self-esteem, perhaps for the first time. Yet the person, when urged to relax the standards, will refuse, saying, "I wish I could, but I can't."

[L] The reason why persons find it difficult to alter the self-ideal is because it came from sources *they dare not question*—parents, teachers, God, or the Bible. Their values have been acquired in the context of an authoritarian relationship, and they are in dread of horrible consequences should they question the "commands." Freud said, "As the child was once compelled to obey its parents, so the ego submits to the categorical imperative pronounced by its superego."

[M] This fear of obscure consequences if one should change one's conscience presents a powerful conserving force in the personality. A person may anesthetize the conscience with alcohol, lull it with self-deceptive arguments and rationalizations, may even repress it; but one rarely changes it. This refusal has disastrous consequences for one's wellbeing and maturity.

GROWTH OF THE SELF

Thus far, we have discussed the myriad ways in which a person maintains a stable identity in the face of experiencing that threatens it. Such stability is not pathology-producing in its own right; everything depends upon the availability of action that serves the person's needs and fulfills the person's projects. If the different aspects of the self are in reasonable harmony, and the person can cope with the challenges of work, leisure, and personal relationships, a stable self-structure is compatible with healthy personality. But there are times when healthy personality can be achieved only by changes in the self. I shall discuss these occasions now.

The Time for Change

There are various indicators of the time for change. These include boredom, sickness, chronic anxiety and guilt, failure in work, and failure in personal relationships. In all these instances, the person's self-structure may have gotten out of touch with the real self, and the person is out of touch with external reality. Something has changed, and he or she has not acknowledged or recognized it.

Boredom. The experience of boredom signifies the person's action is not serving his or her true needs and interests. Boredom also arises from prolonged exposure to monotonous surroundings, unchanging relationships, and repetitive work and leisure activity. Boredom is evidence of unperceived change in the self; the person whom one takes oneself to be *used* to be satisfied by those ways of being. Boredom means that one *no longer is that person,* and it is time to discover new dimensions of the self.

Sickness. Illness may signify that the person was not living in health-engendering ways. If a person is recurrently sick, it means, among other things, that the person does not know what he or she needs to do, or to stop doing, to achieve buoyant health; something must be done besides taking medicines. So-called nervous breakdowns—a radical inability to cope with conflict and responsibility in life—likewise indicate that a change in the structure of the self is overdue. Physical and psychological breakdown are the ultimate price one pays for resisting change in the self when life calls for it. If a person "worships" the present self-concept, public image, or self-ideal and is willing to sicken rather than change, then that person truly is guilty of the sin of idolatry so strongly condemned in the Old Testament.

NOTES

1. **John T. Walsh,** *Interpretation of Reading Materials in the Natural Sciences* (New York: Cambridge & Coules, 1973), p. 27.
2. **James Crockett,** *Foliage House Plants* (New York: Time-Life Books, 1972), p. 18.
3. **Crockett,** p. 18.
4. **Houston, Bee, Hatfield,** and **Rimm,** *Invitation to Psychology* (New York: Academic Press, 1979), p. 211.
5. **Houston, Bee, Hatfield,** and **Rimm,** p. 318.
6. **Rachman** and **Mescon,** *Business Today* (New York: Random House, 1979), p. 224.
7. **James Cicarelli,** *Economics: Macroeconomic Principles and Issues* (Boston: Houghton Mifflin, 1978), p. 27.
8. **Houston, Bee, Hatfield, and Rimm,** p. 583.
9. **Cicarelli,** p. 27.
10. **Sydney M. Jourard** and **Ted Landsman,** *Healthy Personality,* 4th ed. (New York: Macmillan, 1980), pp. 222–226.

Five

MAIN IDEA

The topic of a paragraph is precisely what the whole paragraph is about. The main idea of a paragraph conveys what the writer has to say about the topic. Every well-written paragraph contains a main idea. All other thoughts or details in a paragraph serve to support, prove, or clarify the main idea. The main idea provides the paragraph with meaning and is the most important element in a paragraph. If you want to understand a paragraph you must be able to identify the main idea quickly.

STATED MAIN IDEA

The main idea of a paragraph may be stated directly. When the main idea is stated directly it can be found in the topic sentence, which may be located anywhere in the paragraph.

The topic will lead you to the main idea. Establish the topic and then look for a topic sentence that makes the most important statement about the topic. This topic sentence will convey the main idea.

To find a stated main idea (1) establish a topic, (2) locate the topic sentence.

EXERCISE I

Read the following paragraph. Write the topic. Then find and underline the topic sentence that conveys the main idea. Write the main idea in the space provided.

(1) Our present society is dominated by a large "single" population. (2) Despite their large numbers, singles point out that they are constantly treated unfairly. (3) Single men argue that they do not fare as well as married men in the job market. (4) They claim that raises and promotions are more apt to be given to married men. (5) Singles complain they have more trouble getting credit and insurance is more expensive. (6) "Just think," said one disgruntled single, "you can't even buy a single cemetery plot."

Topic _____

_____

Main idea _____

_____

The topic of this paragraph is obviously problems of "singles."

In looking for a topic sentence we see that each sentence makes some statement about single people. However, the most general statement, and the most important statement, is found in sentence 2, so you should have underlined that as the topic sentence.

The main idea conveyed by this sentence is that singles are constantly being treated unfairly.

UNSTATED MAIN IDEA

The main idea may not be stated directly. In this case the paragraph will not contain a topic sentence. You will have to infer the main idea from the details in the paragraph. In this type of paragraph, almost all the sentences are about one common subject. It is up to you to infer the main idea from these sentences. The main idea, stated in your own words, will bind together the sentences in the paragraph.

To find an unstated main idea:

1. Establish a topic.
2. State the main idea in your own words.

Read the paragraph below. Write the topic and the main idea in your own words.

The first people to use sails many thousands of years ago were the Chinese. Many centuries later sails were reinvented in Europe. The kite and the wheel were also invented and used in China well before their introduction into European life. Other Chinese inventions also show lags of from two to fifteen centuries before they appeared in the West.

Topic _____

_____

Main idea _____

_____

The topic of this paragraph would be inventions.

The main idea of this paragraph is that the Chinese invented and used many things centuries before they were used in Europe.

Read and analyze the following paragraph. Write the topic and the main idea in your own words.

A bill may be a statement of an amount owed or a draft of a law. A loaf may be a portion of bread or a lazy bore. A hand may be an extremity of the arm or a guide to help.

Topic _____

_____

Main idea _____

_____

EXERCISE II

Read the following paragraphs.

1. Write a precise topic.
2. Locate and underline the topic sentence.
3. Write the main idea in your own words. (Use a complete sentence.)

1. Final goods are goods and services purchased by all sectors for final consumption, not for additional processing or resale. Intermediate goods are goods and services that undergo additional processing or are resold. Final goods, thus, are the end result of the nation's productive effort, while intermediate goods are all the goods and services that will be processed further to make final goods. The distinction between final and intermediate goods is not necessarily the same as that between finished products and raw materials. In the previous example, polyethylene is an intermediate good when it is used by the waterbed manufacturer to make his product for households. If the polyethylene is sold directly to the households, it becomes a final good. A product may be either a final good or an intermediate one, depending on who buys it and for what purpose.[1]

Topic _____

_____

Main idea _____

_____

2. Few of us are totally immune from depression, but in most cases our actions and feelings would not warrant the use of the terms depressive neurosis. Thus, periods of grief and mourning following the death of a loved one are perfectly natural. In fact, a person who does not show some such reaction probably would be seen by others as a cold, uncaring person. However, if depression is quite persistent and is severe enough to interfere with our lives in some important way, a psychiatric label would be in order. Whether our depression is seen as neurotic or psychotic depends mainly on how much it incapacitates us. We will have more to say about depression when we deal with psychotic depression later in this chapter.[2]

Topic _____

_____

Main idea _____

_____

3. To further economic knowledge, economists often develop models consisting of logically constructed theories of economic behavior in which the assumptions and conclusions bear some resemblance to reality. These models begin with assumptions designed to simplify reality by focusing on the essential characteristics of an economic situation. At the same time, however, the assumptions must be sufficiently realistic so the conclusions logically derived from them will be relevant and meaningful. Ideally, a model reduces

the analysis of economic activity to manageable proportions, while preserving the significant features of the real-world problem under investigation.[3]

Topic _____

_____

Main idea _____

_____

4.   In national income accounting, it is assumed that households consume all the products they buy; hence, every commodity purchased by the household sector for the first time is considered a final good. Items bought by households after the original sale are *not* final products. For example, the acquisition of a new car is included in personal consumption expenditures, and in GNP. But the purchase of a used car is not included, because the used car was part of GNP in the year in which it was sold for the first time. To include the value of any subsequent sale as part of current production would involve multiple counting (remember, the function of the GNP is to measure *output,* not sales).[4]

Topic _____

_____

Main idea _____

_____

5.   Obsessional thinking cannot be observed directly, but compulsive behavior is public and so it can be studied easily. Compulsive behavior tends to be very stereotyped and ritualistic, so experimentors have tried to find out what produces such behavior in laboratory animals. One way is to give an animal a problem that cannot be solved, for instance one where it gets unpredictable punishment no matter which way it jumps (Maier, 1949). This training does lead to stereotyped behavior, such as always jumping in the same direction.[5]

Topic _____

_____

Main idea _____

_____

The following paragraphs do not contain stated main ideas. Write the topic and main idea in your own words.

6.   About fifteen miles below Monterey, on the wild coast, the Torres family had their farm, a few sloping acres above a cliff that dropped to the brown reefs and to the hissing white waters of the ocean. Behind the farm the stone mountains stood up against the sky. The farm buildings huddled like the clinging aphids on the mountain skirts, crouched low to the ground as though the wind might blow them into the sea. The little shack, the rattling, rotting barn were gray-bitten with sea salt, beaten by the damp wind until they had taken on the color of the granite hills. Two horses, a red cow and a red calf,

half a dozen pigs and a flock of lean, multicolored chickens stocked the place. A little corn was raised on the sterile slope, and it grew short and thick under the wind, and all the cobs formed on the landward sides of the stalks.[6]

Topic _____

_____

Main idea _____

_____

7. A seat in this boat was not unlike a seat upon a bucking bronco, and by the same token a bronco is not much smaller. The craft pranced and reared and plunged like an animal. As each wave came, and she rose for it, she seemed like a horse making at a fence outrageously high. The manner of her scramble over these walls of water is a mystic thing, and, moreover, at the top of them were ordinarily these problems in white water, the foam racing down from the summit of each wave requiring a new leap and a leap from the air. Then, after scornfully bumping a crest, she would slide and race and splash down a long incline, and arrive bobbing and nodding in front of the next menace.[7]

Topic _____

_____

Main idea _____

_____

Read the following paragraphs.

1. Write a precise topic.
2. Underline the topic sentence if one is present.
3. Write the main idea.

8. Fertile, level land and a favorable climate encouraged family size farms, which produced surplus grain (wheat, corn, and oats) for export to the other colonies and to England. The Middle Colonies soon became known as the bread colonies. Long, navigable rivers, such as the Hudson, Susquehanna, and Delaware, promoted trade with the Indians for furs. First-class harbors, such as New York and Philadelphia, stimulated trade with other colonies, England, and the European continent.[8]

Topic _____

_____

Main idea _____

_____

9. Language and writing are the most common media of human communication. Research has proven, however, that we also express a great deal through movements, gestures, as well as the tone of our voice. Children laugh when they are happy, and cry when they are sad. Joy, astonishment, disappointment, fear, and frustration are all expressions of emotion. These nonverbal expressions of emotion are all forms of communication.

Topic _____

_____

Main idea _____

_____

10.   There are 25,000 violent crimes committed in the United States every year. Approximately three people an hour are victims of these crimes. The lives lost through these senseless crimes are estimated at 800,000. All the wars in American history from the Revolution through Vietnam account for the loss of 500,000 lives.

Topic _____

_____

Main idea _____

_____

PROJECT

The reading selection titled "Education" has been selected from a college sociology text. Read the selection. Pay particular attention to the lettered paragraphs and underline the topic sentence found in each. Write the main idea for each lettered paragraph in the space below.

Paragraph	Main Idea
A	_____
B	_____
C	_____
D	_____
E	_____
F	_____
G	_____
H	_____
I	_____
J	_____
K	_____
L	_____
M	_____
N	_____
O	_____

EDUCATION⁹

CHAPTER OUTLINE

Characteristics of American Education
Commitment to Mass Education
Utilitarian Emphasis
Community Control

Education: The Functionalist Perspective
Cultural Transmission
Social Integration
Personal Development
Screening and Selection
Innovation
Latent Functions

Education: The Conflict Perspective
The "Credential Society"
Education and Social Mobility

Inside the School
The Formal Structure of the School
Competitiveness
Declining Academic Standards
The Self-Fulfilling Prophecy

Social Inequality and the Schools
Class, Race, and Education
Class, Race, and Intelligence

Equality of Educational Opportunity
The Coleman Report
Busing and School Integration
Can Education Create Equality?

[A] The word "school" comes from an ancient Greek word meaning "leisure." The link between the two words may not seem obvious today, but in preindustrial societies schooling had little practical use and was undertaken only by those with the time and money to pursue the cultivation of the mind for its own sake. The rest of the population began their working lives at adolescence or even earlier. Most people acquired all the knowledge and skills they needed through ordinary, everyday contacts with parents and other kin.

[B] With the rise of industrialism, however, mass schooling became a necessity. Knowledge expanded rapidly, the pace of social change increased, and many new economic roles were created. In a modern industrial society, people need to acquire specialized knowledge and skills if they are to fill their roles competently. Their education, therefore, cannot be left to chance. It requires attendance at specialized formal organizations such as elementary schools, high schools, and colleges. In all industrial societies, education is a central social institution.

[C] In its broadest sense, "education" is almost synonymous with "socialization," since both involve the passing on of culture from one person or group to another. The distinguishing feature of education in modern industrial societies, however, is that it has become an institutionalized, formal activity. These societies deliberately organize the educational experience, make it compulsory for people in certain age groups, train specialists to act as educators, and provide locations and equipment for the teaching and learning process. For our present purposes, then, *education is the systematic, formalized transmission of knowledge, skills, and values.*

[D] In terms of the number of people involved, education is the largest single industry in the United States. If we include students, teachers, and administrators and other staff, almost one American in three currently participates in the institution—a figure without parallel anywhere else in the world. There are several reasons for this remarkable emphasis on education. First, a large number of skilled and literate people is essential to the survival of such a highly industrialized society. Second, educational credentials, such as high school diplomas and college degrees, have become a valuable resource in the competition for good jobs and high incomes. Third, Americans have historically had a deep faith in the virtues of mass education, even if it means educating millions of people to levels far above those demanded by most jobs in the economy. We tend to regard education as a cure-all for a variety of social ills, and it is no accident that in recent years the schools have been used in controversial attempts to bring about social and racial equalities. As we shall see, the results have been somewhat disappointing, largely because of a failure to make a realistic sociological assessment of the schools' potential for bringing about social reform.

CHARACTERISTICS OF AMERICAN EDUCATION

American education has several characteristics not found in the same combination in any other society. Many of the virtues and problems of our educational system stem from this unique blend of features.

Commitment to Mass Education

[E] It is taken for granted in America that everyone has a basic right to at least some formal education and that the state should therefore provide free elementary and high school education for the masses. Schooling for every child was pioneered by the United States, and by the time of the Civil War most states were offering free education to white residents. This development took place long before similar systems were introduced in Europe. European countries were much less inclined to regard mass education as a virtue in itself; instead, they have always tended to tailor their educational planning to their economic needs.

[F] The expansion of mass education in the United States in the course of this century has been unequaled anywhere. In 1900, about 7 percent of Americans in the appropriate age group were graduated from high school; by 1920 this figure had risen to 17 percent; by 1940, to 50 percent; and it stands today at over 80 percent. More than two-thirds of the present American population has a high school diploma, and the adult population has a median of 12.4 years of education. The proportion of high school graduates attending college has also risen steeply, from 4 percent in 1900 to 16 percent in 1940 to about 40 percent by the beginning of the 1980s. By comparison, in Canada less than 20 percent of the people between the ages of eighteen and twenty-one are in college. In Western Europe opportunities for advanced education are even more scarce: only about 20 percent of the sixteen- and seventeen-year-olds are still in school, and only about 10 percent of all children proceed to college. The less developed nations of the world present an even greater contrast. Although they try to provide all children with a few years of elementary education, only a small minority obtain secondary education, and a person's chances of attending a college are minimal. More than half of the world's population can neither read nor write, and the absolute number of illiterates is actually increasing.

[G] This extension of educational opportunities in America has not been without its price, for mass education on this scale inevitably means some lowering of academic standards. Other industrialized countries, such as Great Britain and France, have generally insisted on high standards, even though this meant denying educational opportunities to the less academically able. Until the late sixties, for example, British schoolchildren were required to take a tough examination at the age of eleven, and on the basis of the results, were sent to one of two quite different kinds of schools. The "secondary modern" schools, to which the vast majority of children went, offered vocational training and only a basic academic curriculum; most of these children left school at the age of fifteen or sixteen. The "grammar" schools, attended by a small minority of children, had very high academic standards, emphasized such subjects as Latin and ancient Greek, and prepared their students for the university. (This system has now been abolished, and British secondary schools increasingly resemble those of America.)

[H] Formal education in America is not merely freely available: it is actually compulsory. There are still many societies where this is not the case, or where schooling is compulsory for only the first few grades. American parents are legally obliged to send their children to school, although they may choose between public and private (including religious) education—choices that are not offered in many other countries. Education in the United States is financed by taxing everyone, including people without children and people whose children attend private schools. The implication is that public education benefits the entire society, not merely those who happen to receive it. Every child is thus entitled to at least twelve years of schooling at public expense, and we even expect some skilled professionals to spend twenty years or more in school—a period equal to half the life expectancy in some of the less developed countries of the world.

Utilitarian Emphasis

[I] Our commitment to mass education arises partly from our historic belief not only that education is valuable and desirable in itself but also that it can serve a variety of social goals. At the founding of the Republic, Thomas Jefferson argued that the schools should be used to ensure the success of democracy. If the voters were merely an ignorant rabble, Jefferson believed, the American experiment was probably doomed.

[J] Since the nineteenth century, there has been a growing belief that the schools can be used for a wide range of utilitarian purposes, including the solving of social problems that were once considered a more appropriate concern for the family or the church. Education was first used as a tool for social engineering in attempts to "Americanize" immigrants and to "civilize" Indian children. Since then we have continued to lay new burdens on the schools. In the sixties the "war on poverty" placed great emphasis on education, in the belief that the culture of the poor, not their lack of money, was the source of their problem. If drug addiction spreads, we immediately start drug-education programs. When the teen-age pregnancy rate soars, the schools are expected to reduce it through effective sex education, and when young drivers cause too many accidents, we rely on the schools to teach them to drive safely.

[K] There is little evidence that these and similar programs have had much effect and a good deal of evidence that they have not, but our faith in education as a cure-all persists anyway. Other societies, of course, have used the schools to change attitudes and behavior—the outstanding examples are probably Nazi Germany and modern China—but they have done so in conjunction with sweeping changes in other social institutions at the same time. The faith that the schools *alone* can bring about social change is distinctively American. As sociologists of education are increasingly pointing out, there seems to be very little empirical justification for this faith, and it may be that we have cherished expectations of the institution that it cannot fulfill alone (Hurn, 1978).

Community Control

[L] Most other countries regard education as a national enterprise, and many have uniform national curriculums, teacher salaries, funding policies, and examinations. Not long ago it was said, a little cynically, that the minister of education in France could state exactly which book every child at a given grade was using during a particular hour of any schoolday. In the United States, however, the schools are regarded as the concern of the community they serve, and most decisions—ranging from the hiring of teachers to the selection or even banning of school library books—are in the hands of a local school board elected by the voters of the community. At present the individual states provide about 40 percent of the funding for the schools, the federal government provides about 10 percent, and the remainder comes from local school districts—most of it derived from property taxes.

[M] Compared with control from a distant national government, community control has many obvious advantages, and it is a tradition that is highly valued and zealously guarded. But it is also one that results in schools in wealthy neighborhoods being far more lavishly funded than schools in poorer areas. When taxable property per pupil is measured, some school districts have as much as ten thousand times the potential income of others (Reischauer et al., 1973). Thus, in one recent year, a district in South Dakota was spending $175 per pupil, while a district in Wyoming was spending $14,554. The average class size in Tennessee was over 23 pupils, while in Vermont it was nearer 16. As Figure 15.3 shows, expenditures per pupil vary widely from state to state. Community control has the drawback, then, that the quality of a child's educational experience may depend on the neighborhood in which he or she happens to live.

EDUCATION: THE FUNCTIONALIST PERSPECTIVE

The functionalist perspective explains the central importance of the schools by emphasizing the part they play in maintaining the social order as a whole. Several distinct functions of education can be identified.

Cultural Transmission

[N] If society is to survive, its culture must be handed down from one generation to the next. The schools are used to provide young people with the knowledge, skills, and values that a complex modern society considers especially important. Thus we learn about our history, geography, and language. We learn how to read, write, and manipulate numbers. We learn about patriotism, the virtues of our political system, and our culture's norms of behavior and morality. This function of education is an essentially conservative one, for the schools are transmitting the culture of the past, or, at best, the present. In a traditional society, this conservatism may not matter much, because culture changes very slowly. In a modern society, however, teachers of the older

Figure 15.3

There is a great variation in the per student expenditure on public schools from one state to another. These variations are closely related to the per capita income in each state. The physical quality of the school environment is therefore dependent on the relative wealth of the state concerned.

PUBLIC SCHOOL EXPENDITURES AND PERSONAL INCOME, 1978, BY STATES

State	Average per Pupil		Per Capita Personal Income	
	Total	Rank	Total	Rank
United States	$1,739	—	$ 7,810	—
Alabama	1,281	44	6,247	47
Alaska	3,341	1	10,851	1
Arizona	1,436	34	7,374	30
Arkansas	1,193	48	6,183	49
California	1,674	20	8,850	5
Colorado	1,649	21	8,001	15
Connecticut	1,914	16	8,914	4
Delaware	2,138	4	8,604	8
Dist. of Columbia	2,368	—	10,022	—
Florida	1,594	22	7,505	27
Georgia	1,189	49	6,700	37
Hawaii	1,963	12	8,380	11
Idaho	1,206	47	6,813	36
Illinois	2,058	8	8,745	7
Indiana	1,449	33	7,696	23
Iowa	2,002	10	7,873	17
Kansas	1,682	19	8,001	15
Kentucky	1,294	43	6,615	40
Louisiana	1,481	30	6,640	38
Maine	1,522	28	6,333	46
Maryland	2,100	6	8,306	12
Massachusetts	2,137	5	8,063	14
Michigan	1,975	11	8,442	10
Minnesota	1,962	13	7,847	18
Mississippi	1,220	45	5,736	50
Missouri	1,425	35	7,342	31
Montana	1,906	17	7,051	33
Nebraska	1,526	26	7,391	29
Nevada	1,526	26	9,032	3
New Hampshire	1,366	38	7,277	32
New Jersey	2,333	3	8,818	6
New Mexico	1,476	31	6,505	43
New York	2,527	2	8,267	13
North Carolina	1,343	41	6,607	41
North Dakota	1,518	29	7,478	28
Ohio	1,581	23	7,812	20
Oklahoma	1,461	32	6,951	34
Oregon	1,929	15	7,839	19
Pennsylvania	2,079	7	7,733	21
Rhode Island	1,840	18	7,526	26
South Carolina	1,340	42	6,242	48
South Dakota	1,385	36	6,841	35
Tennessee	1,209	46	6,489	44
Texas	1,352	40	7,697	22
Utah	1,363	39	6,622	39
Vermont	1,550	25	6,541	42
Virginia	1,560	24	7,624	24
Washington	1,951	14	8,450	9
West Virginia	1,374	37	6,456	45
Wisconsin	(NA)	—	7,597	25
Wyoming	2,007	9	9,096	2

SOURCE: U.S. Bureau of the Census, *Statistical Abstract of the United States,* 1979 (Washington, D.C.: U.S. Government Printing Office), p. 157.

generation may find it impossible to equip students to face a future that can never be fully anticipated. In their transmission of cultural values, too, schools in all societies engage, deliberately or otherwise, in indoctrination. We are well aware of this practice in certain other societies whose values are different from ours, but tend to overlook it in our own because the values we are taught seem so "natural" to us. But if a schoolteacher deals with controversial values—if, for example, he or she tries to present the life and thought of Karl Marx in a favorable light, or discusses sexual practices that are accepted in other societies but considered highly deviant in our own—a community furor is likely to result.

Social Integration

[O] Modern societies frequently contain many different ethnic, racial, religious, or other subcultures. Education can help to integrate the young members of these minorities into a common culture, encouraging the development of a relatively homogeneous society with shared values. In the United States the schools have always been considered an important factor in the "melting pot" process. Children of immigrants may arrive in the first grade unable to speak more than a few words of English, but they emerge from school, at least in theory, able to take their place in the mainstream of American life. This social integration function is particularly important in many of the less developed nations. The borders of these countries were often established by European colonial powers without any regard to tribal, linguistic, or ethnic barriers. Consequently, some new nations contain literally hundreds of different language groups that lack a common cultural tradition and often have a history of mutual hostility. These countries explicitly use the schools to generate a common sense of national loyalty among the young.

Personal Development

The schools teach a variety of facts and skills, most of which are expected to be of some practical use to the students later in their lives. They also provide the students with the opportunity to acquire something more subtle, but at least as important: the habits of thought, the broader perspectives, that are the mark of an educated person. In both the formal curriculum and informal interaction with peers and teachers, students learn a great deal about themselves and about the world that surrounds them. Some of this learning is relevant to their future occupational roles, but much of it is more valuable for personal emotional, social, and intellectual development. To take but one example, level of education has a strong impact on attitudes and opinions. A "don't know" response to questions in national opinion polls is consistently linked to low educational attainment, irrespective of the subject of the poll. The higher one's level of education, the more likely one is to reject prejudice and intolerant thinking. Each additional year of college appears to make a student more democratic in outlook and more tolerant toward civil liberties issues (Feldman and Newcomb, 1969; Nunn et al., 1978; Hyman and Wright, 1979).

Screening and Selection

Education is an important avenue to occupational and financial success in industrial societies because the schools screen and select students for different kinds of jobs. The more desirable a job, the larger the number of people who would like to have it, and an important function of the schools is to limit access to various occupations by granting the necessary diplomas, degrees, or other credentials to some students but not to others. From the elementary years onward, the schools constantly test students and evaluate their achievements, channeling some toward technical vocations, some toward academic subjects, and some straight into the job market. The credentials that people possess at the end of their education have a strong influence on their life chances.

Innovation

Educational institutions do not merely transmit existing knowledge; they add to the cultural heritage by developing new knowledge and skills as well. This function arises partly because the experience of education stimulates intellectual curiosity and critical thought, and partly because college and university teachers are usually expected to conduct research that will increase scientific knowledge. A good deal of research now takes place outside the schools—in government, industry, and specialized research institutes—but the college professor has a double role as teacher and researcher. This role can generate tensions; in fact, many professors complain that they face the choice of neglecting either their research or their students. Colleges and universities remain primarily responsible for *basic* research, which is concerned with establishing new knowledge. *Applied* research, which tries to find practical uses for knowledge, is increasingly pursued outside the college context.

Latent Functions

The functions discussed so far are of the type that sociologists call *manifest*—that is, they are recognized and intended. But education also has functions of a *latent* type, functions that are not generally recognized and were never intended (Merton, 1968). For example, schools serve as "babysitting" agencies. They free parents from child-rearing tasks and permit them to work outside the home. Colleges and even high schools serve as a "marriage market," by giving young people of fairly similar background a chance to interact with one another in a way that would not be possible if their social oribits were restricted to the home and workplace. By isolating the young from the rest of society, the schools also have the latent function of permitting distinctive youth cultures to form. In the sixties and early seventies, for example, many college students adopted political and social norms that were often radically at odds with those of the wider society, and the college campus became a focus of unrest. The schools may also serve the latent function of keeping adolescents—who are not expected to have full-time jobs—occupied and out of trouble. In addition to their formal curricula, the schools also teach habits of punctuality, docility, and obedience to authority, a latent function that has a useful payoff when young people move on to offices and factories. One further latent function of education in the United States, which we shall discuss in more detail below, is that of perpetuating the class and racial inequalities of our society.

EDUCATION: THE CONFLICT PERSPECTIVE

A functionalist analysis of education gives a useful understanding of the role this institution has in society. But the analysis does not tell the whole story, for it tends to ignore the fact that education can become deeply involved in social conflict. The conflict perspective, on the other hand, focuses on the ways different social groups use education as a means of getting or keeping power, wealth, and prestige.

The "Credential Society"

The United States has been described as a "credential society"—one in which overwhelming importance is attached to educational qualifications of various kinds (Collins, 1979). During this century, and particularly since World War II, the proportion of the population with high school diplomas, bachelor's and master's degrees, and even doctorates has increased at an astonishing pace. Why has this happened? The functionalist answer would be that education has expanded in response to economic growth: that new and more challenging jobs have demanded higher levels of skill, and that the schools have helped to keep the social system in balance by producing the necessary trained workers.

Until recently this common-sense explanation was almost unquestioned. The evidence, however, gives it surprisingly little support. Some new jobs that require advanced knowledge and skills have of course appeared (like that of the atomic physicist). But the content of most jobs has not changed in the course of this century. The level of skills required of file clerks, typists, cashiers, assembly-line workers, lawyers, teachers, receptionists, sales representatives, or bus drivers is generally little different than it was decades ago. Yet the same kinds of jobs now demand more advanced qualifications. In fact, upgrading of this nature accounts for most of the increased educational requirements for jobs during this century. Only about 15 percent of the increase results from the appearance of new, high-skill jobs (Berg, 1970; Freeman, 1976; Collins, 1971b, 1979).

Why do employers demand ever higher educational credentials from their workers? There seem to be two reasons. First, they use formal qualifications to make their task of screening and selecting job applicants easier; and when there is an oversupply of job candidates with the necessary credentials, employers simply increase the required qualifications. Second, employers share the widespread belief that better-educated workers are more productive than those who are less educated. Yet numerous studies have shown that, contrary to popular opinion, there is little or no relationship between educational achievement and job performance or productivity. For example, good grades in a graduate school of medicine or education are poor predictors of whether someone will become a good doctor or teacher (Gintis, 1971; Collins, 1979). The skills required to get an A grade in a college course on anatomy or educational philosophy are not the same as the skills needed to deal with a medical emergency or an unruly junior high school class. The schools and colleges teach very little (other than basic literacy and numeracy) that is directly relevant to the world of work. Most people pick up the necessary skills on the job, not in the classroom, and the characteristics that make for a successful career (such as initiative, leadership, drive, negotiating ability, willingness to take risks, and persuasiveness) are not even taught in the schools. It seems that the schools produce graduates with any number of educational credentials but with few specifically job-related skills; in fact, nearly half of the country's college graduates work in fields they consider unrelated to their major subjects (Solomon et al., 1977).

Education and Social Mobility

On the whole, a higher credential means higher earnings—simply because the value the job market places on it makes it a major asset in the competition for the best jobs. . . . the most prestigious jobs tend to be those that are known not only to yield the highest incomes but also to require the longest education. In their landmark study of *social mobility* (movement from one status to another) in the United States, Peter Blau and Otis Duncan (1967) found that the most important factor affecting whether a son achieved a higher status than his father's was the amount of education the son attained. A high level of education is a scarce and valued resource, for which people compete vigorously. According to conflict theorists, the remarkable expansion of American education in recent decades has less to do with the demands of the economy than with competition for power, wealth, and prestige. In their view, the pressure for ever-increasing credentials comes from two main sources: the professions, which insist on high membership qualifications as a means of protecting their own interests, and the consumers of education who want credentials for their own advantage.

A *profession* is an occupation requiring extensive, systematic knowledge of or training in an art or science. Professionals try to maintain a clear distinction between themselves and lay persons, typically by the use of some form of licensing or certification, which is usually awarded only after a long socialization process involving a college degree or other advanced credential. A major purpose of this requirement is to limit entrance into the profession, thereby increasing its prestige, autonomy, and earning power. As hundreds of occupations have become professionalized—first those of the physician and the lawyer, then of the engineer and the accountant, and now those of the police officer, the social worker, and the real estate broker—the demands on the schools for more and higher credentials have increased (Bledstein, 1976; Larson, 1977). (Professions are discussed in more detail in Chapter 18, "The Economic Order.")

The consumers of education, too, are well aware that education is the key to social mobility. When the Gallup poll asked Americans in 1972 why they wanted their children to become educated, the most frequent response was "To get a better job"; only 15 percent felt that education was "To stimulate their minds." Four years later, the poll found that 80 percent of the adult population wanted to see high schools "put more emphasis on careers." And a 1979 survey of college freshmen by the American Council on Education found that nearly two-thirds cite "being very well-off financially" as a "very important goal" of their college education. In recent years Americans have flocked to colleges in such numbers that—as you are no doubt keenly aware—there is now a glut of college graduates on the job market. The competition for credentials, combined with a slowdown in economic growth, has left American society with more graduates than there are "college level" jobs to be filled. As a result, many of today's college students and graduates will have to work at a lower level of skill and income than they had anticipated. By the mid-seventies, in fact, nearly half of the employed college graduates were "underutilized" in this way (Berg et al., 1978). It is not possible to predict precisely how many graduates will be affected by unemployment or underemployment in the next few years, since such an estimate involves guesswork about the future of the economy; but it seems likely that by the mid-eighties a third of all college graduates will be in jobs that would normally not require a degree (Froomkin, 1976; Wiegner, 1978).

In the light of these depressing statistics, is a college degree really worth the effort and expense? Caroline Bird (1975) suggested that, on average, a student who went directly to work after high school and put the equivalent of college tuition fees in a savings account would, by the time of retirement, have earned over half a million dollars more than a college graduate. Other analysts strongly dispute this view, and maintain that a college degree will yield as much as a 30 percent annual return on tuition costs, particularly if the economy improves in the decades ahead (Mincer, 1974; Witmer, 1976). In addition, a college degree offers many benefits, even if it does not lead automatically to a "college-level" job. A graduate has an advantage over nongraduates in the competition for the pleasanter, better-paid, and more prestigious of the remaining jobs. And a college education offers people an opportunity to grow and be challenged in a variety of ways that cannot be measured in dollars and cents (Hyman et al., 1975; Bowen, 1977; Drew, 1978). In fact, young Americans show continuing enthusiasm for college degrees. Most high school graduates with college plans are responding to economic uncertainty, not by abandoning their education, but by switching from such subjects as English and history to engineering or business administration—fields that supposedly offer more potential for social mobility.

NOTES

1. **James Cicarelli,** *Economics: Macroeconomic Principles and Issues* (Boston: Houghton Mifflin, 1978), p. 120.
2. **Houston, Bee, Hatfield,** and **Rimm,** *Invitation to Psychology* (New York: Academic Press, 1979), p. 571.
3. **Cicarelli,** p. 27.
4. **Cicarelli,** p. 120.
5. **Houston, Bee, Hatfield,** and **Rimm,** p. 573.
6. **John Steinbeck,** ''Flight,'' from *The Long Valley* (New York: Viking Press, 1938), p. 45.
7. **Stephen Crane,** *The Open Boat* (New York: Doubleday, 1898), pp. 5–6.
8. **Irving L. Gordon,** *American History Review Text* (New York: Amsco, 1973), p. 21.
9. **Ian Robertson,** *Sociology* (New York: Worth, 1981), pp. 377–386.

Six

DETAILS ... DETAILS

Once you have identified the main idea you may want to look to a paragraph for more details. You must read the details to understand some paragraphs, whereas in other paragraphs the main idea may be sufficient. Details are used to support, clarify, and explain the main idea. Details may be words, phrases, or statements that explain or describe.

Of course, if the main idea is not stated you must read the details to infer the main idea. In these cases it is particularly important to note which main idea the supporting details are proving.

CLUES TO HELP FIND IMPORTANT DETAILS

Writers use a variety of clues to call your attention to important details. These clues can help you identify the details you should read.

1. *Numbering:* Some authors help you locate ideas by numbering: first ... second ... third. ... It is important to give the words that follow special attention. These words will be important details.

   The causes of the War of 1812 were
   1. The impressment of American seamen.
   2. British interference with American commerce.

2. *Examples:* The words *for example, for instance,* and *to illustrate* signal important details.

   Ford, for instance, makes the engine for the American Pinto in its German plant but assembles the transmission in the more cost efficient British plant.

3. *Italics:* Italicized words call your attention to particularly important words and ideas. Italicized words may indicate that you should look up the meaning.

Qualifiers

4. *Negatives:* Watch for negative words. Negative qualifiers such as *no, not, never, neither,* and *hardly* can change the meaning of a sentence. Consider the changes in meaning when using negatives.

   Punishment is the best way to discipline.
   Punishment is not the best way to discipline.
   Punishment is never the best way to discipline.

5. *How many*: Words that tell how many are important qualifiers. These words should alert you to think carefully. *All, every, few, most, some, almost, nearly,* and *several* are examples of these words. Consider the different meanings of these sentences.

Some human behavior is instinctive.

Most human behavior is instinctive.

All human behavior is instinctive.

Punctuation

6. *Colon*: A colon is a signal for you to read what follows. A colon may direct you to a formal list, an explanation, or a long quotation at the end of a sentence.

Add these ingredients in the following order: butter, milk, salt, vanilla, and nutmeg.

The speaker listed the reasons for success: intelligence, desire to learn, and energy.

7. *Semicolon*: Statements that express closely related ideas may be joined by a semicolon.

The old man listened carefully; he heard nothing.

8. *Dashes*: Explanatory details are set off by dashes. The dash says, "The words you see from here to the next dash explain what you have just read or will read."

A drop in the purchasing power of the dollar can mean hardship for people—such as those living on pensions—whose daily comfort depends on the wise investment of capital.

9. *Quotes*: Quotation marks set off a speaker's or writer's exact words. Notice the difference in meaning when quotes are used:

I can't believe the president said that the recession is over.

"I can't believe," the president said, "that the recession is over."

EXERCISE I

The following exercise will help you develop a more precise understanding of details and how they relate to the main idea. Read the following sets of main ideas and details. Label each detail with the letter of the main idea it supports.

A. South America's geography affects its economy.
B. South America's major problem is not overpopulation.

1. _____ South America cannot utilize one-third of her cultivatable land, because of high mountain ranges.

2. _____ South America has a high birth rate, but the population is stabilized because of a high death rate.

3. _____ Productivity lags far behind other countries because of geographic conditions.

4. _____ South America's population increases relatively little every year.

5. _____ South America's high mountain ranges make farmland inaccessible.

6. _____ South America's climate in many regions is too hot for sustained physical effort.

7. _____ There is little iron or coal in South America.

EXERCISE II

Main ideas and details are given below. Label each detail A, B, or C to show which main idea it supports.

A. Our memory systems are less than perfect.
B. The process of focusing our attention plays an important role in memory.
C. Attention as well as repetition will help secure memory.

1. _____ The more you repeat a difficult name, the more likely you will remember it.

2. _____ We can all be frustrated trying to memorize complicated academic material.

3. _____ If we can train ourselves not to be distracted we can improve our chances of remembering.

4. _____ We know the answer to a test item but we cannot retrieve it.

5. _____ Your retention of other types of material, such as course work, can be maximized by focused attention.

6. _____ Attention is necessary, but not necessarily sufficient.

7. _____ At a party you may be too busy talking, looking, smiling, shaking hands, wondering what to say, and worrying about impressions to pay attention to what was said.

EXERCISE III

In the following paragraphs you will encounter many of the detail clues discussed in this chapter. Read each paragraph. Circle each clue the writer uses to call attention to the details. Note the line number in which the clue occurs and the type of clue.

Read the following paragraph about "National Income Accounting." Circle each clue. Write the line number and clue the author uses to highlight details.

1– In national income accounting, it is assumed that
2– households consume the products they buy, hence
3– every commodity purchased by the household sector
4– for the first time is considered a final good.
5– Items bought by households after the original sale
6– are not final products. For example, the acquisition
7– of a new car is included in personal consumption
8– expenditures, and in GNP in the year in which it was
9– sold for the first time. To include the value of
10– subsequent sale as part of current production would
11– involve multiple counting (remember, the function
12– of the GNP is to measure output, not sales.)[1]

( ) _____   ( ) _____   ( ) _____

( ) _____   ( ) _____   ( ) _____

Read the following passage about advertising. Circle each clue. Write the line number and clue used to highlight details.

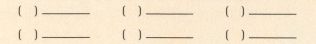

1– Advertising can be classified in three main
2– categories: primary-demand advertising; selective or
3– brand advertising; and institutional advertising
4– The thru categories differ in what they try
5– to accomplish.[2]

( ) _____   ( ) _____   ( ) _____

( ) _____   ( ) _____   ( ) _____

Read the following passage, "National Income Accounts." Circle each clue. Write the line number and clue used to highlight details.

1– The national income accounts . . . are
2– based on the concepts of national output and national income. . . .
3– There are some
4– differences, however, between the actual accounts and the
5– concepts on which they are based, because the concepts are
6– not perfectly translatable into practice. These differences
7– concern: (1) the distinction between final and intermediate
8– goods, (2) the imputation of value to certain commodities not
9– exchanged in the markets, (3) nonincome
10– revenues, and (4) the meaning of the accounts.[3]

( ) _____   ( ) _____   ( ) _____

( ) _____   ( ) _____   ( ) _____

( ) _____   ( ) _____   ( ) _____

PROJECT

Read the selection "The Roots of Modern Industrialism," which follows. For further practice in finding details, use the following outline to complete lettered paragraphs A and B. Complete paragraphs C through J on a separate piece of paper using the diagram outline shown below.

A.

B.

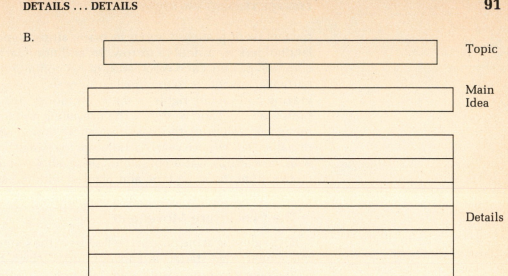

THE ROOTS OF MODERN INDUSTRIALISM[4]

[A] Modern industrialism, quite simply, is the mass production of goods by means of machines driven by generated power and set up in factories. There had been few mechanical inventions before the eighteenth century. During the Middle Ages, consumer goods had been produced by hand and for local consumption. With the Age of Discovery and the "Commercial Revolution" in the sixteenth century, the rate of production had increased to provide goods for export. Since the small artisan did not have the capital to buy large quantities of raw materials, to produce a large stock, and to sell it in a distant market, a class of wealthy capitalists and merchants began to inject themselves into the production process. They supplied the artisan with raw materials and sometimes with tools, and they took over the finished product to sell at a profit. This "domestic," or "putting-out," system had become quite common by the seventeenth century. There were even a few simple machines, but they still had to be operated by humans or animals, or by the natural power of wind or water. During the eighteenth century the trend toward large-scale production was accelerated by numerous mechanical inventions that increased the speed and thus the volume of production. The most important step came with the application of steam power to these new machines. This step brought the decline of the domestic system and the gradual shift of production from home to factory.

[B] It was no accident that modern industrialism should have had its start in the eighteenth century. The intellectual climate of the Enlightenment, its interest in science, and its emphasis on progress and the good life were particularly favorable to such a development. The beginnings of modern industrialism fall into the period after 1760, and the acceleration of industrialism was most pronounced in England. England's parliamentary government gave some voice to the rising commercial and industrial classes; it had large colonial holdings and far-flung commercial interests; it had a sound financial system and sufficient surplus capital; and it had an ample supply of basic raw materials and manpower. The manpower had been made available in part by drastic changes in British agriculture—an "Agricultural Revolution"—which converted farmers into laborers and materially increased Britain's food supply.

THE AGRICULTURAL REVOLUTION

[C] Most of the land in Britain before the eighteenth century was still worked under the open-field system, which meant that the holdings of individual owners were scattered about in many strips, separated from those of other landholders by a double furrow. In addition, each landholder shared in the common pastures and woodlands of his community. This arrangement was of particular advantage to the small farmers and cottagers, who participated in the grazing and fueling rights of the "commons." But the open-field system was both inefficient and wasteful. The prevailing method of cultivation was still the medieval system of three-field rotation under which one-third of the land remained fallow each year. Any attempt to change this routine by experimenting with new crops was impossible, since all strips in a given field had to be cultivated at the same time and planted with the same crop.

The "Enclosure Movement"

[D] Beginning at the time of the Tudors in the sixteenth century, an "enclosure movement" had started in England under which the scattered strips of individual owners were consolidated into compact holdings surrounded by fences or hedges. Enclosure meant a gain of usable land because it did away with the double furrows, and it made cultivation much easier. But since enclosure also entailed a division of the commons, it worked to the detriment of the small farmer, who thereby lost part of his livelihood. As the population of England increased, agricultural production for the general market rather than for local consumption became more profitable. The trend toward more efficient large-scale farming, and especially sheep raising, through enclosures therefore gained momentum. It reached its climax in the eighteenth century. Between 1702 and 1797, Parliament passed some 1776 enclosure acts affecting 3 million acres. In each case the larger landowner profited at the expense of the smaller farmer. Left with too little land of his own and deprived of his share in the commons, the small farmer had no choice but to become a tenant farmer or move to the cities. Many took the latter course, providing some of the manpower without which the rapid growth of Britain's industry could not have taken place.

[E] The enclosure movement brought hardships to many people, but it brought a dramatic improvement in agriculture. Freed from the restrictions of collective cultivation, landowners were now able to try new methods and new crops. This enabled them to grow more food on the same amount of land. The improvement was such as to give substance to the term "Agricultural Revolution." Like its industrial counterpart, the Agricultural Revolution at first was almost entirely restricted to Britain. Only with the advent of industrialization did the larger landholders on the Continent seriously begin to experiment with British methods. The small peasants, on the other hand, continued in their backward ways. As new industrial centers developed, new markets for agricultural produce opened up. Improvements in transportation, furthermore, facilitated marketing; and new scientific discoveries and the use of fertilizers brought larger crop yields. These and other developments brought renewed hope for western Europe's farmers, who were gradually being pushed to the wall by the rising industries and were beginning to feel the competition of the fertile agrarian lands of eastern Europe and America.

THE BEGINNINGS OF INDUSTRIALIZATION

Inventions and the Rise of the Factory System

[F] The early history of industrialization is related to the rise of mechanical inventions. There were few of these at first, but they multiplied as one discovery created the need for another. When John Kay invented his flying shuttle in 1733, enabling one weaver to do the work of two, the need arose for some new device that would speed up spinning. This demand was met in 1764 by James Hargreaves and his spinning jenny, which permitted the simultaneous spinning of eight or more threads. A few years later, Richard Arkwright devised the water frame, and in 1779 Samuel Crompton perfected the "mule," a hybrid that combined features of both Hargreaves' and Arkwright's inventions. These improvements in spinning in turn called for further improvements in weaving. In 1787 Edmund Cartwright patented a new power loom. After it was perfected, the demand for cotton increased. Cotton production received a boost when an American, Eli Whitney, in 1793 developed the cotton "gin," which speeded up and cut the cost of removing the cotton fiber from its boll. Almost all the early inventions were made in the cotton industry: it was a new industry, it had a large overseas market, and cotton lent itself particularly well to mechanical treatment.

[G] Since most of the earlier devices were small, relatively inexpensive, and hand-operated, they could be used as part of the domestic system in the workers' cottages. Arkwright's water frame, however, was large and expensive, and it needed water power to operate. Arkwright, therefore, moved into the heart of the English textile region of Nottingham, where he opened the first spinning mill in 1771. By 1779 he was employing some three hundred workers who operated several thousand spindles. With this important innovation, the modern factory system had been born. Arkwright's example was soon followed by other manufacturers, especially as the steam engine became the major source of power for newer and larger machines.

The Steam Engine

[H] Of all the inventions in the early years of industrialism, the steam engine was the most important. Until the advent of electricity it remained the chief source of power, and even in our atomic age its usefulness has not entirely ended. The development of the steam engine is closely related to the two industries that ultimately proved basic to all modern economic progress—coal and iron. At the beginning of the eighteenth century the smelting of iron was still done by charcoal. The depletion of Britain's wood supply, however, and the discovery, shortly after 1700, of a process for smelting iron with coke, shifted the emphasis to coal. The mining of coal was made considerably easier by a primitive steam engine, developed by Thomas Newcomen, that was used to pump water from the coal mines. This early eighteenth-century engine was a long way from the kind of steam engine that could be used to run other machines. The credit for developing such an engine belongs to the Scotsman James Watt, who patented his first steam engine in 1769. By 1800 some three hundred steam engines were at work in England, mostly in the cotton industry. The use of steam engines, of course, further increased the need for coal and iron. Improvements in iron production, on the other hand, in turn led to improvements in the making of steam engines. The interaction of one discovery with another continued to be a major characteristic of industrial development.

Early Industry on the Continent

Prior to 1815 the "Industrial Revolution," for reasons already stated, was chiefly a British phenomenon. An economic revival in France after 1763, helping to make up for the loss of the French colonies to Britain, had been interrupted by the French Revolution. But the Continental System of Napoleon, which excluded British goods from the Continent, had proved most beneficial to French industry.

[I] In the rest of Europe there were not even the beginnings of modern industrialization. Economic development in Germany was retarded by political disunity. The rich coal fields of the Ruhr and Silesia were hardly worked before 1815, and what little industry there was, especially in textiles, still operated under the "putting-out" system. Russia, Italy, and Austria were almost wholly agrarian. Even after 1815, continental industries were slow to assert themselves against British competition. It was only after the advent of the railroad in the 1830s that the situation began to improve.

THE RAILWAY AGE

Transportation in the Eighteenth Century

[J] Industrial development was closely related to the improvement of transportation. England again had a special advantage in being able to use coastal shipping for the movement of bulky goods. But like any other country it depended on roads and canals for inland transportation. As industrialization increased the need for transport and travel, the construction of toll roads and canals became a profitable business. England added thousands of miles to its system of roads and canals during the eighteenth century, and France before the Revolution had the finest highway system in Europe. Napoleon improved the situation further by pushing highways far into Germany and the Netherlands. In eastern Europe, however, paved roads were rare. Prussia's kings constructed canals and improved riverways, but the movement of goods was hampered by innumerable tools and tariffs. Farther east, dirt roads that regularly turned to mud and rivers that ran shallow during the summer and froze during the winter were the only arteries of communication.

NOTES

1. **James Cicarelli,** *Economics: Macroeconomic Principles and Issues* (Chicago: Rand McNally, 1978), p. 120.
2. **Rachman** and **Mescon,** *Business Today* (New York: Random House, 1979), p. 234.
3. **Cicarelli,** p. 120.
4. **Joseph Strayer** and **Hans Gatzke,** *The Mainstream of Civilization* (New York: Harcourt, 1979), pp. 571–574.

Seven

PARAGRAPH TYPES AND PATTERNS

Paragraphs are usually developed according to an overall plan or structure. A writer has a particular purpose in mind when writing. This purpose will determine the type of paragraph the author uses and the pattern of development.

As a good reader, you should be able to grasp the author's central purpose, identify the type of paragraph, and sense the pattern of paragraph development. In this chapter we review the most common paragraph types and patterns you should be able to identify.

AUTHOR'S PURPOSE

There is no formula to follow when trying to grasp the author's central purpose. The purpose can almost always be clearly determined once the paragraph has been read and the paragraph type has been determined.

PARAGRAPH TYPES

Narrative Paragraphs

Every narrative paragraph contains three essential components that provide the answers to these questions.

1. What happened?
2. Who or what was involved?
3. Where did the incident occur?

The events are presented chronologically. Time and logical order are frequently employed to connect several incidents.

In order to tell the story, the author adopts one of three viewpoints: (1) The first person, in which the author identifies with the character and relates events as they occur. (2) The third person, in which the author describes events from the "outside." (3) A shifting point of view, which shifts between the first and the third person.

You should identify the author's viewpoint and analyze its relationship to the content of the narrative. In a narrative paragraph, there is no stated main idea. All the sentences in a narrative paragraph are needed to develop the main idea.

The following short paragraphs are examples of narratives. A simple analysis of each will reveal that both are similar in purpose and development.

> The preacher preached a wonderful rhythmical sermon, all moans and shouts and lonely cries and dire pictures of hell, and he sang a song about the ninety and nine safe in the fold, but one little lamb was left out in the cold. Then he said: "Won't you come? Won't you come to Jesus? Young lambs, won't you come?" And he held out his arms to all us young sinners there on the mourners' bench. And the little girls cried. And some of them jumped up and went to Jesus right away. But most of us just sat there.[1]

> "Finally, I turned us onto a residental street, wanted to show them some pretty homes, and I ran smack into a dead-end street. When we got to the end, I stopped the car and looked around. I pushed one thing and then the other around the steering wheel, but I didn't know how to put the car in reverse. I cut the engine off, walked around, looked it over good, then told the ladies to step down. After they were off, I put my back up against the front end. I lifted. I was strong as an ox back then. I picked that car up, turned it around, and drove off. I never said a word about that to your Mamma or Nanny. I just acted like it was the thing to do. The next day I learned how to put the car in reverse." He slapped his knees and laughed at himself.[2]

The purpose of each paragraph is to relate an incident. Both paragraphs have a point of view. The first paragraph is written in the third person and the other mainly in the first person. The details of each paragraph follow the natural time sequence common to all narratives. The sentences of both paragraphs share equally in revealing the story; therefore, no topic sentence is evident. All of the above characteristics of the narrative as well as the who, what, and where components are effectively used in both examples.

Expository Paragraphs

Expository paragraphs are used to discuss and explain facts and ideas. Expository paragraphs are the ones encountered most in college textbooks. This type of paragraph consists of a main idea accompanied by details that relate to the main idea and to each other. An author may achieve a certain emphasis by putting the details first and concluding with the main idea.

Let's study the following expository example.

> Proteins are found in the basic structures of all cells. All movement in your body is performed by the contraction of protein fibers in your muscle cells. Blood is red because the red blood cells are filled with a special protein, hemoglobin, that combines easily with oxygen. The cells that line digestive glands produce digestive juices, the active ingredients of which are special proteins, the digestive enzymes.[3]

The purpose of the paragraph is to discuss that proteins are found in the fundamental structures of cells. The procedure is to state this idea in a topic sentence. Supporting sentences are used to explain or support this idea.

Descriptive Paragraphs

Descriptive paragraphs paint a verbal picture. No one sentence expresses the main idea. Directional or spatial order can be noted through the use of transitional words, such as *over, under, around, next to, beside,* and *between.* All descriptive paragraphs have the same purpose, to help you explore and experience the physical world by appealing to the senses. The following examples are presented to help clarify the characteristics of descriptive paragraphs.

> Vendors, ringing their bells, will hawk hot dogs, orange drinks, ice cream; and the caressing but often jarring noise of honking horns, music, chldren's games, and casual quarrels, whistles, singing, will go on late into the night. When you are in it you don't notice the noise, but when you stand away and listen to a taped conversation, the sound suddenly appears as a background roar. This loud stimulation of the senses may produce some of the emotionalism of the poor.[4]

> Our father was an artist in stone. He sculpted the most beautiful figures of Cupid and Psyche, Venus rising from the waves, of little mermaids, dancing girls, urns and baskets of flowers; and visitors came and bought them. My mother was his favorite model and next to her, Francine. I posed for him too. They would never have thought of leaving me out, although I had never had that sylphlike quality of Francine and my mother which lent itself so perfectly to stone. They were the beautiful ones. I resembled my father with hair which was rather nondescript in colour and could be called mid-brown, thick, straight and invariably untidy; I had greenish eyes which changed colour with their surroundings and what Francine called a "pert" nose, and a mouth which was rather large. "Generous," Francine called it. She was a great consoler. My mother had a fairylike beauty which she had passed on to Francine—blond and curly-haired, blue, dark-lashed eyes and that extra fraction of an inch on the nose which was sufficient to make it beautiful, and with all this went a shortish upper lip which revealed ever so slightly prominent pearly teeth.[5]

The author of each paragraph wishes to describe something; each, however, does so in a different manner. The first deals with sights and sounds; the second with the look of a person. Each paragraph is descriptive in form. These examples as well as all descriptive paragraphs share the same purpose. That is to help the reader see, touch, taste, or smell his or her physical environment.

Persuasive Paragraphs

A persuasive paragraph tries to change or alter your beliefs or actions. Such a paragraph may convince you to follow a certain choice of thought or behavior. Persuasive paragraphs are most commonly found in magazine articles, newspaper editorials, or texts where the author feels you will need more than cold facts to accept a point of view. In persuasive paragraphs, the facts are usually presented first with the main idea found in the middle or at the end of a paragraph. Two persuasive paragraphs are presented. The first persuasive paragraph, written by George Washington in his Farewell Address to the people of America, defends a policy.

> The great rule of conduct for us, in regard to foreign nations, is, in extending our commercial relations, to have with them as little political connection as possible. Europe has a set of primary interests, which to us have none, or a remote relation. Hence she must be engaged in frequent controversies, the causes of which are essentially foreign to our concerns. Hence, therefore, it must be unwise in us to implicate ourselves by artificial ties, in the ordinary vicissitudes of her politics or the ordinary combinations and collisions of her friendships and enmities. Our detached and distant situation invites and enables us to pursue a different course. Why forego the advantages of so peculiar a situation? It is our true policy to steer clear of permanent

alliances with any portion of the foreign world. Even our commercial policy should hold an equal and impartial hand; neither seeking nor granting exclusive favors or preferences, constantly keeping in view that it is folly in one nation to look for disinterested favors from any other; that it must pay with a portion of its independence for whatever it may accept under that character.

The second persuasive paragraph, written by Thomas Paine, condemns cowardice.

The summer soldier and the sunshine patriot will, in this crisis, shrink from the service of their country; but he that stands it now, deserves the love and thanks of man and woman. Tyranny, like hell, is not easily conquered; yet we have this consolation with us, that the harder the conflict, the more glorious the triumph. What we obtain too cheap, we esteem too lightly; it is dearness only that gives everything its value. Heaven knows how to put a proper price upon its goods, and it would be strange indeed if so celestial an article as freedom should not be highly rated.

Integrated Paragraphs

Often a paragraph will embody the characteristics of several paragraph types. A writer is concerned with presenting ideas effectively and naturally uses any method or variation that seems to work best. Paragraphs that contain two or more equally prominent paragraph types are called integrated paragraphs. The following paragraph is clearly an example of an integrated paragraph. The author's purpose is to discuss and explain the diatom. This is done through description. The paragraph embodies the characteristics of both the expository and descriptive types mentioned.

Diatom, *DIE uh tahm,* is a tiny water plant of the kind called algae. Unlike some of the other algae, which include large seaweeds, a diatom consists of only one golden-brown cell. There are several thousand species of diatoms, including both salt- and fresh-water types. Some appear as brown, slimy coatings on stones and piles in the water. Many of these one-celled plants may hang together in chains, and in various other arrangements. Still others float free. Diatoms can move by themselves through the water with jerky, creeping, or pendulumlike motions. The cell wall of the individual diatom is made up of two nearly equal halves, called valves. They are joined together somewhat as the two halves of a pillbox. The "glassy" cell wall is largely made up of silica, and forms a shell. Often the shell is very beautiful. Silica will not dissolve in water, so large masses of the tiny shells may be found at the bottom of seas, lakes, and ponds. The free, floating diatoms which grow in midocean and in lakes are a very important food for small sea animals. These, in turn, are eaten by fishes. If there were no diatoms, most of the fish of the world would die.[6]

PATTERNS OF PARAGRAPH DEVELOPMENT

Comparison and Contrast

The comparison and constrast paragraph pattern usually has a topic sentence that describes two subjects as being alike or different. The supporting sentences provide details that compare and contrast. Statistical tables, charts, and graphs are most often found in this type of paragraph. You should follow this pattern by jotting down the major similarities and differences.

An analysis of the comparison and contrast method of paragraph development follows:

> At first glance, then, we would expect the modern interconnected system of Canada to be a carbon copy of that of the United States. After all, both are among the half-dozen largest countries in land area in the world; both were settled about the same time by similar European immigrant groups; both have benefited from the results of the Industrial Revolution and stand among the most advanced industrial countries in the world; both are pulled together by a modern system of transport and communication. Despite these similarities, however, one of the important variables in the geographic equation is different, and that variable has produced a very different version of the modern interconnected system. Canada has only about one-tenth the population of the United States—23 million people, only slightly more than in California, the most populous state in the United States.[7]

> I. Canada and the United States: similarities
>   A. Large in area
>   B. Settled around same time by similar immigrants
>   C. Industrial Revolution: most advanced industrial countries in the world
>   D. Modern transport and communication system
> II. Canada and United States: contrast
>   A. Population variable

Cause and Effect

This paragraph pattern shows a cause–effect chain of events. This pattern is most often found in social studies texts and is closely related to the problem-solving pattern found in many science paragraphs. In both patterns, a cause or problem leads to a certain effect or solution. Transitional words most often found in cause–effect paragraphs are *because, therefore, in conclusion, resulting, consequently, thus,* and *for this reason.*

Cause–effect paragraphs can be outlined as follows.

> After the collapse of the Roman Empire, the trade between Europe and the East was reduced to a trickle. Even trade between various regions of Europe itself was reduced sharply. Because feudal estates in Europe provided most of what was needed for the lord and his household, there was no impetus for a revival of trade. Furthermore, travel between distant points was hindered by lack of roads and by highway robbers, while pirates and unskilled crews made travel by sea hazardous and uncertain. In addition, Moslems had won control of the Mediterranean during the 7th century, and they monopolized most of the commerce on the sea for 400 years.[8]

Main thought—
   Reasons why trade between Europe and the East diminished after the collapse of Roman Empire.

> Cause—feudal estates
>   lack of roads
>   highway robbers
>   sea hazards
>   Moslem monopoly
> Effect—Trade between Europe and East as well as various regions of Europe itself diminished.

ILLUSTRATION AND EXAMPLE

In this pattern, the main idea is supported by general or specific examples. The details are easy to identify since the author usually presents them through the use of transitional phrases, such as *to illustrate*, *for example*, and *for instance*.

In the example that follows the paragraph chosen has a series of specific examples without the use of transitional words. Read and note the use of these examples.

Imported wildlife getting loose also contributes to the growth of our new urban jungle. In Florida, where the climate is hospitable, about 50 such exotic species have been recorded, according to National Geographic Society. These escaped species include giant Colombian iguanas, walking siamese catfish (creatures with stiff fins that permit them to "walk" across roads) and the Amazon flesh-eating piranha fish, brought into Florida under strict control but freed by careless handlers. Rhesus monkeys were imported for early Tarzan films and later freed; today they survive in Florida swamps. Many Western jackrabbits used in Florida training farms for racing greyhounds escaped in 1940. Today they plague the state's cattle ranchers. Armadillos also roam the Florida countryside and ruin lawns by boring into them. These armadillos are descendants of escapees from a private zoo in Cocoa Beach that was destroyed by a hurricane in 1924.[9]

Definition Paragraphs

Writers use the definition pattern to define words or ideas not generally understood. The definition may answer a stated or implied question, and is followed by details and examples to clarify the terms. The following is an example of a definition paragraph and its outline.

Normative economic statements are value judgments: expressions of what ought to be, as opposed to what is. Assertions such as "labor unions ought to be illegal," "everyone should receive a guaranteed annual income," and "the work week ought to be reduced to twenty hours" are examples of declarations that comprise normative economics.[10]

I. Normative economic statements are value judgments.
   A. Labor unions *ought* to be illegal.
   B. Everyone *should receive* a guaranteed annual income.
   C. The work week *ought* to be reduced to twenty hours.

The following exercises will give you an opportunity to practice finding the topic and main idea as well as the author's purpose, the paragraph type, and the pattern of development.

EXERCISE I

1.   The conifers are the largest group of gymnosperms—naked-seed plants— so called in contrast to the angiosperms in which the seed is enclosed in an ovary, which develops to form a fruit. Among conifers, the male gametophyte is formed on modified leaves, the sporophylls, which form a cone. The gametophytes are released in the form of windblown pollen. The female

gametophyte develops on scales of a separate, larger cone within an ovule composed of the tissue of the parent sporophyte. Within the female gametophyte, archegonia form. The male gametophyte germinates and produces a pollen tube through which male reproductive cells (the sperm) enter the archegonium and fertilize the egg cell. The seed consists of the ovule and its contents, including the young embryo and the gametophyte, which serves as nutritive tissue. The seed, which is shed from the female cone, can remain dormant for long periods of time and hence is adapted to withstanding cold and drought.[11]

1. List the topic _____

_____

2. List the main idea _____

_____

3. What was the author's purpose in writing this paragraph? _____

_____

4. What type of paragraph is this? _____

5. What pattern of development did the author use? _____

_____

2.   A good example of creative and profitable programming can be seen at American Airlines, one of the most thoroughly computerized companies in any business field. Computer management has proved especially helpful in the area of fuel consumption—a vital consideration for an enterprise that uses 1.25 billion gallons each year of a commodity that jumped some 230 percent in price between 1973 and 1977. American's flight planning system, for instance, not only charts an aircraft's route—computing wind, payload weight, and other data in the process—but also supplies continuous weather information that enables the pilot to avoid storms and headwinds that would reduce fuel mileage. Meanwhile, a separate fuel management system keeps track of supplies and prices in different areas, advising the flight crew where it can take on fuel at the lowest cost. Computers even monitor the jet's takeoff, constantly adjusting engine thrust and wing flaps to get the plane airborne without wasting fuel.[12]

1. Topic _____

_____

2. Main idea _____

_____

3. Purpose _____

_____

4. Type _____

_____

5. Pattern _____

_____

3. There are two Americas. One is the America of Lincoln and Adlai Stevenson; the other is the America of Teddy Roosevelt and the modern superpatriots. One is generous and humane, the other narrowly egotistical; one is self-critical, the other self-righteous; one is sensible, the other romantic; one is good-humored, the other solemn; one is inquiring, the other pontificating; one is moderate, the other filled with passionate intensity; one is judicious and the other arrogant in the use of great power.[13]

1. Topic _____

_____

2. Main idea _____

_____

3. Purpose _____

_____

4. Type _____

_____

5. Pattern _____

_____

4. We are all used to hearing the refrain: "If poor people showed some ambition and initiative, they could escape from poverty and the slums." There are many reasons for questioning the validity and relevancy of this assertion, but in one field its absurdity is obvious and distressing. No matter how great his aspiration and ambition, neither the poor Negro-American, nor the rich one, can choose where to live. Whether he is moving from a tenement into a city high rise, or from a high rise into a suburban garden apartment; or from a garden apartment into a country split level, the color of his skin bars him from access to a large part of the housing market. No matter how secure and successful he may be, he finds himself judged not on his financial responsibility, or even his personality or the number of children he has, but rather on his pigmentation.[14]

1. Topic _____

_____

2. Main idea _____

_____

3. Purpose _____

_____

4. Type _____

_____

5. Pattern _____

_____

5. We could see the circus performers eating tremendous breakfasts, with all the savage relish of their power and strength: they ate big fried steaks, pork

chops, rashers of bacon, a half-dozen eggs, great slabs of fried ham and great stacks of wheat cakes which a cook kept flipping in the air with the skill of a juggler, and which a husky looking waitress kept rushing to their tables on loaded trays held high and balanced marvelously on the fingers of a brawny hand. And above all the maddening odors of the wholesome succulent food, there brooded forever the sultry and delicious fragrance—that somehow seemed to add a zest and sharpness to all the powerful and thrilling life of morning—of strong boiling coffee, which we could see sending off clouds of steam from an enormous polished urn, and which the circus performers gulped down, cup after cup.[15]

1. Topic _____

_____

2. Main idea _____

_____

3. Purpose _____

_____

4. Type _____

_____

5. Pattern _____

_____

Edgar Allan Poe, in "The Pit and the Pendulum," wrote:

6.   So far, I had not opened my eyes. I felt that I lay upon my back, unbound. I reached out my hand, and it fell heavily upon something damp and hard. There I suffered it to remain for many minutes, while I strove to imagine where and what I could be. I longed, yet dared not to employ my vision. I dreaded the first glance at objects around me. It was not that I feared to look upon things horrible, but that I grew aghast lest there should be nothing to see. At length, with a wild desperation at heart, I quickly unclosed my eyes. My worst thoughts, then, were confirmed. The blackness of eternal night encompassed me. I struggled for breath. The intensity of the darkness seemed to oppress and stifle me. The atmosphere was intolerably close. I still lay quietly, and made effort to exercise my reason.

1. Topic _____

_____

2. Main idea _____

_____

3. Purpose _____

_____

4. Type _____

_____

5. Pattern _____

_____

7.   When the energy crisis of the early 1970s hit, the federal government found itself poorly prepared to cope with the problems of the Arab oil embargo, lagging supplies of natural gas, the need for conservation, and a thousand related situations. As a result, Congress brought together some fifty federal energy agencies under a new Cabinet post—the Department of Energy (DOE). Once started, DOE found that its efforts to coordinate federal energy policies were hampered by a slow-moving Congress. By 1980, the Congress was still struggling to design an overall energy program acceptable to the White House, consumers, energy suppliers, and industry.[16]

1. Topic _____

_____

2. Main idea _____

_____

3. Purpose _____

_____

4. Type _____

_____

5. Pattern _____

_____

PROJECT

Read the following selections from three different college texts with paticular attention to the lettered paragraphs. Write the type and method of development for each lettered paragraph.

A. _____

_____

_____

B. _____

_____

_____

C. _____

_____

_____

D. _____

_____

_____

E. _____

_____

_____

[A] Sponges are somewhere between a colony of cells and a true multicellular organism. The cells are not organized into tissues or organs; each leads an independent existence. Yet there is a form of recognition among the cells that holds them together and organizes them. If the sponge *Microciona prolifera* is squeezed through a fine sieve or a piece of cheesecloth, the body of the sponge is separated into individual cells and small clumps of cells. Within an hour, the isolated sponge cells begin to reaggregate, and as these aggregations get larger, canals, flagellated chambers, and other characteristics of the body organization of the sponge begin to appear. This phenomenon has been used as a model for the analysis of cell adhesion, recognition, and differentiation, all of which are basic biological features of development in higher organisms.

Most kinds of sponges are hermaphroditic; that is, they have male and female reproductive organs in the same individual. Gametes appear to arise from an enlarged amoebocyte, but there are reports that choanocytes can also form gametes. A sperm enters another sponge in a current of water. It is captured by a choanocyte and transferred to an amoebocyte, which then transfers it to a ripe egg (a method of fertilization unique to the sponges). The fertilized egg develops into a ciliated, free-swimming larva. After a short life among the plankton, the larva settles and become sessile.

Sponges also reproduce asexually, either by fragments that break off from the parent animal, or by gemmules, aggregations of amoebalike cells within a hard protective outer layer. Production of such resistant forms is found, in general, only among freshwater organisms. In the ocean, conditions are relatively unchanging but the freshwater environment is much harsher. Invertebrates that live in fresh water are more likely to have protected embryonic forms than even closely related marine species.[17]

Like mitochondria, chloroplasts contain ribosomes and also some DNA. They synthesize some of their proteins. Chloroplasts can also divide and form new chrloroplasts.

chromo-: colored

[B] **Chromoplasts** are plastids of some color other than green—usually yellow, orange, red, or brown. Their pigments are fat-soluble. In higher plants chromoplasts are found largely in flowers and fruits, where they serve no known metabolic function, but the colors attract insects and other animals that transfer pollen or disseminate seeds. In some algae the chromoplasts are photosynthetic.

The large number of shades of color found in various parts of plants is due to the presence of different combinations of several pigments—either vacuolar or plastid or both in the same cell or in the same tissue.

leuco-: white, colorless

[C] **Leucoplasts** are colorless plastids. They store foods—especially starch, but sometimes oils—that represent the excess of food manufactured over food currently required. Starch deposited in the leucoplast forms a **starch grain.** Starch grains may grow so large that they break out of their leucoplasts and lie free in the cytoplasm. Leucoplasts are found mostly in plant parts that are not exposed to light, such as roots and tubers, or in some seeds and fruits. Certain interconversions among plastids are possible. Leucoplasts may become chloroplasts if they receive enough light; chloroplasts in some green fruits become chromoplasts as the fruits ripen.[18]

The old man looked sorrowfully about for a moment, and then, turning with a confidential air to the other, he replied,—

[D] "I passed the spring, summer, and autumn of life among the trees. The winter of my days had come, and found me where I loved to be, in the quiet—ay, and in the honesty of the woods! Teton, then I slept happily, where my eyes could look up through the branches of the pines and the breeches, to the very dwelling of the Good Spirit of my people. If I had need to open my heart to him, while his fires were burning above my head, the door was open and before my eyes. But the axes of the choppers awoke me. For a long time my ears heard nothing but the uproar of clearings. I bore it like a warrior and a man; there was reason that I should bear it: but when that reason ended, I bethought me to get beyond the accursed sounds. It was trying to the courage and to the habits, but I had heard of these vast and naked fields, and, I came hither to escape the wasteful temper of my people. Tell me, Dahcotah, have I not done well?"

[E] The trapper laid his long lean finger on the naked shoulder of the Indian as he ended, and seemed to demand his felicitations on his ingenuity and success, with a ghastly smile, in which triumph was singularly blended with regret. His companion listened intently, and replied to the question by saying, in the sententious manner of his race,—

"The head of my father is very gray; he has always lived with men, and he has seen everything. What he does is good; what he speaks is wise. Now let him say, is he sure that he is a stranger to the Big-knives, who are looking for their beasts on every side of the prairies and cannot find them?"

"Dahcotah, what I have said is true. I live alone, and never do I mingle with men whose skins are white, if—"[19]

NOTES

1. **Langston Hughes,** *The Big Sea* (New York: Hill and Wang, 1940), p. 19.
2. **Wayne Greenshaw,** "Meet Bubba Able," *New York Times,* 6 Aug. 1980.
3. **John T. Walsh,** *Interpretation of Reading Materials in the Social Sciences* (New York: Cambridge Book Co., 1973), p. 27.
4. **Patricia Cayo Sexton,** "Backdrop of Poverty," in *Spanish Harlem: Anatomy of Poverty* (New York: Harper & Row, 1965), pp. 1–2.
5. **Victoria Holt,** *Judas Kiss* (New York: Doubleday, 1982), p. 3.
6. **Lewis Tiffany,** "Diatom," *World Book Encyclopedia,* 1983 ed., IV, p. 152.
7. **Robert Harper** and **Theodore Schmudde,** *Between Two Worlds: An Introduction to Geography* (Boston: Houghton Mifflin, 1978), p. 362.
8. **Wollbank** and **Schrier,** *Living World History* (Chicago: Scott Foresman, 1964), p. 156.
9. **Christopher Nyerges,** "Elect Tarzan Mayor," *New York Times,* 23 July 1979.
10. **James Cicarelli,** *Economics: Macroeconomic Principles and Issues* (Boston: Houghton Mifflin, 1978), p. 27.
11. **Helena Curtis,** *Biology* (New York: Worth, 1979), p. 420.
12. **David J. Rachman** and **Michael M. Mescon,** *Business Today* (New York: Random House, 1979), p. 445.
13. **William J. Fulbright,** "A Fable from Tomorrow," from *Arrogance of Power* (New York: Random House, 1967), pp. 245–246.
14. Taken from the *Congressional Record,* Vol. 113, No. 198, December 5, 1967, p. S1789.
15. **Thomas Wolfe,** "Circus at Dawn," in *From Death to Morning* (New York: Charles Scribner's Sons, 1935), p. 209.
16. **Sanford** and **Green,** *Basic Principles of American Government* (New York: Amsco, 1977), p. 214.
17. **Curtis,** p. 426.
18. **Joan Elma Rahn,** *Biology,* 2nd ed. (New York: Macmillan, 1980), p. 256.
19. **J. F. Cooper,** "The Prairie."

Eight

SKIMMING AND SCANNING

Skimming and scanning are rapid-reading techniques. Skimming and scanning should not be confused with previewing, which is a prereading technique. Skimming and scanning should also not be confused with reading rapidly for high comprehension. Skimming and scanning are low comprehension techniques.

SKIMMING

Skimming should be used when you want to cover large amounts of material quickly and do not intend to read the material completely at a later time. Skimming is used to get a general impression of the material and not for a high level of comprehension. Skimming can be a very valuable reading aid when used properly. You should never skim when reading technical or very detailed material.

Skimming Different Paragraph Types

When you skim a paragraph, you should keep in mind the writer's purpose and paragraph plan. A quick glance will help you identify the paragraph type (see Chapter 7).

Expository paragraphs usually make a statement and then offer support through details. In this case, read the first and last sentence and pick out key words and phrases.

Persuasive paragraphs also contain a stated main idea. When you skim this type of paragraph, note the author's point of view and review the first, middle, and last sentences.

The other paragraph types do not contain a stated main idea. When skimming this type of paragraph, glance at the details to form a quick impression of the topic.

As you read the above it might have seemed an impossible task to vary your skimming method to match the different paragraph types. However, with a little practice varying your skimming method can become second nature.

SKIMMING AN ARTICLE OR CHAPTER

Read the opening paragraph or two at your average reading rate. Leave out nothing. The first several paragraphs contain the idea of the article or chapter.

Reading these first few paragraphs provides you with an overview, a context for skimming the rest of the material.

You should then attempt to get the main idea of the other paragraphs plus a few facts, names, or numbers. Final paragraphs often summarize material and you should read these more carefully.

You must skim as rapidly as you can. It is necessary to leave out large sections of information and to avoid getting interested as you read. Read only the information that will give you an idea of the general content.

You should skim entire magazines, newspapers, and supplementary readings. This will help to keep you generally informed. Occasionally, regular reading assignments can be skimmed with good results. Use your discretion for regular assignments, which usually require careful reading.

Reference sources can also be skimmed. A regular check of periodicals and reports in your field will help to keep you up to date. Make a habit of skimming everything you can. You will be surprised how much useful information will come to your attention.

Follow these steps when skimming:

1. Examine the material to decide whether you want to read it.
2. Examine the table of contents and the index to identify where material of interest to you may be found.
3. Preview the material you want to skim.
4. Skim.

Read texts or factual material to grasp general content. Read light material or fiction for impressions only.

ACTIVITY I

Practice skimming as a rapid-reading technique in the selections below. Use the following guide:

1. Read the title.
2. Read the first sentence of each paragraph.
3. Read the italic print.

The Memory Unit

After the computer has translated input data into binary language the data can then be stored. The *memory unit* of a computer is where items are stored and called for when needed. Many of today's computers use magnetic cores for storage. *Magnetic cores* are like tiny doughnuts that can be magnetized either clockwise or counter clockwise. The binary 0 is represented by one direction, and the binary 1 by the other.

All data processed by the computer pass through memory, where they are either stored permanently or on a temporary basis to be recalled as needed. The *access time* for this information, the amount of time that elapses from the moment the data are asked for until the moment they appear, is what determines the speed of the computer, its efficiency, and its capability.

Magnetic-core storage has many advantages. The equipment is easily magnetized, does not wear out, and has much faster access time than most other media. It is, however, more costly than other media and provides only a limited amount of storage.[1]

Without looking back, answer these questions.

1. What is the main idea? _____

_____

2. Define:

   A. Memory unit: _____

_____

   B. Magnetic cores: _____

_____

   C. Access time: _____

_____

SCANNING

Scanning is closely related to skimming. But when you scan you already have a purpose in mind. Scanning means searching for particular information.

   The most common form of scanning you use is scanning the telephone directory. You also scan when you search for answers to questions such as when you take a reading comprehension test or an open book examination.

   To scan effectively, pick out the key words in the questions you want answers for and keep these key words in mind. Run your eyes through the lines of print looking for the specific fact or idea that will answer the question. You may have to scan lengthy passages to find the appropriate part of the passage. If you are scanning properly, you will not be aware of the ideas presented in a particular selection. Your goal is to find a particular name, number, word, or idea. Scanning requires practice, but it is worth the effort to be able to locate material rapidly. Follow these steps when you scan.

1. Read the question.
2. Keep the key words of the question in mind.
3. Scan until you find the answer to the question. Stop! Write the answer. Move on to the next question.

ACTIVITY II

Scan the following paragraphs.

1. What country consumes three times more beef than it exports?_____

_____

2. Over 80% of iron ore exports come from what countries?_____

_____

3. What exports are lower today than forty years ago?_____

_____

4. What new export industry has developed since World War II?_____
_____

5. In what years were the exports of wool and hides high?_____
_____

Changes in the Trade Structure

Considerable shifts in the relative importance of particular export commodities have, in turn, affected particular producing areas. Today Europeans are less interested in midlatitude staple foods—wheat, corn, and meat. They have higher per acre yields, depend on more intra-European trade, and draw imports from Canada and Australia. At the same time, with the population increase at home, Argentina now consumes three times as much beef as it exports. Exports of agricultural raw materials, particularly wool and hides, are only half the totals of the early 1930's. Lead, zinc, tin, and nitrate exports are also lower today than forty years ago.

The greatest gains by far have come in petroleum exports. Crude oil production in Venezuela in 1971 was ten times that of the early 1930's. Over 90 percent of Venezuelan oil was exported. Iron ore exports, though much less in total, also increased sharply in the past forty years. Over 80 percent of this output comes from Brazil, Venezuela, and Chile.

One remarkable new export industry in the period since World War II has been the fish meal and fish oil industry of Peru and, to a lesser degree, Chile. The industry is based on the demand for high-protein livestock feed in the United States and Western Europe and the presence of vast quantities of a single variety of fish.[2]

ACTIVITY III

Scan the following table. Fill in each blank on p. 111.

INTRA-EUROPEAN TRADE OF COUNTRIES OUTSIDE EASTERN EUROPE, 1973[3]

Trade with	Western Europe (Percent)	Northern Europe (Percent)	Southern Europe (Percent)	Eastern Europe (Percent)	Value of Total Trade in Europe ($ Billion)
EEC countries					
West Germany	67	8	20	5	83.0
France	72	4	21	3	49.5
Netherlands	82	4	9	2	36.8
Belgium and Luxembourg	87	4	8	1	35.4
United Kingdom	66	17	14	3	33.9
Italy	82	3	10	5	30.8
Denmark	57	31	8	3	10.5
Ireland	90	4	5	1	4.0
Other Western European countries					
Switzerland	73	6	17	3	15.7
Austria	70	6	15	9	10.4
Northern European countries					
Sweden	70	19	8	3	17.7
Norway	63	26	7	3	8.1
Finland	62	28	7	3	5.7

1. Which country conducted 90% of its trade with Western Europe? _____

2. Trade between _____ and Western Europe was 66%.

3. Trade between Spain and Northern Europe was _____%.

4. Which country had value of total trade in Europe of $15.7 billion? _____

ACTIVITY IV

Skim and then scan. The scanning questions are given at the end of the selection.

What Does a Computer Do?[4]

Despite the amazing capabilities of today's ultrasophisticated computers, their operations still boil down to a few very basic function-tasks not harder in principle than those performed every day by millions of schoolchildren. (The chief difference, of course, is that computers perform the tasks with superhuman speed and accuracy. Any time you hear the phrase "computer error"—when the electric company bills you for $25 million instead of $25, say—you can safely translate it to mean a computer operator's error.) These basic computer functions can be broken down into four categories.

First of all, computers perform arithmetic tasks—that is, they add, subtract, multiply, and divide numbers. A computer could, for example, instantly balance your checkbook—making sure the bank's figures were right, then adding any subsequent deposits, totaling all the outstanding checks, and subtracting them from the balance. You could do this too, of course, but a properly programmed computer could do it for you and everyone you know in, say, a hundredth of a second, without making a mistake.

Second, computers perform logical tasks—tasks requiring reasoning. This frequently involves making objective comparisons between things—determining, say, whether a given item is the same size as another item, or larger or smaller than the other item. The computer handling your checking account, for instance, would see whether the balance in your checkbook is the same amount as the one shown in your bank statement. Similarly, a computer can determine whether an item logically fits into a particular category—whether a number entered in your checking account, for example, is a withdrawal (that is, a check that's been cashed) or a deposit.

Third, a computer can follow a program, a prearranged sequence of arithmetic and logic operations. Whether the program is simple or complicated, it is carried out just one step at a time (though, again, the speed is phenomenal: new computers work at rates measured in billionths of a second), and what is done at each step depends on the result of the preceding step. The programming for your checkbook would instruct the computer to determine what category each entry falls into before going to the next step: if it is a withdrawal, then the next step will be to subtract it from the balance; if it's a deposit, the computer will add it to the balance.

Fourth, a computer can keep information stored in its memory, as if in a filing cabinet, and retrieve it rapidly whenever needed. If you want to see how many checks you wrote last August or how many deposits you've made since then, the data will be readily available.

Milestones in Computer Development

Since the debut in 1946 of the first all-electronic computer, ENIAC (short for Electronic Numerical Integration and Calculator), technological advances have brought about a dramatic increase in the speed and capability of computers, along with an equally drastic reduction in size and cost. Five million on/off computations by a computer in the early 1950s, for example, took three minutes and cost the user about $42; today the same amount of electronic brainwork takes one eightieth of a second and costs less than half a cent. By most standards, such an improvement in any service especially accompanied by such a reduction in price would seem little short of miracles. In this case, though, there are no miracles involved—only ingenuity, combined with an ever-more-sophisticated arsenal of tools and techniques.

Batch Processing

In batch processing, data are collected over a fixed interval of time (a day, a week, a month) before they are processed. For example, at the end of every day a company might process invoices for the orders it received that day. The daily group of invoices is referred to as a batch. Batch processing is used for keeping historical records and producing output on a regular basis.

Parts of the Computer and How They Are Used

Basically, a computer is made up of two types of equipment: the central processing unit (CPU), the part that does the "thinking," and the peripheral, or secondary, equipment, the input and output devices through which a computer and its operator communicate with each other. In principle, this system can be compared to an old-fashioned adding machine.

If you want to add up a column of numbers, you punch the appropriate keys (input), the adding machine calculates the answer (processing), and the figures are typed out on paper tape (output). A computer likewise receives input, processes it, and gives out the result. The computer's electronic equipment, of course, is considerably more sophisticated, and each function is carried out by a different component.

Computer Software; Programs and People

Years ago, the term "computer" meant the machine itself, the hardware. But in recent years people have recognized that the machine is only as good as the procedures given it for solving problems. Therefore, the definition of computer has been altered to include both the machine and its programs, both the hardware and the software. Software includes the materials and procedures used with computers. It's a category which covers checklists, forms, programs, and written diagrams and instructions.

Answer these questions.

1. What are the four basic functions of a computer? _____

_____

_____

_____

_____

2. What are the four major innovations in the field of computers since 1946? _____

_____

_____

_____

3. What are the basic components of a computer system? _____

_____

_____

_____

4. When would batch processing be used? _____

_____

_____

5. What is software? _____

_____

_____

_____

PROJECT

Skim and scan "Retailing." Apply the skills of skimming and scanning and write the answers to the following questions about this selection.

1. Define retailing. _____

_____

_____

2. Why do final consumers usually visit retail stores when organizational consumers generally have salespeople call on them? _____

_____

_____

_____

3. How can independents successfully compete with chains? _____

_____

_____

_____

4. How is ease of entry in retailing both good and bad? _____

_____

_____

_____

5. Give two examples of the wheel of retailing working in your area. _____

_____

_____

_____

RETAILING[5]

CHAPTER OBJECTIVES

1. To define retailing and consider the special characteristics that distinguish it from other areas of marketing
2. To study the importance of retailing, including its impact on the economy, functions in distribution, and relationships with suppliers
3. To examine the different types of retailing categorized by ownership, strategy mix, nonstore operations, services, and location
4. To delineate three major considerations in retail marketing planning: atmosphere, scrambled merchandising, and the wheel of retailing
5. To explore the responses of retailers to recent trends involving consumers, inflation, costs, and technology

In 1968 Morrie Mages Sports store opened on Chicago's North Side. Today it is the biggest sporting-goods store in Chicago. It is located in a loft building with eight floors and a basement. Mages stocks 250 types of fishing rods, 400 kinds of sleeping bags, 12,000 pairs of skis (in season), and a full range of other sporting goods from scuba gear to pogo sticks.

The success of Mages is founded on sound retailing principles and years of experience: large inventories are maintained, there is a mixture of discount and brand-name merchandise, and heavy advertising emphasizes wide selections and low prices. Mages buys in large quantities to obtain reduced costs. He also purchases "off-priced" items, which include irregular clothing, manufacturers' surplus inventories, and the merchandise of retailers going out of business.[1]

RETAILING DEFINED

Retailing, the final stage in a channel of distribution, includes the business activities involved in sales to the final consumer.

Retailing encompasses those business activities that involve the sale of goods and services to the ultimate (final) consumer for personal, family, or household use. It is the final stage in a channel of distribution.

Retailing includes products, such as automobiles and televisions, as well as services, such as life insurance and appliance repair. It involves store and nonstore (vending machine, door-to-door, mail order) sales. Manufacturers, importers, and wholesalers act as retailers when they sell products directly to the ultimate consumer.

The average size of a retail sale is small, $14.52 for department stores and $28.77 for specialty stores in 1979.[2] Convenience stores, like 7-Eleven, have average sales under $2.00.[3] Medium-sized supermarkets average $10.07.[4] Accordingly, retailers need to increase sales through one-stop shopping appeals, broadened merchandise assortments, increased frequency of shopping, and attracting more family members to go on shopping trips. Inventory controls, automated material handling, and electronic cash registers are needed to reduce transaction costs.

Despite low average sales, 56 per cent of department and specialty store sales are on credit.[5] For example, in 1979 Sears had credit sales of $6 billion.[6] The use

---

[1]Dick Griffin, "The Second Heaven of Morrie Mages," *Fortune* (August 13, 1979), pp. 189–190.
[2]"The Good and the Not-So-Good News FOR," *Stores* (October 1980), p. 21.
[3]Pamela G. Hollie, "Food Is Pumping Up Net at Arco," *New York Times* (March 3, 1980), p. D5.
[4]"Grocery Industry Report for 1979," *Progressive Grocer* (April 1980), p. 130.
[5]"Good and Not-So-Good News FOR," p. 21.
[6]"Retailers and Banks Tighten Availability of Credit in Reaction to Economic Plan," *Wall Street Journal* (March 20, 1980), p. 3.

of credit necessitates bank or store credit plans and reasonable credit terms but leads to increased sales.

Whereas salespeople regularly visit organizational consumers to initiate and consummate transactions, most final consumers patronize stores. This makes the location of the store, product assortment, store hours, store fixtures, sales personnel, delivery, and other factors critical tools in drawing customers to the store.

Final consumers make many unplanned purchases. In contrast, those who buy for resale or use in manufacturing are more systematic in their purchasing. Therefore, retailers need to place impulse items in high-traffic locations, organize store layout, train sales personnel in suggestion selling, place related items next to each other, and sponsor special events.

IMPORTANCE OF RETAILING

Among the major reasons for studying retailing are its impact on the economy, functions in distribution, and relationships with suppliers.

Impact on the Economy

Retail sales and employment comprise substantial amounts of total U.S. sales and employment. According to the Department of Commerce, in 1979 retail sales volume was over $886 billion; this does not include nonstore sales (vending machines, door-to-door sales, and mail-order sales) and retail services. See Table 13–1 for financial data on selected retailers.

Retailing is also a major source of employment. According to the Department of Labor, about 17 per cent of the nation's total nonagricultural workforce was employed in 2.5 million retail establishments in the United States in 1979. A wide range of retailing career opportunities is available, including store management, merchandising, and owning one's own retail business.[7]

From another perspective—costs—retailing is a significant field of study. On the average, in 1979, about 41 cents of every dollar spent in a department store went to the store as compensation for the functions it performed.[8] The corresponding figures for other stores were 41 cents for specialty stores[9] and 23 cents for supermarkets.[10] This compensation, known as gross margin, went for rent, taxes, fuel, advertising, inventory management, personnel, and other retail costs, as well as profits (which are shown in Table 13–1).

Retail Functions in Distribution

The *functions of retailing* include collecting an assortment, circulating information, and preparing items for sale.

Chapter 11 outlined the basic roles of retailers and wholesalers in distribution. In general, retailers perform three functions: they collect an assortment of products and services from a wide variety of suppliers and offer them for sale; they disseminate information to consumers, as well as to other channel members; and they frequently store merchandise, mark prices on it, and pay for items prior to selling them to final consumers.

Relationship of Retailers and Suppliers

Retailers have suppliers who sell products or services for resale or for use by the retailers.

Retailers deal with two broad categories of suppliers: those selling products or services for use by retailers and those selling products or services for resale.

[7] A further discussion of careers in retailing can be found in Barry Berman and Joel R. Evans, *Retail Management: A Strategic Approach* (New York: Macmillan, 1979), pp. 8–15.
[8] "Good and Not-So-Good News FOR," p. 21.
[9] Ibid.
[10] "Grocery Industry Report for 1979," p. 132.

TABLE 13–1 FINANCIAL DATA ON SELECTED RETAILERS, 1979
A. Food Retailers

Name	Sales ($ mil)	Net Income ($ mil)	Net Income (as a % of sales)
Safeway Stores	$13,717.9	$143.3	1.0%
Kroger	9,029.3	85.7	0.9
Great Atlantic & Pacific Tea (A&P)	7,469.7	-52.2	-0.7
Lucky Stores	5,815.9	98.0	1.7
Winn-Dixie Stores	4,930.5	94.4	1.9
Southland (7-Eleven)	3,856.2	83.1	2.2
Jewel	3,764.3	50.7	1.3
Albertson's	2,673.8	38.3	1.4
Grand Union	2,398.9	21.8	0.9
Supermakets General (Pathmark)	2,372.6	23.4	1.0

B. Nonfood retailers: department, discount, mail-order, variety, and specialty stores

Name	Sales ($ mil)	Net Income ($ mil)	Net Income (as a % of sales)
Sears, Roebuck	$17,514.3	$810.1	4.6%
K Mart	12,858.6	358.0	2.8
J. C. Penney	11,274.0	244.0	2.2
F. W. Woolworth	6,785.0	180.0	2.7
Federated Department Stores	5,806.4	203.2	3.5
Montgomery Ward	5,251.1	73.4	1.4
Dayton-Hudson	3,384.8	192.1	5.7
May Department Stores	2,977.2	114.0	3.8
Carter Hawley Hale Stores	2,408.0	69.7	2.9
Rapid-American	2,132.2	34.6	1.5

SOURCE: Adapted from "The 50 Largest Retailing Companies," *Fortune* (July 14, 1980), pp. 154–155.

Examples of products and services purchased by retailers for their use are store fixtures, data-processing equipment, management consulting, and insurance. Resale purchases depend on the lines sold by the retailer.

Suppliers must have knowledge of retailer's goals, strategies, and methods of business operation in order to sell and service accounts effectively. Frequently, retailers and their suppliers have divergent viewpoints, which must be reconciled.

When Waltham, Gruen, Elgin, and Hamilton started discounting their watches to mass merchandisers, traditional jewelers began dropping the brands because their retail prices were no longer competitive.[11]

The success of General Electric bulbs in supermarkets is the result of the large number of supermarkets that stock the line. Because consumers do not perceive much difference among brands of bulbs, store managers like to carry only one brand—in many cases, General Electric.[12]

Manufacturers usually find that retailers do not want to stock new products prior to the start of the firm's advertising campaign. The retailers want brand recognition before tying up valuable floor space.[13]

TYPES OF RETAILERS

Retailers can be categorized by ownership, strategy mix, nonstore operations, service retailing,[14] and location. These groupings are detailed in Figure 13–1.

[11]"Seiko's Smash," *Business Week* (June 5, 1978), pp. 86–93.
[12]Iver Peterson, "Bulb Snatching in Supermarkets," *New York Times* (May 14, 1978), Business and Finance Section, pp. 1, 11.
[13]See Geri Hirshey, "The Supermarket That's Eating Manhattan," *New York Times* (March 17, 1980), p. 48.
[14]Service retailing is discussed fully in Chapter 22. Types of services were classified in Chapter 8. This chapter does not deal with service retailing.

Figure 13–1
A Classification Method
for Retailers

I. By ownership	III. By nonstore retailing
A. Independent	A. Vending machines
B. Chain	B. Door-to-door
C. Franchise	C. Mail order
D. Leased department	
E. Cooperative	IV. By service retailing*
	A. Rented goods services
II. By retail strategy mix	B. Owned goods services
	C. Nongoods services
A. Convenience store	
B. Supermarket	V. By location
C. Superstore	
D. Specialty store	A. Isolated store
E. Variety store	B. Unplanned business district
F. Full-line discount store	C. Planned shopping center
G. Department store	
H. Retail catalog showroom	

*Discussed in Chapters 8 and 22

The categories are not mutually exclusive; that is, a retailer can be correctly placed in more than one grouping. For example, 7-Eleven can be classified as a chain, a franchise, and a convenience store and by its use of isolated store locations.

An examination of retail types provides information about the characteristics of retailers, shows their relative sizes, outlines different strategies, and explores the impact of economic, social, and competitive environments on various kinds of retailers.

By Ownership

Retail ownership can be independent, chain, franchise, leased department, and/or cooperative. Figure 13–2 outlines the advantages and disadvantages of each form of ownership.

An *independent retailer* operates only one retail outlet. It offers personal service, a convenient location, and close customer contact. Dry cleaners, butcher shops, furniture stores, independent service stations, barber shops, and many neighborhood stores are independents. About 85 per cent of all retailers are independents. This large number is the result of the *ease of entry* in retailing. For many kinds of retailing, capital requirements, state licensing standards, and technical knowledge requirements are low, and, therefore, competition is plentiful. Many retailers also fail because of ease of entry, poor management skills, and inadequate capital. In 1979, 3,183 retailers of all types failed, including 33.5 per cent of those in business three years or less.[15]

A *chain* is the common ownership of multiple retail units. It usually employs centralized purchasing and decision making. Independents have simple organizations, but chains have specialization, standardization, and elaborate control systems. Because of these factors, chains are able to serve a large, geographically dispersed target market and maintain a well-known company name. Whereas chains comprise only about 15 per cent of all retailers, they account for over 45 per cent of total retail store sales. Only a few hundred chains operate one hundred or more units, yet they are responsible for one quarter of total store sales. Chains are widespread for supermarkets, department stores, variety stores, and fast-food restaurants, among others. Examples of large chains are Sears, K mart, and Safeway.

An independent retailer operates one retail outlet and offers personal service and a good location. Independent retailers comprise 85 per cent of all retailers; this is attributable to ease of entry.

A chain involves common ownership of multiple retail units. They are efficient and represent over 45 per cent of sales despite operating 15 per cent of the units.

[15]*The Business Failure Record* (New York: Dun & Bradstreet, 1981), pp. 9–10.

Figure 13–2
Advantages and Disadvantages of Retail Ownership Forms

Advantages	Disadvantages
Independent	
1. Personal contact with customers and flexibility in operation	1. Limits in bargaining power
2. Low required investment	2. Labor intensiveness the result of low mechanization and computerization
3. Ability to concentrate efforts	3. Inability to use all media—geographic coverage is too broad
4. No unionization and close supervision of employees	4. Overdependence on owner
5. Neighborhood locations	5. Lack of capital and managerial expertise
Chain	
1. Use of specialists	1. Inflexibility—need for common image in all branches
2. Lower operating costs the result of computerization, personnel specialization, centralized decision making	2. High investment costs—each branch must be stocked
3. High bargaining power	3. Store managers with less incentive than independent owners
4. Ability to use regional and national media	4. Limited independence the result of unionized employees, stockholders, and boards of directors
5. Use of private labels and wide geographic recognition	
Franchising (to franchise)	
1. Well-known name provided	1. Some disreputable franchisors provide an incorrect statement of income potential, required managerial ability, and investment
2. Utilization of national advertising program and cooperative ventures	2. Requirements for "exclusive dealing" or tying arrangements
3. A well-integrated business program—including training, management controls, and trouble shooting	3. Attempts by franchisor to cancel or refuse to renew franchise agreement
4. Prototype stores and standardized product lines	4. Inflexibility
Leased department (to leasee)	
1. Utilization of traffic of store	1. Conformity with restrictions in lease agreements relating to store hours and days open, return policy, etc.
2. Investment lowered because of shared facilities—such as a central checkout area	2. Dependence on store and other leased departments for traffic and image
3. Economies through pooled advertising, central air conditioning, and central packing services	3. Receipts possibly kept by leasor until bookkeeping period
4. Appeal to one-stop shopping motive of consumers	
Retailer cooperative	
1. Shared planning and expenses	1. Competing firms not allowed to participate legally in the same cooperative
2. Ability to use many media and purchase in larger quantities	2. Different objectives and management styles of member firms
3. Private labels developed	3. Difficulty in coordinating
4. Bargaining power	
Consumer cooperative	
1. Savings to members	1. Difficulty in organizing
2. Social experience	2. Problems occurring in recruitment of members and member turnover
3. Way of demonstrating dissatisfaction with current retail institution	3. Time-consuming nature of tasks

Franchising is an arrangement between a franchisor and a franchisee that employs an established name and operates under a specific set of rules.

Franchising is a contractual arrangement between a franchisor (who may be a manufacturer, wholesaler, or service sponsor) and a retail franchisee, which allows the franchisee to conduct a certain form of business under an established name and according to a specific set of rules. It is a form of chain ownership. Franchising allows a small businessperson to benefit from the experience, buying capabilities, and image of a large multiunit chain retailer. The franchisee also receives management training, participates in cooperative buying and advertising, and acquires a well-established company name. The franchisor benefits by obtaining franchise fees and royalties, fast payments for goods and services, strict controls over operations, consistency among outlets, and motivated owner-operators. In 1981 franchises were expected to account for about $376 billion in sales and represent about 476,000 establishments.[16] Franchising is particularly prevalent for auto and truck dealers, fast-food outlets, health spas, and convenience-food stores. Examples of franchises are McDonald's, Carvel, and Jack LaLanne health spas.

A *leased department* is rented to an outside party that provides expertise and management skills and absorbs risks.

A *leased department* is a department in a retail store (usually a department, discount, or specialty store) that is rented to an outside party. The proprietor of a leased department is responsible for all aspects of operation and pays a percentage of sales as rent. As in franchising, the owner places strict rules on the leased department operator. Leasors benefit because of the expertise of department operators, reduced risk and inventory investment, and lucrative lease terms. Leasees benefit because they do not have to build a store, traffic is generated, and customers are attracted by one-stop shopping. Leased departments are popular for beauty salons, jewelry, photographic studios, shoe repairs, and cosmetics. On average, leased departments contribute 7.0 per cent of department store sales and 11.0 per cent of specialty store sales.[17]

With a *retail cooperative,* independents form an organization to share costs, functions, and planning.

A *cooperative* is a retail organization that is operated by several independent retailers or by a group of consumers. In a *retail cooperative,* independent retailers form an organization in order to share purchases, advertising, planning, and other functions. The individual stores retain their independence but agree on broad, common policies. Retail cooperatives are growing in response to the domination of independents by chains. Retail cooperatives are common for liquor stores, hardware stores, and some grocery stores. Ace Hardware, Associated Food Stores, and Western Auto are all retail cooperatives. As pointed out in Chapter 12, wholesalers frequently aid retailers in setting up cooperatives.

With a *consumer cooperative,* a retailer is owned by consumer members who invest in and operate the firm.

A *consumer cooperative* is a retailer that is owned by consumer members. A group of consumers invests, receives stock certificates, elects officers, manages operations, and shares profits or savings. The goal is to offer reduced prices to members. Consumer cooperatives have been most prevalent with food products, particularly produce items. However, the cooperatives represent less than 1 per cent of total supermarket sales or supermarket produce sales. They have not grown further because they involve a lot of consumer initiative, profits have been low, and consumer expertise as owner-operators has been lacking.

By Strategy Mix

Retailers can be classified by *retail strategy mix,* the combination of prices, products, sales personnel, displays, and other factors. Retail strategy mixes differ for convenience stores, supermarkets, superstores, specialty stores, variety stores, full-line discount stores, department stores, and retail catalog showrooms. Figure 13–3 outlines the advantages and disadvantages of these strategy mixes.

A *convenience store* is open long hours and carries a limited number of items. It is patronized for fill-in items during off-hours.

A *convenience store* is a food store that is open long hours and carries a limited number of items. In 1979 the average convenience store had total sales of $371,000 (including gasoline), while the average supermarket had sales over $1.4 million.[18] Consumers use a convenience store for fill-in merchandise, often at off-hours. Bread, milk, ice cream, and newspapers are popular items for convenience stores. Nonfood stores that place their emphasis on long store hours, convenient locations, and fill-in merchandise also can be considered

[16]"Restaurant Franchising in the Economy," *Restaurant Business* (March 15, 1981), p. 87.
[17]"Leased Departments," *Stores* (December 1977), p. 44.
[18]"Grocery Industry Report for 1979," pp. 85, 93, 113.

Figure 13–3
*Advantages and Disadvantages
of Retail Strategy Mixes*

Advantages	Disadvantages

Convenience Store

Advantages	Disadvantages
1. High turnover of items in stock 2. Higher profit margin than supermarkets 3. Relatively low investment required 4. No long lines for consumers 5. Neighborhood location 6. Convenient hours	1. Long hours of operation for employees 2. Low average purchase 3. Small size of store limits merchandise selection 4. Higher prices and less selection than supermarkets

Supermarket

Advantages	Disadvantages
1. Self-service operation reducing overhead 2. Large supermarkets utilize private-label merchandizing for greater control and to develop store loyalty 3. Nonfood items increasing profit margins 4. Successful in price competition over smaller groceries and convenience stores 5. Large proportion of impulse sales 6. Substantial economies in price marking, checkout operations, and inventory management possible because of Universal Product Code 7. Great appeal to females	1. Difficulty of national and regional chains in adapting to local needs (e.g., ethnic tastes) 2. Diversification into nonfood items not as great as superstores 3. Lowest net profit after taxes of any retail form 4. Vulnerability of supermarket sales to fast-food stores 5. Large inventory and store investments

Superstore

Advantages	Disadvantages
1. High one-stop shopping appeal 2. Appeal for entire family 3. Larger trading areas than supermarkets 4. Higher profit margins on general merchandise than on groceries	1. Large investment 2. Extensive merchandising experience required for large-ticket, nonfood items 3. Larger population base needed

Specialty Store

Advantages	Disadvantages
1. Special expertise in a limited product line 2. Reliance on product knowledge and extensive selection, instead of price competition 3. Exclusive merchandise lines 4. May be trend setter 5. High assortment 6. Strategy tailored to consumers	1. Limited product line susceptible to extensive competition and negative environmental factors 2. No appeal to one-stop shopping—except for limited shopping purposes 3. High labor costs because of high service levels

Variety Store

Advantages	Disadvantages
1. Reduced labor costs the result of self-service merchandising 2. Appeal of wide assortment to one-stop shopping needs 3. Sale of fill-in merchandise 4. Attractive source of low-priced items	1. Locations in central business districts, where success rates have been spotty 2. Negative fashion image 3. Use of high-rent locations 4. Low average sales

Full-line Discount Store

Advantages	Disadvantages
1. Low prices 2. Low-rent location 3. Emphasis on self-service 4. Merchandise selection limited to high turnover items 5. Low operating costs	1. Low pedestrian traffic in many locations 2. No fashion leadership 3. Lots of price competition 4. Easy replication of a low-price strategy by others

Figure 13—3
(Continued)

Advantages	Disadvantages

Department Store

1. Wide variety and assortment	1. Management may not be receptive to unique needs of branches because of centralized buying
2. Improved merchandising the result of departmentalization	2. Relatively high labor costs
3. Reduced costs the result of centralized decision making	3. Extensive commitment to central business districts, some of which have spotty performance records
4. Improved efficiency through specialists	4. Lack of a specialty image
5. Fashion leadership	5. Competition from specialty and discount stores
6. Good credit-card penetration	
7. Excitement in merchandising	
8. Use of good retail locations	
9. Full services	

Retail Catalog Showroom

1. Low prices	1. No delivery
2. High profit margins on jewelry lines	2. No phone ordering
3. Low shoplifting costs	3. Low level of customer service
4. Fewer salespeople required	4. Stockouts
5. Preselling of much merchandise—name brands	5. Secondary location
6. Ease of selling	

convenience stores. These would include neighborhood stationery/candy stores, 24-hour gasoline stations that carry some food products, and roadside motels. 7-Eleven, Arco, and Dairy Barn operate convenience stores.

A *supermarket* is departmentalized with minimum annual sales of $1 million. It is self-service and offers low prices.

A *supermarket* is a departmentalized food store with minimum annual sales of $1 million. The supermarket originated in the 1930s, when food retailers realized that a large-scale operation would enable them to combine volume sales, self-service, low prices, impulse buying, and one-stop food shopping. The automobile and refrigerator contributed to the supermarket's success by lowering travel costs and adding to the life span of perishable items. During the past twenty years, supermarket sales have stabilized at about 72 to 75 per cent of total grocery sales. In 1979 total supermarket sales were $155 billion, 60 percent of which was provided by chains.[19] In response to convenience stores, some supermarkets have lengthened their hours of operation. The largest supermarkets are Safeway, Kroger, and A&P.

A *superstore* stocks supermarket items and a variety of other products to attract one-stop shoppers.

A *superstore* is a large retailer that is much more diversified than a supermarket. Superstores typically carry garden supplies, televisions, clothing, wine, boutique items, bakery products, and household appliances—in addition to a full line of supermarket items. While the average supermarket occupies 18,000 square feet of space, the typical superstore utilizes 30,000 square feet. Several factors are causing a number of supermarkets to switch to superstores: an interest in total one-stop shopping, the leveling off of food sales as a result of population stability and competition from restaurants and fast-food stores, improved transportation networks, and the higher margins on general merchandise (more than double those of food items).[20] Grand Bazaar in Chicago and Hyper-Marche Laval in Montreal, Canada, are two superstores.

A *specialty store* emphasizes one type of merchandise.

A *specialty store* concentrates on the sale of one merchandise line, such as apparel and its accessories, sewing machines, or high-fidelity equipment. Consumers like specialty stores because they are not confronted with racks of merchandise, do not have to walk or search through several departments, can

---

[19]Robert Dietrich, "Super Market Census—Entering the 1980's," *Progressive Grocer* (September 1979), p. 34.
[20]See "Safeway: Selling Nongrocery Items to Cure the Supermarket Blahs," *Business Week* (March 7, 1977), p. 54.

select from tailored assortments, and usually avoid crowds. Specialty stores are most successful in the apparel, gourmet food, appliance, and sports product lines. In some cases department stores have reacted by creating boutiques and specialty shops within their stores.[21] Specialty store sales exceed $50 billion per year. Successful specialty stores include Radio Shack, The Limited, and Toys-R-Us.

A *variety store* sells an assortment of lower-priced merchandise.

A *variety store* sells a wide assortment of low and popularly priced merchandise. It features stationery, gift items, women's accessories, toilet articles, light hardware, toys, housewares, and confectionaries. Variety-store sales are about $8 billion per year. With the growth of other retail strategy mixes, variety stores have fallen on hard times. In the mid-1970s W. T. Grant went bankrupt, the largest bankruptcy in retailing history. F. W. Woolworth, the country's seventh largest retailer, dominates the variety-store category.

A *full-line discount store* has a broad assortment, inexpensive location, self-service, popular merchandise, and displays most merchandise on the selling floor.

A *full-line discount store* is characterized by a broad merchandise assortment, low-rent location, self-service, brand-name merchandise, wide aisles, shopping carts, and most merchandise displayed on the selling floor.[22] In 1979, 7,226 discount stores sold almost $50 billion in general merchandise. Discount stores are the largest retailers of general merchandise, housewares, sporting goods, luggage, linens and domestics, toys, and children's wear, and they account for one third of apparel sales.[23] Other low-price retailers are discount-food supermarkets, discount-apparel dealers, combination supermarket/discount stores, and drug/discount stores. These retailers reduce prices by using inexpensive fixtures and limited inventory. Major discount stores are Zayre, Wal-Mart, The Treasury, and Caldor.

A *department store* offers the best assortment and customer services of any retailer, is a fashion leader, and dominates nearby stores.

A *department store* is a retailer that employs at least 25 people, has apparel and soft goods sales equal at least 20 per cent of total sales, and sells a general line of apparel for the family, household linens and dry goods, and furniture, home furnishings, appliances, radios, and television sets. It is organized into separate departments for purposes of buying, promotion, service, and control. A department store has the greatest assortment of any retailer, provides many customer services, is a fashion leader, and dominates the stores around it. Because most department stores are parts of chains, they have high name recognition and can utilize all forms of media. In recent years department stores have set up many boutiques, theme displays, and designer departments to compete with other retailers. In 1979 total department store sales, excluding mail order, were about $89 billion. Figure 13–4 contrasts the strategies of discount and department stores. Examples of department stores are Macy's, Nieman-Marcus, and Rich's.

In a *retail catalog showroom* consumers shop from a catalog at a warehouse location.

A *retail catalog showroom* is an operation in which consumers select merchandise from a catalog and shop at a warehouse location. Customers frequently write up their own orders, products are usually stocked in a back room, and there are limited displays. Catalog showrooms specialize in national brands. A major expense for catalog showrooms is the catalog, which costs an average of $1.60 to produce and $.37 to distribute. In 1980, 1,828 catalog showrooms sold $8 billion of merchandise.[24] During the 1970s the industry grew at an annual rate of 20 percent; however, in 1980 this slowed down to 11 per cent because of competition from other types of retailers, increasing costs of goods and operations, and a decreased demand for jewelry.[25] Best Products, Service Merchandise, and Modern Merchandising are the largest catalog showrooms.

[21]See Eleanor G. May and Malcolm P. McNair, "Department Stores Face Stiff Challenge in Next Decade," *Journal of Retailing,* Vol. 53 (Fall 1977), pp. 54–55.
[22]See Morris L. Mayer and J. Barry Mason, "Discount Department Stores Will Prosper in '80 Despite Intense Competition," *Marketing News* (March 7, 1980), p. 6.
[23]"Discount Stores," *Retailing: Standard & Poor's Industry Surveys* (December 6, 1979), Section 2, p. R122.
[24]"Catalog Showrooms," *Retailing: Standard & Poor's Industry Surveys* (December 11, 1980), Section 2, p. R126.
[25]"No Christmas Cheer for Catalog Showrooms," *Business Week* (November 24, 1980), pp. 137, 141.

Figure 13—4:
Retail Strategy Mixes—a
Discount Store Versus a
Department Store

Discount-store strategy	Department-store strategy
1. Inexpensive rental location—low level of pedestrian traffic	1. Expensive rental location in shopping center or district—high level of pedestrian traffic
2. Spartan fixtures, linoleum floor, centralized dressing room, few interior or window displays	2. Elaborate fixtures, carpeted floor, individual dressing rooms, many interior and exterior displays
3. Promotional emphasis on price	3. Promotional emphasis on full-service, quality brands, and fashion leadership
4. No alterations, telephone orders, delivery, or gift wrapping; limited credit	4. Alterations included in clothing prices, telephone ordering, and home delivery at little or no fee; credit widely available
5. Reliance on self-service, dump-bin displays (plain cases with piles of merchandise), and rack displays; all merchandise visible	5. Extensive sales force assistance, attractive merchandise displays, most storage in back room
6. Emphasis on branded merchandise. Selection probably not complete (not all models and colors); featuring "seconds," removal of labels from merchandise if required by manufacturer, and stocking of nonbranded items which priced low	6. Emphasis on a full selection of branded and privately branded first-quality merchandise; will not stock closeouts, discontinued lines, or seconds
7. Frequent use of sales to generate store traffic throughout the year	7. Sales limited to end-of-season clearance and special events

By Nonstore Operations

Nonstore retailing refers to retailers who do not utilize conventional store facilities. It includes vending machines, door-to-door sales, and mail order. Figure 13—5 outlines the advantages and disadvantages of nonstore retailing.

Coin-operated *vending machines* eliminate sales personnel, allow 24-hour sales, and can be placed outside or inside a store.

A *vending machine* involves coin-operated machinery, eliminates the use of sales personnel, allows around-the-clock sales, and can be placed outside rather than inside a store. Vending-machine sales are concentrated in a narrow product line. Beverages and cigarettes yield two thirds of sales. Less than 10 per cent of sales come from nonfood items.[26] They require intensive servicing because of breakdowns, stock outs, and vandalism. Annual sales exceed $13 billion.

Door-to-door retailers use cold canvassing, referrals, or party plans to sell directly to consumers in their homes.

Door-to-door retailers sell directly to consumers in their homes. Cosmetics, vacuum cleaners, encyclopedias, dairy products, and newspapers are successfully sold door-to-door. This form of retailing can be either on a cold canvass (Electrolux), referral (Avon), or party (Tupperware) basis. In a cold canvass the salesperson goes through an area and knocks on each door in search of customers. With a referral system, past buyers recommend friends for the salesperson to call on. In the party method one consumer acts as host and invites friends and acquaintances to a sales demonstration in his or her home. It is estimated that door-to-door sales are about $8 to $10 billion per year.

With *mail order* the seller solicits through the media and ships merchandise to the consumer at home.

Mail order is a type of retailing where the seller solicits orders through television, radio, printed media, or the mail, receives orders through the mail or telephone, and ships merchandise to the customer's home. There are general-

[26]"Restaurants and Food Services," *Standard & Poor's Industry Surveys* (September 18, 1980), Section 2, p. R176.

Figure 13–5:
Advantages and Disadvantages
of Nonstore Retailing

Advantages	Disadvantages
Vending Machines	
1. Convenient locations	1. Sales in narrow product lines
2. Use during off-hours	2. High servicing requirements
3. Supplement to regular business	3. Reluctance of consumers to purchase certain items from vending machines
4. Limited personnel needed	4. High rental fees for use of space
5. Stimulus for impulse purchases	5. Theft and vandalism
Door-to-Door	
1. Personal contact with consumers	1. Consumers suspicious of door-to-door salespeople
2. Convenience for consumers	2. High personal selling costs
3. Ability to conduct detailed demonstrations	3. Legal restrictions
4. Consumers exposed to only one brand	4. Poor product image
5. No store overhead	5. Consumers not home
Mail Order	
1. Low investment and operating costs	1. Reluctance of consumers to purchase many items from mail order
2. No need for store hours and sales force	2. Poor image of mail order
3. Convenience for consumers	3. Delivery delays
4. Supplement to regular business	4. Legal restrictions
5. Wide trading area	

merchandise mail-order firms, stores offering mail order as a supplement to regular business, and novelty or specialty mail-order firms. The most popular mail-order items are ready-to-wear clothing, insurance, magazines, and books. Annual mail-order sales are approximately $30 billion, including nearly 12 per cent of all general merchandise sales. More than 10,000 firms in the United States use mail order.[27] This form of retailing offers convenience for consumers, low operating costs, coverage of a wide geographic area, and new market segments.

By Location

The last classification of retailers is based on *location*. There are three basic types of location: the isolated store, the unplanned business district, and the planned shopping center. Each of these has its own attributes regarding the composition of competing stores, parking facilities, pedestrian traffic, costs, and ease of reaching. Figure 13–6 outlines the advantages and disadvantages of the three retail locations.

An *isolated store* is a free-standing retail outlet located on either a highway or side street. Although there are no adjacent stores with which the firm must compete, there are also no stores to help draw consumer traffic. The difficulty of attracting and holding consumers is the reason why large retailers are usually best suited for an isolated location. Customers are unwilling to travel to an isolated store that does not have a wide assortment of products and an established reputation.

An *unplanned business district* exists where a group of stores are located in close proximity to one another and the combination of stores is not based on prior planning. There are four types of unplanned business district: central business district, secondary business district, neighborhood business district, and string.

An *isolated store* is a free-standing outlet on a highway or side street. There are no other stores next to this outlet.

In an *unplanned business district,* stores are located close together without prior planning.

[27]Maxwell Sroge, "Socioeconomic Trends Cause High Growth in Nonstore Marketing Field," *Marketing News* (February 8, 1980), pp. 1, 3, and Barbara Ettore, "Catalogues of Christmas Cheer," *New York Times* (November 23, 1979), pp. D1, D4.

	Advantages	**Disadvantages**

Figure 13–6:
Advantages and Disadvantages
of Retail Locations

Isolated Store

Advantages	Disadvantages
1. No competition	1. Difficult to attract initial customers
2. Low rental costs	2. Extensive product line needed
3. Flexibility in operations	3. No one-stop shopping appeal to customers
4. Good road and traffic visibility	4. High advertising costs
5. Facilities adapted to individual specifications	5. No shared operating costs, such as security and outside lighting
6. Easy parking	6. Zoning law restrictions
7. Reasonable purchase terms	7. Store may have to be built from scratch, rather than rented in an existing building
8. Space	

Unplanned Business District

A. Central Business District

Advantages	Disadvantages
1. Good product assortment	1. Inadequate parking
2. Access to public transportation	2. High real-estate taxes
3. Variety of store types and price lines	3. Older stores and fixtures
4. Location of chain headquarters	4. Unbalanced product offerings
5. Nearness to commercial, social, and cultural facilities	5. Crowding and traffic congestion
6. Few restrictions on merchandise lines carried	6. Theft and vandalism
7. Pedestrian traffic	7. Urban blight
	8. Limited business on weekends and evenings

B. Secondary Business District and

C. Neighborhood Business District

Advantages	Disadvantages
1. Closeness to population	1. Inadequate parking
2. Nearness to commercial, social, and cultural facilities	2. Older stores
3. Access to public transportation	3. Traffic congestion
4. Fill-in sales	4. Unbalanced product offerings
5. Few restrictions on merchandise lines carried	5. Theft and vandalism

D. String

Advantages	Disadvantages
1. Low rent	1. Zoning law restrictions
2. Complementary stores increase trading area	2. Few shared operating costs, such as security and outside lighting
3. Store visibility	3. Lack of one-stop shopping
4. Space	4. High advertising costs

Planned Shopping Center

A. Regional Shopping Center

Advantages	Disadvantages
1. Good product assortment	1. Restrictions on store hours and merchandise lines
2. Balanced tenancy	2. Domination by largest store or stores
3. Ample parking	3. Payment for services that may be of little value to an individual store, such as membership in a merchants' association
4. Modern facilities	
5. One-stop family shopping	
6. Maximization of pedestrian traffic	4. High rent
7. Access to highways	5. Population must travel to center
8. Low theft rates	6. Limited public transportation
9. Distinctive, unified image	
10. Sharing of common costs, such as security, advertising, exterior lighting	
11. Temperature control in enclosed malls	

B. Community Shopping Center and

C. Neighborhood Shopping Center

Advantages	Disadvantages
1. Balanced tenancy	1. Restrictions on store hours and merchandise lines
2. Fill-in merchandise	2. Domination by largest stores
3. Sharing of common costs	3. High rent
4. Ample parking	4. Competition from regional centers
5. Access to major throughfares	
6. Distinctive, unified image	
7. Modern facilities	
8. Near consumers	

A *central business district* (CBD) is the largest "downtown" area of a city with commercial and shopping facilities.

A *central business district* (CBD) is the hub of retailing in a city and is synonymous with the term *downtown*. It contains the largest commercial and shopping facilities in a city. Cultural, employment, and entertainment facilities surround it. There is at least one major department store and a broad grouping of specialty and convenience stores. CBDs have had some problems with crowding, lack of parking, old buildings, crime, and other factors.[28] However, CBD sales remain strong. Among the innovations used to strengthen CBDs are closing streets to vehicular traffic, modernizing storefronts and equipment, developing strong merchant associations, planting trees to make the area more attractive, improving transportation, and integrating a commercial and residential environment.[29]

A *secondary business district* (SBD) is bounded by two major streets. It has a junior department store.

A *secondary business district* (SBD) is a shopping area that is usually bounded by the intersection of two major streets. Cities generally have several SBDs, each having at least one junior department store, a variety store, and several small service shops. In comparison with the CBD, the SBD has less merchandise assortment, a smaller *trading area* (the geographic area from which a store draws its customers), and sells more convenience items.

A *neighborhood business district* (NBD) satisfies local needs.

A *neighborhood business district* (NBD) satisfies the convenience shopping needs of a neighborhood. The NBD contains a number of small stores, with the major retailer being a supermarket or variety store. An NBD is located on the major street in a residential area.

A *string* contains closely grouped stores which usually sell compatible products.

A *string* is usually composed of a group of stores with similar or compatible product lines. However, because this location is unplanned, various store combinations are possible. It is located along a street or highway. Car dealers, antique stores, and clothing stores are retailers that frequently locate in a string.

A *planned shopping center* is centrally planned, suits the surrounding area, and has *balanced tenancy*, which relates the stores to the needs of the population.

A *planned shopping center* is centrally owned or managed, planned and operated as an entity, surrounded by parking, and based on balanced tenancy. *Balanced tenancy* means that the type and number of stores within any planned center are related to the overall needs of the surrounding population. The various stores complement each other in the quality and variety of merchandise. To ensure balance, a center may limit the merchandise lines any store carries. Planned centers account for approximately 43 per cent of total retail store sales; isolated stores and unplanned business districts account for the remaining 57 per cent. The three types of planned center are regional, community, and neighborhood.

A *regional shopping center* sells shopping goods to a dispersed market.

A *regional shopping center* sells predominantly shopping goods to a geographically dispersed market. A regional center has at least one or two department stores and up to one hundred or more small retailers. More than 50 per cent of the customers live within ten minutes' driving time of the center, another 25 per cent within twenty minutes of it.[30]

A *community center* has a moderate variety of stores; a *neighborhood center* sells convenience goods.

A *community shopping center* has a variety store and/or small department store as its major retailer, with several smaller stores. This center sells both convenience and shopping items. A *neighborhood shopping center* sells mostly convenience products. The largest store is a supermarket and/or drugstore, with a few smaller stores.

CONSIDERATIONS IN RETAIL PLANNING

There are many factors for retailers to consider when developing and implementing their marketing plans. Three of the most important factors that need to be understood are atmosphere, scrambled merchandising, and the wheel of retailing.

[28]See Barry Berman (Editor), *An Evaluation of Selected Business Districts in Nassau, Suffolk and Queens Counties* (Hempstead, N.Y.: Hofstra University Press, 1980).
[29]See Frederick C. Klein, "Chicago Pins Hopes of Downtown Revival on Big Shopping Mall," *Wall Street Journal* (March 11, 1980), pp. 1, 24.
[30]"Regional Shopping Malls Recover from Gas Crunch," *Marketing News* (August 10, 1979), p. 14.

Atmosphere

Atmosphere refers to the physical characteristics of a store that are used to develop an image and to draw customers. It consists of a store's exterior, general interior, layout, and displays.

Atmosphere is the sum total of the physical characteristics of a store that are used to develop an image and draw customers. The overall atmosphere of a store helps determine the customers it will attract, sets the mood for shopping, encourages impulse purchases, and sets a long-term image for the store. Atmosphere is closely related to the strategy mix a retailer selects, as described earlier in the chapter. For example, a discounter will have linoleum floors, crowded displays, centrally located cash registers, and shopping carts. A prestige department store will have carpeted floors, wide aisles and attractive displays, recessed cash registers, and sales personnel to help carry purchases.

There are four components of a store's atmosphere: exterior, general interior, store layout, and interior displays. The *exterior* of a store encompasses its storefront, marquee, entrances, display windows, visibility from the street or highway, uniqueness, surrounding area, surrounding stores, and traffic congestion. The *general interior* includes a store's flooring, colors, scents, lighting, fixtures, wall textures, temperature, width of aisles, dressing facilities, vertical transportation, personnel, and placement of cash registers.

Store layout refers to the floor space allocated for customers, selling, and storage, the groupings of products, department locations, and arrangements within departments. *Interior (or point-of-purchase) displays* involve the types of cases and racks used to show merchandise, mobiles, in-store advertising, mannequins, and wall decorations.

The renovation of Macy's Herald Square store in the late 1970s demonstrates how atmosphere can affect a retailer's success. From a struggling position in the mid-1970s, prior to its renovation, Macy's now stands at the peak of its success:

> Gone are the dreary bargain-basement tables of budget dresses and sportswear with which pre-Finkelstein leadership tried to forestall the competitive pull of nearby Korvettes and Gimbels. As elsewhere in the store, Finkelstein has deemphasized budget shopping—here with a repeat of a California success called "The Cellar."
>
> Instead of sales tables or display cases cluttered with various sorts of coffee pots, for example, along with sundry accessories, a full inventory of one carefully selected product may be stacked from the floor so that its packaging alone creates a casual, eye-catching display.[31]

Scrambled Merchandising

In *scrambled merchandising*, a retailer adds products that are unrelated to each other and to its regular merchandise, in order to obtain one-stop shopping, higher margins, and more impulse purchases.

Scrambled merchandising occurs when a retailer adds products or product lines that are unrelated to each other and the retailer's original business. Examples of scrambled merchandising are supermarkets carrying nonfood items like toys, panty hose, nonprescription drugs, and magazines; gasoline service stations selling food items; and drugstores selling film and gift items.

There are three reasons for the popularity of scrambled merchandising: retailers seek to convert their stores to one-stop shopping centers; scrambled merchandise is often fast selling, generates store traffic, and yields high profit margins;[32] and impulse purchasing is increased.

Scrambled merchandising is self-perpetuating and frequently leads to competition among unrelated stores. For example, when supermarkets branched into nonfood personal care items, they created a decline in drugstore sales. Drugstores were then forced to scramble into small appliances and toys. This caused a drop in specialty store sales, and so on.

There are limits to scrambled merchandising, especially if the lack of buying, selling, and servicing expertise is considered. In addition, low turnover of certain products can occur, should the retailer expand into too many diverse

---

[31]James O'Hanlon, "This Is Show Biz," *Forbes* (February 20, 1978), p. 72.
[32]See Deborah A. Randolph, "Convenience Stores Battle Lagging Sales by Adding Items and Cleaning Up Image," *Wall Street Journal* (March 28, 1980), p. 16.

product categories. Finally, store image may become fuzzy as consumers fail to see a retailer stressing any one product category or group.

Wheel of Retailing

The *wheel of retailing* describes how low-end strategies evolve into high-end strategies and thus provide opportunities for new firms.

The differences between the department store (high-end) and discount store (low-end) strategies illustrated in Figure 13–4 are explained by the *wheel of retailing*.[33] According to this theory, some retail innovators first appear as low-price operators with low profit-margin requirements. As time passes, these innovators upgrade product offerings, facilities, and services and develop into more traditional retailers. They may enlarge sales force support, utilize a more costly location, and introduce delivery, credit, and alterations. These improvements lead to higher costs, which in turn lead to higher prices. This creates opportunities for new retailers to emerge by appealing to price-conscious consumers.

An example of the wheel of retailing occurs when full-line discount stores become like department stores. This provides opportunities for retail catalog showrooms and new full-line discounters to enter the price-conscious market.

RECENT TRENDS IN RETAILING

Retailers are affected by demographic and life-style changes, inflation, increases in capital costs and business expenses, and technological advances. This section analyzes retailers' responses to these elements.

Responses to Demographic and Life-Style Trends

The *slowdown in suburban population growth* is leading retailers to develop additional regional and cross-country branches.

The slowdown in suburban population growth and the poverty of time are two consumer trends that influence retailers. The *slowdown in suburban population growth* is causing retailers to develop more regional and cross-country branches. For instance, Federated Stores' Los Angeles-based Bullock's is looking for opportunities anywhere in the western United States. Its West Coast-based I. Magnin announced plans to become national. During one recent ten-year period, Carter Hawley Hale obtained nine major retailers throughout the United States, including Bergdorf Goodman (New York), Nieman-Marcus (Dallas), and John Wanamaker (Philadelphia). These expansions require more decentralized planning and budgeting, otherwise management personnel will be stretched to the limit, local adaptations overlooked, and the popularity of individual store names diminished.

Poverty of time states that greater affluence can result in reduced free time as a result of the rise in alternative activities.

The increase in the number of females performing the joint roles of working woman, wife, and mother; the greater desire for personal fulfillment; increased distances between home and work; and the large number of people working at second jobs contribute to the concept of *poverty of time*.[34] This concept states that greater affluence can result in less free time, because the alternatives competing for a consumer's time rise significantly. Retailers can respond to the poverty of time by stocking labor-saving devices, such as microwave ovens and ready-to-eat foods; lengthening store hours and opening additional days; expanding catalog sales efforts; prewrapping gift items to eliminate waiting on lines; setting up comprehensive specialty boutiques to minimize the number of

---

[33]The pioneering works on the wheel of retailing are Malcolm P. McNair, "Significant Trends and Developments in the Postwar Period," in A. B. Smith (Editor), *Competitive Distribution in a Free High Level Economy and Its Implications for the University* (Pittsburgh: University of Pittsburgh Press, 1958), pp. 17–18, and Stanley Hollander, "The Wheel of Retailing," *Journal of Marketing,* Vol. 25 (July 1960), pp. 37–42.

[34]See Leonard L. Berry, "The Time-Buying Consumer," *Journal of Retailing,* Vol. 55 (Winter 1979), pp. 58–69.

departments a consumer must visit; and adding special services, such as fashion coordinators.[35]

Responses to Inflation

Inflation has had a dramatic impact on both the attitudes and shopping habits of consumers. During an inflationary period, people feel that their standard of living is adversely affected, stock up on bargains and lower priced brands, and use leftovers more frequently.

One response to inflation has been A&P's development of the PLUS store. These limited-assortment outlets offer a no-frills approach to grocery shopping. Customers must bag their own purchases, choose from only 900 shelf items (compared with 8,000 to 10,000 in a typical supermarket), cannot use coupons or checks, and select items out of packing cartons. Merchandise is not unpacked and sorted onto shelves. Labor and overhead cost reductions result in prices that are 20 to 30 per cent below standard supermarket prices.[36]

Responses to Increases in Costs

Retailers have implemented various strategies to combat rising costs. These include subleasing and cutting expenses.

Rising capital and other costs (such as labor, heat, and air conditioning) are forcing some retailers to reevaluate their past policies, as the following examples demonstrate.

Abraham and Straus has decided to sublease space in its large Brooklyn headquarters store. Two Associated Dry Goods divisions also sublease excess space. Many other retailers are cutting expenses by reducing inventories because high interest rates cause inventory costs to increase if retailers need to borrow funds to purchase goods. In addition, excessive inventories can lead to markdowns if consumer purchases are not made. J. C. Penney is eliminating many stockroom jobs by requiring manufacturers to adhere price labels to merchandise. Credit policies of banks and retailers are tightened when the cost of credit to these firms increases rapidly, as it did in 1980 when interest rates exceeded 20 per cent. Credit charges reflect the interest rates that prevail in the marketplace.

Responses to Technological Advances

With *computerized-checkouts*, a retailer is able to employ a total inventory control and lower costs.

An important technological advance utilized by many large retailers (it is currently too expensive for smaller firms) is the computerized checkout or electronic point-of-purchase system.

With the *computerized-checkout system* (*electronic point-of-purchase*), a retailer is using a total inventory control system. A cashier passes an item over or past an optical scanner and a computer system instantly records and displays a sale. The customer is given a receipt, and all inventory information is stored in the computer's memory bank.

The food industry uses a coding classification system known as the *Universal Product Code* (UPC), whereas department and specialty stores apply *Optical Character Recognition* (OCR-A) for coding information onto merchandise. The UPC requires manufacturers to premark packages with a series of thick and thin vertical lines. Price and inventory data contained in the UPC are not readable by employees or customers. OCR-A is readable by both machines and humans and handles greater information than the UPC.

A computerized checkout lowers costs through reductions in checkout time

[35]See Marion Burk Rothman, "Personal Shopping: New Needs, New Tactics," *Stores* (November 1979), pp. 38–43.

[36]John M. Geddes, "A&P German Owners Bullish," *New York Times* (January 2, 1980), pp. D1, D4, and Richard Sandomir, "A No-Frills Store Makes Cents," *Newsday* (February 4, 1980), p. 33.

and employee training, fewer misrings, and the elimination of price marking on merchandise. In addition, the system generates a current listing of the types and quantities of merchandise in stock without taking a physical inventory, improves inventory control, reduces spoilage, and enhances ordering. The system is also able to verify and change transactions, provide instantaneous sales and profit reports, compute discounts, and determine the prices of items with missing tags.[37] The major obstacles to computerized checkouts are their high purchase costs and consumers' insistence that price tags be adhered to each item.

SUMMARY

Retailing encompasses those business activities involved with the sale of goods and services to the ultimate (final) consumer for personal, family, or household use. Average retail sales are small, yet the use of credit is widespread. Final consumers make many unplanned purchases and generally visit a retail store to make a purchase.

Retailing has an impact on the economy because of its total sales and the number of people employed. Retailers provide a variety of functions, including collecting an assortment of items from a supplier, selling items, disseminating information, and storing merchandise. Retailers deal with one group of suppliers that sell products the retailers use in operating their businesses and a second group selling items the retailers will resell.

Retailers may be categorized in several ways. Ownership types are independent, chain, franchise, leased department, and cooperative. The ease of entry into retailing fosters competition and results in many new firms failing. Different strategy mixes are used by convenience stores, supermarkets, superstores, specialty stores, variety stores, full-line discount stores, department stores, and retail catalog showrooms. Nonstore retailing involves vending machines, door-to-door, and mail order. Service retailing includes rental goods, owned goods, and nongoods categories (discussed in Chapters 8 and 22). Locational alternatives are isolated stores, unplanned business districts, and planned shopping centers. Only the planned centers utilize balanced tenancy.

In retail planning, atmosphere, scrambled merchandising, and the wheel of retailing need to be understood. Atmosphere is the sum total of a store's physical characteristics that help develop an image and attract customers. Scrambled merchandising is the addition of products unrelated to the retailer's original business. The wheel of retailing explains low-end and high-end retail strategies and how they evolve.

Retailers have adapted to recent population trends by broadening their locations. They have responded to the poverty of time by making shopping more convenient. They have responded to inflation by adding no-frills stores. In order to reduce rising costs, retailers have sublet space, lowered inventories, tightened credit, and eliminated personnel. The computerized checkout (electronic point-of-purchase) is used by large retailers to tabulate data, control inventory, reduce costs, and conclude transactions.

QUESTIONS FOR DISCUSSION

1. Define *retailing*.
2. Why do final consumers usually visit retail stores, when organizational consumers generally have salespeople call on them?

[37] See Cyrus C. Wilson and William D. Harreisen, "Retail Information Systems Can Help Provide Profits Needed for Growth," *Marketing News* (March 7, 1980), p. 4.

3. Table 13–1 shows the profit margins of retailers. How can these be so low if 41 cents of every sales dollar in department stores and 23 cents of every sales dollar in supermarkets go to the retailers?
4. Explain how a tavern owner and one of his or her beer suppliers could have different goals.
5. How can independents successfully compete with claims?
6. How is ease of entry in retailing both good and bad?
7. At one time most of McDonald's outlets operated under franchise agreements. Today about half of all McDonald's outlets are owned by the firm itself.
   a. Why was franchising a correct strategy for McDonald's in its early years?
   b. Why would McDonald's want to buy back its franchises now?
8. Why have consumer cooperatives not become a more important factor in food marketing?
9. Compare the strategies of convenience stores, supermarkets, and superstores.
10. Develop a discount store strategy for high-fidelity equipment. How would it compete with a high-priced specialty store?
11. Why is nonstore retailing growing so rapidly? Are all forms of nonstore retailing increasing? Why or why not?
12. Compare the attributes of a central business district with those of a regional shopping center.
13. Describe the disadvantages of a small retailer locating in a regional shopping center.
14. Explain the appropriate atmosphere for a retailer of fine jewelry.
15. Give two examples of the wheel of retailing working in your area.
16. Describe several ways in which a large home improvement retailer can respond to the poverty of time when developing its marketing strategy.

NOTES

1. **David Rachman** and **Michael Mescon,** *Business Today* (New York: Random House, 1979), p. 440.
2. **Robert Harper** and **Theodore Schmudde,** *Between Two Worlds: An Introduction to Geography* (Boston: Houghton Mifflin, 1978), p. 441.
3. **Harper** and **Schmudde,** p. 269.
4. **Rachman** and **Mescon,** pp. 434–440, 443–445.
5. **Joel R. Evans** and **Barry Berman,** *Marketing* (New York: Macmillan, 1982), pp. 353–377.

Nine

THE ART OF READING RAPIDLY

Many college students believe that speed reading itself is the goal. These readers erroneously reason that the faster they complete an assigned reading, the faster they can move on to another assignment or to some leisure activity. Often these same readers close the book and suddenly realize that they do not understand or remember much of what they have read. Clearly, comprehension and understanding are the most important goals when reading.

This chapter presents ways for you to increase your reading rate while you are striving for a high level of comprehension. Remember, previewing is a prereading activity; it should be undertaken before any reading activity. Skimming and scanning are low comprehension techniques for covering large amounts of material that you do not intend to read completely.

Reading rapidly with good comprehension is a skill that you develop gradually, not suddenly. Once you have this skill, though, it is yours for life. All the skills you have learned in previous chapters come into play here. Rapid reading means applying these skills efficiently. Below is a review of the steps you should follow when reading.

1. Preview.
   A. Read all headings and subheadings.
   B. Read all typographical aids such as italics and boldface.
   C. Review graphs, tables, charts, and illustrations.
   D. Read the first and last sentence of each paragraph.
   E. Read the questions at the end of the chapter.
   F. Read the summary.
2. Formulate prereading questions based on your preview to answer as you read.
3. Read for main ideas. Apply what you know about understanding the meaning of a sentence and finding the topic of a paragraph.
4. Read for appropriate details. When the main idea is unstated you must read details to infer the main idea. When the main idea is stated, read enough details to understand the paragraph and to answer your prereading questions.
5. Use the paragraph type and pattern to help you read efficiently for main ideas and details.
6. Scan tables and charts to answer prereading questions. Skim over ancillary material.

There are several other techniques you can use to improve your reading speed while maintaining effective comprehension. Here are some more specific suggestions:

7. Read alone where you will not be distracted. Read in a sitting position.
8. Set realistic time limits for each reading assignment.
   A. Adhere to these time limits and read the entire assignment.
   B. If there is a section you do not understand, return to it later. (Make sure you return to it!)
9. Read at a speed which is appropriate for the material you are reading and for the level of comprehension expected by the instructor.
10. If you have read a passage several times and you still don't understand it, *ask* before reading on!

The rest of this chapter presents some activities to help you increase your reading speed.

ACTIVITY I

You should vary your reading rate. The rate will depend on the difficulty of the material and the desired level of comprehension. The list below shows four categories of reading rates. Use these rates as a guide when you read.

Review each category. In the space provided, write the name of a selection you have read, or are reading now; that should be read at that rate.

1. *Skimming and scanning:* Reading rate 2–4 pages per minute; about 1000 words per minute. These techniques are used to locate specific information, main ideas, or details. Usually, a limited comprehension of the material is desired.

   _____

   _____

2. *General reading:* Reading rate 1–2 pages per minute; about 500 words per minute. The general reading rate is used for easy reading such as newspapers, journals, fiction, and light textbook content. Much of the material can be understood without intense concentration.

   _____

   _____

3. *Efficient study reading:* Reading rate about 1 page per minute; about 250 words per minute. This reading rate is used when you are reading textbooks which contain new or difficult material. Usually, you want to understand the material completely and retain the information.

   _____

   _____

4. *Intensive reading:* Reading rate less than 1 page per minute; about 50–100

words per minute. This rate is used when you need to "read between the lines" for critical evaluation and for complete mastery of the subject. This rate is also used to read material that you will have to apply to other subjects.

ACTIVITY II

When you read, your eyes glance across the page and stop or fixate two or three times on each line. During these instantaneous *fixations*, you look at a group or *span* of words. As you couple together groups of words from fixation to fixation, you start to make sense out of the material. At the end of the line, your eyes drop and *return sweep* back to the beginning of the next line.

One way to increase your reading speed is to decrease the number of fixations and increase the span of words in each fixation. In addition, you should not reread words or regress as you read. Addressing these factors alone can result in a significant increase in reading rate.

The peep hole test will help you learn more about your fixations, return sweeps, and regressions.

The Peep Hole Test

Work with a partner. In the peep hole test you will observe your partner's eye movements while he or she is reading.

1. Choose a book. Each of you will read the same page in the book.
2. Poke a small hole in a piece of paper with a pen or pencil.
3. Hold the paper close to your eye. Look through the hole and focus on your partner's eyes as they read the words.
4. Observe your partner's eyes as they make regressions and return sweeps.
5. Tally these fixations, regressions, and return sweeps on the chart below. Discuss the results with your partner and the instructor. What did you see?
6. Set specific goals for improving and write these goals below.

TALLY CHART

Fixations	Regressions	Return sweeps

ACTIVITY III

This self-quiz will help you identify the other poor reading habits that are preventing you from reading as rapidly as you can. Discuss your responses to this quiz with your teacher and decide what you should do to increase your reading speed. Set specific goals. A = always; S = sometimes; N = never.

Poor Reading Habit	A	S	N	Improvement goals
1. Vocalizing—saying the word and moving your mouth as you read silently.				
2. Finger following—pointing to each word as you read.				
3. Word by word reading—reading individual words.				
4. Monotonous plodding—using a consistently slow reading rate.				
5. Backtracking—rereading words or phrases.				
6. Regressions—rereading sections and paragraphs.				
7. Word blocking—over analysis of unfamiliar words and their parts.				
8. Number attraction—careful reading of all numbers.				
9. Clue blindness—ignoring print aids in textbooks.				
10. Daydreaming—letting your mind wander as you read.				

SUMMARY

By now you have a good idea of what you must do to become an effective, rapid reader. Ten steps to follow when reading are outlined at the beginning of this chapter. Activity I gives you some guidelines to follow when deciding on a reading rate. In Activity II you set some goals for decreasing your fixations, increasing your span, and eliminating your regressions. In Activity III you identified your other poor reading habits and set goals for improvement.

One last word about reading rate. What counts is that you read as rapidly as *you* can read. Do not compare yourself with others. You want to make the most of your potential. *Rapid reading is a useful technique only if you understand and remember what you have read.*

Activity IV will help you determine your current reading rate.

ACTIVITY IV

Just before you begin reading the following selection, note the time and mark it next to "beginning time" in the chart below. Start on the minute.

Then read the selection about being bitten by a rattlesnake at your usual rate. Don't try to rush the reading. You want accurate information.

When you finish, note the time next to "ending time" in the chart below. Subtract the beginning time from the ending time to find the total time. Enter the total time to the nearest quarter minute.

Write the total time as a decimal (every quarter minute is 0.25) and divide that into the total number of words. The answer is your average reading speed.

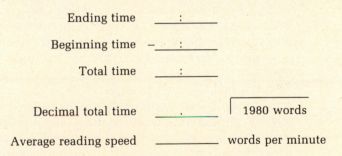

Ending time   _____ : _____

Beginning time   – _____ : _____

Total time   _____ : _____

Decimal total time   _____ . _____ ⟌ 1980 words

Average reading speed   _____ words per minute

SNAKE BIT! PERSONAL ACCOUNT OF BEING BIT BY A RATTLER[1]

by Milan D. Fiske

The snake seemed to share my feeling of incredulity: what had happened just could not happen. He paused after the strike, his mouth still open (I noted his fangs were light green), and he eyed me as if to say, "I really didn't mean that." And then I released him, and he dropped into the garbage can. I banged the lid on and ruefully studied the two bloody spots on my middle finger. It was by no means certain that it had been much of a bite: certain it was that I had scarcely felt it. Perhaps the punctures were just through the skin; perhaps it was not a real bite at all, but just surface scratch; perhaps a simple disinfectant would do the trick and I woundn't have to waste an hour or two going to a physician; perhaps . . .

My wife Kay had dashed into the house for the snakebite kit, and now had the lance ready only a couple of minutes after the strike. But in that couple of minutes it became clear that the bite was more than superficial, for the finger was swelling. The conventional wisdom called for a shallow cut through the fang marks to expose the venom, followed by suction to extract it. However, the bite was into my middle finger, and any cut deep enough to expose the venom would risk cutting tendons and doing lasting damage. Surely, all that was really needed was a shot of antivenin and everything would be okay. At least, so spoke my ignorance. What I should do was suck hard on the wound and go get that shot.

Kay and I had come to our cottage at Lake George for a stay of several days. We had just arrived and carried several loads of groceries, linens, etc. to the house. I had returned for a cleanup load when I heard alongside the path the familiar buzz of a rattler. He was not hard to spot, coiled up partly concealed by a shrub, and steadily rattling away his hissing buzz warning.

Timber rattlesnakes (*Crotalus horridus*) were no strangers in camp: we had seen one or two, sometimes none, each year over the 28 years we had the place. At first I had killed them as protection to the children and ourselves, but in recent years it had increasingly seemed pointless to kill these really fascinating animals. Instead, I had caught them with a loop-bearing stick, put them into a small garbage can, and transported them a quarter mile or so back up to the rocks higher on the mountain whence they had presumably come. Aside from the brief flurry attending capture and relocation, the occasional presence of a rattler at our camp was no big deal.

This time, however, I could not locate my loop stick. So I had grabbed a 6-foot long stick with the intention of lifting the snake under his midriff and dropping him into the can. He had been far too active for that and had promptly slid off the stick each time I had tried lifting him. The prospect had loomed of his getting away under the house and remaining as a most unwelcome intruder. Somehow it had not occurred to me to kill him and be done with it.

The solution—the epitome of foolishness—had been to pick up the snake by pinning him to the ground with the stick and grasping him right behind the head for a quick lift into the garbage can. This would have worked had the snake not managed to wriggle a spare inch or so of neck room, enough to swing his head sideways and strike. As I dropped him I wondered for a brief moment how I could have been so careless.

When the swelling made it clear that the bite was for real, we dropped everything, slammed the cottage door shut, and drove to the nearest physician.

138

It was my expectation then to get an antivenin shot and be back in camp in an hour or so. The local physician, however, had no antivenin: he had been practicing there for 35 years and he had never seen a snakebite! He urged me to go to the nearest hospital, some 20 miles away in Glens Falls, and he called ahead for us.

By this time it looked as if the snakebite might ruin the better part of the day. The full danger of it really had not struck me yet, but it had Kay. About this time the first systemic effects showed up, perhaps a half-hour after the bite. I had moments of light-headedness, my hand was now swelling appreciably, and the pain attending the edema was becoming insistent. Therefore, rather than wait for an ambulance, we decided to drive directly to the hospital, and Kay's driving skills had a high-speed workout. (No police car showed up to escort us—we had not taken the time to call for one.) During the half-hour drive, I fainted and revived repeatedly and arrived at the hospital in a very woozy state.

Although the emergency room at Glens Falls Hospital had been alerted, they also had seen no snakebites, at least during the previous five years or so. The start of treatment waited on hasty consultations of medical literature and following a test for horse serum sensitivity (antivenin is produced in a horse), I was given two intramuscular shots of antivenin. The decision was soon made, however, to transfer me to Albany Medical Center Hospital (AMCH) where there was greater experience in treating snake venom poisoning. So off we went to Albany, this time in an ambulance with one attendant keeping the intravenous drip and cardiac monitoring equipment going and another making soothing sounds while keeping my head iced and handling occasional vomiting spells. Kay followed behind at speeds of doubtful legality.

By great good fortune and/or laudable curiosity, one of the staff physicians at AMCH had become interested in snakebite poisoning some months previously, and she had absorbed much of the current medical literature on the subject. Her timely knowledge was a bulwark for the treatment begun promptly on arrival at the emergency room. Beyond the treatment actually used, the staff planned systems and procedures to cover various contingencies which might develop if things did not go as planned. I was only vaguely aware of all this background, and not too cognizant of the foreground either.

Swelling had advanced up the arm, and the hand, now some five hours after the bite, was swollen almost beyond recognition. The pain had become rather severe as the skin tightened toward its limit of stretch. Intravenous administration of antivenin was started almost at once and continued for the next 12 hours or so, and discontinued only when the swelling was arrested and blood tests indicated the venom had been neutralized.

One of the effects of the rattlesnake venom is to reduce the ability of the blood to clot, while at the same time perforating the small blood vessels. In severe cases it is possible for a person to bleed to death internally, with blood leaving the circulatory system and entering body tissues and cavities. The medical people watched for this possibility very carefully, and it took until early the following morning for them to be sure that internal blood loss was under control.

There followed another day of intensive care and three more of "ordinary" care before I was released. The swelling was now confined largely to the finger. The remaining pain, although present, was quite manageable. I was given physical therapy instructions for restoring the finger to full use. What was pointed out, however, was my liability for serum sickness.

I had received 17 units of antivenin, as required for the "severe" envenomization I had received. The amount of horse serum in that much antivenin almost guaranteed a massive bodily reaction as the blood went about cleaning up the foreign protein. The typical reaction resembles a case of common flu, with aches in the joints, some nausea, and a generally blah feeling, but there is great individual variation in the reaction. In my case, I simply had off-and-on bouts of lassitude and weakness lasting for several weeks, often obliging me to enjoy a summer day or two in a hammock or a deck chair.

In retrospect, there are a number of points worth mentioning about the affair:

- No one should try to handle a rattler without the proper equipment and training any more than he would try to restrain a wild raccoon or a bobcat barehanded. The lack of proper tools and proper techniques can have very unpleasant consequences.
- Snakebite from the timber rattler is a very rare event, at least in New York State. Only four bites were reported statewide by hospitals in the most recent years (1958–1959) surveyed in the literature. Local inquiry revealed no Lake George resident who could recall a single rattler bite around the lake within the last 20 years, an account supported by medical people of the area. This despite the annual influx of thousands of visitors, many of whom tramp the woods with little thought of snakes. The timber rattler is a very shy animal, and given half a chance, he'll get out of your way.
- Modern medical treatment, particularly the intravenous injection of anti-venin, removes virtually any prospect of death from a rattlesnake bite. Of an estimated 8,000 bites by venomous snakes which occur each year in the U.S. only about 10 are fatal. Almost all of these are due to lack of proper treatment. In the most recent (1966) report for New York State, H. M. Parrish stated that "there were no deaths from snakebites from 1950 through 1959" although there were roughly 400 venomous snakebites during that decade.
- The sooner snakebite treatment can be started, the better, yet antivenin administered 12 hours after the bite can be helpful. Nevertheless, the bite of any poisonous snake should be regarded as a medical emergency, and treatment should be sought as quickly as possible from the nearest hospital.

1980 words

A Procedure for Estimating the Total Number of Words in a Selection

At times you may want to estimate the total number of words in a selection to compute your reading speed. Follow these steps to estimate the total number of words.

1. Select three "typical" lines of print from the selection. Count the total number of words in these lines. Divide the total number of words by three to find the *average number of words per line.*
2. Next, count the total number of lines in the selection. Multiply the total number of lines by the average number of words (from step 1). Your answer is the estimated number of words.
3. If the selection continues for several pages, do step 1, then count the number of lines on a "typical" page. Next, multiply the number of lines on a typical page by the number of pages in the selection. Estimate partial pages as half or quarter pages and count these, too. Your answer is the total number of lines in the selection. Multiply this by the average words per line from step 1.
4. The answer to step 2 or to step 3 is the estimated total words in the selection.
5. Time how many minutes it takes to read the selection and divide the total number of words by the total minutes (round to one-half or one-quarter minute) it takes to read the selection.
6. Your answer is your reading speed in words per minute.

ACTIVITY V

Use the following technique from time to time to keep track of your reading speed. The chart below gives you room to figure out your reading speed for 12 different readings. Check your reading speed with your instructor as the term continues.

Selection	Begin time	Ending time	Total time	Number of words	Average reading speed
1.					
2.					
3.					
4.					
5.					
6.					
7.					
8.					
9.					
10.					
11.					
12.					

PROJECT

Now that you have begun to read rapidly, here are three selections for you to practice on. The first is from a textbook about human sexuality (p. 143). The second selection is from a text about personality (p. 150), and the third is from a short story (p. 155).

When you read each selection, note beginning and ending times on the chart below. Compute your total reading time by subtracting the beginning time from the ending time to find how many minutes you have been reading. Divide the number of words by the number of minutes to find your average reading speed.

Selection I		Selection II		Selection III	
Ending time	___:___	Ending time	___:___	Ending time	___:___
Beginning time	___:___	Beginning time	___:___	Beginning time	___:___
Total time (minutes)	_____	Total time (minutes)	_____	Total time (minutes)	_____
Total words	3200 est.	Total words	2400 est.	Total words	5200 est.
Average reading speed	_____	Average reading speed	_____	Average reading speed	_____

Next, try your rapid reading on some other selections that you have picked. You can use the procedure already given for estimating the total number of words in a selection. Make a chart like the one above to calculate your reading speed. Graph your reading speed and you will see your speed improve.

SELECTION I: BIRTH DEFECTS[2]

Birth defects occur in significant numbers (Volpe, 1971): one baby in every 100 born enters postnatal life with a serious congenital malformation. In the United States each year, approximately 250,000 infants are born with defects of grave consequence. These infants will either die soon after birth or will carry with them, for a lifetime, a severe handicap. And this is to say nothing of the many malformed embryos lost naturally through spontaneous abortion.

It is difficult to appreciate either the grief and the emotional stress that birth defects cause parents and expectant parents or the suffering of the congenitally deformed themselves. In general, such malformations are caused either by genetic and/or developmental errors or by unfavorable environmental conditions. Under the former, we can include abnormal or deleterious genes that are destined to produce their devastating effects from the moment fertilization occurs. These traits can be passed from one generation to the next. In fact, the deleterious genes are sometimes harbored by "normal" individuals and express themselves in future generations. Developmental errors can be produced, for instance, by degenerative changes in the egg, which affect its chromosomes, prior to fertilization. Defects produced by such changes are generally not heritable. Nor are most environmentally produced defects able to be passed genetically from one generation to the next. These errors arise from unsatisfactory conditions imposed on the embryo, usually early in pregnancy.

It is not our purpose here to provide a thorough review of birth defects and their causes. But there are three areas that are of particular relevance to the discussion here: environmentally produced defects, maternal-fetal blood incompatibility, and phenylketonuria.

ENVIRONMENTALLY PRODUCED DEFECTS

Most congenital malformations originate early in pregnancy when the embryo is in its most crucial stages of formation. Thus, it is extremely important to maintain an appropriate environment for the embryo in the first trimester. It is especially important for the pregnant woman to maintain an adequate diet and to avoid exposure to substances and conditions that can affect embryogenesis. Alcoholism and excessive smoking, for instance, can affect the well-being of the embryo. Birth defects can be caused by contraction of German measles; by exposure to influenza, polio, and other viruses and to radiation of more than ten roentgens; and by any of numerous drugs taken by the expectant mother. With the exception of irradiation, which penetrates the mother and embryo directly from an external source—such as from an X-ray machine—all factors that are potentially dangerous for the embryo must cross the placenta. Although the placenta may serve as a barrier to the movement of some things from the mother to the embryo, such as bacteria, it readily permits the movement of many other things. This is no more dramatically demonstrated than when babies born of mothers addicted to narcotics are also addicted.

Fetal Alcohol Syndrome

Recent evidence indicates the existence of a **fetal alcohol syndrome,** an umbrella term that includes a set of physical and mental abnormalities in children who were exposed to alcohol while in the uterus. More specifically, these deficiencies include mental retardation, learning difficulties, smaller than normal head size, and defects in body organs. This should not be of concern just to heavy drinkers, for these conditions can be prompted by an intake of as little as three ounces of alcohol a day by the expectant mother. In fact, some defects are induced by a single drinking binge during pregnancy. The identification of alcohol as a cause of birth defects has stimulated government agencies to hold hearings on the possibility of requiring a label on alcoholic beverages warning women of the implications of drinking while pregnant (Smith, 1978; Witti, 1978).

Cigarette Smoking

Smoking in pregnant women is correlated with an increase in miscarriage, stillbirths, and premature births. In one study, the incidence of miscarriage was 12.6 per cent in smokers and 8.8 per cent in nonsmokers. Another study proved even more convincing. The spontaneous abortion rate among smokers was 22.5 per cent but only 7.4 per cent among nonsmokers. As for stillbirths, one group of scientists found the fetal death rate in smokers to be 15.5 per thousand and 6.4 per thousand in nonsmokers. A study of 4,440 postpartum women representing 16,158 pregnancies revealed that there was a twofold increase in premature births in smokers. The statistics build: the death rate among newborns is higher for babies born of mothers who smoke, and infants of smokers are smaller and weigh less. Why smoking adversely affects the fetus is not completely understood, but nicotine no doubt crosses the placenta because fetal heartbeat increases when the pregnant woman smokes. Some researchers believe that the fetus is affected primarily by a decrease in placental circulation, which in turn means that the fetus is receiving fewer nutrients. Whatever the mechanisms, smoking most definitely has a negative effect on the well-being of the fetus (Ochsner, 1971).

Viruses

That viruses or their toxic products can cross the placenta is clearly shown in the case of German measles, or rubella. If the expectant mother contracts measles in early pregnancy, the developing embryo may suffer severe defects, including blindness, deafness, mental retardation, and a malformed heart (Volpe, 1971). The chances of contracting German measles should be significantly reduced now that a rubella vaccine is available; however, health authorities recently expressed the concern that far fewer children are being immunized than should be.

Irradiation

Irradiation of all types, but particularly X-ray irradiation should be avoided following conception, except where medically unavoidable. Although the dangers of X-ray irradiation are not thoroughly understood, there is enough evidence to suspect that under certain circumstances the dangers are considerable. Certainly pelvic irradiation of pregnant women is likely to produce developmental defects in the embryo.

Such irradiation can produce physical deformities and alter the genes in both the mother's and the embryo's gonads. Although such deformities are not usually heritable, the changes in the genetic information are. For this reason, it is not wise to experience excessive irradiation of the pelvic region, even when not pregnant.

Drugs

Drugs represent the most common hazard for the developing embryo, and in the United States this hazard is amplified because medication is extensively and often irresponsibly prescribed and used. The average physician in the United

States writes 7,934 prescriptions a year! Often drugs are prescribed at considerable risk to the patient without sufficient compensating benefits. A good example of this was the use of DES, discussed in Chapter 5, to prevent spontaneous abortion. Not only did the drug prove ineffective to its purpose, but it proved to be carcinogenic, as well (Maugh, 1976).

A classic, but unfortunate, example of the teratogenic (a teratogen is a chemical or physical agent capable of producing congenital malformations) effect of drugs is that of thalidomide, a sedative and hypnotic drug. In 1957 a German pharmaceutical company introduced this drug, which found widespread acceptance in many countries. Although advertised as safe for pregnant women, it was soon discovered that the drug was the cause of many new cases of a rare congenital condition called **phocomelia,** a word that literally means "seal limbs." Use of thalidomide during pregnancy was found to be the one thing that women who bore infants with phocomelia had in common. In phocomelia an infant's arms are either absent or reduced to flipperlike appendages. Sometimes the legs are similarly affected. The embryo is most sensitive to thalidomide in approximately the third to fourth week of development. This is early enough in pregnancy that some women who took thalidomide did not even know they were pregnant. Because the drug was not generally available in the United States, the incidence of thalidomide-induced phocomelia was low, but in Germany at least 5,000 such deformed babies were born. The price, in terms of human suffering was and still is enormous (Volpe, 1971).

What can we expect in the future? The answer may be disappointing. Even though hormonelike drugs used to prevent miscarriage appear to be ineffective, and may produce birth defects, they are still being prescribed. In 1973 and 1974 the Food and Drug Administration (FDA) withdrew approval for the use of these drugs during pregnancy. In addition it sent a special letter to physicians warning against the use of these drugs during pregnancy early in 1975. In 1975 physicians wrote 533,000 prescriptions for the use of the hormones during pregnancy, a reduction of only 10 per cent of those written in 1972 (Maugh, 1976). Perhaps the best advice when confronted with this situation is "no barbiturates, opiates, sedatives, or hypnotics should be prescribed for, or taken by, mothers-to-be" (Volpe, 1971).

MATERNAL-FETAL BLOOD INCOMPATIBILITY

The red blood cells carry on their surfaces chemical substances called **antigens.** The types of antigens found there are genetically determined and vary from individual to individual. However, antigens fall primarily into one of two categories: the **ABO system** and the **Rh system.** The kinds of antigens present on an individual's red blood cells represent the blood group to which the individual belongs. If the blood possesses A antigen, it is grouped as type A blood; if it has B antigen, it is type B; if it possesses both A and B, it is AB; and if it possesses neither, it is type O. The antigen in the Rh system is referred to as the Rh factor; it received this letter designation because it was first found in the rhesus monkey. It is also referred to as type D antigen. Individuals with the Rh factor present are said to be **Rh-positive;** those without it are **Rh-negative.** Because both systems are inherited independently of one another, both are tested for in blood typing. Thus, an individual whose red blood cells carry both the A antigen and Rh factor, is typed A-positive.

Understanding Blood Types

But to understand the concept of blood types, one must also comprehend something about the plasma, or liquid, portion of the blood. Plasma contains **antibodies,** at least for the ABO system, that correspond to the antigens on the cells. How these antibodies get there is not germane here. These antibodies are designated anti-A and anti-B. What is important to recognize is the fact that the antibody present in the plasma of any one individual is the reciprocal of the antigen. That is, if the cells carry A-antigen, the plasma contains anti-B antibody; type B blood has anti-A; AB has no antibodies; and type O blood contains both anti-A and anti-B. Knowledge of blood types is essential for transfusing whole blood from one individual to another. Ideally a donor's blood should be the same as the recipient's. But if this is not possible, one can transfuse other combinations. The rule is that if the plasma of the recipient contains an antibody that corresponds to the antigen carried by the donor's blood, the transfusion should not be made. Why? Because as the donor's red blood cells enter the recipient's system, the antibodies of the recipient will cause the donor's red cells to clump together. This can be fatal. So, for example, type A blood, with its A antigen, should not be transfused into a recipient with type B blood, because the plasma of this blood contains anti-A antibody.

Rh Disease

The Rh system is again different. In this sytem Rh-negative individuals also do not carry anti-Rh antibodies in their plasma. Only if Rh individuals are exposed to Rh-positive blood will they develop the antibodies. If they receive a second Rh-positive transfusion, the results can be fatal, for now they have the antibodies present in their blood.

So what does this have to do with the mother and fetus? In the United States each year the wife in about 200,000 marriages is Rh-negative and the husband is Rh-positive (Volpe, 1971). If the Rh-negative female carries an Rh-positive embryo (there is a good chance for this, given the genetics of the situation), some of the Rh antigens will leak into the maternal system from the fetus. Most fetal blood probably enters the maternal system at the time the afterbirth, or placenta, shears from the uterus following the birth of the infant. This presumably occurs through wounds in the uterine wall created by the placental separation. What happens is that the mother is "sensitized" to the presence of Rh-positive cells in her blood. In other words, she begins to produce anti-Rh antibodies that may persist in her body for long periods of time. The first baby escapes any harm. But if the mother should carry a second Rh-positive baby, her antibodies may cross the placenta, enter the fetal blood, and destroy the fetal red blood cells. This is maternal-fetal blood incompatibility, a disorder referred to as **erythroblastosis fetalis,** or **Rh disease.**

This disease results in about 5,000 stillbirths (infants born dead) a year in the United States and produces 20,000 living infants that suffer with anemia, heart failure, jaundice, and sometimes mental retardation (Volpe, 1971). These symptoms are all related to the destruction of the fetal red blood cells by the maternal antibodies. When the fetal cells break down they release their **hemoglobin,** or oxygen-carrying chemical, which then circulates in the blood plasma. The hemoglobin is normally transformed into a yellow pigment called **bilirubin,** which is then added to the bile by the liver. But the liver cannot process so much bilirubin and it accumulates in the blood to produce in the baby's skin a yellow-orange color—a **jaundice.** At the same time, prolonged exposure to excessive bilirubin will permanently damage tissue in the fetal brain.

Couples can anticipate the problem of Rh maternal-fetal blood incompatibility by knowing their blood types. About 85 per cent of white Americans and 88 per cent of black Americans are Rh-positive. At one time the only treatment for the fetus suspected of having erythroblastosis fetalis was an injection of type O, Rh-negative blood into its abdominal cavity while it was in the uterus. If Rh disease were confirmed after birth, an exchange transfusion of O, Rh-negative blood was performed, completely replacing the infant's blood—a flushing out, so-to-speak. Now drugs are available that desensitize the mother—that is, they stop the maternal system from producing the anti-Rh antibodies. The therapy consists of massive doses of anti-D gamma globulin with the trade names Rho-GAM (Ortho Diagnostics) and RhoImmune (Lederle Laboratories). Given within 72 hours of birth, the anti-D gamma globulin reacts with the fetal antigens that are circulating about in the maternal system to form a chemical complex that is excreted by the kidney. With the fetal antigens out of the way, the mother will not manufacture the antibodies. A second Rh-positive embryo then can be carried without fear of it developing Rh disease.

ABO INCOMPATIBILITY

ABO incompatibility may also develop; it is twice as common as RH disease. However, the ABO disease is milder, because anti-A and anti-B antibodies do not readily cross the placenta into the fetal system. These antibodies, of course, are already present in the maternal system. If, for instance, a mother with type A blood conceives an embryo of type B blood, incompatibility exists. She possesses anti-B that may cross the placenta and attack the fetal red blood cells. The main result of this ABO incompatibility is jaundice (Volpe, 1971).

Phenylketonuria

Phenylketonuria (PKU) is an inherited biochemical disease. Because the disease impairs the production of a pigment called **melanin,** individuals suffering from this malady have light complexions, blond hair, and blue eyes. Most tragically, they are severely mentally retarded. Although the incidence of the disease in populations varies, it is estimated that among Caucasians in the United States one child in 10,000 to one in 20,000 is born with this disease. It is much lower in frequency among U.S. blacks. This means that about five hundred white PKU babies are born per year in the United States (Lerner and Libby, 1976).

Specifically, there is a defect in or absence of an enzyme that converts the amino acid phenylalanine into a compound called tyrosine. Thus, phenylalanine accumulates in the newborn's tissues, as do several related side products. These side products probably account for the mental retardation (Singer, 1978).

Why discuss PKU here? PKU is an excellent example of a genetically determined metabolic disease that can be "cured" if appropriate measures are taken immediately after the PKU infant is born. A simple, inexpensive test can identify PKU in the newborn. All that it involves is pricking the baby's heel to collect a drop or two of blood. The blood is subjected to the Guthrie test, which is based on the ability of some strains of bacteria to grow only in a phenylalanine-rich medium. If they grow in the infant's blood, PKU is indicated. About 37 states now make the Guthrie test compulsory for all newborn babies (Lerner and Libby, 1976).

Once a PKU baby is identified, it can be placed on a special phenylalanine-low diet. Although it is not a particularly appealing diet, babies survive on it. PKU children are generally kept on the diet until they are at least five years old. In this way, mental retardation is prevented (Singer, 1978). The PKU example gives hope that preventive and treatment procedures can be developed for other diseases, even those that are genetically based.

Amniocentesis

The possibility of genetic diseases and congenital malformations worries many prospective parents. However, relatively inexpensive screening tests for some genetic diseases are available. Tay-Sachs disease, Cooley's anemia (thalassemia), and sickle cell anemia are all hereditary diseases that can be tested for in an individual's blood. However, the tests usually only identify individuals as *genetic carriers* of the diseases. In other words, these normal individuals carry the genes that cause the disease and can pass them on to their offspring. While this information may be helpful, it may also create an emotional crisis for couples who wish to have children. Tay-Sachs, for example, is a cruel, debilitating, and ultimately fatal disease in infants that appears primarily in Jewish babies whose parents are of Eastern European origin. If a couple who desire children find that they are both carriers of the disease, they can be warned that any child they might have has a one in four chance of having the disease (Pines, 1978). These are not comfortable odds. The couple's problem is whether they should take the chance of producing a Tay-Sachs child.

Many such parents now can take this chance because there is a test that can be performed during pregnancy that can identify Tay-Sachs in the fetus. This test is performed on loose fetal cells that are collected from the amniotic fluid. The fluid, in turn, is collected by means of an important technique called **amniocentesis.** Simply put, amniocentesis is a procedure, usually performed during the second trimester, in which a hypodermic syringe is inserted through the mother's abdominal wall into the fluid-filled amniotic cavity. Some of the fluid is then withdrawn through the needle. This can be done without touching or damaging the fetus. If, in our example, the test for Tay-Sachs proves positive, the prospective parents can choose to abort the fetus or to prepare themselves for the death of their child before it reaches the age of five.

Because abortion is an alternative for parents who find that they have produced a defective fetus, amniocentesis—the identifying procedure—has become controversial. The procedure is particularly anathema to the right-to-life groups that see it as the first step to abortion. However, in 1975, the U.S. Department of Health, Education and Welfare (HEW) officially endorsed amniocentesis as a safe, accurate procedure by which genetic disorders can be identified in the fetus. Amniocentesis might be appropriate for as many as 400,000 women a year in the United States. But in 1974 it was performed on only 3,000 women and detected about 100 or so defective fetuses (Culliton, 1975).

At the moment it is true that although a defective fetus can be diagnosed, it cannot be cured. A woman must either have a defective child or submit to an abortion. Although the development of techniques for the prenatal diagnosis of birth defects has required tremendous research efforts, little can yet be offered in the way of therapy for birth defects. Therapy, however, is the ultimate goal of this research, because, as one HEW official put it, "a preventative technique dependent on elective abortion is not a final answer to the problem of birth defects" (Culliton, 1975). Even without a treatment available, amniocentesis and diagnosis of birth defects in the uterus is a source of relief to carriers of genetic diseases. It is also of great importance to pregnant women over thirty-five years of age who, because of their age, run the risk of bearing a child with Down's syndrome (mongolism).

But amniocentesis is not only a problem for antiabortion groups. Physicians, primarily obstetricians, still look with distrust on the procedure. Their distrust is based in part on the fact that midtrimester amniocentesis is a relatively new procedure (amniocentesis in the late stages of pregnancy to detect Rh disease has been available for decades). Many obstetricians fear that the needle might injure the fetus, but recent evidence indicates that the risk is quite low (Culliton, 1975). However, some obstetricians fail to warn their patients about the dangers of hereditary diseases. In fact, several obstetricians have been sued for malpractice because such omissions led to the birth of babies with Tay-Sachs and other diseases. A case in point follows:

Some children have even sued doctors for giving them "wrongful life," on the theory that their suffering is so great they should never have been born. Last year, for instance, a New York judge ruled in favor of parents who presented such a claim on behalf of their second child, a little girl who died at three from a painful inherited disorder called polycistic kidneys. Although their first child had died of the same disease, the obstetrician had encouraged them to conceive again and— without ever bothering to make any tests—assured them that their next child would not be afflicted [Pines, 1978].

The detection of more than one hundred chromosomal and metabolic disorders is now possible through the use of diagnostic amniocentesis, and this list continues to grow. Detection is achieved through either an analysis of the composition of the amniotic fluid or a chromosomal and biochemical analysis of the fetal cells that are found in the fluid. Perhaps someday it will also be possible to treat genetic and chromosomal diseases in the fetus. This certainly cannot be achieved, however, without the invaluable aid of the procedure called amniocentesis.

SELECTION II: SOME BASIC NEEDS IN HUMANS[3]

TO VALUE LIFE ITSELF

Most basic of all human needs is the affirmation of life, the desire to continue living. When life is under threat, a person will do almost anything, break laws, kill others, and sacrifice wealth, to eliminate the threat and preserve existence. Such occasions are rare. It will suffice merely to remind the reader that the wish to live is the most powerful determiner of action that we can know. A person may, however, decide to sacrifice his or her life for love of another or for country.

Paradoxically enough, a person can be persuaded that further existence is neither meaningful nor possible. A long period of suffering or joylessness may so dispirit someone that he or she resigns from life. This person may commit suicide or yield to a sickness that would not be lethal had he or she retained the desire to live. Loss of zest for life and the choice for sickness or death can be induced in a person by misfortune and tragedy such as prolonged illness, failure, or an intense sense of lack of worth. One's choice of friends and companions takes on added significance when you consider that good choices of friends can help one through these otherwise lethal crises.

PHYSICAL NEEDS

Physical needs refer to food, drink, relief from pain and discomfort, and adequate shelter. Modern society does a better job of satisfying these needs than was true in earlier times, and so the quests for food, shelter, and comfort are less powerful determiners of everyday action than they used to be. However, when we experience a threat to our supplies, or to our access to supplies, of food and shelter, we may take desperate measures to secure these vital things.

LOVE

It is not only the poets who think of love as having fundamental significance in one's fate. Two fundamental kinds of love may be identified: natural or unconditional love, and earned or conditional love. The former is seen in the parent's love for the child, which is unconditional, in that the love exists regardless of how "bad" the child is. It is not "earned," in that the child ordinarily receives it without reciprocation. In ordinary development this love proceeds to become reciprocal, with the maturing person recognizing that he or she must do things for the other person, parent, peer, or even later, lover. This is the earned, conditional love of most of contemporary human relationships—despite the myth of unconditional love among adults.

The first phase of learning to love—receiving parental or adult love—is fundamental; a child needs it to survive, to grow, and to know how to carry on that most joyous of human activities: loving, giving and receiving love from peers. If the person has been deprived of parental love, his or her ability to participate in the adult conditional love may be seriously impaired. The early Freudian psychologists felt that such love was irreplaceable and that withholding such love by the parent led to serious personality problems in the child.

Many contemporary psychologists, however, while they also feel such love to be critical, desirable, and nurturant, also feel that one can learn to love on an adult level, while an adult, even if one is originally deprived. It is nevertheless clear that parental love, unconditional and spontaneous, as seen in the dignity-devoid father or mother playing with and cooing to an infant, is crucially important for a happy adult life and for the healthy personality.

STATUS, SUCCESS, SELF-ESTEEM, AND COMPETENCE

Human beings need to feel recognized and approved by other members of the groups within which they live. Without such recognition they tend to feel inferior. The quest for power and prestige is universal, though the means of attaining status differ from society to society. A man or woman may work to the point of exhaustion, neglecting personal health and the needs of his or her family, in order to purchase a Rolls Royce. The status symbolized by the Rolls seems worth the cost. The person may not enjoy the work, may not enjoy seeing his or her family suffer from neglect, the limousine may not transport the family any better than a less costly vehicle, but so urgent is the quest for status that the person is willing to pay the price.

Let us not underrate the strength of the status drive in modern humans. The puzzling thing is, how does it become so powerful? One hypothesis is that the fanatic quest for status is in compensation for lack of love or for physical deprivations associated with poverty. It is as if the "success-starved" person is trying to make up in adult years for childhood privations and can never get enough. Related is human beings' need for a feeling and experience of competence, a confidence that they can control their environment.

FREEDOM AND SPACE

Humans need varying degrees of freedom to conduct their lives according to their own wishes and plans. Many wars have been fought in the name of freedom. We can distinguish between *objective* freedom, which refers to the relative absence of real restrictions on one's behavior, and the *feeling* of freedom. The latter refers to persons' estimates of how free they are to express themselves. Healthy personalities find an environment within which there is the greatest possible amount of objective freedom. Unhealthy personalities may dread both objective freedom and the feeling of freedom. They find it anxiety-producing. They can only carry on as long as they feel that they are under authoritarian rule or in surrender to charismatic leadership.

Human beings not only need room to move and to express their unique ways; they need personal space for solitude and to facilitate uninterrupted intimacy with others. In the absence of such assured space, people tend to become irritable and chronically defensive. As we enter an age of vastly increased population and the concentration of this population in crowded cities, the need for more space becomes increasingly urgent.

SOLITUDE

Parallel to the need to love and care for others is the need to be alone for predictable periods of time. The crowding of cities, the constant interaction with other humans, require periods of time for an individual to contemplate the self, to consider personal growth, and to place self in perspective with the rest of the world. It is for this reason that monks and other ascetics seek long periods of solitude. The popularity of transcendental meditation is partly ascribable to the deprivation from the solitude experience. This solitude is not the same as loneliness, which is a result of deprivation from the company of others. A solitude experience is created by a healthy person out of a positive need to be alone for contemplation or intense meditation. Solitude is harder to create for oneself than is the companionship of a good friend and requires careful planning in our heavily socialized culture. Moustakas has suggested that such experience is essential to the development of the healthy personality.

INTIMACY

To be close to another person physically and emotionally, to be held tightly, to share one's deepest self-secrets—all of these represent a basic need largely ignored by most behavioral scientists. This tender need seems to be uniquely human in its manifestation. Obviously related to the sexual needs, intimacy yet has a meaning of its own that includes the physical union, but that can be expressed and can be experienced in the psychological realm alone. Its opposite is true loneliness—just being in the presence of others is insufficient. The need is for a real closeness that affirms the existence of the person. One's existence as an individual is not only highlighted, like a back-lit photograph, in separation from others, but is also manifested in the phenomenon of intimate closeness.

CHALLENGE

Deprivation of challenge is experienced as boredom, or as emptiness in existence. The need for challenge manifests itself most keenly when a person has made a "successful adjustment" to life, when he or she has been able to fulfill the material needs, and cannot then find anything to do. Without challenging goals, people eat or drink to excess or pass the time getting high on marijuana.

MEDITATION AND DISENGAGEMENT

Just as human beings need intense involvement to foster full functioning and growth, they also need disengagement. They need to get away from their customary consciousness of themselves and their world. The "getting away" can be literal, as in travel; but it can also take the form of what are now called *altered states of consciousness*. There are two ways to alter one's consciousness of one's situation. One of these is literally to change situations. The other is to suspend the customary way of experiencing a situation, to allow new modes of consciousness to appear. One's situation functions hypnotically, influencing a person to perceive, recall, think and even imagine in stereotyped ways. One way to break the quasihypnotic spell is to engage in meditation. Za-zen, or sitting-Zen meditation, is one such method. It entails sitting cross-legged, or in any comfortable position, letting one's stream of consciousness simply "happen." Another technique is that of transcendental meditation, which also calls for the attainment of a state of quiescence, where one's "chattering" mind is stilled. Hatha Yoga, together with deep, slow breathing, is yet another method through which a person can disengage from the usual situation. The significant aspect of these meditative disciplines is not the state itself, but rather the effect they have on persons' awareness of their situation when they return to it. New aspects of the situation are perceived, and they can imagine, think, and remember in more flexible ways.

Psychedelic drugs, such as lysergic acid diethylamide (LSD), cannabis derivatives (marijuana and hashish), mescaline, psylocybin, and peyote, are all pharmacological means by which persons can leave their situations (in a metaphorical sense). Indeed, in current jargon persons who ingest LSD or mescaline are said to be "tripping." Although these drugs often produce an absorbing and sometimes pleasant change in experience, they can have deleterious effects upon the capacity to cope effectively with problems.

COGNITIVE CLARITY

Human beings cannot endure ambiguity or contradiction in their knowledge. In the face of uncertainty, they seem impelled to construct answers, because they can act only when they have made a satisfactory interpretation of the situation. Their interpretation may not be valid, but it seems true that humans prefer a false interpretation to none. Thus, a person may hear unidentifiable noises in the sky. The experience of not knowing may fill the person with anxiety. He or she may be virtually paralyzed until the noise is explained.

In addition to the need for some interpretation of situations, human beings need consistency among their presently held beliefs. When new cognitions—perceptions and knowledge—are not compatible with those already held, the state of *cognitive dissonance* is said to exist. Cognitive dissonance influences behavior like any other basic need. When there is a conflict between present knowledge and new information, people may deny and distort truth to eliminate dissonance. Healthier personalities can tolerate ambiguity better than unhealthy personalities; they resolve cognitive dissonance in ways that do the most justice to logic and evidence (see Chapter 4).

MEANING AND PURPOSE

To ask about the purpose of human life is to raise an existential question, rather than one answerable through experiment or logic. Existential questions are answered by the way one lives. Every person's life, and the daily actions and decisions that comprise it, represent that person's answer to the question, "How, then, shall I live?"

These answers are almost by definition the embodiment of a person's religion. The chief function of religion is to provide ultimate answers to the questions that existence poses (see Chapter 15). In the absence of credible and lifegiving answers to the questions, "How shall I live, and why?" a person enters the state Frankl calls noögenic neurosis—a kind of despair or cynicism. Much depression and neurotic suffering stem from a failure to find meaning in life or to find new meaning when old goals have been consummated or have lost their inspiriting power.

Fromm regards "a frame of orientation and devotion" to be as essential to healthy personality as food. The process of self-actualizing, of which Maslow wrote, and the achievement of selfhood (in Jung's sense) appear to be impossible without such a religious orientation. Of course, it does not matter whether the religion is theistic, and it is possible to judge whether or not a person's objects and ways of worshiping are life-giving. But life for human beings is impossible without something to live *for*.

VARIED EXPERIENCE

The human needs varied stimulation, not just to avoid boredom but actually to preserve the ability to perceive and to act adequately. When a person is radically deprived of the customary variety of sights, sounds, smells, conversation, and so on—as happens in solitary confinement—he or she begins to feel strange and may show signs of deteriorating as a person. "Sensory deprivation" experiments show that when volunteer subjects are placed in a special room that is soundless, with their vision closed off by special goggles, and immersed in warm water kept at body temperature (to reduce the experience of tactile stimulation), some begin to hallucinate and go through other psychoticlike experiences. I have been in such an isolation chamber, and I found it tranquil and conducive to meditation. Variety in "stimulus input," then, may be regarded as a basic need, even though deprivation as extreme as that produced in the laboratory seldom occurs in everyday life.

The "evil twin" of varied experience is boredom—a form of dispiriting in style of life. Travel, risk-taking excitement, and simply trying something new in the way of clothes, reading, vacations, or challenges are the antitheses of boredom—varying one's experience of life. Even moonrises and sunsets can get monotonous for the jaded taste of the daily skywatcher. The healthy personality is also nurtured by meaningful variety.

Excitement has often been thought of as a need for the young only. We now recognize that it is part of the fullest of lives in all generations. The excitement experience is one of the most difficult to create. Not all excitements involve risk-taking, and excitements are quite individually determined. One person may be thrilled by the first parachute jump—another is equally excited about the first sighting of the sandhill crane.

SELECTION III:
THE BIG BEAR OF ARKANSAS[4]

A steamboat on the Mississippi frequently, in making her regular trips, carries between places varying from one to two thousand miles apart; and as these boats advertise to land passengers and freight at "all intermediate landings," the heterogeneous character of the passengers of one of these up-country boats can scarcely be imagined by one who has never seen it with his own eyes. Starting from New Orleans in one of these boats, you will find yourself associated with men from every State in the Union, and from every portion of the globe: and a man of observation need not lack for amusement or instruction in such a crowd, if he will take the trouble to read the great book of character so favorably opened before him. Here may be seen jostling together the wealthy Southern planter, and the pedlar of tin-ware from New England—the Northern merchant, and the Southern jockey—a venerable bishop, and a desperate gambler—the land speculator, and the honest farmer—professional men of all creeds and characters—Wolvereens, Suckers, Hoosiers, Buckeyes, and Corncrackers, beside a "plentiful sprinkling" of the half-horse and half-alligator species of men, who are peculiar to "old Mississippi," and who appear to gain a livelihood simply by going up and down the river. In the pursuit of pleasure or business, I have frequently found myself in such a crowd.

On one occasion, when in New Orleans, I had occasion to take a trip of a few miles up the Mississippi, and I hurried on board the well-known, "high-pressure-and-beat-every-thing" steamboat "Invincible," just as the last note of the last bell was sounding, and when the confusion and bustle that is natural to a boat's getting under way has subsided, I discovered that I was associated in as heterogeneous a crowd as was ever got together. As my trip was to be of a few hours duration only, I made no endeavors to become acquainted with my fellow passengers, most of whom would be together many days. Instead of this, I took out of my pocket the "latest paper," and more critically than usual examined its contents; my fellow passengers at the same time disposed of themselves in little groups. While I was thus busily employed in reading, and my companions were more busily still employed in discussing such subjects as suited their humors best, we were startled most unexpectedly by a loud Indian whoop, uttered in the "social hall," that part of the cabin fitted off for a bar; then was to be heard a loud crowing, which would not have continued to have interested us—such sounds being quite common in that *place of spirits*—had not the hero of these windy accomplishments stuck his head into the cabin and hallooed out, "Hurra for the big Bar of Arkansaw!" and then might be heard a confused hum of voices, unintelligible, save in such broken sentences as "horse," "screamer," "light-ning is slow," &c. As might have been expected, this continued interruption attracted the attention of every one in the cabin; all conversation dropped, and in the midst of this surprise the "big Bar" walked into the cabin, took a chair, put his feet on the stove, and looking back over his shoulder, passed the general and familiar salute of "Strangers, how are you?" He then expressed himself as much at home as if he had been at "the Forks of Cypress," and "prehaps a little more so." Some of the company at this familiarity looked a little angry, and some astonished, but in a moment every face was wreathed in smile. There was something about the intruder that won the heart on sight. He appeared to be a man enjoying perfect health and contentment—his eyes were as sparking as diamonds, and good natured to simplicity. Then his perfect confidence in himself was irresistibly droll. "Prehaps," said he, "gentlemen," running on without a person speaking, "prehaps you have been to New Orleans often; I never made *the first visit before,* and I don't intend to make another in a crow's life. I am thrown away in that ar place, and useless, that ar a fact. Some of the gentlemen thar called me *green*—well, prehaps I am, said I, *but I arn't so at home;* and if I aint off my trail much, the heads of them perlite chaps themselves wern't much the hardest, for according to my notion, they were *real know-nothings,* green as a pumpkin-vine—couldn't, in farming, I'll bet, raise a crop of turnips—and as for shooting, they'd miss a barn if the door was swinging, and that, too, with the best rifle in the country. And then they talked to me 'bout hunting, and laughed at my calling the principal game in Arkansaw poker, and high-low-jack. 'Prehaps,' said I, 'you prefer chickens and rolette;' at this they laughed harder than ever, and asked me if I lived in the woods, and didn't know what *game* was? At this I rather think I laughed. 'Yes,' I roared, and says, 'Strangers, if you'd asked me *how we got our meat* in Arkansaw, I'd a told you at once, and given you a list of varmints that would make a caravan, beginning with the bar and ending off with the cat; that's *meat* though, not game.' Game, indeed, that's what city folks call it, and with them it means chippen-birds and shite-pokes; maybe such trash live in my diggings, but I arn't noticed them yet—a bird any way is too trifling. I never did shoot at but one, and I'd never forgiven myself for that had it weighed less than forty pounds; I wouldn't draw a rifle on anything less than that; and when I meet with another wild turkey of the same weight I will drap him.''

''A wild turkey weighing forty pounds?'' exclaimed twenty voices in the cabin at once.

''Yes, strangers, and wasn't it a whopper? You see, the thing was so fat that he couldn't fly far, and when he fell out of the tree, after I shot him, on striking the ground he bust open behind, and the way the pound gobs of tallow rolled out of the opening was perfectly beautiful.''

''Where did all that happen?'' asked a cynical looking hoosier.

''Happen! hapened in Arkansaw; where else could it have happened, but in the creation State, the finishing up country; a State where the *sile* runs down to the centre of the 'arth, and government gives you a title to every inch of it. Then its airs, just breathe them, and they will make you snort like a horse. It's a State without a fault, it is.''

''Excepting mosquitoes,'' cried the hoosier.

''Well, stranger, except them, for it ar a fact that they are rather *enormous,* and do push themselves in somewhat troublesome. But, stranger, they never stick twice in the same place, and give them a fair chance for a few months, and you will get as much above noting them as an alligator. They can't hurt my feelings, for they lay under the skin; and I never knew but one case of injury resulting from them, and that was to a Yankee: and they take worse to foreigners anyhow than they do to natives. But the way they used that fellow up! first they punched him until he swelled up and busted, then he sup-per-a-ted, as the doctor called it, until he was as raw as beef; then he took the ager, owing to the warm weather, and finally he took a steamboat and left the country. He was the only man that ever took mosquitoes at heart that I know of. But mosquitoes is natur, and I never find fault with her; if they ar large, Arkansaw is large, her varmints ar large, her trees ar large, her rivers ar large, and a small mosquito would be of no more use in Arkansaw than preaching in a cane-brake.''

This knock-down argument in favor of big mosquitoes used the hoosier up, and the logician started on a new track, to explain how numerous bear were in his ''diggings,'' where he represented them to be ''about as plenty as blackberries, and a little plentifuler.''

Upon the utterance of this assertion, a timid little man near me enquired if the bear in Arkansaw ever attacked the settlers in numbers.

''No,'' said our hero, warming with the subject, ''No, stranger, for you see it ain't the natur of bar to go in droves, but the way they squander about in pairs and single ones is edifying. And then the way I hunt them—the old black rascals know the crack of my gun as well as they know a pig's squealing. They grow thin in our parts, it frightens them so, and they do take the noise dreadfully, poor things. That gun of mine is a perfect *epidemic among bar*—if not watched closely, it will go off as quick on a warm scent as my dog Bowie-knife will; and then that dog, whew! why the fellow thinks that the world is full of bar, he finds them so easy. It's lucky he don't talk as well as think, for with his natural modesty, if he should suddenly learn how much he is acknowledged to be ahead of all other dogs in the universe, he would be astonished to death in two minutes. Strangers, that dog knows a bar's way as well as a horse-jockey knows a woman's; he always barks at the right time—bites at the exact place—and whips without getting a scratch. I never could tell whether he was made expressly to hunt bar, or whether bar was made expressly for him to hunt; any way, I believe they were ordained to go together as naturally as Squire Jones says a man and woman is, when he moralizes in marrying a couple. In fact, Jones once said, said he, 'Marriage according to law is a civil contract of divine origin, it's common to all countries as well as Arkansaw, and people take to it as naturally as Jim Doggett's Bowie-knife takes to bar.'"

"What season of the year do your hunts take place?" enquired a gentlemanly foreigner, who, from some peculiarities of his baggage, I suspected to be an Englishman, on some hunting expedition, probably, at the foot of the Rocky Mountains.

"The season for bar hunting, stranger," said the man of Arkansaw, "is generally all the year round, and the hunts take place about as regular. I read in history that varmints have their fat season, and their lean season. That is not the case in Arkansaw, feeding as they do upon the *spontenacious* productions of the sile, they have one continued fat season the year round—though in winter things in this way is rather more greasy than in summer, I must admit. For that reason bar with us run in warm weather, but in winter they only waddle. Fat, fat! it's an enemy to speed—it tames everything that has plenty of it. I have seen wild turkies, from its influence, as gentle as chickens. Run a bar in this fat condition, and the way it improves the critter for eating is amazing; it sort of mixes the ile up with the meat until you can't tell t'other from which. I've done this often. I recollect one perty morning in particular, of putting an old he fellow on the stretch, and considering the weight he carried, he run well. But the dogs soon tired him down, and when I came up with him wasn't he in a beautiful sweat—I might say fever; and then to see his tongue sticking out of his mouth a feet, and his sides sinking and opening like a bellows, and his cheeks so fat he couldn't look cross. In this fix I blazed at him, and pitch me naked into a briar patch if the steam didn't come out of the bullet hole ten foot in a straight line. The fellow, I reckon, was made on the high-pressure system, and the lead sort of bust his biler."

"That column of steam was rather curious, or else the bear must have been *warm*," observed the foreigner with a laugh.

"Stranger, as you observe, that bar was WARM, and the blowing off of the steam show'd it, and also how hard the varmint had been run. I have no doubt if he had kept on two miles farther his insides would have been stewed; and I expect to meet with a varmint yet of extra bottom, who will run himself into a skin full of bar's-grease: it is possible, much onlikelier things have happened."

"Where abouts are these bear so abundant?" enquired the foreigner, with increasing interest.

"Why, stranger, they inhabit the neighborhood of my settlement, one of the prettiest places on Old Mississippi—a perfect location, and no mistake; a place that had some defects until the river made the 'cut-off' at 'Shirt-tail bend,' and that remedied the evil, as it brought my cabin on the edge of the river—a great advantage in wet weather, I assure you, as you can now roll a barrel of whiskey into my yard in high water, from a boat, as easy as falling off a log; it's a great improvement, as toting it by land in a jug, as I used to do, *evaporated* it too fast, and it became expensive. Just stop with me, stranger, a month or two, or a year if you like, and you will appreciate my place. I can give you plenty to eat, for beside hog and hominy, you can have bar ham, and bar sausages, and a mattrass of bar-skins to sleep on, and a wildcat-skin, pulled off hull, stuffed with cornshucks for a pillow. That bed would put you to sleep if you had the rheumatics in every joint in your body. I call that ar bed a *quietus*. Then look at my land, the government ain't got another such a piece to dispose of. Such timber, and such bottom land, why you can't preserve anything natural you plant in it, unless you pick it young, things thar will grow out of shape so quick. I once planted in those diggings a few potatoes and beets, they took a fine start, and after that an ox team couldn't have kept them from growing. About that time I went off to old Kentuck on bisiness, and did not hear from them things in three months, when I accidentally stumbled on a fellow who had stopped at my place, with an idea of buying me out. 'How did you like things?' said I. 'Pretty well,' said he; 'the cabin is convenient, and the timber land is good, but that bottom land ain't worth the first red cent.' 'Why?' said I. ' 'Cause,' said he, ' 'Cause what?' said I. ' 'Cause it's full of cedar stumps and Indian mounds,' said he, 'and *it can't be cleared*.' 'Lord,' said I, 'them ar "cedar stumps" is beets, and them ar "Indian mounds" ar tater hills,'—as I expected the crop was overgrown and useless; the sile is too rich, *and planting in Arkansaw is dangerous*. I had a good sized sow killed in that same bottom land; the old thief stole an ear of corn, and took it down where she slept at night to eat; well, she left a grain or two on the ground, and lay down on them; before morning the corn shot up, and the percussion killed her dead. I don't plant any more; natur intended Arkansaw for a hunting ground, and I go according to natur."

The questioner, who thus elicited the description of our hero's settlement, seemed to be perfectly satisfied, and said no more; but the "big bar of Arkansaw" rambled on from one thing to another with a volubility perfectly astonishing, occasionally disputing with those around him, particularly with a "live sucker" from Illinois, who had the daring to say that our Arkansaw friend's stories "smelt rather tall."

In this manner the evening was spent, but conscious that my own association with so singular a personage would probably end before morning, I asked him if he would not give me a description of some particular bear hunt—adding that I took great interest in such things, though I was no sportsman. The desire seemed to please him, and he squared himself round towards me, saying, that he could give me an idea of a bar hunt that was never beat in this world, or in any other. His manner was so singular, that half of his story consisted in his excellent way of telling it, the great peculiarity of which was, the happy manner he had of emphasizing the prominent parts of his conversation. As near as I can recollect, I have italicized them, and given the story in his own words.

"Stranger," said he, "in bar hunts *I am numerous*, and which particular one as you say I shall tell puzzles me. There was the old she devil I shot at the hurricane last fall—then there was the old hog thief I popped over at the Bloody Crossing; and then—Yes. I have it, I will give you an idea of a hunt, in which the greatest bar was killed that ever lived, *non excepted*; about an old fellow that I hunted, more or less, for two or three years, and if that ain't a *particular bar hunt*, I ain't got one to tell. But in the first place, stranger, let me say, I am pleased with you, because you ain't ashamed to gain information by asking, and listening, and that's what I say to Countess's pups every day when I'm home—and I have got great hopes of them ar pups, because they are continually *nosing* about, and though they stick it sometimes in the wrong place, they gain experience anyhow, and may learn something useful to boot. Well, as I was saying about this big bar, you see when I and some more first settled in our region, we were drivin to hunting naturally; we soon liked it, and after that we found it an easy matter to make the thing our business. One old chap who had pioneered 'afore us, gave us to understand that we had settled in the right place. He dwelt upon its merits until it was affecting, and showed us, to prove his assertions, more marks on the sassafras trees than I ever saw on a tavern door 'lection time. 'Who keeps that ar reckoning?' said I. 'The bar,' said he. 'What for?' said I. 'Can't tell,' said he, 'but so it is, the bar bite the bark and wood too, at the highest point from the ground they can reach, and you can tell by the marks,' said he, 'the length of the bar to an inch.' 'Enough,' said I, 'I've learned something here a'ready, and I'll put it in practice.' Well, stranger, just one month from that time I killed a bar, and told its exact length before I measured it by those very marks—and when I did that I swelled up considerable—I've been a prouder man ever since. So I went on, larning something every day, until I was reckoned a buster, and allowed to be decidedly the best bar hunter in my district; and that is a reputation as much harder to earn than to be reckoned first man in Congress, as an iron rod is harder than a toad-stool. Did the varmints grow over cunning, by being fooled with by green-horn hunters, and by this means get troublesome, they send for me as a matter of course, and thus I do my own hunting, and most of my neighbors'. I walk into the varmints though, and it has become about as much the same to me as drinking. It is told in two sentences—a bar is started, and he is killed. The thing is somewhat monotonous now—I know just how much they will run, where they will tire, how much they will growl, and what a thundering time I will have in getting them home. I could give you this history of the chase with all the particulars at the commencement, I know the signs so well. *Stranger, I'm certain.* Once I met with a match, though, and I will tell you about it, for a common hunt would not be worth relating.

"On a fine fall day, long time ago, I was trailing about for bar, and what should I see but fresh marks on the sassafras trees, about eight inches above any in the forests that I knew of. Says I, them marks is a hoax, or it indicates the d——t bar that was ever grown. In fact, stranger, I couldn't believe it was real, and I went on. Again I saw the same marks, at the same height, and *I knew the thing lived.* That conviction came home to my soul like an earthquake. Says I, here is something a-purpose for me—that bar is mine, or I give up the hunting business. The very next morning what should I see but a number of buzzards hovering over my corn-field. The rascal has been there, said I, for that sign is certain; and, sure enough, on examining, I found the bones of what had been as beautiful a hog the day before, as was ever raised by a Buck-eye. Then I tracked the critter out of the field to the woods, and all the marks he left behind, showed me that he was *the Bar.*

"Well, stranger, the first fair chase I ever had with that big critter, I saw him no less than three distinct times at a distance; the dogs run him over eighteen miles and broke down; my horse gave out, and I was as nearly used up as a man can be, made on *my* principle, *which is patent.* Before this adventure, such things were unknown to me as possible; but, strange as it was, that bar got me used to it, before I was done with him,—for he got so at last, that he would leave me on a long chase *quite easy.* How he did it, I never could understand. That a bar runs at all, is puzzling; but how this one could tire down and bust up a pack of hounds and a horse, that were used to overhauling every thing they started after in no time, was past my understanding. Well, stranger, that bar finally got so sassy, that he used to help himself to a hog off my premises whenever he wanted one—the buzzards followed after what he left, and so between *bar and buzzard,* I rather think I was *out of pork.* Well, missing that bar so often, took hold of my vitals, and I wasted away. The thing had been carried too far, and it reduced me in flesh faster than an ager. I would see that bar in every thing I did—*he hunted me,* and that, too, like a devil, which I began to think he was. While in this fix, I made preparations to give him a last brush, and be done with it. Having completed every thing to my satisfaction, I started at sun-rise, and to my great joy, I discovered from the way the dogs run, that they were near him—finding his trail was nothing, for that had become as plain to the pack as a turnpike-road. On we went, and coming to an open country, what should I see but the bar very leisurely ascending a hill, and the dogs close at his heels, either a match for him this time in speed, or else he did not care to get out of their way—I don't know which. But, wasn't he a beauty though? I loved him like a brother. On he went, until coming to a tree, the limbs of which formed a crotch about six feet from the ground—into this crotch he got and seated himself—the dogs yelling all around it—and there he sat eyeing them, as quiet as a pond in low water. A green-horn friend of mine, in company, reached shooting distance before me, and blazed away, hitting the critter in the centre of his forehead. The bar shook his head as the ball struck it, and then he walked down from that tree as gently as a lady would from a carriage. 'Twas a beautiful sight to see him do that—he was in such a rage, that he seemed to be as little afraid of the dogs, as if they had been sucking pigs; and the dogs warn't slow in making a ring around him at a respectful distance, I tell you; even Bowie-knife himself stood off. Then the way his eyes flashed—why the fire of them would have singed a cat's hair; in fact, that bar was in a *wrath all over*. Only one pup came near him, and he was brushed out so totally with the bar's left paw, that he entirely disappeared; and that made the old dogs more cautious still. In the mean time, I came up, and taking deliberate aim as a man should do, at his side, just back of his foreleg, *if my gun did not snap*, call me a coward, and I won't take it personal. Yes, stranger, *it snapped*, and I could not find a cap about my person. While in this predicament, I turned round to my fool friend—says I, 'Bill,' says I, 'you're an ass—you're a fool—you might as well have tried to kill that bar by barking the tree under his belly, as to have done it by hitting him in the head. Your shot has made a tiger of him, and blast me, if a dog gets killed or wounded when they come to blows, I will stick my knife into your liver. I will—' my wrath was up. I had lost my caps, my gun had snapped, the fellow with me had fired at the bar's head, and I expected every moment to see him close in with the dogs, and kill a dozen of them at least. In this thing I was mistaken, for the bar leaped over the ring formed by the dogs, and giving a fierce growl, was off—the pack of course in full cry after him. The run this time was short, for coming to the edge of a lake the varmint jumped in, and swam to a little island in the lake, which it reached just a moment before the dogs. I'll have him now, said I, for I had found my caps in the *lining of my coat*—so, rolling a log into the lake, I paddled myself across to the island, just as the dogs had cornered the bar in a thicket. I rushed up and fired—at the same time the critter leaped over the dogs and came within three feet of me, running like mad; he jumped into the lake, and tried to mount the log I had just deserted, but every time he got half his body on it, it would roll over and send him under; the dogs, too, got around him, and pulled him about, and finally Bowie-knife clenched with him, and they sunk into the lake together. Stranger, about this time I was excited, and I stripped off my coat, drew my knife, and intended to have taken a part with Bowie-knife myself when the bar rose to the surface. But the varmint staid under—Bowie-knife came up alone, more dead than alive, and with the pack came ashore. Thank God, said I, the old villain has got his deserts at last. Determined to have the body, I cut a grape-vine for a rope, and dove down where I could see the bar in the water, fastened my queer rope to his leg, and fished him, with great difficulty, ashore. Stranger, may I be chawed to death by young alligators, if the thing I looked at wasn't a *she bar, and not the old critter after all*. The way matters got mixed on that island was unaccountably curious, and thinking of it made me more than ever convinced that I was hunting the devil himself. I went home that night and took to my bed— the thing was killing me. The entire team of Arkansaw in bar-hunting, acknowledged himself used up, and the fact sunk into my feelings like a snagged boat will in the Mississippi. I grew as cross as a bar with two cubs and a sore tail. The thing got out 'mong my neighbors, and I was asked how come on that individ-u-al that never lost a bar when once started? and if that same individ-u-al didn't wear telescopes when he turned a she bar, of ordinary size, into an old he one, a little larger than a horse? Prehaps, said I, friends—getting wrathy—prehaps you want to call somebody a liar. Oh, no, said they, we only heard such things as being *rather common* of late, but we don't believe one word of it; oh, no—and then they would ride off and laugh like so many hyenas over a dead nigger. It was too much, and I determined to catch that bar, go to Texas, or die—and I made my preparations accordin'. I had the pack shut up and rested. I took my rifle to pieces, and iled it. I put caps in every pocket about my person, *for fear of the lining*. I then told my neighbors that on Monday morning—naming the day—I would start THAT BAR, and bring him home with me, or they might divide my settlement among them, the owner having disappeared. Well, stranger, on the morning previous to the great day of my hunting expedition, I went into the woods near my house, taking my gun and bowie-knife along, just *from habit*, and there sitting down also from habit, what should I see, getting over my fence, but *the bar*! Yes, the old varmint was within a hundred yards of me, and the way he walked *over that fence*—stranger, he loomed up like a *black mist*, he seemed so large, and he walked right towards me. I raised myself, took deliberate aim, and fired. Instantly the varmint wheeled, gave a yell, and *walked through the fence* like a falling tree would through a cobweb. I started after, but was tripped up by my inexpressibles, which either from habit, or the excitement of the moment, were about my heels, and before I had really gathered myself up, I heard the old varmint groaning in a thicket near by, like a thousand sinners, and by the time I reached him he was a corpse. Stranger, it took five niggers and myself to put that carcase on a mule's back, and old long ears waddled under his load as if he was foundered in every leg of his body, and with a common whopper of a bar, he would have trotted off, and enjoyed himself. 'Twould astonish you to know how big he was—I made a *bed spread of his skin,* and the way it used to cover my bar mattrass, and leave several feet on each side to tuck up, would have delighted you. It was in fact a creation bar, and if it had lived in Sampson's time, and had met him, in a fair fight, it would have licked him in the twinkling of a dice-box. But, stranger, I never liked the way I hunted him, *and missed him*. There is something curious about it, I could never understand— and I never was satisfied at his giving in so *easy at the last*. Prehaps, he had heard of my preparations to hunt him the next day, so he jist come in, like Capt. Scott's coon, to save his wind to grunt with in dying; but that ain't likely. My private opinion is, that that bar was an *unhuntable bar, and died when his time come.*"

When the story was ended, our hero sat some minutes with his auditors in a grave silence; I saw that there was a mystery to him connected with the bear whose death he had just related, that had evidently made a strong impression on his mind. It was also evident that there was some superstitious awe connected with the affair—a feeling common with all "children of the wood," when they meet with any thing out of their every day experience. He was the first one, however, to break the silence, and jumping up he asked all present to "liquor" before going to bed—a thing which he did, with a number of companions, evidently to his heart's content.

Long before day, I was put ashore at my place of destination, and I can only follow with the reader, in imagination, our Arkansas friend, in his adventures at the "Forks of Cypress" on the Mississippi.

NOTES

1. **Milan Fiske,** "Snake Bit! A Personal Account of Being Bitten by a Rattler," *The Conservationist,* 36, No. 1, July–Aug. 1981, pp. 30–31.

2. **William Gotwold** and **Gale Golden,** *Sexuality: The Human Experience* (New York: Macmillan, 1981). pp. 155–167.

3. **Sidney M. Jourard** and **Ted Landsman,** *Healthy Personality,* 4th ed. (New York: Macmillan, 1980), pp. 92–98.

4. **Thomas Thorpe,** "The Big Bear of Arkansas," in *Anthology of American Literature,* ed. George McMichael, I, 2nd ed. (New York: Macmillan, 1980), pp. 608–616. Originally published in *The Spirit of the Times,* XI, 27 Mar. 1841, pp. 43–44.

Ten

STEPS IN TEXTBOOK STUDY

In previous chapters, you learned how to read efficiently and study shorter selections and chapters. In the following, you will build on these skills and learn how to study entire textbooks efficiently.

There are many proven techniques for studying college texts. Educators shorten the names for these techniques by letting each letter stand for one step in the technique. PQRST (preview, question, read, summarize, test), SQ3R (survey, question, read, recite, review), PQ4R (preview, question, read, recite, review, reflect) are some of the more popular techniques. The approach that follows incorporates all the best parts of these approaches.

Select one of your textbooks to use for the rest of this chapter.

KNOWING YOUR TEXTBOOK

Before you begin to study any textbook, you should take a few minutes and get to know it better. Pick it up and look at it. Get a feel for it. Flip through the pages from front to back and back to front. You and your textbook will probably be together for a long time—better as friends than as enemies.

ACTIVITY I

Use one of your textbooks to answer these questions.

1. What is the title? _____

_____

2. Who wrote the text? _____

_____

3. What is the copyright date? _____

4. Where is the table of contents? _____

5. Where is the index? _____

6. Where is the glossary? _____

7. Read the preface and/or introduction. What does the preface or introduction tell you

about the book? _____

_____

_____

8. What does your instructor expect you to learn from this book? _____

_____

AN EFFECTIVE TEXTBOOK STUDY TECHNIQUE

You can markedly increase your textbook study skills by deliberately applying the strategy given below.

Step 1: Preview, Survey, Overview

Preview the entire chapter or assignment you are to read for five minutes. Complete the entire assignment in five minutes! If you cannot preview the chapter in this time, break it into segments. Use the preview techniques discussed earlier.

Step 2: Prereading Questions and Key Ideas

Take five or ten minutes to write questions in your notebook that you expect to have answered in this selection. You want to list the key ideas that you will encounter while reading. This important step sets your purpose for reading. You should formulate these prereading questions by turning each of the following into a question:

1. Chapter title.
2. Headings and subheadings.
3. Review questions.

and where appropriate:

4. Highlighted words.
5. Graphs, charts, and illustrations.
6. The first and last sentences of paragraphs.

Step 3: Read

Carefully read the parts of the chapter that answer your prereading questions. Concentrate on getting the main ideas in these sections. Attach details to these main ideas when the details answer your prereading questions. Do not underline or take notes now. You should allow about thirty minutes to read the assignment and answer your prereading questions.

About 45 minutes have elapsed and you have "read" the selection three times. This is very efficient reading indeed.

Step 4: Answer Questions, Recite, and Recall

Close your eyes and think about what you have read. Ask yourself and answer each prereading question. You will probably have to reread some sections of the text to clarify what you did not understand.

Begin your study guide by briefly writing the answers to your prereading questions. You are restating these important ideas in your own words and taking notes on the reading. Follow these steps;

1. Restate main ideas and important details in your own words in your notebook.
2. Next to each highlighted word, write a brief definition and possibly an example.
3. Actively remember what you have written down.
4. Write your notes crisply, using phrases and words. Do not use complete sentences.
5. Concentrate on the relationship among the main ideas and between main ideas and details.

This step often takes 30 minutes. You have read an assignment four times in a little over an hour—and you have taken notes! Effective studying at this rate will guarantee that all your work can be successfully completed during a term.

Step 5: Review, Reflect, and Test

Once you have finished all sections of a reading assignment, you must review what you have read and learned. This immediate five- to ten-minute review is a key to remembering.

After a few days, go back to your notebook study guide and quiz yourself. Reread the sections you have forgotten or still do not understand. The more effectively you read, the less you will have to reread.

CHECKLIST: TEXTBOOK STUDY

Follow these steps as you study your textbook:

1. Preview, survey, and overview.
2. Write prereading questions and key ideas.
3. Read.
4. Answer questions, recite, and recall.
5. Review, reflect, and test.

As you use this study technique it will become more and more familiar until it is almost second nature. You can be assured that the continued, deliberate use of this technique will dramatically improve your reading and studying efficiency.

ACTIVITY II

A text chapter titled "Varieties of Consciousness" appears on the following pages. Use the study technique to read this selection.

1. Preview the selection.
2. Turn to the study guide on the page following the reading. This study guide supplies your prereading questions and vocabulary. In the exercises that follow and in your own reading you will supply this information.
3. Read the selection with the study guide in mind.
4. Complete and review the study guide.
5. Review the material immediately and again tomorrow.

VARIETIES OF CONSCIOUSNESS[1]

THE PARADOXES OF REM SLEEP

One curious fact abut REM sleep is that in some respects it seems similar to being awake. The EEG pattern during REM sleep looks very much like that of someone who is awake, as do other physiological patterns: heartbeat, breathing rate, and blood pressure are irregular and vary enormously, and there is evidence of sexual arousal. Normally this would be the total pattern of a person who is not only awake, but excited—and yet the person is sound asleep. To add to the paradox, certain medical catastrophes seem to occur during REM sleep, including heart attacks and acute worsening of duodenal ulcers and emphysema (Snyder, 1965; Armstrong et al., 1965; Trask and Cree, 1962).

Other measures, however, indicate that REM is a deeper stage of sleep than the other stages. During REM sleep, people are very difficult to awaken and do not respond to touch or sound as readily as during stages 2 and 3. In addition, while all the erratic physiological activity mentioned above is going on, virtually all the major body muscles lose their tone and become flaccid (limp). For these reasons REM is sometimes called "paradoxical sleep": people seem to be awake and yet deeply asleep at the same time.

The loss of muscle tone makes us temporarily paralyzed during REM sleep, whereas in stage 4 the muscles still have some tone. The marked drop in muscle tension levels is the surest indicator of REM sleep. Michael Jouvet (1967) has shown that stimulation of a specific part of the brain causes this loss of motor control. When he removed this small part of the brain in cats, REM sleep still occurred, but during it the cats no longer lay still. Instead, they jumped up and moved about—asleep all the while. The cats' behavior suggests that if our muscles weren't paralyzed during REM, our bodies might act out our dreams.

DO WE NEED REM SLEEP?

Suspecting that dreams might in some way be essential to our psychological well-being, Dement (1974) deprived sleepers of REM sleep over a series of nights. Whenever he saw the beginning of a REM period, he would awaken the sleeper. He found that it became harder and harder to arouse the sleeper with the onset of each subsequent REM stage, and that the longer he denied REM, the more frequent its appearance became. When, on the fifth night, he let the sleeper go into REM without interruption, he found a "REM rebound" effect: the total time spent in REM doubled over the person's normal level.

Although we apparently have a need for REM sleep, judging from the fact that our bodies automatically compensate for a loss of it, what REM sleep actually does for us is not clear. Any deprivation of sleep—whether of REM or other sleep stages—may make a person somewhat irritable or tired. But loss of our dream time seems to be no more psychologically troubling than loss of other kinds of sleep. Still REM sleep may be of special value. Some evidence suggests that REM sleep may be a time when the brain adapts to life experiences. In one study, for example, some medical students wore goggles with distorting lenses for several days. The students slept at night in the laboratory. While they were adapting to the weird lenses, they showed a greater than usual amount of REM sleep; but once they had become accustomed to the lenses, REM sleep dropped back to normal (Luce, 1971).

Indirect evidence that REM sleep helps maintain the responsiveness of the brain comes from the fact that REM time steadily lessens as people age. Newborns spend about half their sleep time in REM, infants under two years 30 to 40 percent, adolescents and adults about 20 to 25 percent, and old people less

Figure 14–1
The amount of time the average person spends each day in three states: awake, non-REM sleep, and REM (dreaming) sleep, as it changes over the years. In order to show the changes more clearly, the time intervals shown here are wider for younger people than for older people. As people get older, they tend to need less sleep. (Adapted from Hartman, 1967)

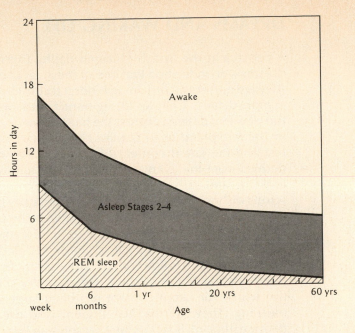

than 5 percent. The average amount of time spent awake and asleep as a function of age is shown in Figure 14.1; some researchers suggest that dreams offer the brain an internal source of mental stimulation, which enhances the growth and maintenance of neural tissue (Anders and Roffwarg, 1972). Such stimulation may allow key sensory and motor areas to prepare to handle the enormous rush of stimulation from the outside environment during waking. The need for such "rehearsal" time is greatest in the newborn and decreases with age, just as does REM time (Roffwarg, Muzio, and Dement, 1966).

THE CONTENT OF DREAMS

One researcher estimates that by age seventy the average person will have had about 150,000 dreams (Snyder, 1970). Does this mean 150,000 fascinating adventures? Not at all. We have selective recall for our dreams, remembering the more exciting ones and forgetting the rest. When people are awakened randomly during REM sleep and asked what they had just been dreaming, the reports generally are commonplace, even dull (Hall and Van de Castle, 1966). The dreams we remember and talk about "are more coherent, sexier, and generally more interesting" than those collected in systematic research (Webb, 1975, p. 140). Even so, psychologists (especially psychoanalysts) find great symbolic meaning in the most prosaic of dreams. From where does the stuff of dreams come?

DREAMS AND EXTERNAL STIMULI

The realization that the bell persistently ringing in your dream is really your alarm clock is a fairly common occurrence. Some of the content of a dream is simply incorporated from what is happening near the sleeping person—events such as sounds, temperature changes, or touches. Dement and Wolpert (1958) sprayed water on the faces of some sleep-lab volunteers and left a control group of volunteers undisturbed. Those who were sprayed reported more dreams about water than did those who were left dry. This incorporation of environmental stimuli into dreams may serve to "protect" sleep to some extent (Bradley and Meddis, 1974).

DREAMS AND WAKING LIFE

A papyrus in the British Museum dating from 1350 B.C. is about interpreting dreams—an indication that one of the most ancient beliefs about dreams is that they are portents, containing hidden truths about our lives. As we shall discuss in more detail in Chapter 18, Sigmund Freud formulated for modern psychology the view that dreams express the hidden needs and desires of the subconscious. In *The Interpretation of Dreams* (1900), Freud distinguished between the manifest and the latent content of a dream. The *manifest content* of a dream is derived from the events of the day, sensations during sleep (such as bladder tension), and early memories. *The latent content* is a reflection of our unconscious wishes, primarily from unresolved early psychosexual conflicts. Through "dream work," the manifest content veils the unconscious wishes in symbolic images that are more acceptable to the dreamer.

Over the years, psychoanalysts have modified Freud's theory of dreams; only his most ardent followers still adhere strictly to Freud's method of dream interpretation. Among others (for example, Ullman, 1962, and Foulkes, 1964), the search for latent content has been largely abandoned in favor of direct meaning. They say that the student who dreams about writing an exam in disappearing ink is not trying to resolve an infantile sexual conflict but is simply worried about his or her upcoming final. The dream is not saying one thing and meaning another.

STUDY GUIDE: "VARIETIES OF CONSCIOUSNESS" PREREADING QUESTIONS

From the title:

1. What are the varieties of consciousness? _____

_____

From the topic headings and subheadings:

2. What are the paradoxes of REM sleep? _____

_____

_____

3. Why do we need REM sleep? _____

_____

_____

4. What is the content of dreams? _____

_____

_____

5. How are dreams and external stimuli related? _____

_____

_____

6. How are dreams related to waking life? _____

_____

_____

From graphic aids:

7. What does the graph tell about the relationship between age and sleep? _____

_____

_____

8. Why do different people of different ages need different amounts of sleep? _____

_____

_____

From highlighted words; define:

REM sleep _____

_____

Deeper stage of sleep _____

_____

EEG pattern _____

_____

External stimuli _____

_____

Manifest content _____

_____

Latent content _____

_____

PROJECT

The following selection is a complete chapter taken from a college textbook on marketing. The text is used in many business classes. Using the techniques taught to you in this chapter, efficiently read this selection.

Remember to follow these steps:

1. Preview, survey, and overview.
2. Write prereading questions and key ideas in your notebook.
3. Read.
4. Answer your questions, recite, and recall.
5. Review, reflect, and self-test.

Use your notebook to write important vocabulary, questions to read for, and review and rereading notes.

CONSUMER DEMOGRAPHICS²

CHAPTER OBJECTIVES

1. To show the importance and scope of consumer analysis
2. To define and enumerate important demographics in the United States: population size, gender, and age; location, housing, and mobility of the population; income and expenditures of the population; occupations and education of the population; and marital status of the population
3. To examine trends and future projections of important demographics and study their marketing implications
4. To describe several applications of consumer demographics and consider the limitations of demographics

Recently, A. C. Nielsen conducted a marketing research study to determine the characteristics of households consuming diet products. The study was important because of the increase in sales of dietary products. For example, diet soft drink sales now account for almost 20 per cent of total soft drink sales. Nielsen found that the per cent of dieters increased with income and education, and that women dieted substantially more than men.[1]

By studying consumers, a firm can determine its most appropriate audience and the combination of marketing factors that will satisfy it.

By understanding consumers, a firm is able to ascertain the most appropriate audience to which to appeal and the combination of marketing factors that will satisfy this audience. Without consumer analysis, a firm may identify the wrong market, aim at too small a segment of the market, not perceive differences among consumer groups, produce an undesirable product or service, sell through the wrong outlets, or otherwise fail to attract and keep customers. With the apparent rise in the popularity of diet soft drinks, how would a company fare with only regular drinks to offer? Or, how successful would a marketing campaign clearly aimed at a male audience be in light of Nielsen's findings?

CONSUMER ANALYSIS: IMPORTANCE AND SCOPE

As noted in Chapters 1 and 2, the central focus of marketing is the consumer. In order to develop appropriate marketing plans, it is necessary to determine the characteristics and needs of consumers, the social and psychological factors affecting consumers, and the process consumers go through when making a purchase.

The scope of consumer analysis includes the study of who buys, what they buy, why they buy, how they buy, when they buy, where they buy, and how often they buy.[2] Figure 4–1 shows the scope of consumer analysis for different types of products and services.

In Chapters 4 through 7, the basic elements necessary for understanding and responding to consumers are detailed. Chapters 4 and 5 examine the demographics, social and psychological characteristics, and the decision process used by final consumers. *Final consumers* purchase products and services for personal, family, or household use. Chapter 6 centers on the characteristics and behavior of organizational consumers. *Organizational consumers* purchase products and services for further production, usage in operating the organization, or resale to other consumers. Chapter 7 explains how to develop a target

Final consumers purchase for personal, family, or household use; *organizational consumers* purchase for further production, usage in operating the organization, or resale to other consumers.

---

[1]"Who's Dieting and Why?" *The Nielsen Researcher* (Number 4, 1978), pp. 16–25.
[2]Adapted from Leon G. Schiffman and Leslie Lazar Kanuk, *Consumer Behavior* (Englewood Cliffs, N.J.: Prentice-Hall, 1978), p. 4.

Who	What	Why	How	When	Where	How Often
Middle-aged male	Hair cut	Messy hair	Use regular barber or hair stylist	Saturday morning	Regular hair salon	Every two months
Young female college graduate	Suit	Job interview	Read newspaper for sale, select a conservative suit	Next day	Store with lowest price and fastest alterations	Once per year
Husband	Watch	Gift	Browse through a store	In two weeks	Local jeweler	Once
College freshman	College textbook	Required for course	Obtain book title from course syllabus	At the beginning of the term	College bookstore	Every term
Working woman, with husband and two children	Automobile	Transportation and status	Talk to friends, read advertisements, test drive alternatives, evaluate alternatives	In two months	Nearby authorized dealer	Every four years
Hospital	Hospital beds	Equipment replacement	Review catalogs, talk to salespeople, determine specifications, evaluate alternatives	In three months	Regular supplier	Every seven years

Figure 4–1
The Scope of Consumer Analysis

market and the generation and uses of sales forecasts. By developing a profile of consumer characteristics, needs, and behavior patterns, an individual marketer is better able to satisfy the demands of consumers and remain ahead of the competition.

DEMOGRAPHICS DEFINED AND ENUMERATED[3]

Consumer demographics are easily identifiable and measurable statistics that describe population.

Consumer demographics are statistics that are used to describe the population. They are easy to identify, collect, measure, and analyze. The demographics discussed in this chapter are population size, gender, and age; location, housing, and mobility; income and expenditures; occupations and education; and marital status.

In combination, demographics can establish consumer profiles that may present attractive market opportunities. For example, the potential market for a unisex hair salon may be composed of young, college-educated, urban single people. The potential market for instant soup may be comprised of young, white-collar working women in a northern climate. Figure 4–2 shows the

Consumer profiles combine demographics in ways that are useful to marketers.

Figure 4–2
Factors Determining a Consumer's Demographic Profile

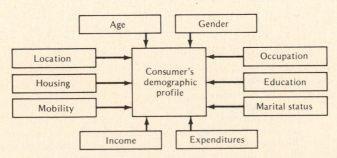

---

[3]Two good discussions of demographics in the 1980s are Walter Guzzardi, Jr., "Demography's Good News for the Eighties," *Fortune* (November 5, 1979), pp. 92–106 and "Population Changes That Help for a While," *Business Week* (September 3, 1979), pp. 180–187.

individual factors that determine a consumer demographic profile for a single consumer. By summing individual profiles, the firm can determine the size of a potential consumer market.

POPULATION SIZE, GENDER, AND AGE

The United States has more than 221 million people, and will contain 260 million by the year 2000. Nonetheless, the *rate* of population growth has slowed greatly since the 1950s.

Selected characteristics of the U.S. population, for the period 1960–2000, are shown in Table 4–1. As of 1980, the population of the United States was more than 221 million people; this is projected to grow to 260 million by the year 2000. Despite the increase in the number of people, the rate of population growth has slowed considerably since the decade of the 1950s. Between 1980 and 2000, population will increase by less than 1 per cent each year.

The annual number of births peaked at 4.3 million in 1957; the number exceeded 4 million per year, from 1954 to 1964. By the mid-1970s, the annual number of births fell to under 3.2 million. Beginning in 1977 the annual number of births rose again. During the 1980s and early 1990s, the annual number of births is expected to surpass 3.5 million. A large proportion of the births in the 1980s will be first-borns. During the 1960s, 25 per cent of all babies were first-born. In 1980, first-borns were estimated to be 40 per cent of all births.

Females comprise 51.3 per cent of the population and males comprise 48.7 per cent.

In 1980, females comprised 51.3 per cent of the population, almost 114 million people, and males represented 48.7 per cent of the population, almost 108 million people. The life expectancy for females born in 1980 is 77.3 years; for males born in 1980, it is 69.4 years. The median age of the population reached a low point of 27.9 years in 1970. The median age is expected to rise to 35.5 years by the year 2000.

Population age changes include the shrinkage of the under 5 and five to thirteen age groups and the enlargement of the thirty-five to forty-four, forty-five to fifty-four, and sixty-five-and-over age groups.

Figure 4–3 shows the changing age distribution in the population of the United States from 1960–2000. The under five and five through thirteen age groups are becoming a much smaller percentage of the overall population. In 1960 these two groups accounted for 29.5 per cent of the population. In 2000 they will represent 20.4 per cent. On the other end of the age scale, the thirty-five to forty-four, forty-five to fifty-four, and sixty-five-and-over age groups are projected to have large growth during the last part of this century.

TABLE 4–1: SELECTED CHARACTERISTICS OF U.S. POPULATION, 1960–2000

Characteristic	1960	1970	1980	1990	2000
Population size	180,671,000	204,878,000	221,651,000	243,004,000	259,869,000
Rate of population increase over prior decade	18.5%	13.4%	8.2%	9.6%	6.9%
Annual number of births	4,257,850	3,731,386[a]	3,575,000	3,868,000[b]	3,676,000
Per cent males	—	48.7	48.7	48.7	48.6
Per cent females	—	51.3	51.3	51.3	51.4
Life expectancy of males	66.6	67.1	69.4[c]	69.7[c]	70.0[c]
Life expectancy of females	73.1	74.6	77.3[c]	77.8	78.3[c]
Median age of population	29.4	27.9	30.2	32.8	35.5

[a]The annual number of births reached a low point in 1973 (3,136,965).
[b]Based on average annual birth rate for five-year period.
[c]Based on linear interpolation of 1976 and 2050 Bureau of Census estimates.
SOURCE: *Current Population Reports* (Washington, D.C.: U.S. Bureau of the Census), series P-25. Projections are based on Series II assumptions.

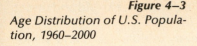

Figure 4–3
Age Distribution of U.S. Population, 1960–2000

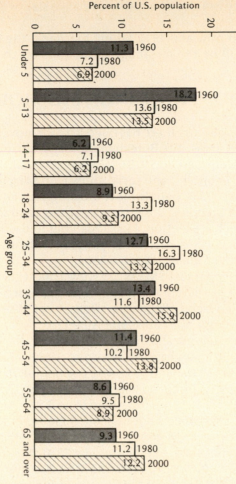

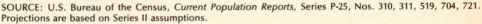

SOURCE: U.S. Bureau of the Census, *Current Population Reports*, Series P-25, Nos. 310, 311, 519, 704, 721. Projections are based on Series II assumptions.

Marketing Implications

Population demographics hold several implications for marketers: the large and growing population can sustain a long-run rise in sales and offer new opportunities; with the slow growth rate firms must strive to satisfy existing markets with better products; and it will be necessary for firms to be innovative.

Population size, gender, and age hold several implications for marketers. The large and growing population can sustain a long-run rise in product and service sales and offer new opportunities of various kinds. The slow growth rate (percentage increase) of the population means that firms must strive to satisfy further existing markets and realize that sales growth must be tied to superior products and services. In addition, it may be necessary for firms with high sales-growth objectives to enter new markets (such as international), develop related product lines, diversify, or delete some products aimed at declining markets.

The baby market is a significant one, representing almost 2 per cent of the overall population. This market will be strong in the 1980s and 1990s. Contrary to prior predictions, firms making baby products should not have major difficulties as long as they display a marketing orientation. The greater proportion of first-borns is important to marketers because several hundred dollars are spent on start-up costs for the first child, such as furniture and a car seat.

There are six million more females than males in the total population, despite the birth of more males. This is the result of the large and growing older female market. Although life expectancy is increasing for both females and males, female life expectancy is seven years longer than that for males. Lengthening life expectancy will also diminish the relative size of the thirteen-year-old and under markets.

Between now and 1990, young marrieds, the early middle-aged, and senior citizens will be the major age groups on which marketers ought to focus.

LOCATION, HOUSING, AND MOBILITY

Standard Metropolitan Statistical Areas (SMSAs) are urban centers with these features: integrated and large population base; a central city with at least 50,000 people; and the name of a major city.

During this century there has been a major movement of the U.S. population to large urban areas. The Bureau of the Census has defined these urban centers as *Standard Metropolitan Statistical Areas* (SMSAs). An SMSA has these features: an integrated economic and social entity with a large population base, a central city with at least 50,000 people (or two contiguous cities with a total population of at least 50,000 people), the inclusion of the central city and adjacent counties or towns (which are metropolitan and integrated with the city), and the name of the major city. SMSAs may cross state boundaries, if the city(ies) and adjacent counties meet the other provisions.

Among the largest SMSAs are New York, Chicago, Los Angeles-Long Beach, Chicago, Philadelphia, Detroit, San Francisco-Oakland, Washington, D.C., Boston, Cleveland, Baltimore, Dallas-Fort Worth, Houston, Minneapolis-St. Paul, Pittsburgh, St. Louis, and Atlanta.

Although urbanization has increased in the United States throughout the 1900s, major changes have occurred since 1950. The number of SMSAs has grown from 169 to nearly 300. The population in SMSAs has risen from 56.1 per cent to nearly three quarters of the total U.S. population. The land area contained in SMSAs has expanded from 5.9 to about 15 per cent of the total U.S. land area. This reflects not only the increase in the number of SMSAs, but also the urban sprawl, or greater size, of each SMSA as central cities and suburbs have become more contiguous. In 1950 the average SMSA contained 1,225 square miles. Now, the average SMSA has more than 1,850 square miles.

Standard Consolidated Statistical Areas (SCSAs) are made up of two or more contiguous SMSAs. An SCSA is synonymous with the term *megalopolis*.

Recently the Bureau of the Census added a new urban classification known as *Standard Consolidated Statistical Areas* (SCSAs). SCSAs are two or more continuous SMSAs with the size, urban character, integration, and contiguity set forth for single SMSAs. An SCSA is also called a *megalopolis*. As cities and their suburbs have drawn closer to neighboring cities and suburbs, the SCSA classification has taken on considerable importance. At present, thirteen SCSAs exist. They are

Boston-Lawrence-Lowell, Massachusetts-New Hampshire
Chicago-Gary, Illinois-Indiana
Cincinnati-Hamilton, Ohio-Kentucky-Indiana
Cleveland-Akron-Lorain, Ohio
Detroit-Ann Arbor, Michigan
Houston-Galveston, Texas
Los Angeles-Long Beach-Anaheim, California
Miami-Fort Lauderdale, Florida
Milwaukee-Racine, Wisconsin
New York-Newark-Jersey City, New York-New Jersey-Connecticut
Philadelphia-Wilmington-Trenton, Pennsylvania-Delaware-New Jersey-Maryland
San Francisco-Oakland-San Jose, California
Seattle-Tacoma, Washington

About two thirds of American households reside in the home they own.

The housing characteristics of the U.S. population are owner oriented. About two thirds of American households reside in a home they own. This rate has increased over the last twenty years. On the negative side, many units that were constructed have not been occupied. Several million units, about 8 to 10 per cent of all housing units, are unoccupied at any point in time.

Since 1960 there has been a change in the mix of housing. The proportion of households residing in multiple-unit structures has grown from one quarter to more than one third. It is not a paradox for ownership to increase and the per cent of single-unit housing to decline at the same time; this is explained by the growth in condominiums (ownership of a single unit in a multiple-unit dwelling).

About 12 to 15 per cent of the population moves each year, most within the same SMSA.

The mobility of the U.S. population is quite high. According to the Bureau of the Census, about 12 to 15 per cent of the population moves each year. To properly view mobility, it must be defined precisely, because different types of movement are possible. The Bureau of the Census uses these categories to describe movers:

1. Within the same SMSA (example, from Brooklyn to Queens).
2. Between SMSAs (example, from Chicago to Los Angeles).
3. From outside an SMSA to an SMSA (example, from Flat Rock, Michigan, to Detroit).
4. From an SMSA to outside an SMSA (example, from Dallas-Fort Worth to Kilgore, Texas).
5. Between two areas that are both outside SMSAs (example, from Ardmore to Clinton, Oklahoma).
6. From abroad.

The greatest amount of mobility (about half) occurs for people moving within the same SMSA. The least mobility is for people moving from abroad. In addition, few people move from an SMSA to outside an SMSA or from outside an SMSA to an SMSA.

The mobility of the U.S. population varies by geographic region. Some regions are gaining in size, whereas others are declining. Figure 4–4 shows the regional distribution of the population for the period of 1970 to 2000. Major growth is occurring in the South Atlantic, West South Central, and Mountain regions. Moderate growth exists in the Pacific region. The New England and East-South-Central Regions are stable. The relative sizes of the Middle Atlantic, East North Central, and West North Central are declining.

Marketing Implications

The location, housing, and mobility of the population will make marketing programs more cost efficient and available to larger markets, encourage branch outlets in suburbs, enlarge trading areas, and require improved transportation and delivery services.

The location, housing, and mobility of the population have various marketing implications. The growth of urban areas makes marketing programs more cost efficient and available to larger markets. Branch outlets in suburbs are possible and necessary. Trading areas are becoming larger, requiring improved transportation and delivery services. The similarities and differences of contiguous cities in SCSAs must be studied and exploited.

The continuing interest in home ownership may lead to further declines in the central cities of SMSAs, as people move to the outskirts of cities. This may be partially remedied by the construction of condominiums in densely populated regions. With resource shortages, high inflation, and high mortgage rates, many housing units will remain unoccupied.

The mobility of consumers must be broken into types. Almost half of all movers stay within the same SMSA. Purchase levels for some items, such as clothing and home products, will be high for movers, because many people discard them when moving to new environments (particularly those involving changes in climate or long-distance moves). Increasing mobility creates opportunities for national chains, franchises, national brands, and nationwide credit systems. Regional trends also indicate growth/decline possibilities.

Figure 4—4

Distribution of U.S.Population by Geographic Regions, 1970– 2000

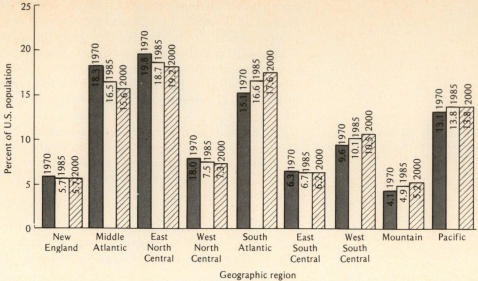

KEY OF REGIONS

New England = Maine, New Hampshire, Vermont, Massachusetts, Rhode Island, Connecticut
Middle Atlantic = New York, New Jersey, Pennsylvania
East North Central = Ohio, Indiana, Illinois, Michigan, Wisconsin
West North Central = Minnesota, Iowa, Missouri, North Dakota, South Dakota, Nebraska, Kansas
South Atlantic = Delaware, Maryland, District of Columbia, Virginia, West Virginia, North Carolina, South Carolina,
                   Georgia, Florida
East South Central = Kentucky, Tennessee, Alabama, Mississippi
West South Central = Arkansas, Louisiana, Oklahoma, Texas
Mountain = Montana, Idaho, Wyoming, Colorado, New Mexico, Arizona, Utah, Nevada
Pacific = Washington, Oregon, California, Alaska, Hawaii

SOURCE: U.S. Bureau of the Census, *Current Population Reports,* Series P-25, Nos. 310, 311, 519, 704, 721. Projections are based on Series II assumptions.

INCOME AND EXPENDITURES

Real annual family income doubled from 1950 to 1979; one third of U.S. families had incomes of $25,000 or more in 1979.

From 1950 to 1979, real annual family income almost doubled from $10,008 to $19,684 (expressed in 1979 dollars). The number of families with annual incomes under $5,000 dropped from about one in five in 1950 to one in fourteen in 1979. In 1950, 50.4 per cent of all families had incomes of less than $10,000 per year. For 1979, only one fifth fit in this category. At the upper end of the income scale, 9.2 per cent of all families had annual incomes of $15,000 or higher in 1950. This rose to over 64 per cent of all families in 1979 and one third of all families had annual incomes of $25,000 and higher.[4]

By 1990 two of every five families will have annual incomes of $25,000 and higher. Families with incomes over $50,000 will more than double, from 1.8 to 3.9 million. Although incomes will rise between 1980 and 1990, the growth rate will be 20 per cent, as compared with 38 and 39 per cent increases in the 1950s and 1960s.[5] Because of inflation, real income growth will not approach that of the 1950s and 1960s.

The per cent of income spent on food, beverages, tobacco, clothing, accessories, and jewelry has declined while the per cent of income spent on housing, medical care, personal business, recreation, and transportation has risen.

As income levels have changed, so have consumption patterns. The per cent of income spent on food, beverages, tobacco, and on clothing, accessories, and jewelry has declined substantially. The per cent spent on housing, medical care,

[4]*Current Population Reports* (Washington D.C.: U.S. Bureau of the Census), series P-60, No. 118.
[5]A. F. Ehrbar, "The Upbeat Outlook for Family Incomes," *Fortune* (Feb. 25, 1980), pp. 122–130.

TABLE 4–2: CONSUMPTION EXPENDITURES, U.S. POPULATION, 1950–1979 (IN BILLIONS)

Expenditure	1930 $	1930 %	1960 $	1960 %	1970 $	1970 %	1979 $	1979 %
Food, beverages, tobacco	58.1	30.3	88.0	27.1	147.1	23.8	321.3	21.3
Clothing, accessories, jewelry	23.7	12.4	32.2	9.9	55.6	9.0	117.5	7.8
Personal care	2.4	1.3	5.2	1.6	10.9	1.8	20.3	1.3
Housing	21.7	11.3	48.1	14.8	94.0	15.2	241.5	16.0
Household operations	29.1	15.2	46.1	14.2	87.8	14.2	219.5	14.5
Medical care expenses	9.1	4.7	20.0	6.2	49.9	8.1	146.8	9.7
Personal business	6.6	3.4	14.2	4.4	31.3	5.1	82.2	5.4
Transportation	25.4	13.2	42.4	13.1	78.0	12.6	212.2	14.1
Recreation	11.1	5.8	17.9	5.5	41.0	6.6	101.0*	6.7
Other	4.7	2.4	10.7	3.3	23.1	3.7	47.5	3.2
Total	191.9	100.0	324.8	100.0*	618.7	100.0*	1,509.8	100.0*

*Because of rounding errors, totals do not equal 100.
SOURCE: *The National Income and Product Accounts of the United States, 1929–1974* (Washington, D.C.: U.S. Bureau of Economic Analysis) and *Survey of Business.*

personal business, recreation and, recently, transportation has increased substantially. Since 1950 total annual consumption expenditures have risen from $192 billion to over $1.5 trillion.[6] See Table 4–2.

Consumers own a large and varied number of appliances and automobiles. For example, according to the Bureau of the Census, almost all homes are equipped with coffeemakers, radios, televisions (black and white), and refrigerators. More than 80 per cent of American families have automobiles and color televisions and more than 50 per cent have air conditioners. Between 7 and 10 per cent of American families own a microwave oven.

The growth for some of these items has been substantial. In fact, many products now taken for granted (such as a blender, clothing iron, toaster, and vacuum cleaner) have only recently been bought by many consumers. (See Table 4–3.)

Although family income and expenditures have increased dramatically over the last few decades, the rate of inflation (the yearly percentage increase in prices of products and services) has recently dampened the effects of higher

The *Consumer Price Index (CPI)* measures changes in prices; it has demonstrated that the rate of inflation recently dampened the effects of higher income by causing rises in the cost of living.

TABLE 4–3: OWNERSHIP OF SELECTED PRODUCTS, 1960–1979

Product	No. homes owned as of 1960 (millions)	No. homes owned as of 1979 (millions)	1979 Saturation level*
Air conditioner (room)	7.8	44.0	55.5%
Blender	4.2	41.6	52.4
Coffeemaker (total)	30.2	79.3	99.9
Dishwasher	3.7	34.1	43.0
Freezer	12.1	35.5	44.7
Iron (total)	45.7	79.3	99.9
Microwave oven	none	6.1	7.6
Mixer (food)	29.0	73.7	92.8
Television (color)	negligible	71.3	89.8
Toaster (total)	37.2	79.3	99.9
Vacuum cleaner	38.4	79.3	99.9
Washer	28.6	61.4	77.3

*Per cent of wired homes with these products, based upon 79,398,569 total wired homes.
SOURCE: Adapted from "Saturation Levels: 1979 Percentages and Totals of Wired Homes with These Products," *Merchandising* (March 1980), pp. 60–61. Reprinted with permission.

[6]*The National Income and Product Accounts of the United States, 1929–1974* (Washington, D.C.: U.S. Bureau of Economic Analysis) and *Survey of Current Business.*

income by causing rises in the cost of living (prices consumers pay for products and services). The federal government monitors the cost of living through the *Consumer Price Index (CPI)*. The CPI measures the changes in the prices of selected consumer items in different product categories, expressing the changes in terms of a base year.

At present the base year is 1967; and the price index for all items and individual items sold in 1967 is 100. Changes are measured against this base. For example, if monthly food costs were $200 in 1967 and $476 in 1981, the 1981 consumer price index for food would be 238 (100 × $476/$200). This would represent a 138 per cent rise in food prices from 1967 to 1981.

Since 1967 the greatest price increases have occurred in medical services, food, housing, and transportation. The smallest price increases have taken place for apparel and upkeep and reading and recreation. The South and Northeast have experienced greater price hikes than the North-Central or West regions. Among major cities, New York, Boston, and Washington, D.C., have incurred higher prices; Chicago, Kansas City, Atlanta, and Los Angeles have seen smaller increases since 1967.

Marketing Implications

The income and expenditures of the population lead to several marketing implications. With the overall growth in family income and the rising per cent of families with annual incomes above $25,000, large markets are available for a wide range of products and services.

Disposable income is used for spending and/or savings; *discretionary income* is used for luxuries after necessities are bought.

Disposable income (aftertax income to be used for spending and/or savings) and *discretionary income* (earnings remaining for luxuries, such as a vacation or dining out, after necessities such as food, clothing, and shelter are bought) have grown as the result of increases in family income.

There are major new opportunities in the areas of personal care, recreation, health care, housing, and others. In addition, consumers are fascinated with mechanical devices, such as appliances and automobiles. For example, ten years ago, the sales of microwave ovens were quite low. Currently, one out of fourteen homes has one. In fact, more microwave ovens are now sold than conventional ones.

Marketers must understand the cost of living and the CPI for three reasons. First, in measuring changes in family income, these increases must be gauged against prices. Real income must be examined. Second, the CPI differs by product, region, and city. This may necessitate different selling prices in different areas; for example, a watch selling for $185 in New York might be priced at $175 in Chicago. Third, it may be difficult to raise prices to reflect increased costs without consumer dissatisfaction.

OCCUPATIONS AND EDUCATION

There is a continuing trend toward white-collar and service occupations.

The labor force in the United States is continuing its steady movement toward white-collar and service occupations and away from blue-collar and farm occupations. In 1979, the total labor force was 97 million people. See Table 4–4.

From 1960 to 1979 the per cent of those employed in professional, technical, and clerical white-collar jobs rose substantially. The per cent of managers, administrators, and sales workers remained relatively constant. During the same period, the per cent of people employed as operatives and nonfarm laborers declined substantially, while craft and kindred workers were fairly constant. By 1979 only 2.7 million people were employed as farm workers.

For the 1980s the U.S. Bureau of Labor Statistics predicts strong gains in these occupational categories: engineering, science, medicine, computers, social

TABLE 4–4: U.S. POPULATION BY OCCUPATION, 1960–1979 (000)*

Occupation	1960 #	1960 %	1970 #	1970 %	1979 #	1979 %
White-collar workers	28,522	43.4	37,997	48.3	49,343	50.9
Professional and technical	7,469	11.4	11,140	14.2	15,050	15.5
Managers and administrators	7,067	10.7	8,289	10.5	10,517	10.8
Salesworkers	4,224	6.4	4,854	6.2	6,163	6.4
Clerical workers	9,762	14.8	13,714	17.4	17,614	18.2
Blue-collar workers	24,057	36.6	27,791	35.3	32,065	33.1
Craft and kindred workers	8,554	13.0	10,158	12.9	12,880	13.3
Operatives	11,950	18.2	13,909	17.7	14,521	15.0
Nonfarm laborers	3,553	5.4	3,724	4.7	4,664	4.8
Service workers	8,023	12.2	9,712	12.4	12,834	13.2
Farm workers	5,176	7.9	3,126	4.0	2,703	2.8
Total*	65,778	100.0	78,627	100.0	96,945	100.0

*There are rounding errors within categories and totals.
SOURCE: *Employment and Earnings* (Washington, D.C.: U.S. Bureau of Labor Statistics), monthly.

science, buying, selling, secretarial, construction, refrigeration, health service, personal service, and protection. These categories will have limited growth or decline: education, office-machine operations, printing trades, baking, jewelry, shoe repair, tailoring, barbering, and farming.

Women represent a large and growing percentage of the U.S. labor force.

Another important change in the U.S. labor force has been the increase in the number and per cent of working women. In 1960, 22.5 million women comprised 31.2 per cent of the employed labor force. By 1979, 43.0 million women accounted for 41.4 per cent of the employed labor force, and 50.7 per cent of all adult women were employed.

The growth in the number and per cent of married women in the labor force has been substantial. In 1960, 12.3 million married women, 30.5 per cent of married women, were employed. As of 1979, 23.8 million married women, 49.4 per cent of all married women, were employed. The per cent of married women with children under six who were working jumped from 18.6 per cent in 1960 to 43.2 per cent in 1979. The statistics on working women are contained in Table 4–5.

TABLE 4–5. WOMEN IN THE U.S. LABOR FORCE, 1960–1979 (PERSONS SIXTEEN YEARS OLD AND OLDER)

Factor	1960	1970	1979
Women employed in the labor force	22,516,000	31,233,000	42,971,000
Per cent of people employed in the labor force who are women	31.2	36.7	41.4
Per cent of all women employed in the labor force	34.8	42.6	50.7
Married women employed in the labor force	12,300,000	18,400,000	23,800,000
With no children under eighteen	5,700,000	8,200,000	11,000,000
With children ages six to seventeen only	4,100,000	6,300,000	8,100,000
With children under six	2,500,000	3,900,000	4,800,000
Per cent of all married women employed in the labor force	30.5	40.8	49.4
With no children under eighteen	34.7	42.2	46.7
With children ages six to seventeen only	39.0	49.2	59.1
With children under six	18.6	30.3	43.2

SOURCES: *Employment and Earnings* (Washington, D.C.: U.S. Bureau of Labor Statistics, U.S. Bureau of the Census), monthly, and *Current Population Survey* (Washington, D.C.: U.S. Bureau of the Census), and *Special Labor Force Reports* (Washington, D.C.: U.S. Bureau of the Census).

Almost 86 per cent of young adults have graduated from high school; 46 per cent have gone to college.

The educational attainment of Americans continued its upward trend in the 1960s and 1970s. As of 1960, 58.8 per cent of all adults twenty-five years old and older were not high school graduates. This figure dropped to 32.3 per cent in 1979. As of 1960 only 16.5 per cent of all adults twenty-five years old and older had received some college education. This rose to 31.1 per cent in 1979. Of those adults at ages twenty-five to twenty-nine in 1979, 85.6 per cent had graduated high school, 46.3 per cent had received some college education, and 23.1 per cent were college graduates. . . .

The sharp increase in the prevalence of working wives and increased educational attainment both contribute to the growing population of the upper-income brackets.

Marketing Implications

The occupations and education of the population indicate these marketing implications. A greater number and percentage of the total populations are working than ever before. The larger work force requires transportation, clothing, restaurants, and personal services.

The modern U.S. labor force requires convenient store hours, wider services, convenience foods, and job-centered products and services.

Working wives may be unable to shop during regular retail hours. This has meaning for mail-order and round-the-clock retailers. Advertising, particularly that on television, may have to be placed in evening time periods. Services, such as repairs, may have to be offered during evenings and weekends. Working wives spend large amounts for major appliances and household equipment, especially when they are time-saving products. The market for prepared foods, convenience foods, fast-food restaurants, and child-care centers will expand.

Stores have opportunities in major commercial centers. The market for job-oriented products and services is growing and the shift in occupations means different needs and aspirations in consumer purchases.

As the education level rises, the needs for honesty, information, clear-cut product or service attributes, safety, environmental controls, and other factors also rise.

MARITAL STATUS

Despite some literature to the contrary, the data indicate that marriage and family remain important in the United States. (See Table 4–6.) Well over two million couples get married each year. The per cent of the population 18 and older which was married remained relatively stable between 1950 and 1979 at about two thirds of this population group. In 1950 the median age at first marriage was 22.8 years for males and 20.3 years for females. For 1979, these figures were 24.4 and 22.1, respectively. Therefore, in recent years adults have been waiting somewhat longer to be married. The size of the average family has declined slightly, from 3.5 members in 1950 to 3.3 in 1979.

A *family* is a group of two or more persons residing together who are related by blood, marriage, or adoption; a *household* is a housing unit with one or more people. The number of single-person households has increased substantially.

A *family* is defined as a group of two or more persons residing together who are related by blood, marriage, or adoption. A *household* is defined as a housing unit with one or more people. There have been two important changes in family and marital status. First, the number of single-person households has gone from 4.7 million in 1950 to 17.2 million in 1979. More than 20 per cent of all American households are now comprised of one-person units. Singles account for roughly one eighth of total consumer spending for goods and services.[7] (See Table 4–7 for any analysis of expenditures by singles.)

Second, the size of the average household dropped from 3.4 in 1950 to 2.8 in 1979, because fewer single adults now live with their parents and divorces have

[7]Fabian Linden, ''Singles: Spending Patterns,'' *Consumer Markets* (July 1979), p. 1.

TABLE 4–6: MARITAL STATUS OF U.S. POPULATION, 1950–1979

Factor	1950	1960	1970	1979
Number of marriages	1,667,000	1,523,000	2,159,000	2,359,000
Rate of marriages per 1,000 population	11.1	8.5	10.6	10.7
Per cent of population, eighteen and older, married	67.0	67.3	71.7	66.2
Median age at first marriage:				
Males	22.8	22.8	23.2	24.4
Females	20.3	20.3	20.8	22.1
Average size of family	3.5	3.7	3.6	3.3
Number of single-person households (ages fourteen and older)	4,700,000	7,064,000	10,851,000	17,201,000
Single-person households as a per cent of all households	10.8	13.4	17.1	22.2
Average size of household	3.4	3.3	3.1	2.8
Number of divorces	385,000	393,000	708,000	1,170,000
Rate of divorce per 1,000 population	2.6	2.2	3.5	5.3
Per cent of population, eighteen and older, widowed	8.3	8.4	8.9	8.1

SOURCES: *Vital Statistics of the United States* (Washington, D.C.: U.S. National Center for Health Statistics), annual, and *U.S. Census of Population and Current Population Reports* (Washington, D.C.: U.S. Bureau of the Census), series P-20, Nos. 144, 255, 271, 287, 306, 313, 323.

TABLE 4–7: HOW "SINGLES" SPEND THEIR MONEY (TOTAL EXPENDITURES EACH GROUP EQUAL 100 PER CENT)

	Total U.S. households	Singles					Singles expenditures as % total, U.S.
		Total	One-person household		Two-person household		
			Under 25	24–34	Under 25	25–34	
Total U.S. expenditures	100.0%	12.4	1.2	2.7	2.9	5.6	12.4%
Distribution expenditure	100.0%	100.0%	100.0%	100.0%	100.0%	100.0%	
Food	21.3	14.4	11.8	15.0	13.9	14.8	8.4
At home	16.4	8.2	5.7	6.8	8.3	9.2	6.1
Away from home	4.6	5.8	5.4	7.7	5.2	5.4	15.5
Alcoholic beverages	.9	1.5	2.0	2.8	.9	1.1	20.0
Tobacco products	1.6	1.5	1.7	1.7	1.4	1.5	11.9
Housing	30.2	34.7	35.2	34.4	34.3	34.9	14.2
Shelter	16.5	22.8	26.4	25.0	22.4	21.3	17.2
Rented dwellings	7.2	19.0	25.9	23.4	20.2	15.1	33.0
Owned dwellings	9.0	3.7	.4	1.5	2.1	6.1	5.0
Fuel and utilities	5.1	3.0	2.3	2.4	3.1	3.3	7.2
Housing expenses	3.8	3.4	2.7	3.1	3.1	3.7	11.0
Home furnishings & equipment	4.8	5.6	3.8	4.0	5.6	6.6	14.1
Clothing	8.1	8.6	7.3	8.5	8.2	9.2	13.1
Male	2.7	2.8	2.5	3.0	2.5	2.8	12.6
Female	3.9	3.9	2.7	3.2	3.9	4.4	12.4
Clothing care, etc.	1.5	2.0	2.2	2.3	1.8	1.9	16.0
Transportation	19.8	22.5	28.1	20.5	25.4	20.7	14.0
Vehicle purchases & finance charges	9.8	12.2	16.4	10.9	14.4	10.9	15.4
Vehicle operations	9.3	9.4	10.8	8.7	10.3	9.1	12.6
Health and personal care	7.3	4.5	3.1	4.0	4.1	5.2	7.7
Recreation	8.0	9.8	9.0	10.3	9.2	10.0	15.2
Vacation trips	3.1	3.4	2.4	3.8	2.6	3.8	13.3
Other*	4.9	6.4	6.6	6.5	6.6	6.2	16.2
All other	2.8	2.5	1.8	2.8	2.6	2.6	11.2

*Includes owned vacation homes, television, boats, aircraft, wheeled goods and other.
NOTE: Distribution of expenditures based on U.S. Department of Labor Consumer Survey, 1972–73. Subitems do not always add up to the major category total because of minor items not shown separately.
SOURCE: Fabian Linden, "Singles: Spending Patterns," *Consumer Markets* (July 1979), p. 2. Reprinted by permission.

risen substantially. From 1950 to 1979 the number of divorces jumped from 385,000 to 1.2 million annually. During the same period, the per cent of adults widowed went from 8.3 to 8.1. However, the number of widowed adults rose considerably because of the greater number of adults in the overall population.

Marketing Implications

Marriage and family are important institutions in the United States, in spite of the high divorce rate. The marketing implications of marital and family status include the following. There are opportunities for product and service industries associated with weddings (such as caterers and travel agents), family life (such as full-sized automobiles), and divorce (such as attorneys).

Because marriage is occurring slightly later in an individual's life, people have better financial resources and two-income families are prevalent. This leaves opportunities for organizations involved with travel, furniture, and entertainment.

The growth of single-person households provides opportunities for home and home furnishings industries and manufacturers who produce single-serving packages. These implications also apply to divorced and widowed persons.

Marital and family trends present diverse opportunities such as catering, travel, and single-serving packages.

USES OF DEMOGRAPHIC DATA

After examining each of the demographics separately, the marketer should develop a *consumer demographic profile* based on a composite of the most important demographics. In this section, some examples of demographic profiles are shown.

Generic products, no frills, and unbranded merchandise have grown in popularity. A study recently conducted on consumer characteristics showed these shoppers to represent large families, to be female, and to spend a lot of money. Income and race have no impact on generic brand behavior.[8]

An expanding market for maternity clothes are the women who work full-time. Not long ago, 20 per cent of maternity clothes sales were made to working women. Now, half of maternity clothes sales, or more than $400 million per year, are sold to this market. These women are between the ages of twenty-six and thirty-four and spend considerably more than nonworkers, $500 versus $350.[9]

B. Dalton Bookseller, a nationwide book store chain, uses demographic studies of 36,000 cities with information broken down by census tract. It defines heavy readers as those between twenty-one and forty-nine years of age, some college, high income, female, and employed in a management or professional position.[10]

Advertisers frequently collect and update demographic data about consumers in order to set advertising rates and attract clients. For instance, television, newspaper, and other advertising rates are set on the basis of audience size, age, income, location, occupation, and other statistics.

LIMITATIONS OF DEMOGRAPHIC DATA

Demographic data have limitations: information may be dated, opportunities and risks may be hidden, single demographic statistics are often not useful, and demographic data do not consider consumer behavior.

When using demographic data, these limitations should be noted. One, demographic information may be dated. The national census is conducted only once

[8]"Rich Shopper, Poor Shopper, They're All Buying Generics," *Progressive Grocer* (March 1979), pp. 92–106.
[9]"The Svelte Look: Rebirth for Maternity Retailing," *Business Week* (December 19, 1978), pp. 100–103.
[10]John Mutter, "B. Dalton Bookseller: A Novel Approach to Retailing," *Sales & Marketing Management* (May 14, 1979), pp. 49–51.

every ten years. Regular statistical updates normally have time lags—for example, 1981 data will not be widely available until mid-1983. Two, aggregate data and trends may hide opportunities and risks in small markets or specialized product categories. Three, single demographic statistics are often not very useful. A consumer demographic profile is needed.

Four, demographic data do not consider the psychological or the social factors influencing consumers. They do not explain the decision process consumers utilize when making purchases. Most importantly, demographics do not delve into the reasons why consumers make particular decisions; demographics are descriptive in nature. For example, why do people with similar demographic profiles buy different products or brands? For these reasons, Chapter 5 examines the psychological and social factors affecting consumer behavior and the decision process consumers use.

SUMMARY

By understanding consumers, a firm is able to determine the most appropriate audience to which to appeal and the combination of marketing factors that will satisfy this audience. The scope of consumer analysis includes who, what, why, how, when, where, and how often. This chapter examined consumer demographics. Chapters 5 to 7 focus on social and psychological factors affecting behavior, the consumer's decision process, organizational consumers, the development of a target market, and sales forecasting.

Demographics are easily identifiable and measurable statistics that are used to describe the population. In combination, demographics can establish consumer profiles that may present attractive market opportunities. The United States has more than 221 million people and a growth rate of less than 1 per cent per year. The annual birth rate will exceed 3.5 million during the 1980s and early 1990s. There are approximately 5.7 million more women than men, due in large part to a life expectancy for women that is 7.9 years longer than for men. By the year 2000 the median age of the U.S. population will be 35.5 years.

During the 1900s there has been a strong movement to large urban areas, known as Standard Metropolitan Statistical Areas (SMSAs). About three quarters of the population now live in SMSAs. Urban sprawl has caused the overlapping of cities and their suburbs. In addition, several SMSAs have merged into contiguous, homogeneous regions. This has led the federal government to develop a new classification known as the Standard Consolidated Statistical Area (SCSA). At present, there are thirteen SCSAs.

Almost two thirds of all households own the home in which they live. Multiple-unit housing has grown, as have condominiums. Mobility remains high, with 12 to 15 per cent of the population moving each year. The greatest mobility is for persons moving within the same SMSA. Rapidly growing regions are the South Atlantic, West, South Central, and Mountain regions.

From 1950 to 1979 annual family income (in constant 1979 dollars) doubled, going from $10,008 to $19,684. By 1979, one third of families had annual incomes of $25,000 or more. As income has risen, the per cent spent on food and clothing has declined, while the per cent spent on housing, medical care, personal care, and recreation has increased. The ownership of automobiles and major appliances is quite high. The rate of inflation, as expressed in the Consumer Price Index (CPI), has become a hindrance for marketers. The CPI varies by product, region, and city.

The U.S. labor force contains 97 million people. More workers are now employed in white-collar and service jobs; fewer work in blue-collar and farm jobs. The number and per cent of working women and working mothers have expanded greatly. The educational attainment of the total population has improved significantly, particularly among young adults.

Marriage and family continue as important institutions. Two thirds of adults are married. The median age of first marriage has risen somewhat since 1950. The size of the average family has declined slightly. More than one of every five American households is a single-person household, and the average household size has declined significantly. The divorce rate has risen substantially. The number of widowed people has increased, while the percentage has dropped.

These limitations of demographics are noted: obsolete data, hidden trends or implications, limited use of single demographic statistics, and lack of explanation of the factors affecting behavior, consumer decision making, and motivation.

QUESTIONS FOR DISCUSSION

1. How does the use of demographics aid marketing decision making?
2. The population in the United States will grow from 221 million in 1980 to 260 million in 2000. Why is the rate of population growth considered low? What does this signify for marketers?
3. If you worked for Gerbers' baby food division, what conclusions would you draw about birth projections from now until the year 2000?
4. Name several potential product and service opportunities in the senior-citizen market.
5. Differentiate between an SMSA and an SCSA.
6. Describe the six types of population mobility. How can a local firm retain a customer following with so much moving?
7. Few families have annual incomes under $5,000 per year. What does this signify for marketers?
8. Nearly all homes have radios, refrigerators, and televisions. What does this signify for marketers?
9. Explain the concept of the consumer price index (CPI). What does it measure?
10. Distinguish between disposable income and discretionary income. During inflationary times, what occurs to the level of each?
11. Describe the major changes in the occupations of the U.S. labor force.
12. What products and services should grow as the number of working women and working mothers expands?
13. Describe the marketing implications of selling to better-educated Americans.
14. Distinguish between *family* and *household*.
15. Explain the consumer demographic profile.
16. What are the limitations of demographics?

NOTES

1. **Jay Braun** and **D. Linder**, *Psychology Today: An Introduction*, 4th ed. (New York: Random House, 1979), pp. 323–324.
2. **Joel R. Evans** and **Barry Berman**, *Marketing* (New York: Macmillan, 1982), pp. 85–109.

Eleven

NOTE TAKING IN THE TEXTBOOK

You can read and study your textbook most effectively by taking notes right in the book. In-text note taking helps you identify the main ideas, organize the material, and remember the facts and details included in the selection. In-text notes are most useful when preparing for tests. You should make in-text note taking a part of the reading study technique described in Chapter 9.

Follow the steps given below for taking in-text notes.

1. Write in the margins. Make up a key word outline in your own words (you will be shown how to make this outline later in the chapter). Write capsule summaries after several related paragraphs have been read.

IN-TEXT NOTE-TAKING TECHNIQUES

Device or Symbol	Meaning or Use in Notes
A. Keyword outline	A brief summary of the most important information using only the key nouns and verbs.
B. Vertical lines	Written in the margin, these indicate important passages of details and examples
C. Underlining	Underline key words or phrases while reading.
D. See-through color highlighting	During a second reading, use color accent to highlight underlined material.
E. Checkmarks	Use these to indicate information to be checked and verified.
F. Question marks	Question marks identify things you don't understand that need to be reread or explained by the teacher.
G. Stars and asterisks	These mark information which must be memorized.
H. Circles	Circle important words.
I. X's	"X" information you don't agree with.
J. Capsule summary	On each page, briefly summarize the important information.

2. Selectively underline and highlight important points. Concentrate on the beginning sentences in paragraphs and the main idea, topic headings, highlighted words, graphic aids, and lists of important ideas or details.
3. Use your own coding and shorthand system. Consistently use your own system to note important ideas, details, and vocabulary. Here are some suggestions:
    a. Vocabulary—circle important words. Write your definitions in the margin.
    b. Main ideas—underline or highlight main idea statements. Write a summary phrase in the margin.
    c. Misunderstood ideas—show these with a question mark so that you can ask about them later.
    d. Other shorthand suggestions are given later.
4. Use your textbook notes. You can quickly review textbook information by using the notes you have written. Use these notes as the basis for your review.

ACTIVITY I

Read the following passage. Label each in-text note-taking technique with the appropriate letter.

REALISM AND NATURALISM[1]

By the mid-nineteenth century the Romantic standard had come to seem meaningless. The belief in man's idealistic nature had received setbacks. For example, after the downfall of Napoleon around 1815, most European countries reinstated political conditions which were in many ways more oppressive than those in existence during the eighteenth century. The ideals of liberty, equality, and fraternity no longer seemed to have any reality. Furthermore, the general misery of a large part of humanity was being emphasized in the results of the Industrial Revolution. The factory system was pouring workers into the centers of population where living conditions were daily more inadequate. Crime and poverty were all too prevalent.

The Backgrounds of Realism

In the face of such political and economic conditions the Romanticist's tendency to search for a solution to problems in an idealized notion of man's capacity for infinite good seemed both too vague and too impractical. Many came to argue that dreams must be abandoned for a systematic and scientific search into man's actual state and for solutions based upon discoverable facts. Observation, prediction, and control of society became the new ideals. * Among the major influences on the new thought were the writings of Auguste Comte (1798–1857), whose philosophy came to be called positivism. In his writings, published between 1830 and 1854, he argued that sociology is the highest form of science and that all knowledge should ultimately be used for the improvement of society. He found the key to such improvement in observation and experimentation precise enough to explain all happenings in terms of natural cause and effect. Comte's concept places primary emphasis upon those facts which can be experienced through the five senses, and it thereby limits concern to the observation of contemporary events.

Positivism was reinforced by *The Origin of Species* by Charles Darwin (1809–1882). The doctrine set forth there had two main parts: (1) evolution, or the idea

Margin handwritten notes:

BACKGROUND
About 1850's
DOWNFALL OF
NAPOLEON

INDUSTRIAL
REVOLUTION

DEFINITION
SOLUTION to
Problems based
ON MAN'S
CAPACITY FOR ??
good.

Strive for
1) observation
2) Prediction } of society
3) Control

Comte
Positivism = Science
uses to improve
Society

Example

that all forms of life have developed gradually from a common ancestry; and (2) the survival of the fittest, as an explanation of the reason for evolution.

(1) Heredity
(2) Heredity + Environment

✻ This point of view has several consequences. First, heredity and environment become the determining factors of existence. Everything that man is or can be is the result of the physical makeup with which he is born and of the conditions under which he lives. Second, heredity and environment become explanations for all character traits and actions. Furthermore, since behavior is determined by factors beyond the individual's control, he cannot be blamed for his behavior. If blame is to be assigned it must go to the society which has allowed such undesirable hereditary and environmental factors to exist. While few believers in these theories advocated trying to control heredity, many turned their attentions to ways of improving the social environment.

(3) Effect on Religions

✻ Third, the ideas of evolution and the survival of the fittest cast considerable doubt upon the existence of God as conceived in most religions. If He existed, according to the new views, it was as a totally indifferent and impersonal force. The idea of immortality was seriously challenged at the same time. If there is no future life, man can reach fulfillment only in the present one, and, to many, science seemed to offer the greatest possibilities of achieving the maximum human good.

(4) Progress

✻ Fourth, Darwin's ideas strengthened the idea of progress. If man has evolved from an infinitesimal grain of being to the complex creature he now is, greater and greater improvement and inevitable progress seemed to him to be clearly indicated. Although progress came to be thought of as inevitable, it was also believed that desirable change can be hastened by the consistent application of the scientific method to all phases of human life.

(5) Man in Nature

??? ✻ Fifth, man treated as a natural object is subject to the same laws and conditions as all other things in nature. Prior to the nineteenth century man had been viewed generally as somehow distinct from and superior to the rest of creation. Now, by this concept, he tended to lose this privileged status and to become merely another object for study and control.

Like most movements, then, realism was attempting to improve the lot of mankind by coming to grips with truth. The new school, however, saw truth as being limited to knowledge gained through the five senses (sight, hearing, taste, smell, and touch). Such a marked change in the view of truth inevitably influenced the conception of art and the theatre.

ACTIVITY II

Use the in-book note-taking devices listed on the previous page to take notes for this selection. Demonstrate each note-taking device in this selection.

THE HEART'S WEAKEST LINK[2]

The body's most used muscles need to have a constant supply of oxygen and must be able to get rid of potentially toxic by-products of metabolism. To achieve this, the heart has a tremendous supply of blood vessels. Three large coronary arteries branching right off the aorta send a multitude of branches to the heart's oxygen-consuming muscle fibers. Unfortunately, these three arteries' branches don't overlap one another, and if one artery (or its branches) gets plugged up there is no way of providing an alternative blood supply to that part of the heart. Deprived of oxygen-rich blood, heart muscle stops beating and dies. If the extent of the damage is not too great, the dead heart tissues will be phagocytized, and tough scar tissue will form a strong patch. Autopsies of young soldiers killed in combat have revealed that many of them had patches of scar tissue on their hearts. If the blockage is a gradual process, new vessels develop in young people and there is no harmful effect. It has also been found that exercise promotes the growth of new coronary vessels. Perhaps this is why many cardiologists (heart specialists) recommend a continuous program of exercise that increases cardiac output.

Two problems can arise with the coronary arteries: one is the deposition of cholesterol plaques (plates) on the inner lining of the vessels, a condition called *atherosclerosis*. In time, atherosclerosis may progress to the point where the vessel's diameter becomes very narrow and its capacity to carry blood is decreased (see Fig. 13–1). The patient now has a coronary insufficiency, and the needs of the heart muscle, which uses 80 per cent of the available oxygen, are barely being met. If this person is subject to any kind of stress that requires an increased cardiac output, the heart muscle will experience an oxygen crisis. Heart muscle signals such an oxygen crisis by sending pain signals, a generally nonlethal condition called *angina pectoris*. Angina can be treated by oral medications (such as nitroglycerine) that open up the coronary vessels. The strange thing about anoxia (lack of oxygen) of heart muscle is that the pain is not always felt in the chest but is often referred to some other region, the lower jaw, throat, shoulder, elbow, or little fingers. . . .

Another problem with cholesterol plaques in the arteries is that they sometimes cause the formation of internal clots. If the clot or thrombus breaks loose and is carried into the smaller branches of the coronary circulation, it may plug a vessel and cause death to the heart muscle supplied by that vessel. This is called a *cardiac infarct* or *coronary thrombosis*, and it is a major cause of death. Heart disease will be discussed later.

CONTROL OF THE HEART

The rate and strength of the heartbeat are regulated by both neural and endocrine inputs. These inputs modify the intrinsic pacemaker activity and either accelerate or slow the heart. The two major control centers are in the medulla oblongata of the brain. One of these centers slows the heart via parasympathetic nerves whose secretion, acetylcholine, depresses pacemaker

Figure 13–1

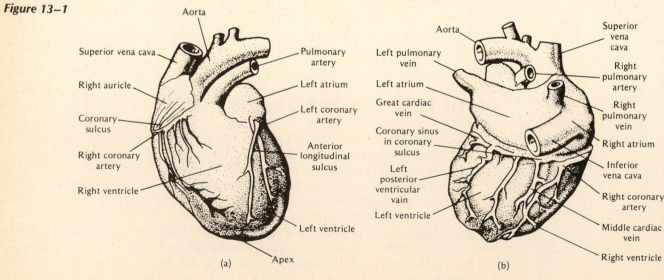

activity. The other center accelerates heartbeat via signals conducted by the sympathetic nervous system and its synaptic transmitter norepinephrine. Actually these two centers are always both active. Slowing the heart involves an increase in parasympathetic signals and a simultaneous decrease in sympathetic signals. It is like driving a car—when you slow down you take your foot off the accelerator and step down on the brake. Obviously these control centers process a variety of sensory signals before issuing their commands to the heart. These signals come from sensory receptors that monitor blood flow, blood pressure, blood chemistry, and conditions in the outside world.

The Heart Monitors and Controls   Love songs are written about the heart, and we are all aware that a variety of emotions can cause the heart to beat faster and even skip a few beats now and then. This zany behavior of our hearts stems from our higher brain centers, which modify the activity of the medulla's **cardiac-control centers.** This particular pathway is of value in that it prepares the body to cope with some anticipated environmental stress. However, the internal signals to the cardiac-control centers are more important. We have an array of sensors that make sure enough oxygen-rich blood is pumped to the critical organs, particularly the brain. These receptors strategically located in the great veins leading to the heart, in the aorta, and in the carotid arteries that carry blood to the brain. There are two basic types of receptors: (1) *pressure receptors* and (2) *chemoreceptors*.

Both types of receptors are in the aorta and carotid body, a receptor-rich bulge on the carotid artery. If the blood pressure drops, these receptors fire more slowly, signaling the cardiac accelerator center to speed the heart up. If the blood pressure goes way up the pressure receptors signal the cardiac-control centers to slow the heart down. If there is too little oxygen in the blood, the chemoreceptors detect this lack and signal the cardiac command post to have the heart pump more blood. In so doing, they also signal the respiratory center to increase the rate and depth of breathing. Even the cardiac-control centers themselves can act as chemoreceptors. Elevation of carbon dioxide levels activates the accelerator center, more blood is pumped to the lungs, and CO_2 is eliminated. All these events occur beyond the limits of our consciousness; they are purely reflex acts. . . .

One other important reflex is the so-called *Bainbridge reflex*. When we exercise, more blood returns to the heart and the great veins are stretched. In the great veins are stretch receptors that increase their rate of firing when activated. These volleys of neural signals are then relayed to the cardiac-control centers, the accelerator center increases its rate of firing, and the heart speeds up to handle the increased load.

Another neat trick the heart muscle picked up in the process of evolution was discovered by the English physiologist Starling. He noticed that stretched heart muscle contracts harder than unstretched heart muscle. Thus was born Richard Starling's *Law of the Heart*, which states (simplistically) that increased filling of the heart causes it to beat harder. Not content with this myriad of controlling influences, a series of endocrine regulators also evolved as back-up and supplemental systems to the neural controls.

Endocrine Influences on the Heart   In any stress situation, our adrenal glands secrete epinephrine and norepinephrine . . . , both of which increase cardiac output and heart rate. Such a response has obvious relevance in any fight or flight situation, but as we shall see later, there is a possible price to be paid. Thyroid hormone also affects heart rate by modifying overall metabolism, but the main hormones to remember in this connection are epinephrine and norepinephrine.

PROJECT

The following article is a part of a chapter from a biology textbook. Read the selection and use the note-taking techniques suggested in this chapter. Write your notes from this sample textbook chapter on the pages in this book. Be sure to include the following in-text note-taking techniques.

A. Key-word outlines of sections.
B. Vertical lines in the margin to note important passages.
C. Underlining of key words or phrases.
D. Color highlighting.
E. Checkmarks to show information to be verified.
F. Question marks to show things you don't understand and that need to be reread or explained by the teacher.
G. Stars and asterisks that show information that must be memorized.
H. Circles around important vocabulary.
I. Xs next to things you don't agree with.
J. Capsule summaries in the margin that summarize each page or section.

SOCIAL STRUCTURE IN VERTEBRATE SOCIETIES[3]

Social Dominance

Vertebrate societies are often arranged in hierarchies. One type of social dominance that has been studied in some detail is the *pecking order* in chickens. A pecking order is established whenever a flock of hens is kept together over any period of time. In any one flock, one hen usually dominates all the others; she can peck any other hen without being pecked in return. A second hen can peck all hens but the first one; a third, all hens but the first two; and so on through the flock, down to the unfortunate pullet that is pecked by all and can peck none in return.

Hens that rank high in pecking order have privileges such as first chance at the food trough, the roost, and the nest boxes. As a consequence, they can usually be recognized at sight by their sleek appearance and confident demeanor. Low-ranking hens tend to look dowdy and unpreened and to hover timidly on the fringes of the group.

During the period when a pecking order is being established, frequent and sometimes bloody battles may ensue, but once rank is fixed in the group, a mere raising or lowering of the head is sufficient to acknowledge the dominance or submission of one hen in relation to another. Life then proceeds in harmony. If a number of new members are added to a flock, the entire pecking order must be reestablished, and the subsequent disorganization results in more fighting, less eating, and less tending to the essential business, from the poultry dealer's point of view, of growth and egg laying.

Pecking orders reduce the breeding population. Cocks and hens low in the pecking order copulate much less frequently than socially superior chickens. Thus the final outcome is the same as if the social structure did not exist. The stronger and otherwise superior animals eat better, sleep better, and leave the most offspring. However, because of the social hierarchy, this comes about with a minimum expenditure of lives and energy.

Territories and Territoriality

Most vertebrates stay close to their birthplaces, occupying a home range that is likely to be the same home range occupied by their parents. Even migratory birds that travel great distances are likely to return year after year to the same area. Often these home ranges are defended, either by individuals (or more likely mating pairs) or by groups against other individuals or groups of the same species. Areas so defended are known as *territories,* and the behavior of defending an area against intruders of the same species is known as *territoriality.*

Territoriality in some form has now been recognized in animals as diverse as crickets, howler monkeys, fur seals, dragonflies, red deer, beaver, dogs, many types of lizards, and a large number of species of birds and fish.

A territory may be an area of a plain, a corner of a small wood, or a few meters at the bottom of a pond. Sometimes the territory consists of little more than the nest itself and the immediate area around it. For the male bitterling, a small fish, the territory is an area immediately surrounding a freshwater mussel. The bitterling admits only egg-laden females into his territory, then leads them to the mussel where they lay their eggs within its gills. The male then injects his sperm while swimming over the siphon of the mussel.

Territoriality in Birds   Territoriality was first recognized by an English amateur naturalist and bird watcher, Eliot Howard, who observed that the spring songs of male birds served not only to court the females but also to warn other males of the same species away from the terrain that the prospective father had selected for his own. In general, territory is established by a male. Courtship of the female, nest building, raising of the young, and often feeding are carried out within this territory. Frequently the female also participates in territory defense.

In some species of birds, the usual sex roles are reversed. The female red-necked phalarope establishes and defends the territory, while the drab defends the nest, incubates the eggs, and takes care of the young. Some birds, such as the American robin and the European swallow, tend to return to the same territory year after year, often with the same mate. Storks and night herons, however, are attached to a nesting place rather than to a mate, and if the mate of the previous year does not return the following year, he or she is readily exchanged for a new incumbent.

By virtue of territoriality, a mating pair is assured of a monopoly of food and nesting materials in the area and of a safe place to carry on all the activities associated with reproduction and care of the young. Some pairs carry out all their domestic activities within the territory. Others perform the mating and nesting activities in the territories, which are defended vigorously by the males, but do their food gathering on a nearby communal feeding ground, where the birds congregate amicably together. A third type of territory functions only for courtship and mating, as in the bower of the bowerbird or the arena of the prairie chicken In these territories, the males prance, strut, and posture—but very rarely fight—while the females look on and eventually indicate their choice of a mate by entering the territory. Males that have not been able to secure a territory for themselves are not able to reproduce; in fact, there is evidence from studies of some territorial species, such as the Australian magpie, that adults that do not secure territories do not mature sexually.

Bird territories vary greatly in size. The golden eagle, for instance, defends a territory of about 90 square kilometers; the European robin, a territory of about 6 square kilometers; and the king penguin, a territory of only ½ square meter. Individuals of the same species often have territories of somewhat different sizes, depending partly upon the density of food and shelter in a given area, partly upon population pressure, and partly upon the aggressiveness of the individual.

Territorial Defense Even though territorial boundaries may be invisible, they are clearly defined and recognized by the territory owner. With birds, for example, it is not the mere proximity of another bird of the same species that elicits aggression, but his presence within a part of a particular area. The territory owner patrols his territory by flying from tree to tree. He will ignore a nearby rival outside his territory, but he will fly off to attack a more distant one that has crossed the border. Animals of other species are generally ignored unless they are prey or predators.

Once an animal has taken possession of a territory, he is virtually undefeatable on it. Among territory owners, prancing, posturing, scent marking, and singing and other types of calls usually suffice to dispel intruders, which are at a great psychological disadvantage. If a male stickleback, for example, is placed in a test tube and moved into the territory of a rival male, he visibly wilts, his posture becoming less and less aggressive the farther within the territory he is transported. Similarly, a male cichlid will dart toward a rival male within his territory but as he chases the rival back into its own territory, he begins to swim more slowly, the caudal fin seemingly working harder and harder, just as if he were making his way against a current that increases in strength the farther he pushes into the other male's home ground. The fish know just where the boundaries are and, after chasing each other back and forth across them, will usually end up with each one trembling and victorious on his own side of the truce line.

Similarly, the expulsion from communal territories is typically accomplished by ritual rather than by force. For example, among the red grouse of Scotland, the males crow and threaten only very early in the morning, and then only when the weather is good. This ceremony may become so threatening that weaker members of the group leave the moor. Those that leave often starve or are killed by predators. Once the early-morning contest is over, the remaining birds flock together and feed side by side for the rest of the day.

Territories and Population Regulation As we mentioned previously, animals that do not gain possession of territories or that are excluded from the "home range" or breeding area do not produce young. As older animals die, younger ones will contend for their places, keeping the breeding population stabilized. If conditions are particularly favorable, or if the range is enlarged, more animals can gain access to the breeding community. However, many never gain territories.

The submissive acceptance of an inferior social position would seem to be little reward in terms of "fitness" to those deprived of a territory and therefore an opportunity to reproduce. Would not it be advisable for such individuals to fight with their last calorie of strength rather than to give up the struggle? What, after all, have they got to lose? This question is such a seductive one that it is the formulation of the hypothesis that populations regulate their own size and individuals that do not reproduce do so for the good of the group. We shall discuss this largely discarded hypothesis at the end of the chapter, but for the moment note only that submission here serves the same function as it does in ritual combat—the loser survives and so has a second chance. For territorial animals, this may be worthwhile.

Some years ago, for example, a group of scientists undertook a study to determine whether or not the warblers nesting in the spruce trees exerted a controlling effect on the caterpillars of the spruce bud worm. They mapped the position of the singing males within an area of 16 hectares (40 acres), found 48 pairs, and began to shoot them all. After 3 weeks, they had shot 302 male warblers (and a lesser number of females), and there were still male warblers throughout the 16 hectares. The moral of this story, among others, is that animals that do not have territories are always ready to claim them and sometimes succeed in doing so. Thus, in the long run, waiting may be a better evolutionary bet than engaging in a probably unsuccessful combat. Territoriality is a successful strategy, in short, because it ritualizes competition and secures for the winner adequate resources for the breeding of young. The limitation of the size of the population is a side effect of these activities.

NOTES

1. **Oscar Brockett,** *The Theatre: An Introduction* (New York: Holt, Rinehart and Winston, 1964), pp. 260–261.
2. **Charles Kingsley Levy,** *Biology: Human Perspectives* (Glenview, Ill.: Scott, Foresman, 1979), pp. 298–303.
3. **Helena Curtis,** *Biology,* 3rd ed. (New York: Worth, 1979), pp. 923–928.

Twelve

READING MATHEMATICS

Reading mathematics can seem confusing. There are words, but scattered in among the words are symbols and equations. Sometimes these symbols and equations take up the entire page. When we get to this part of our reading we slow down or stop. Often we are tempted to skip the symbols or equations and go on reading. This doesn't work because the part we skipped is usually needed to understand the rest of the passage.

Let's stop and think for a second. Symbols and equations actually can make things easier. They are a kind of shorthand. To write out these ideas would often take many sentences—even many paragraphs or pages. Mathematical symbols or equations will make things easier once we know how to read them.

MATHEMATICAL SYMBOLS

Mathematical symbols include numerals, operation signs, symbols that show a relationship, and other symbols with special meanings.

EXERCISE I

Given below is a list of the most common mathematical symbols. Write a letter for each symbol next to the words that describe it. Look up the answers if you're not sure.

a. 400

b. $\div$

c. $=$

d. π

e. $\sqrt{}$

f. a^2

g. %

h. $|a|$

i. $c < d$

j. $c > d$

k. ∞

l. cm

____ the probability of A

____ percent

____ divide by

____ centimeter

____ c is greater than d

____ a times x

____ pi (3.14159)

____ a squared

____ plus or minus

____ equals

____ c is less than d

____ infinity

m. ±   _____ four hundreths

n. 0.04   _____ absolute value of a

o. $c \le d$ _____ three eighths

p. ≅   _____ square root

q. 3/8   _____ c is less than or equal to d

r. ax _____ congruent

s. $P(A)$ _____ four hundred

ARITHMETIC

Much of the mathematics you will be studying is based on the arithmetic you learned in elementary school and high school. Even though you learned arithmetic in the past, you may have forgotten arithmetic operations that you don't use often. However, you will almost certainly have to know arithmetic as well as the symbols above to read mathematics successfully.

EXERCISE II

A list of arithmetic skills is listed below. One problem is given for each skill. Complete each problem. Write the answers in the space provided. Use the right-hand part of the page to show your work.

WHOLE NUMBERS

1. Adding
   $378 + 6 + 92 = $ _____
2. Subtracting
   $2057 - 978 = $ _____
3. Multiplying
   $38 \times 305 = $ _____
4. Dividing
   $2044 \div 73 = $ _____

INTEGERS

5. Adding
   $-3 + -5 = $ _____
6. Subtracting
   $+3 - -5 = $ _____
7. Multiplying
   $-27 \times -48 = $ _____
8. Dividing
   $+368 \div -46 = $ _____

FRACTIONS AND MIXED NUMERALS

9. Adding
   $3/8 + 5/6 = $ _____
10. Subtracting
    $8\ 1/4 - 3\ 4/5 = $ _____
11. Multiplying
    $4/7 \times 3\ 1/4 = $ _____
12. Dividing
    $2\ 1/4 \div 4/9 = $ _____

DECIMALS

13. Adding
    1.7 + 0.08 + 7 = _____
14. Subtracting
    5.08 − 0.29 = _____
15. Multiplying
    4.78 × 0.37 = _____
16. Dividing
    15.12 ÷ 4.2 = _____

PERCENTS

17. Finding the percent of a number.
    What is 25% of 18? _____
18. Finding the percent one number is of another.
    What percent of 55 is 22? _____
19. Finding a number when a percent is known.
    30% of what number is 28? _____
20. Finding a discount.
    Find the price of a dress which is 30% off
    the original price of $28. _____
21. Finding the interest or tax.
    What is the total cost of a $15
    meal if the tax is 7%? _____

STATISTICS

  Use these numbers: 3, 5, 8, 7, 3, 4
22. Find the mean: _____

23. Find the median: _____

24. Find the mode: _____

Check your answers with the instructor. Circle those skills you have not mastered. You should seek additional help for those arithmetic skills you have not mastered. Check with your instructor to find out where to get additional help. Bring this book with you when you go.

Using a Calculator

A calculator can help you find the answers to arithmetic problems. You should buy a calculator if you don't already have one. The Texas Instruments TI-30 calculator and TI-30II are the most popular calculators and include all the operations you will need for college work. These calculators should be available for under $15.00. Sold along with the calculator is an excellent booklet that shows how to use the calculator to solve many different kinds of problems. Other useful, inexpensive calculators are available.

Remember, though, that the calculator is not the answer to all of your problems. In many classes you won't be able to use the calculator during tests and it is imperative that you master the arithmetic skills listed above.

SOLVING WORD PROBLEMS

Mathematics word problems must be read carefully. It is important for you to know exactly what you are supposed to find out and which arithmetic operation you should use. Follow these steps when reading mathematics word problems.

1. Read the problem carefully and completely.

2. Write the question that you must answer to solve the problem.
3. Write the facts that will help you solve the problem.
4. Decide which operation you should use. If the problem involves several steps, decide which order to follow.
5. Solve the problem and write the answer.

Clue Words

There are a number of clue words that will help you decide which operation to use. These words are listed below under the operation they indicate.

1. Addition: added, altogether, increased, total.
2. Subtraction: decreased, difference, fewer, left, less, remain.
3. Multiplication: at, of, times.
4. Division: divide, for each, share.

ACTIVITY I

Follow the steps given above to solve each problem

A.   The Apex Corporation earned $1,987,876 last year. The corporation had expenses of $1,834,687. How much was left after the expenses had been paid?

1. Read
2. Question _How much is left after expenses ?_
3. Facts _Earned $1,987,876; expenses $1,834,687_
4. Operation _Subtraction_
5. Solve _$1,987,876 − $1,834,687 = $153,189_

B.   There are 12,000 people to be surveyed as part of an opinion poll. 12% of the people have already been surveyed. How many people have been surveyed?

1. Read
2. Question _____
3. Facts _____
4. Operation _____
5. Solve _____

C.   A computer firm spent $61,668 on six computers. Each of these computers cost the same amount of money. How much did the firm spend for each computer?

1. Read
2. Question _____
3. Facts _____

4. Operation _____

5. Solve _____

D.   The Big Dome sports arena seats 14,987 people. There were three basketball games held there last week. 8,945 people attended the first game. 13,879 came to each of the last two games. What was the total number of people at these games?

1. Read
2. Question _____

3. Facts _____

4. Operation _____

5. Solve _____

EQUATIONS

You will often encounter equations when reading mathematics. Equations tell us that two numbers or expressions are equal. Equations should be read and understood just as we read and understand words and sentences.

When you encounter an equation while reading, slow down your reading rate and go over the equation several times. Try to understand what the equation means—what it is saying.

You will encounter three main types of equations:

1.   Some equations will be equations to be *solved*. If this is the case, you would use the rules of algebra to solve the equation. Usually, equations to be solved are not found in the body of a text.
2.   Some equations show a *relationship*. For example, an equation that shows how to convert from centigrade to Fahrenheit temperature ($F = 9/5C + 32$) shows a relationship. When you encounter an equation that shows a relationship, you should try to understand the relationship.
3.   Some equations state a *fact*. For example, the equation $P(B) = 2/3$ states a fact about the probability of B.

You are most likely to encounter equations that show a relationship.

Reading Equations

The method explained below will help you undersand equations you read in a text. Use this method only when you do not understand the equation. This method should not be used for *exercises* in a mathematics book or other texts.

If you use the method and you still don't understand the equation, get help! If the equation is central to understanding the material, get an explanation before you read further.

The RATS Method

1.   *Read*: Slow down your reading rate. The equal sign tells you that the numbers or expressions on either side mean the same thing. *Write out the equation.*

2. *Ask:* Is this an equation (a) to be solved, (b) which shows a relationship, (c) which states a fact?

   a. The equation below is to be solved. You want to find the value of x.

$$4x + 5 = 3x + 14$$

   b. The equation below shows a relationship between the length of the side and the area of a square.

$$s = \sqrt{A}$$

   c. The equation below states a fact about the probability of an event *A*.

$$P(A) = \tfrac{1}{2}$$

3. *Think:* What does the equation mean? Write out the meaning.

   a. The equation below means the product of 4 and x added to 5 equals the product of 3 and x added to 14.

$$4x + 5 = 3x + 14$$

   b. The equation below means the length of the side of a square equals the square root of the area.

$$s = \sqrt{A}$$

   c. The equation below means the probability of some event called *A* is 1/2.

$$P(A) = \tfrac{1}{2}$$

4. *Stop:* Before going on, be sure that you understand the equation. Reread your written meaning and solve if necessary.

ACTIVITY II

Use the RATS method to examine these equations.

1. $C = \pi d$

   R   *C = 𝜋 d*

   A   *Shows a relationship*

   T *Circumference equals pi times diameter*
   S

2. $9y - 7 \leq 38$

   R

   A

   T
   S

3. $P(A \text{ and } B) = 0.17$

   R

   A

   T
   S

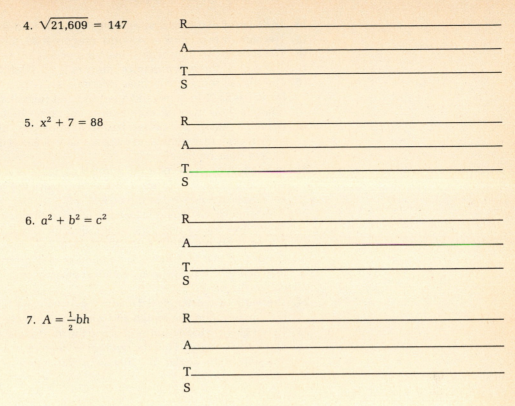

4. $\sqrt{21{,}609} = 147$

R_____

A_____

T_____
S

5. $x^2 + 7 = 88$

R_____

A_____

T_____
S

6. $a^2 + b^2 = c^2$

R_____

A_____

T_____
S

7. $A = \frac{1}{2}bh$

R_____

A_____

T_____
S

PROJECTS

Read and solve the word problems in Project I. Use a separate sheet of paper and show the steps used to solve each problem.

In Project II, you will find six short excerpts from a mathematics text. Each excerpt has a formula to be read and understood. On a separate piece of paper, write out each step of the RATS method for each equation.

PROJECT I

Solve each of the following problems.[1] Only an algebraic solution will be accepted.

1. Three more than a certain number is 10. Find the number.
2. Four less than a certain number is 10. Find the number.
3. The sum of a certain number and 5 is 12. Find the number.
4. Two more than twice a certain number is 6. Find the number.
5. The sum of two consecutive integers is 15. Find the numbers.
6. Mary is 5 years older than Tom and the sum of their ages is 51. How old is each?
7. Julia is 7 years younger than Lewis and the sum of their ages is 53. How old is each?
8. Seven less than 4 times a number is 41. Find the number.
9. The sum of 5 times a number and 8 is 63. Find the number.
10. The sum of one-half of a number and 5 is 12. Find the number.
11. The width of a rectangle is 3 feet less than its length. If the perimeter of the rectangle is 50 feet, find the dimensions of the rectangle.
12. The length of a rectangle is 4 metres longer than its width. If the perimeter of the rectangle is 60 metres, find the dimensions of the rectangle.
13. The length of a rectangle is 2 metres longer than twice its width. If the perimeter of the rectangle is 100 metres, find the dimensions of the rectangle.

14. The sum of two consecutive integers is 101. Find the numbers.
15. The sum of two consecutive odd integers is 40. Find the numbers.
16. The sum of two consecutive even integers is 38. Find the numbers.
17. The sum of three consecutive integers is 93. Find the numbers.
18. The sum of three consecutive odd integers is 123. Find the numbers.
19. David has $2.25 in dimes and quarters in his pocket. If he has twice as many dimes as quarters, how many of each type of coin does he have?
20. Daniel, a newspaper carrier, has $2.90 in nickels, dimes, and quarters. If he has 3 more nickels than dimes and twice as many dimes as quarters, how many of each type of coin does he have?
21. In a collection of 60 coins the number of quarters is one-third the number of dimes and the number of nickels is 10 less than twice the number of dimes. How many of each type of coins are in the collection?
22. A rectangular garden is enclosed by 460 feet of fencing. If the length of the garden is 10 feet less than 3 times the width, find the dimensions of the garden.
23. Joe emptied his bank, which contained only nickels, dimes, and quarters. Joe discovered that he had the same number of quarters and dimes and 5 more nickels than quarters. If the total value of the coins was $4.25, how many of each type of coin was in the bank?
24. The width of a rectangle is 3 inches more than one-half of its length. If the perimeter is 60 inches, find the length and width of the rectangle.
25. Two angles of a triangle are equal and the third angle is 20 degrees less than twice one of the equal angles. Find the number of degrees in each angle of the triangle. (*Hint:* The sum of the angles of a triangle is 180 degrees.)

PROJECT II

Read each excerpt and equation. On a separate piece of paper, write out each step of the RATS method for each equation.

A.   The boiling point of water is 212°F or 100°C, and the freezing point of water is 32°F or 0°C. Most of us will be able to remember these comparative temperatures on the Celsius thermometer. But we would like to be able to interpret other Celsius thermometer readings as well. When someone tells us that their temperature is 37°C, we should be aware that this is normal, or 98.6°F. A room temperature of 68°F is the same as a room temperature of 20°C. It is obviously important to identify a degree measurement as degrees Celsius or degrees Fahrenheit.

The following two formulas will enable you to convert from Fahrenheit to Celsius and vice versa. When you know the Fahrenheit temperature and wish to convert to Celsius, you should use the formula

$$C = \frac{5}{9}(F - 32)$$

B.   When you find the sum of 4 and 5, whether you add them as $4 + 5$, or as $5 + 4$, the answer is 9. That is, $4 + 5 = 5 + 4$. Similarly, if you multiply 4 and 5 together, you can multiply 4×5 or 5×4, and the answer is 20. So $4 \times 5 = 5 \times 4$. No matter what order you do the operation in, the answer is the same. In other words, we can switch the elements around; we can *commute* them. When we can do this for all elements in a system using a given operation, we say that the operation is *commutative*.

Given a system consisting of a set of elements {*a, b, c, . . .*} and an operation ∗, we say that the operation is *commutative* if for all elements *a* and *b* in the system,

$$a * b = b * a$$

C.   How do we combine rational numbers? Since 2 and 3 are rational numbers and 2 + 3 = 5, we already know how to combine some rationals. But consider the problem of adding the rational numbers ⅕ + ⅔. In section 8.3 we discussed the process of adding and subtracting fractions. However, those problems were considered only with regard to the use of the least common multiple. Let's state a general rule for adding any two rational numbers:

If ⅗ and ⅗ are rational numbers, then

$$\frac{a}{b} + \frac{c}{d} = \frac{ad + bc}{bd}$$

Therefore, for the example ⅕ + ⅔, we have the following:

$$\frac{1}{5} + \frac{2}{3} = \frac{(1 \times 3) + (5 \times 2)}{5 \times 3} = \frac{3 + 10}{15} = \frac{13}{15}$$

D.   An ordered pair is always of the form (x, y); that is, the x value is listed first and the y value is listed second. The x value is formally called the **abscissa** and the y value is called the **ordinate,** but in our discussion we shall refer to them as the x and y values.

It should be noted that the ordered pair $(2, 4)$ is not the only ordered pair that will make the open sentence $x + 2y = 10$ a true statement; it is not the only solution for the given equation. In fact, there are infinitely many ordered pairs in the solution set of the equation $x + 2y = 10$.

Any equation of the form

$$Ax + By = C$$

where A, B, and C are real numbers is called a **linear equation.** Thus $x + 2y = 10$ is a linear equation. It is called a linear equation because when we graph such an equation in the Cartesian plane, we get a straight line.

E.   If bank A offers 5% interest on its deposits compounded quarterly and Bank B offers 5½% interest on its deposits compounded semiannually, we can find the effective annual rate for each bank to determine which offers the best investment. We can also compare effective rates when borrowing money. In this case, we would select the lowest effective rate.

We can determine the effective annual rate by means of the formula

$$E = (1 + r)^n - 1$$

where

E = effective rate
n = number of payment periods per year
r = interest rate per period

F.   In 1969, Congress passed a Truth in Lending Act which requires all sellers to reveal the true annual interest rate that they charge. However, the Act does not establish any maximums on interest rates or finance charges.

There is a formula that can be used to determine the **true annual interest rate** on installment loans. It is:

$$i = \frac{2nr}{n+1} \quad \text{where} \quad \begin{aligned} i &= \text{the true interest} \\ n &= \text{number of payments} \\ r &= \text{the nominal rate of interest} \end{aligned}$$

NOTES

1. **William Setek,** *Fundamentals of Mathematics* (New York: Macmillan, 1979), pp. 259, 278, 394, 442–444, 553, 562.

Thirteen

READING SCIENCE

In many ways, reading a science book is very much like reading any textbook. You use the same steps and procedures described in earlier chapters of this book. However, there are some unique features found in science books. Reading a science book often means understanding some technical process or pattern. You often come across technical symbols or terms. You must understand what these symbols and terms mean before you can make sense out of the rest of the material.

If you come across a symbol or term you do not understand, you must discipline yourself not to skip it. You must take the time to look it up in a glossary or reference or to ask your professor. This can be a time-consuming process and, initially, it will break into the the flow of your reading. But this approach works, so put up with the initial frustration and always look up every term or symbol you don't understand.

Often a science text contains charts or diagrams designed to clarify the material presented in the text. *Do not skip these charts or diagrams.* Charts and diagrams should be studied carefully. They are often the best summary of the written material.

SCIENTIFIC TERMS

There are many different types of technical terms and it is not possible here to provide a unified way of dealing with them all. Perhaps the most important thing to remember about these terms is that they are designed to bring a high level of precision to the passage. It is this emphasis on precision that makes it almost impossible to decipher the meaning of a term from its context. *You must look it up.*

On occasion, these terms are of long standing and may be adapted from Greek or Latin words, such as the terms used to classify insects. On other occasions, the terms may be combinations of chemical names, such as the term represented by the abbreviation DNA. In these cases, it may be possible to understand or remember the term by understanding its roots. However, many other scientific terms do not have this structured origin and must be remembered or understood by looking up and studying their meanings.

It is always worthwhile to keep a list of scientific terms. You may want to keep a stack of 3×5 cards or write the terms in your notebook or on the pages of the textbook.

One more thing about scientific terms. You are probably more likely to come across unfamiliar terms in a science text than in any other textbook. This can be frustrating . . . and frightening. All those unfamiliar words—every page brings more of them. Everyone feels the same way. Don't panic or give up in frustration. Take your time as you work through the text—use the suggestions in this book—and you will understand.

SCIENTIFIC SYMBOLS

Among the most common scientific symbols are those showing the composition of different compounds. The letter or letters name the individual elements. Your science text will usually have a table showing the elements, their properties, and the abbreviation used to identify each element. The subscripted number following an element's abbreviation tells how many atoms of that element are in the compound—for example, H_2O is the symbol for water: two atoms of hydrogen for each atom of oxygen.

You will encounter other scientific symbols. Usually, these symbols will be explained in the text or in the glossary. If you can't find the explanation there, you must look it up in the dictionary before proceeding.

As in mathematics, these symbols are actually a shorthand which makes ideas easier to present and to grasp. With a little work, you will come to understand this shorthand and reading science will be easier.

CHARTS AND DIAGRAMS

Science books are full of charts and diagrams. I can remember well a science text I had in college. The text had a diagram which labeled all the parts of the brain. We were expected to be able to correctly label each part and give its function as well. The task, at first, seemed impossible.

Then someone showed me how to learn these difficult diagrams, and I would commend this approach to you. This person took the page with the diagram and made a copy on a duplicating machine. Then she cut out all the descriptive information and pasted the now wordless chart onto a piece of paper. The names of the parts were pasted on cards. I spent some time matching the names to the parts, and what seemed an impossible task became easier. Try this method when studying diagrams.

Take the time to carefully examine each chart and diagram you encounter. Try to understand what important information the chart or diagram is intended to convey. Relate this information to your reading.

STEPS FOR READING SCIENCE

1. Preview the material. Make sure that you understand all the technical terms and symbols. Underline all terms and symbols that you don't understand. Look up the meanings of terms and symbols if necessary. Make a note of each meaning. I recommend that you write these notes in your book for easy reference.
2. Follow the other reading steps outlined in this book. Once you understand the terms and symbols, it's almost easy reading. Preview and read for topic, main idea, and supporting details.
3. Carefully study all charts and diagrams. You will actually do this at each step of your reading. Remember to use the study approach mentioned above for diagrams you must "memorize."

4. Prepare a brief outline. Outline the important points only. The outline is a powerful study tool, and you may want to outline readings other than science readings. Use the outline as the basis for further study.

ACTIVITY I

Carefully read this science selection. Preview first and underline all terms or symbols you do not understand. Write the meaning or definition in the margin near the term or symbol. Read, paying careful attention to any diagrams. Use the format provided on the page following the selection to prepare an outline.

THE LIFE-GIVING PROPERTIES OF WATER[1]

Water is a highly polar molecule with the oxygen end having a partial negative electric charge. The water molecule is not symmetrical, and because it is asymmetrical, electric charges are located at different points in space. Being a polar molecule, water can latch onto charged parts of other molecules, allowing them to dissolve readily. Thus water is a superb solvent. Sodium chloride, a salt, assumes a crystalline lattice shape when dry, but in water the positively charged sodium and the negatively charged chlorine ions separate (or dissociate) completely because they are more attracted to the polar water molecules than to each other. Many substances dissolve in water to form ions (electrically charged atoms or molecules). Acids are substances that dissociate in water to produce an excess of free hydrogen (H^+) ions. Bases dissolve in water to produce an excess of free hydroxide (OH^-) ions. Some acids, called strong acids, dissociate completely and thereby produce large numbers of free H^+ ions; other acids, called weak acids, only partly dissociate in water, giving relatively few H^+ ions. Water itself produces equal but relatively small numbers of free H^+ and OH^- ions. Later the importance of these free H^+ ions will be apparent.

Water molecules, because of their electric charges, are held together by weak hydrogen bonds. However, water molecules at the surface cannot react with air and are drawn downward, creating a film of inwardly directed hydrogen bonds. These bonds create a surface tension, and anything penetrating that surface film must have enough energy to break those bonds. This surface tension is of particular importance in plants, for without it water would not flow from the root system to the top of the plant.

For two reasons, water is also critical in maintaining our constant body temperature. First, water can absorb a considerable amount of heat energy without increasing its temperature very much; thus water has a high heat capacity. However, if you heat water enough, the hydrogen bonds on the surface can be broken and those surface molecules can break away and fly off into the air. This is called vaporization of water. As they depart from the surface they carry with them a considerable amount of heat and cause a tremendous cooling effect. Thus the second temperature-regulating characteristic of water is cooling by evaporative water loss; in humans this is called perspiration.

Not all substances dissolve in water. Substances that interact with water and form hydrogen bonds or ionic (electric) attraction are called hydrophilic ("water-loving") compounds. Unpolarized compounds cannot react with water, are insoluble, and are called hydrophobic ("water-dreading") compounds. The lipid molecules, which have both hydrophilic and hydrophobic ends, were essential in the creation of the boundary layer that surrounds all cells, the cell membrane.

Figure 3–1

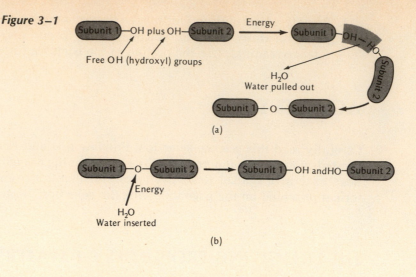

(a)

(b)

Finally, water is not only the medium in which life exists but also an active participant in many chemical reactions. In the complex reactions of photosynthesis that ultimately provide us with all of our fuels, the energy from sunlight is trapped to split water and provide hydrogen for the manufacture of sugars. In other chemical reactions water is removed to form a link between two other molecules in a process called dehydration synthesis. In other reactions water is added to cause two molecules to separate; this is called hydrolysis (-*lysis* means "to split") (Fig. 3–1).

Complete the outline for "Life-Giving Properties of Water." Some main ideas are given. Write the other main ideas and the supporting details for each main idea.

OUTLINE: "LIFE-GIVING PROPERTIES OF WATER"

I. Water

    A.

    B.

    C. Acids

    D. Bases

    E. Surface Tension

F. High Heat Capacity

G.

H.

I.

PROJECT

A science reading about plant hormones follows. First, read the selection using the steps outlined in this chapter. Remember to write a definition in the margin of each term and symbol you do not understand.

On a separate piece of paper, prepare an outline for the reading.

PLANT HORMONES[2]

1. The function of plant hormones is the integration of processes in the plant body.
2. Among the processes controlled by plant hormones are **a.** cell division **b.** cell (and therefore organ) elongation **c.** differentiation of tissues and organs **d.** initiation and breaking of dormancy in buds, seeds, and cambium **e.** tropisms

The fact that an organism as complicated as a flowering plant functions smoothly implies the existence of some regulatory mechanism that integrates the many processes going on within the plant. Hormones contribute to this integration by causing growth to start, stop, or proceed faster or slower and by regulating the differentiation of tissues and organs.

Hormones are defined as organic compounds that are produced in one part of an organism and that move to another part where they exert their effects. In this way they provide communication between the parts of an organism. The distances hormones travel may vary from exceedingly small distances to the length of an organ or even the entire organism. The mechanisms by which some hormones exert their effects have begun to become clear only recently, and this field continues to reveal much interesting new information. Hormones act in such low concentrations that they must have enzyme-related effects. There is evidence that at least some hormones initiate the production of certain enzymes by influencing the genetic material that carries the genetic code for the synthesis of these enzymes. . . . Probably many plant hormones act in this fashion, but others well may be found to function in other ways.

MAJOR PLANT HORMONES

Five groups of plant hormones will be discussed here in some detail: auxins, gibberellins, cytokinins, abscisic acid, and ethylene. Each of these hormones has several functions, only the more important or better known of which are discussed here. Other plant hormones are known, too, and additional ones undoubtedly will be discovered.

Auxins

The **auxins** probably are the best known of the plant hormones. They were discovered late in the 1920s and since then have been the subject of intensive research. The most common auxin in plants is **indole-3-acetic acid (IAA)**; Figure 29.1 shows its molecular structure. Produced by active apical meristems, young leaves, and other tissues with dividing cells, IAA moves primarily in a **basipetal** direction in stems (from stem tip toward the base of the stem) and affects growth and differentiation in several ways. There is conflicting evidence regarding the direction of movement of IAA in roots. It is now believed that it moves in the **acropetal** direction: from the base of the root (where it joins the stem) toward the tip.

basi-: base
-petal: moving toward
acro-: tip

IAA and Elongation Discovered early was the ability of IAA to stimulate elongation of cells. When the apices of oat coleoptiles (which respond to auxin in much the same way as stems do) are removed, the decapitated coleoptiles soon cease to elongate; but if the apices are replaced, the coleoptiles continue to elongate for a while. Applying IAA extracted from coleoptile tips to decapitated coleoptiles also restores their ability to elongate, as does synthetic auxin.

Fig. 29.1
Molecular structures of some plant hormones, including three synthetic auxins.

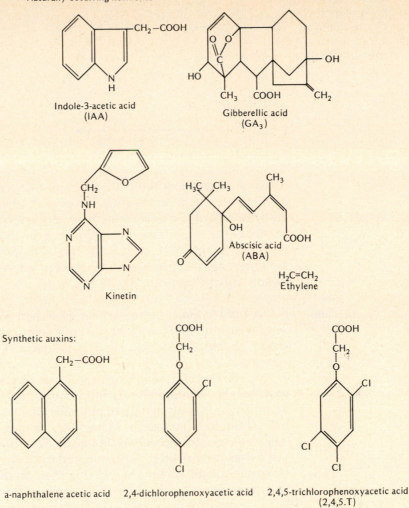

Naturally-occurring hormones

Indole-3-acetic acid
(IAA)

Gibberellic acid
(GA$_3$)

Kinetin

Abscisic acid
(ABA)

$H_2C=CH_2$
Ethylene

Synthetic auxins:

CH_2-COOH

a-naphthalene acetic acid

2,4-dichlorophenoxyacetic acid

2,4,5-trichlorophenoxyacetic acid
(2,4,5.T)

IAA moves basipetally from the apical meristem of a stem to the region of elongation, where it exerts its effect (Fig. 29.2). The cell walls become more plastic as the bonds between the cellulose molecules break, and the walls then can stretch when water enters the cells. It is likely that IAA exerts its effect indirectly by affecting some step in the basic metabolism rather than acting directly on cellulose molecules.

Fig. 29.2
IAA moving basipetally in the stem from the apical meristem causes elongation of the cells below. Diagrammatic.

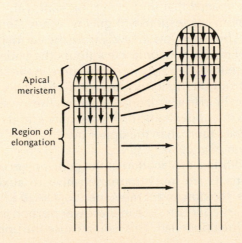

Apical meristem

Region of elongation

Fig. 29.3

Effect of auxin on elongation of roots and stems. Concentrations of IAA that inhibit the growth of roots promote the growth of stems.

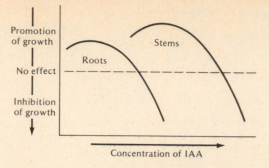

For each organ of the plant there is a concentration of IAA that promotes maximum elongation. Slightly lower or higher concentrations also promote elongation, but to a lesser extent. At very low concentrations there is no effect; at very high concentrations not only is growth inhibited, but various deformations and even death may result. The optimum concentrations for elongation are different in different organs; concentrations that stimulate growth of stems inhibit growth of roots (Fig. 29.3).

trop-: turn, turning (Do not confuse with *troph-*, which refers to nutrition.)

IAA and Tropisms A **tropism** is a growth movement of a plant part toward or away from a stimulus. A tropism is spoken of as being positive if the moving part grows toward the stimulus and as negative if the part grows away from the stimulus.

Through its role in cell elongation, auxin functions in several tropisms (growth movements). **Phototropism** is the bending response of an organ to unilateral illumination. Young stems and petioles, which are positively phototropic, bend toward bright illumination. Many roots do not respond to light, but some are negatively phototropic, bending away from bright illumination.

If a stem is more brightly illuminated from one side, a higher concentration of IAA accumulates on the shaded side than on the illuminated side because the IAA produced in the tip moves laterally *away* from the light as well as basipetally. Because the cells in the shaded side then elongate more than do the cells in the illuminated side the stem bends toward the light source (Fig. 29.4).

A petiole responds similarly if only one side of the leaf blade is illuminated. IAA moves from the blade to the petiole, and more moves from the shaded side than from the illuminated side. The higher IAA concentration on one side of the petiole causes the petiole to bend in such a way that it moves the blade into brighter light. Inspection of most plants shows the leaves so oriented that the blades shade each other as little as possible. Boston ivy and other vines often show patterns called **leaf mosaics** when they grow on walls; the leaves are so uniformly spaced that they cover the wall with little overlapping.

Geotropism is a response to gravity. Many stems and petioles are negatively geotropic, bending upward away from the earth. If growing stems are placed in a horizontal position, in only a few hours the young portion of the stem and the younger petioles bend upward, the curve in the stems usually occurring an inch or more from the tip in the region of elongation.

In a stem held in a horizontal position, the lower half contains much more IAA than does the upper half. The higher concentration in the lower portion causes it to elongate more than the upper portion. This results in the upward bending of the stem (Fig. 29.5).

The traditional explanation of the geotropism of roots has been based on the fact that roots are much more sensitive to auxin than are stems (Fig. 29.3). Therefore, the downward movement of IAA in a horizontal root would produce an inhibitory concentration in the lower portion and leave a stimulatory concentration in the upper half. This would cause the upper part to grow more than the

Fig. 29.4
Positive phototropism of stems and leaves. IAA moves both basipetally and away from a light source. Because cells receiving more IAA elongate more than those receiving less, the stem or petiole bends toward the light. Diagrammatic.

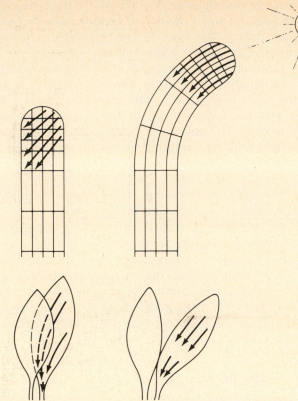

lower part and produce the positive geotropic response. It is also possible that some other hormone may affect geotropism in the root. (See the section on abscisic acid later in this chapter.)

IAA and Apical Dominance Under some conditions IAA promotes cell division; the IAA moving downward from reactivated terminal buds early in the year causes the vascular cambium to begin its divisions. On the other hand, IAA produced by a terminal bud inhibits the growth of lateral buds, whose apical meristems produce no IAA as long as they are dormant. This phenomenon, called **apical dominance,** prevents plants from becoming excessively bushy. Should a terminal bud be removed from a stem or should it be damaged by

Fig. 29.5
Negative geotropism of stems. IAA moves downward as well as basipetally in stems placed in a horizontal position. Because the lower cells elongate more than the upper ones, the stem bends upward. Diagrammatic.

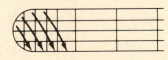

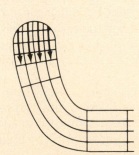

disease, one or more lateral buds on that stem will be released from inhibition and will resume growth and produce a branch. When the terminal bud of this new branch becomes active, it produces its own IAA, and it exerts apical dominance over any lateral buds below it.

Untrimmed, undamaged plants do have some branches, however. With increasing distance from a terminal bud, the concentration of its auxin diminishes. Eventually, a point is reached where the concentration is so low that it exerts no dominance over the lateral buds, which then can develop into branches. The characteristic shapes of many species of trees and shrubs are affected by the amount of IAA produced by their terminal buds and the sensitivity of their lateral buds to it.

IAA and Leaf Abscission   The seasonal dropping of leaves (or fruits) is called **abscission.** The leaves are said to acscise.

In autumn, the formation of a layer of weak, thin-walled cells called the **abscission zone** precedes the dropping of leaves of many species. The base of the petiole, where this zone forms, receives IAA moving downward from the blade and from the terminal bud. As long as the IAA from the blade exceeds that from the terminal bud, as it does early in the growing season, the abscission zone does not form. Later in the year, as the blade ages, it produces less IAA and the abscission zone forms. (See also the discussion of abscisic acid later in this chapter.)

Synthetic Auxins

After naturally occurring auxins were discovered, several additional auxins were synthesized.

Synthetic auxins, such as α-naphthalene acetic acid, find use as rooting agents. Many commercially valuable plants once were difficult to propagate by cuttings, because they do not form adventitious roots readily. Dipping the cuttings into a dilute solution of an auxin or allowing the cut ends to soak in it for several hours usually overcomes the difficulty and induces copious rooting.

The buds ("eyes") of untreated Irish, or white, potatoes often sprout while they are in storage. Because the potatoes ordinarily are stored in darkness, the food they contain is the only energy source that the sprouting buds might use. Therefore, any sprouting represents a loss in food value to the owner of the potatoes. Spraying storage potatoes with synthetic auxins retards or completely prevents sprouting and its concomitant food loss.

In some species auxins also can be used to induce ovaries of unpollinated pistils to mature into fruits. No seeds form because pollination and fertilization did not occur. Seedless tomatoes, watermelons, and cucumbers have been produced this way. In Hawaii, pineapple fields are sprayed with auxin to induce flowering at any desired time of year.

Among the synthetic auxins are 2,4-D and 2,4,5-T (Fig. 29.1). When used at appropriate concentrations, 2,4-D kills broad-leaved weeds by disrupting their metabolism, but it does not affect the grasses, which include not only lawn grass, but the cereal grains and sugar cane. Therefore, it became a favorite weed killer for use on lawns and many farm fields. Because they decompose readily, 2,4-D and 2,4,5-T were believed to be good choices for the purpose, for they would not affect broad-leaved crops or ornamentals planted later in treated areas.

Then, in the war in Vietnam, 2,4,5-T gained notoriety when it was used as a defoliating agent. Mangrove and rubber trees sprayed several times with it show few signs of recovery. The ecological damage in southeastern Asia was extensive and apparently will be long-lasting. The assumption that these substances were harmless to human beings is now brought into question, too. There are reports of births of deformed babies in previously sprayed areas, and United States personnel who were exposed to the spray have complained of an assortment of medical problems. The offending substance may not be 2,4,5-T itself, but dioxin, a contaminant formed in the manufacture of 2,4,5-T. Dioxin is one of the most toxic substances known, and it can do a great deal of damage even at extremely low concentrations.

Gibberellins

Gibberellins were named for the fungus *Gibberella fujikuroi,* from which they were first obtained. *G. fujikuroi* infects rice plants and causes them to grow too tall and too slender to support the rice grains.

Discovery of the **gibberellins** in the 1920s preceded that of auxins by only a few years. The discovery was made in Japan; but because communications between scientists of distant countries were not the best in those days and because World War II later disrupted them, it was only in the mid-1950s that Western scientists became aware of the existence of this new class of plant hormones. At first considered mere curiosities, gibberellins gradually commanded more and more interest when it was learned that they perform important functions in the growth and reproduction of flowering plants. At least 35 gibberellins have been discovered; gibberellic acid (GA_3), illustrated in Figure 29.1, has been used in many experiments. Unlike the auxins, gibberellins move either upward or downward in stems and roots.

Gibberellins cause cell elongation, and marked elongation of stems is one of the startling effects of gibberellin. Dwarf varieties of several plants exist because of their possession of genetic defects that keep them small. External applications of gibberellin to the stem tip of a dwarf or bush variety of bean convert it into the tall climbing vine of the pole variety.

Gibberellin also has a noticeable effect on several biennial rosette plants. In its first year, one of these plants produces a short stem that barely rises above the surface of the ground and a rosette of leaves also near the ground. The second year, after the plant has been exposed to a cold winter, the stem elongates markedly and produces flowers. In nature the exposure to cold temperatures seems to be a requisite for stem elongation and flowering, but applications of gibberellin can substitute for cold treatment. The gibberellin stimulates the cells of the apical meristem to divide and the resulting cells to elongate. Applications of gibberellin to the rosette plant cause stem elongation and flowering even though there has been no exposure to low temperatures (other conditions must be favorable for flowering, of course). In this way, carrots, radishes, and other biennials can be made to flower in their first years.

Another important function of gibberellin is its role in germination. Produced by the embryo, it stimulates the production of several enzymes, including amylase, in the endosperm of corn; thus it promotes the digestion of starch to the sugars that the embryo requires for germination. Gibberellin indirectly stimulates production of auxin, which, in turn, promotes growth of the embryo.

Gibberellin also inhibits the formation of adventitious roots on cuttings.

Cytokinins

The name of this group of hormones derives from the word *cytokinesis.*

The **cytokinins** (or simply kinins) comprise a third group of plant hormones, of which kinetin (Fig. 29.1) is perhaps the best known. They are most abundant in young fruits and seeds and in plant tumors.

Cytokinins are formed primarily in apical meristems of roots and in growing fruits. These hormones stimulate cell division, and in some cases they cause cell elongation. It is known that they stimulate protein synthesis, probably through some action on the genetic system of the cell. When applied to tissue cultures (tissues isolated from living organisms and grown under sterile conditions in test tubes), they cause the initiation of buds from previously undifferentiated tissue. They inhibit rooting of cuttings, but they promote the germination of some seeds.

Abscisic Acid

Other names for abscisic acid are abscisin and dormin.

Abscisic acid (ABA) is found in many different plant parts, among them maturing leaves and fruits. It promotes the formation of abscission layers at the bases of leaves and fruits and so leads to their dropping. Too rapid a production of ABA can cause premature leaf or fruit drop.

ABA also promotes the onset of dormancy in the buds of perennial plants of the temperate zone. It inhibits the germination of some seeds, and in some species it promotes formation of adventitious roots on cuttings.

Roots are positively geotropic, and it was once thought that IAA played a role in the bending of roots—a hypothesis that is not wholly discarded. But there is also some evidence that the root cap produces an inhibitor that moves basipetally in the root (from the root cap up toward the base of the root). The rate of elongation of the root depends on the relative proportions of IAA and this inhibitor. According to one theory, if the root is placed on its side, the inhibitor accumulates to higher concentrations on the lower side. The lower side then grows more slowly than the upper, and so the root tip bends down (Fig. 29.6). The identity of the inhibitor is not known with certainty, but it is thought to be abscisic acid.

Ethylene

Ethylene has two unusual features for a hormone: It is a gas, and it is a small, rather simple molecule (Fig. 29.1). It is perhaps best known for its promotion of ripening of fleshy fruits, such as apples, oranges, and bananas. Young green fruits produce little ethylene. As they ripen, fruits produce more and more ethylene, and that ethylene further hastens ripening. Because it is a gas, ethylene can escape from the fruit; but in a closed container, the ethylene released from one fruit may hasten the ripening of other pieces of fruit.

Today many fruits are picked while still green because they are firmer than when fully ripe and thus suffer fewer bruises during transport from farm to

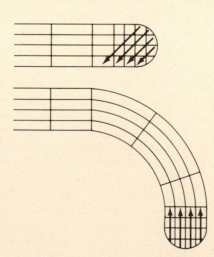

Fig. 29.6
Positive geotropism in roots. It is believed that a growth inhibitor produced in the root tip moves basipetally in the root and also downward in a root placed horizontally. Because cells on the lower side elongate less than those on the upper side, the root bends down. Diagrammatic.

market. These fruits may be stored and/or transported in a container filled with an ethylene atmosphere to hasten their ripening before being offered for sale.

Ethylene also promotes the abscission of leaves and fruits.

INTERRELATIONSHIPS AMONG PLANT HORMONES

From the foregoing it is obvious that each plant hormone does not have a single, specific function but has several. Two or three hormones may have several functions in common, but they also have some antagonistic effects. For instance, IAA and abscisic acid promote rooting of cuttings and inhibit growth of lateral buds; gibberellin and cytokinin inhibit rooting and promote growth of lateral buds. IAA, gibberellin, and cytokinin stimulate active elongation of stems, but by promoting dormancy of apical buds, abscisic acid indirectly brings about a cessation of elongation.

The several groups of hormones do not function separately. Two or more are likely to be present simultaneously in a given tissue. The absolute amount of a given hormone is usually not so important as the relative concentrations of the different hormones. With relatively low cytokinin concentrations in combination with relatively high IAA concentrations, root formation is initiated; but buds are produced by tissues with high concentrations of cytokinin and low concentrations of IAA.

In addition to the hormones discussed in this chapter, several other plant hormones are known: traumatic acid, which is produced by wounded tissue and promotes cell division and healing of the wound; thiamin (vitamin B_1), which roots require for normal growth; and perhaps florigen, the flowering hormone, whose existence has been postulated but not yet proved.

QUESTIONS

1. Define or describe the following terms:
   hormone
   tropism
   apical dominance
2. In a general sense, what is the function of hormones?
3. Give the functions of several plant hormones.
4. If you were to apply auxin to one side of a stem in the region of elongation, what result would you expect? If you applied it to one side of a tree trunk, would you expect the same result? Explain.
5. Name some common uses of synthetic auxin.
6. Explain why roots and stems have opposite geotropic responses.
7. If someone says his potted plant kept on a window sill is searching for light, how would you explain to him what his plant is really doing? Could you suggest a simple way that he might prevent the plant from "searching" for light?
8. What effect would you expect if you sprayed a gibberellin on a biennial plant in its first year?
9. If a cutting removed from a plant of a species that roots readily is placed in water, the lower end of the cutting develops roots and the uppermost lateral bud of the cut stump will grow into a branch. Therefore, if a cut is made at A in the accompanying illustration, the bud in the shaded area is likely to grow, but the formation of roots on that part of the stem is most unlikely. If, on the other hand, a cut is made at B, the shaded area will produce roots, but the bud in that region probably will not grow into a branch. Can you explain why this segment of stem would respond differently under the two conditions?

NOTES

1. **Charles Kingsley Levy,** *Biology: Human Perspectives* (Glenview, Ill: Scott, Foresman, 1979), pp. 46–48.
2. **Joan Elma Rahn,** *Biology,* 2nd ed. (New York: Macmillan, 1980), pp. 377–384.

Fourteen

READING HISTORY

When reading a history textbook, you should follow the steps outlined in the first nine chapters of this book. Previewing, finding the topic, main idea, and details, skimming and scanning, and the steps in textbook study outlined in Chapter 10 should form the basis for studying any book. You should actively employ these techniques in the work of this chapter. However, you will find it much easier to study history texts if you use some additional techniques.

Usually, history texts give an overview of major events. These texts try to help us understand why the major events happened and tell us about the central personalities.

So when you read a history text, you usually want to know:

1. The event: What happened?
2. The date: When did it happen?
3. The cause: Why did it happen?
4. The people: Who were the major personalities?

As you read any history text, you must always keep these questions in mind and constantly be searching for the answers. The most difficult task is to relate the events, causes, and personalities to the dates. This section will show you how to use a time line, in conjunction with your other study skills, to help you remember these dates as well as the events, causes, and personalities associated with them.

Start by dividing a piece of notebook paper into four columns as shown below.

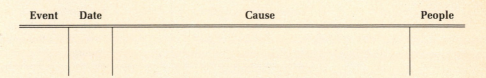

Event	Date	Cause	People

As you read, enter the dates with their associated events, causes, and personalities. Be sure to leave ample room between dates so that you can fill in additional information if necessary. Depending on the subject matter being studied, the dates may be centuries, years, months, days, or, in an event such as the assassination of a president, hours, minutes, and seconds.

Entering dates and events is usually the easiest task in preparing the time line. Authors usually present these facts in a clear manner. Of course, these facts can usually be established fairly precisely. This may be why writers of social studies texts are so preoccupied with events and dates.

Establishing and then entering the cause of an event may be trickier. The cause may be clearly stated in the text or it may be stated in some ambiguous way.

Perhaps the author of a text only implies the cause of an event and you must read carefully to find it. There may be many causes complexly intertwined or the cause may not be known.

Take as an example the assassination of John F. Kennedy. What was the cause? Well, that depends on which book you read and which theory you are exposed to. When you are reading a passage where the cause of an event is not clearly stated, read carefully to infer the cause from the text. If the cause is not known, write this in the "cause" column. If a number of possible causes are given, list them all, preceded by the word "possibly."

Texts usually identify clearly the people involved in an event. It may be useful to write down in the "people" column how the person was involved in the event. Do not list every name you see, but rather list the names of the central figures.

When complete, the time line should present a clear, unified summary of the chapter or selection. It should present an unbroken progression of the important events. The time line should be a flexible note-taking device. You should make any other entries that you think will help you study the material.

You will spend time making up a time line. Don't just put it away once it is complete. Bring it to class and check it against the instructor's interpretation of the book. Make additional notes in class. Be sure you use the time line when you study for tests!

Below is a yearly time line for the Civil War. Read it through and you will get a quick review of the war's progress. Notice that this time line is very general and covers only major events. You will have to decide how general or specific a time line should be.

Event	Date	Cause	People
Southern states secede Civil War begins	1861	Disagreement over slavery. Economic and political rivalry.	Jefferson Davis, President, CSA
War continues. The South gains strength	1862	More commitment from the South's leaders and citizens	Gen. Robert E. Lee, CSA
Lee's army defeated at Gettysburg—turning point of the Civil War.	1863	The North has more resources and industries than the South	Gen. Lee, CSA Gen. Meade, USA
Many Southern defeats	1864	Increasing superiority of North's resources	Gen. Ulysses Grant, USA
Lee surrenders to Grant	1865	Industrial power of the resource-rich North overcomes the agrarian South	Robert E. Lee Ulysses Grant Abraham Lincoln

When reading a history text, you should make your own time line and use it as a study guide. Remember, just preparing the time line is not enough. You must actually study the time line for it to be of real use.

ACTIVITY I

Carefully read the following selection about "Campaigns Against the Indians." Then use the time line format provided on the last page of this section to prepare a time line for this selection.

CAMPAIGNS AGAINST THE INDIANS[1]

George Washington considered himself scrupulously fair in his dealings with Indians. "Brothers," he told one tribe, "you do well to wish to learn our arts and ways of like, and above all the religion of Jesus Christ. These will make you a greater and happier people than you are." To Washington, and most other whites, Indians were either good or bad, depending on whether they were friendly or hostile, which largely depended on whether they honored treaties abdicating their lands to settlers. Friendly Indians, Washington promised, would receive the protection of Congress. Hostile Indians would be suppressed by force.

After the American Revolution, tribes of Indians ravaged settlements throughout the old Northwest. Urged on by the British and undeterred by previous defeats, Shawnees, Miamis, and Kickapoos plundered boats on the Wabash and Ohio rivers and crossed over into Kentucky to continue their raids. Frontiersmen called upon George Rogers Clark to lead a punitive expedition in 1786, but the magic of his name was not enough—the expedition failed, Clark's militiamen first rebelling and then retreating in disorder. The Indians, more determined than ever, announced that all prior treaties with the white men were repudiated and that henceforth "the Ohio shall be the boundary between them and the Big Knives." Such was the situation when George Washington was sworn in as America's first president.

The First Indian Campaign

Without hesitation Washington used his powers as commander in chief to order a military campaign against the Indians. He selected General Josiah Harmar in 1790 to lead some fifteen hundred men from the vicinity of Cincinnati into the Maumee Valley to crush all opposition. The Indians were forewarned, however, and faded into the forests; Harmar's men searched in vain for the main tribes. Then, while marching south, Harmar hoped to surprise the Indians by sending a detachment of troops doubling back to the Maumee. The tribes waited in ambush, and the detachment was badly mauled; their losses totaled 188 dead and 81 wounded. The court of inquiry vindicated Harmar's actions as "honorable" and meriting "high approbation." He then resigned from the army.

The Second Indian Campaign

The second commander Washington chose was Major General Arthur St. Clair, who was instructed to build a fortification at Miami Village (Fort Wayne, Indiana), and then to "seek the enemy" and "endeavor by all possible means to strike them with great severity." Washington personally warned St. Clair to beware of Indian deceptions and to be alert to sudden attacks and ambushes, but he proved as incompetent as his predecessor. On November 4, 1791, St. Clair camped with fourteen hundred men near the site of Harmar's defeat, without adequate guards posted and with tents pitched haphazardly. Throughout the night Indians led by Chief Little Turtle slipped into the camp. They completely surrounded the soldiers and then at dawn fell upon their victims: 632 men were killed and 264 wounded. The rest of the troops fled, leaving behind their cannon and strewing the forest paths with abandoned arms. The troops had spent ten days marching into Maumee country; their retreat to safety, covering the same ground, took twenty-four hours. St. Clair, Washington roared, allowed his army "to be cut to pieces, hacked, butchered, tomahawked. He is worse than a murderer! How can he answer to his country?" Yet an investigation absolved St. Clair of blame. He then resigned his commission, but was retained as governor of the Northwest Territory.

The Third Indian Campaign

The confidence of the Indians soared. Settlers left their homes and sought the refuge of frontier posts at Marietta and Cincinnati. Several officers sent to negotiate with belligerent Indians were murdered. Several previously neutral tribes decided to join the belligerents. Spanish agents in the Southwest, hoping to capitalize on these disasters, began to incite the Creeks to attack American outposts. The British did the same in the Northwest, fueling the fires of Indian expectations by promising them aid. A new British fort was constructed in 1794 at Fort Miami (near Toledo), clearly within American territory.

Meanwhile, the third commander Washington picked, Major General "Mad Anthony" Wayne, thoroughly trained and properly equipped his soldiers. He was determined not to repeat the blunders of Harmar and St. Clair. During the winter of 1793–1794 Wayne built Fort Greenville, and he remained there drilling and disciplining his men in preparation for a spring offensive. Indian warriors were also gathering, 2000 strong, waiting for the Americans, convinced that with British aid victory would be theirs. Chief Little Turtle saw the uselessness of resisting Wayne's army, but his counsel to seek peace was rejected. Thus on August 20, 1794, in the Battle of Fallen Timbers, a fight lasting no more than two hours, the Indians were decisively beaten. Only fifty were killed, but their spirit was shattered when the British commander at Fort Miami refused to help them. Wayne dictated the terms of the treaty; signed by the Indians in 1795, it brought peace to the Northwest for a generation and opened a new stretch of territory for American expansion.

Indians continued to fight in the nineteenth century, but their delaying actions could not stem the flow of white settlers. "If we want it," wrote Thomas Hutchins, referring to the West, "I warrant it will soon be ours." Indians were invisible men to those who dreamed of America's continental destiny. As Wayne opened the Northwest, the New England poet Timothy Dwight rhapsodized on the blessings of western expansion in "Greenheld Hill":

All hail, thou western world! By heaven designed
The example bright to renovate mankind—
Soon shall thy sons across the mainland roam
And claim our far Pacific for their home,
Their rule, religion, manners, arts convey
And spread their freedom to the Asian Sea.

TIME LINE: "CAMPAIGNS AGAINST THE INDIANS"

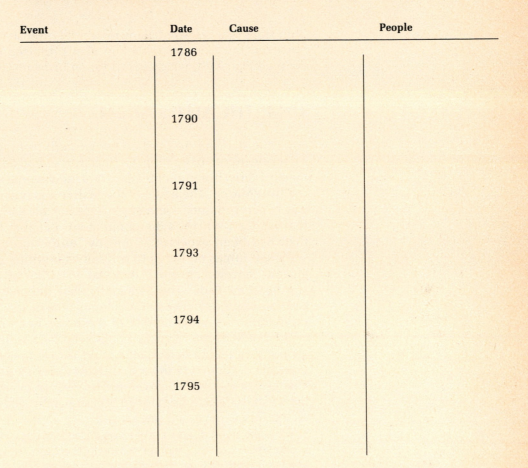

Event	Date	Cause	People
	1786		
	1790		
	1791		
	1793		
	1794		
	1795		

PROJECTS

The first history reading, a relatively short one, is "The Great Stalemate, 1914–1916." Divide a notebook pad into four columns and prepare a time line for this selection.

The second reading on p. 227 is a longer history selection titled "Mohammed and the Rise of the Arab Empire." Read this selection and prepare a time line. You will have to leave some room in your time line to summarize the Koran and any other topics which are discussed at great length.

THE GREAT STALEMATE, 1914–1916[2]

Both sides had prepared plans for a brief offensive war. In its grand simplicity, however, the German Schlieffen Plan promised a far quicker decision than France's Plan XVII, which called for an invasion of Alsace-Lorraine.

1914: THE ALLIES AHEAD

From the start of hostilities on the western front, Germany held the initiative. After one month of fighting, German forces had advanced to within twenty-five miles of Paris. In early September 1914, however, the German drive was halted at the river Marne. The battle of the Marne was one of the decisive events of the war, since it dashed Germany's hope for an early victory. There were many reasons for Germany's disappointment. Belgium had put up more resistance than had been expected. Germany, furthermore, had failed to concentrate sufficient forces on the right wing of its invading armies to make possible the gigantic enveloping move that was to strike at the rear of France's forces southeast of Paris. The Schlieffen Plan depended on the closest possible communications between field commanders and the high command, and on rapid lines of supply; neither of these had been provided for.

The battle of the Marne was followed by a series of engagements in which each side hoped to outflank the other, and in the course of which the front was gradually extended to the sea. By November 1914 the fighting in the West had changed from a war of movement to a war of position. Until the spring of 1918 the western front, except for an occasional thrust of a few miles in one direction or the other, remained unchanged.

With the bulk of Germany's forces tied down in the West, Russia was able to score some unexpected successes in the East. In mid-August 1914 two Russian armies invaded East Prussia and within a few days overran almost half of Germany's easternmost province. At the height of danger, the kaiser recalled from retirement General Paul von Hindenburg, a specialist on conditions in the East, and appointed as Hindenburg's chief of staff the younger and more capable Erich Ludendorff. These men soon reversed the situation on the eastern front. In two major battles, at Tannenberg and the Masurian Lakes, Russia lost close to 250,000 men. Russia's reversals in the north were balanced by successes in the southeast against Austria. In a sweeping campaign under Russia's commander in chief, Grand Duke Nicholas, Russian forces in September took most of Galicia and advanced to the Carpathian frontier of Hungary.

In the East, as in the West, the end of 1914 found the Allied and Central Powers locked in a stalemate. But since Germany had failed to deliver a knockout blow in the West and appeared to be stalled in the East, the advantage was felt to lie with the Allies. In addition, British naval superiority had been responsible for the sinking of a German naval squadron off the coast of South America and for the seizure of most of the colonies that had belonged to Germany.

1915: Allied Reverses

But Allied dreams of victory were premature. The new Italian ally they gained in the spring of 1915 proved to be of little use. Furthermore, a British attack against the Gallipoli Peninsula and the Turkish Straits failed. Had it succeeded,

The First World War, 1914–1918

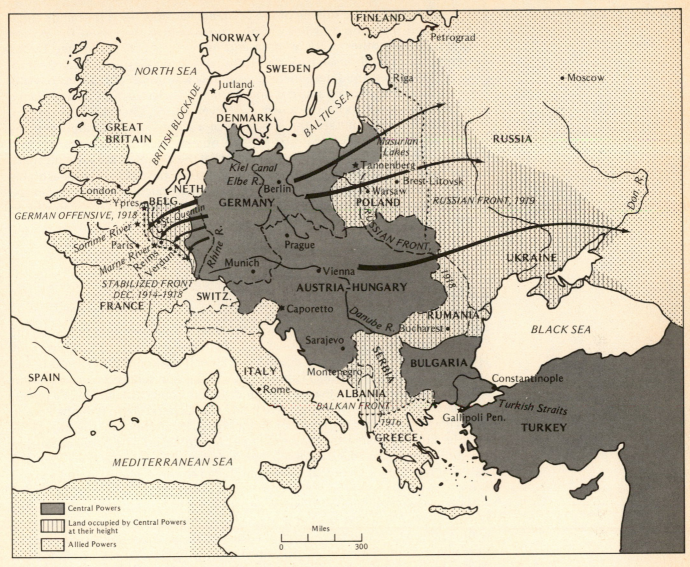

Turkey would have been seriously weakened and the Black Sea opened to Allied shipping. Instead, the Straits remained closed for the rest of the war.

The most serious Allied reverses during 1915 were on the eastern front and in the Balkans. In the spring and summer, German forces in the north and combined Austro-German forces in the south advanced in a series of offensives that cost the Russians Poland, Lithuania, and Courland, drove them out of Galicia, and lost them almost a million men. All of central and eastern Europe was now in German and Austrian hands. In October the Central Powers turned against Serbia; and in November they moved into Montenegro and Albania.

By the beginning of 1916 the tide of war on land seemed definitely to have turned against the Allies. Even on the high seas the Germans were able to make some gains. To counteract Britain's blockade, the German government, in early 1915, imposed a submarine blockade against the British Isles. The first phase of German submarine warfare came to a head with the sinking of the British liner *Lusitania* in May 1915. The loss of 139 American passengers caused a serious crisis in American-German relations. It was settled only after Germany promised to restrict its submarine tactics in the future.

The Sinking of the *Lusitania*

The full horror of the sinking of the *Lusitania* has now been revealed; and it has stirred the people of this country more deeply than even the poison clouds, or any other of the wanton and murderous acts committed by the Germans. . . . By thousands of dastardly crimes the Germans have demonstrated that they are determined to wage this war under conditions of cold-blooded and deliberate murder and outrage, of destruction and brutality, such as the world has never known. . . . Never before, since the world began, has there been witnessed the spectacle of a whole race, numbering many millions, scientifically organised for the objects of wholesale murder and devastation. . . . It is universally seen now that the Germans are a nation apart, that their civilisation is a mere veneer, that they have fallen immeasurably lower than their tribal forbears, and that their calculated and organised barbarity is without precedent in history. Nations, we perceive, can sink to unprecedented depths. No nation has ever fallen so low in infamy. . . .

From an editorial in *The Times* (London), May 10, 1915.

1916: STALEMATE

Since time was clearly on the side of the Allies, it seemed imperative to the Germans to force a major showdown. In February 1916, therefore, they launched an all-out offensive against the French stronghold of Verdun. The battle of Verdun was the most famous battle of the war. It lasted more than four months and caused more than seven hundred thousand casualties; yet it ended undecided. Its chief hero on the French side was General Henri Philippe Pétain. Like Hindenburg after the battle of Tannenberg, Pétain became the idol of his people. Both men were to play fateful roles in later years. The battle of Verdun was followed by an Allied counteroffensive along the Somme River. But the battle of the Somme, like that of Verdun, failed to force a final decision in the West.

Events elsewhere during 1916 were equally indecisive. In June, Russian forces under General Brusilov started a major drive against the Austrian lines and within a few weeks had taken most of eastern Galicia. These successes brought Rumania into the war. But its participation only made matters worse for the Allies. In late September, Austro-German forces invaded Rumania, and by January 1917 most of that country's rich resources were in the hands of the Central Powers. In the East as in the West, the outcome of the war continued to hang in the balance.

The year 1916 also saw the one great naval battle of the war between Germany and Britain. The German navy, to have a chance of success, had to fight in its home waters. But the British refused to venture forth that far. On several occasions the Germans went out into the North Sea, hoping to entice the British into battle. It was on one of these sallies that the two fleets made contact off the coast of Jutland in May 1916. The battle of Jutland was costly and indecisive. The British lost more naval tonnage than the Germans, but they could better afford to. The German fleet henceforth remained safely at home.

By the end of 1916 a stalemate had been reached on all fronts, and victory for either side seemed far away. Meanwhile losses and material costs of the war had been staggering, and the strain of war had begun to tell on the home fronts as well as on the battlefields.

MOHAMMED AND THE RISE OF THE ARAB EMPIRE[3]

A few years after the death of Justinian in 565, a child was born in Arabia who was to found a religion that spread more rapidly than Christianity and an empire that was larger than that of Rome at the height of its power. Few men have had more impact on history than Mohammed. His religion split the old Mediterranean world and transformed the civilization of the Middle East; his influence is felt today in a broad belt of territory stretching from West Africa to the East Indies. Islam was the last of the three great world religions to emerge, and for many centuries it was more vigorous than either of its rivals—Christianity in the West and Buddhism in the East.

THE EARLY ARABS

Arabia had played no important role in history before the time of Mohammed. The huge peninsula, about one-third the size of the United States, was like an arid wedge driven into the fertile lands of the Middle East. Most Arabs were nomads, driving their herds from one scanty patch of vegetation to another. A much smaller, but very influential, group was made up of traders who dealt in products from the southern part of the peninsula, notably frankincense, and in goods imported from India and the Far East. Overland trade through Arabia was not extensive, but there was enough to support a few small towns along the southern and western sides of the peninsula.

The early Arabs were thus in touch with all the civilizations of the East and had learned something from all of them. Since they themselves spoke a Semitic language, they had been most influenced by other peoples of this language group who lived in the Fertile Crescent north of the peninsula. The Arabs developed a system of writing related, at least indirectly, to the Phoenician alphabet. They had the usual Semitic interest in religion, although it was expressed in almost indiscriminate polytheism. They had numerous tribal deities, and they had had contacts with the Christians and Jews who inhabited the northern part of the Arabian Peninsula. They honored poets, and the ideal Arab leader was as ready to make verses as he was to make war. They knew a good deal about astronomy, for knowledge of the stars is as helpful in crossing the desert as it is in navigating the seas. At their best, the Arabs were imaginative and eager to absorb new knowledge. They assimilated and profited from Greco-Roman civilization far more rapidly than did the Germans who took over the western part of the Roman Empire.

And yet there were grave defects in the social and political organization of the early Arabs. The nature of the country forced them to live in small, scattered tribes, and each tribe was almost constantly at war with its neighbors. The leading families within each tribe were often jealous of one another, so that blood-feuds were frequent and persistent. Weaker members of each tribe, and indeed of each family, were harshly treated by their stronger relatives. Sickly children were often killed, and orphans had little hope of receiving their parents' property. Women had almost no rights; their fathers or their husbands controlled their lives and their property. Men who could afford it had many wives and could divorce any of them whenever they wished. The divorced woman was usually left without any property or regular income.

In spite of all this disunity, certain strong ties bound the Arabs together. They were great geneologists; the leaders of many tribes could trace their ancestry back to the same ancient families—families that were known and respected throughout Arabia. Most of the tribes accepted a few common religious observances. There was a sacred period in each year, for example, when fighting was suspended and when many Arabs made a pilgrimage to the religious center of Mecca, a trading town near the west coast. In Mecca was the Kaaba, an ancient building full of images, including one of Christ. Here almost every god known to the Arabs could be worshiped. Here, too, was the most venerated object in the Arab world, the sacred Black Stone that had come from heaven. This habit of worshiping together at Mecca was the strongest unifying force in Arabia and one that was carefully preserved by Mohammed.

Mohammed's Teaching

Mohammed was born about 570 in Mecca. We know little about his early years, except that he was a poor orphan. When he reached adolescence he began to work for a woman named Khadija, the widow of a rich merchant. In her service he made many caravan trips, during which he may have accumulated his information about the Jewish and Christian religions and his knowledge of the legends and traditions of other Arab tribes. He eventually married his employer, though she was considerably older than he, and the marriage gave him the wealth and leisure to meditate on religious problems.

Like many other Arabs, Mohammed had a sensitive mind, a deep appreciation of the wonders of nature, and a strong interest in religion. These qualities were enhanced by mysterious seizures, to which he had been subject since childhood. During these attacks he seemed to be struggling to express ideas that were not yet fully formed in his own mind. He gradually came to believe that this was God's way of trying to communicate with him, but until he was about forty he had no clear idea of what he was meant to do. Then he had his first revelation: a vision of the angel Gabriel, who commanded him to speak "in the name of the Lord, the Creator . . . the Lord who taught man what he did not know."

Mohammed was still doubtful about his mission, but as revelation succeeded revelation he became filled with the vision of the one, eternal God, the Lord of the world. He began to appeal to his fellow citizens of Mecca to abandon their host of false deities and to worship the one, true God. These early revelations bear some resemblance to the Psalms, both in their poetic quality and in their appeal to the wonders of nature as proofs of God's greatness and mercy. The stars in the heavens, sunshine and rain, the fruits of the earth—"all are signs of God's power if you would only understand."

By now Mohammed was convinced that he was a prophet, the last and greatest in the succession of prophets whom God had sent to enlighten and save mankind. He never claimed to be more than a prophet and even denied that he could work miracles, although he admitted that some of his predecessors had had this gift. He also admitted the divine mission of the Jewish prophets and of Jesus, but he claimed that their teachings had been distorted or misinterpreted. He was quite certain that the revelations he received superseded everything that had come before. The earlier prophets had had glimpses of the true religion, but he alone had received the full message. Their teachings were to be accepted only when they agreed with the final word of God, which had been revealed to him.

An Early Revelation to Mohammed

> *By the white forenoon*
> *and the brooding night!*
> *Thy Lord has neither forsaken thee nor hates thee*
> *and the Last shall be better for thee than the First.*
> *Thy Lord shall give thee, and thou shalt be satisfied.*

Did He not find thee an orphan, and shelter thee?
Did He not find thee erring, and guide thee?
Did He not find thee needy, and suffice thee?

As for the orphan, do not oppress him,
and as for the beggar, scold him not;
and as for thy Lord's blessing, declare it.

From A. J. Arberry, *The Koran Interpreted* (London: George Allen and Unwin, 1955), Vol. II, p. 342, Ch. 93.

Mohammed at first made little progress in converting his countrymen. His wife, Khadija, believed in him and comforted him when he was despondent, and his cousin Ali was one of his first converts. But most Meccans of good family were hostile; most of his early followers were from poor and uninfluential families. Mohammed's attacks on idols angered those who believed that the prosperity of Mecca depended on its being the center of worship of all the known gods. Mohammed's followers were persecuted, and his own life was threatened. Finally he fled with his supporters to the city of Yathrib, some distance north of Mecca. The Mohammedan era begins with this flight, or Hegira, which took place in 622 A.D.*

Mohammed was welcomed as an arbitrator of local disputes in Yathrib. The town was renamed Medinet-en-Nabi (Medina), the City of the Prophet. Jewish influence was strong there, and the Arabs of Medina found nothing strange in the doctrine of a single, all-powerful God. Mohammed soon gained many converts among the pagan and half-Jewish Arabs and became virtually the ruler of the community. He now became involved in political problems, and the revelations he received during this period dealt largely with law and government. For example, it was at Medina that the rules about marriage, inheritance, and the punishment of criminals were laid down.

During the stay at Medina, Mohammed's reputation and power increased steadily. A desultory war between Medina and Mecca gradually became more serious, and by 630 Mohammed had gained so many supporters that he was able to capture Mecca with little difficulty. He immediately destroyed the idols in the Kaaba, except for the Black Stone, and made the temple the center of his religion. He had long asserted that the Kaaba had been built by Abraham and that Abraham had placed the heavenly Stone there as a sign of God's power. Thus he was able to preserve Mecca as the religious center of Arabia.

The fall of Mecca convinced many Arabs that Mohammed really was a prophet or at least that he was too strong to oppose. During his last years, most of the tribes of the peninsula acknowledged his spiritual and political leadership. Nevertheless, when Mohammed died in 632 Arabia was far from being a unified state, and many Arabs had only vague ideas about the religion they had accepted.

THE KORAN

Mohammed, however, had left behind the Koran, a collection of his revelations. He had taught that the Koran was God's guide for the human race, that it had always existed in heaven, but that no one had been worthy of receiving it before his own appearance on earth. Although he had received the Koran piece by piece, as circumstances made its teachings applicable, it formed a consistent and coherent whole. It contained all that man needed to know, and it was to be followed without question. Mohammed said: "Let the Koran always be your guide. Do what it commands or permits; shun what it forbids."

*This does not mean that dates of the Moslem era can be converted to our reckoning simply by adding 622 years. The Moslem year is based on a lunar calendar, and so does not coincide with ours. Our year 1978 was 1398 A.H.

From the very start of Mohammed's mission, his followers had carefully written down his revelations on parchment, palm leaves, or whatever else was available. The task of sorting out and arranging this mass of sayings was begun soon after Mohammed's death by Abu-Bekr, but his version was not universally accepted. Othman, who ruled the Arab Empire from 644 to 656, ended the disputes that arose by compiling an authoritative version and banning all other collections. Othman's version has remained almost unchanged down to the present.

In no other major religion was there such early agreement on the official version of the founder's teachings. In fact, the Koran was put together so hurriedly that it seems somewhat confused and illogical to a non-Moslem. The basic rule was to put the longer passages first. Thus the earliest revelation, in which Mohammed was ordered to begin his mission, comes in Chapter 96, after many of the long, prosaic Medina passages. Seemingly repetitious and even contradictory statements were never harmonized. But these flaws are not admitted by orthodox Moslems, who consider the Koran a masterpiece of Arabic literature as well as the ultimate word of God to man.

The religion taught in the Koran was easy to understand and easy to follow. The basic creed was simple: "There is no God but Allah and Mohammed is his prophet." The faithful must also believe in the resurrection and the day of judgment, when every man will be rewarded according to his merits. The Mohammedan hell is very like the Christian one, but the Mohammedan paradise is unmistakably Arabian—a green garden full of running water and fruit trees with beautiful damsels to wait on the souls in bliss. Finally, the Koran teaches predestination: "Every man's fate have We bound around his neck"— that is, all human events have been determined, once and for all, by the will of God. Mohammed's own name for his religion was Islam—"submission to the will of God"—and his followers were called Moslems—"those who submit."

The principal religious practices of Islam were as simple as its theology. Every Moslem was to pray five times a day and to fast during the daylight hours of the month of Ramadan. Alms giving was a religious duty. Finally, every believer was to make a pilgrimage, if possible, to Mecca. But "only he shall visit the Mosque of God who believes in God and the Last Day, and is constant in prayer, and gives alms and fears God alone."

The Koran forbade wine drinking, usury, and gambling, and a dietary law, somewhat like that of the Jews, banned certain foods, especially pork. There was also a rudimentary code of law designed to check the selfishness and violence that had prevailed among the Arabs. Arbitration was to take the place of the bloodfeud, infanticide was condemned, and elaborate rules of inheritance safeguarded the rights of orphans and widows. Mohammed also made an effort to limit polygamy by ruling that no man might have more than four wives simultaneously. Divorce was still easy, but the divorced wife could no longer be sent away penniless. These and other provisions were enough to furnish a framework for a judicial system.

There were obvious resemblances between Islam and Christianity, especially between Islam and the Christian heresies that denied or minimized the divinity of Christ. Since Mohammed admitted that Jesus was a major prophet, many heretics could accept Islam without feeling that they had greatly changed their beliefs. Other unorthodox Christians in Asia and Africa were so angered by their persecution by the Greek Church that they turned to Islam as a lesser evil. And in the competition for the loyalty of groups with little knowledge of either religion, Islam had a great advantage. It needed no organized church, for it had neither a priesthood nor a sacramental system. Each individual had to assure his salvation by his own right belief and good conduct. Every essential act of the religion could be accomplished by a man living quite by himself. It was customary for the faithful to meet together for prayers, especially on Friday, and from the earliest

*The Growth of the Islamic
Caliphate 632–750*

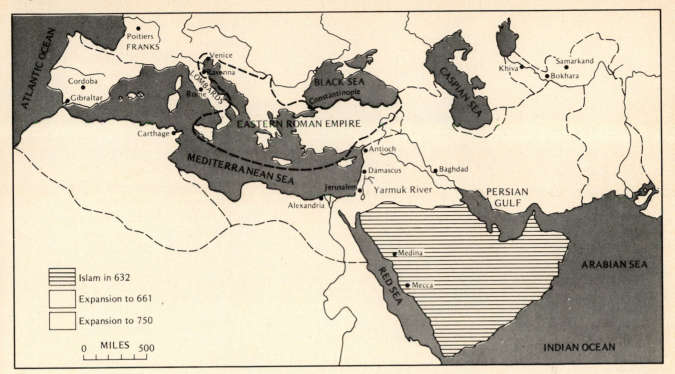

period certain men devoted themselves to explaining the Koran. But none of this was essential; anyone could accept Islam without waiting for the organization of a religious community, and any believer could make converts without waiting for an ordained priest to come and validate his action. Simple and uncomplicated monotheism was easier to explain than the doctrine of the Trinity.

These advantages often gave Islam the victory in competition with Christianity. On several occasions in the Middle Ages the Moslems were able to move in and convert a pagan people while the Christians were still trying to recruit a troop of missionary priests. And even today Islam is spreading more rapidly among the peoples of Asia and Africa than is Christianity.

The Caliphate

Mohammed left no very clear instructions about how his successor should be chosen. At his death there was confusion in the ranks of his followers and rebellion on the part of recently converted tribes. The faithful finally decided to choose a caliph, or successor to the prophet, who would act as both spiritual and political leader of Islam. The first caliph was Abu-Bekr, one of the earliest and most pious of Mohammed's converts. Though he ruled only two years (632–634), he succeeded in suppressing the revolts and in completing the unification of Arabia. Under his successor, Omar (634–644), the great conquests began. The Arabs had long been in the habit of raiding their wealthier neighbors to the north. Now they found themselves united for the first time, while both the Byzantine and the Persian states had been weakened by disastrous wars. In their first probing attacks, the Arabs met such slight resistance that they soon turned to wars of conquest. Their defeat of a Byzantine army at the Yarmuk River in 636 determined the fate of all the eastern provinces. Some fortified towns held out for a few years, but by 649 the Arabs had conquered

Syria, Armenia, Palestine, and Egypt. Persia gave even less trouble and was completely in Arab hands by 642. Only the outbreak of civil war in Arabia slowed this first wave of conquest.

The civil war was caused by bad feeling between the early converts and some of the leading Arab families who had accepted Islam only after Mohammed's triumph was assured. The trouble began under the caliph Othman (644–656), who was an early convert himself but who was not so opposed to the latecomers as were some of the prophet's other companions. He was accused of favoring recent converts and of pushing forward his kinsmen, the Ommiads, who had at one time led the Meccan opposition to Mohammed. The accusation was largely true, but it is hard to see what else Othman could have done. He now had an empire to govern, and he needed the help of every man who displayed qualities of leadership, whatever his past religious behavior had been.

Quarrels between the two factions led to the assassination of Othman in 656. He was succeeded by an old believer, Ali, the son-in-law and adopted son of Mohammed. But since Ali was accused of condoning Othman's murder, the Ommiads soon revolted and secured the nomination of one of their family as caliph. Ali held Persia and Mesopotamia for a while but was assassinated in 661 by a member of a small, fanatical sect that believed the office of caliph was unnecessary. After Ali's death, the Ommiad caliph, who had taken no part in the assassination, was accepted as ruler by the entire Moslem world.

The Ommiad Dynasty

The first Ommiad caliph transferred the capital of the Arab Empire from Mecca to Damascus. This act was typical of the family, which put far more emphasis on politics than on religion. Damascus was not the prophet's city, but it had public buildings, a large group of educated and experienced civil servants, and a central location. It was far more satisfactory as a capital than Mecca, and it had the additional advantage of containing few of the prophet's early companions. The Ommiads bestowed key positions on members of the Arab aristocracy rather than on the early converts, and they filled the government bureaus with Christian Syrians and Egyptians. Thus the Arab Empire began to change from a loosely organized tribal theocracy into a centralized state employing many Byzantine administrative techniques. Finally, the office of caliph ceased to be elective and was made hereditary in the Ommiad family.

The policy of the Ommiads toward conquered peoples was also based on purely political considerations. The Arabs, like most tribal peoples, had never paid taxes, and they had no intention of doing so now that they were lords of a large part of the civilized world. In any case, the Arabs were not in actual possession of farms and businesses; they were administrators, not property owners. Thus the government was financed by tribute exacted from unbelievers, which meant that mass conversions would be a threat to its financial stability. So, instead of forcing Islam on their subjects, the Ommiad caliphs did not encourage conversion. New converts had to pay a heavy land tax, from which Arabs were exempt, and they were seldom given responsible positions in the government.

This policy caused little trouble in Syria, where the Arab aristocracy was satisfied with its special privileges and where Christians were numerous. But in both Persia and Mesopotamia, where Ommiad control was less secure, most of the population became converted to Islam. The new converts resented their inferior position and often revolted against the rule of Ommiad officials. They were encouraged in their resistance by the more pious Arabs, who felt that the Ommiads were far too worldly, and by survivors of the faction that had supported Ali.

570	632	661		750	1268
Life of Mohammed	First Four Caliphs	Ommiad Dynasty		Abbasid Dynasty	

In spite of hidden weaknesses in their state, the Ommiad caliphs profited more from the late Roman civilization they had taken over than did the Germanic kings of the West. Syria, the heart of the Ommiad state, had always been more advanced intellectually and economically than Gaul, the heart of the strongest Germanic kingdom. The Ommiads began to draw on their heritage from the older civilization almost as soon as they gained power. They organized their administrative services on Roman and Persian models. They welcomed scholars of all nationalities to their court and urged them to undertake the task of translating philosophical, scientific, and medical works into Arabic. They built impressive mosques at Damascus and Jerusalem, adapting Syrian architecture to the needs of the Mohammedan religion. A new civilization began to grow up around the Ommiad court, a civilization based on Greek, Syrian, Egyptian, and Persian traditions and yet with a style and a spirit of its own. This new civilization reached its peak only after the Ommiads had lost the throne and the capital had been moved from Damascus to Baghdad. Much of the work of the Ommiads was either absorbed in or surpassed by the accomplishments of their successors. But the Ommiads laid the foundations, and they did so at a time when western kings had almost no administrative services, when western scholars had almost no books but compendia and epitomes, and when western architects showed almost no skill in designing large buildings.

New Conquests

The stability and prosperity assured by the early Ommiads soon made it possible for the Arabs to undertake further conquests. In the East the Ommiads took Khiva, Bokhara, and Samarkand, thus gaining control of one of the oldest and most important trade routes in Eurasia—the silk road from China. These conquests in turn opened the way to the occupation of Afghanistan and the valley of the Indus. The strong Moslem position on the northwest frontier was a permanent threat to India, as the invasions of the next thousand years were to demonstrate.

In the West the Arabs advanced steadily along the southern shore of the Mediterranean. North Africa was their first objective, and here, as often before, the invaders profited from the fact that the native population hated Byzantine government. Justinian's reconquest of the Vandal kingdom had been followed by heavy taxation and persecution of heretics. Many of the Romanized Africans had fled the country; the Berbers, who remained, were neither Romanized nor obedient to the orders of Byzantine officials. When the Arab attack came, both the Roman cities and the Berber countryside resisted bravely, but there was little cooperation between them. The Arabs quickly defeated their divided enemies, taking Carthage in 697 and winning control of the entire North African coast by 708.

Although the Berbers had fought fiercely to preserve their independence, they felt no particular antipathy to Islam. Many of them became converts and joined the victorious army in the hope of sharing in the spoils of the next conquest. This addition to their strength enabled the Arabs to pass over into Spain. The Visigothic rulers of Spain had been weakened by quarrels over the succession and had not been able (or willing) to build up strong local forces. A single victory over the royal army in 711 was enough to open the whole country to Tarik, who commanded the invading forces, and from whom Gibraltar takes its name.* The largest part of his army was probably composed of recently converted Berbers, and now many Visigothic nobles joined the victors—an illustration of the Arabs' ability to gain the cooperation of conquered peoples in a remarkably short time. Only the support of thousands of non-Arabs made possible Islam's rapid conquests.

The Moslem army quickly overran the entire Iberian Peninsula except for the extreme northwest, where a few Christians maintained their independence. The Moslems then pushed on across the Pyrenees into the Frankish kingdom, which was not quite so helpless as Spain. The Franks could not defend the south, but when the raiders pushed north the Frankish leader, Charles Martel, assembled an effective army that checked the invasion. Charles' victory at Poitiers in 732 was not very decisive, for the Moslems withdrew in good order and held towns in southern Gaul for another thirty years. But they made no more raids on the north.

During the early years of the eighth century the Ommiads reached the height of their power. They had created the largest Moslem state that ever existed, and in less than a hundred years they had built an empire larger than that of Rome. But they had reached their limit; their setback at Poitiers in 732 had its counterpart in an earlier failure to take Constantinople in a great siege in 716 to 717. Although the Byzantine Empire had lost almost all of its outlying provinces, it had preserved the most important part of its territories. Like the Frankish kingdom, Byzantium grew stronger after the early eighth century, and the Moslems were long unable to make any headway against these two bulwarks of Europe.

The Rise of the Abbasids

The Ommiad state had also begun to weaken internally. It was difficult to rule a vast empire that stretched from Spain to India and that embraced dozens of different peoples. Moreover, many Moslems continued to distrust and oppose the Ommiads. There was still a party that honored the memory of Ali and considered the Ommiads usurpers; there were also puritanical Moslems who loathed Ommiad luxury and worldliness; and there were recent converts, especially in Mesopotamia and Persia, who resented the domination of the Arab aristocracy.

All these groups were united by Abu'l Abbas, who was to found the Abbasid dynasty. By claiming one of Mohammed's uncles as an ancestor, he satisfied most of the legitimists; by making himself appear more devout than the Ommiads, he gained the support of most of the inhabitants of Mesopotamia and Persia. By 750 Abu'l Abbas was strong enough to risk rebellion. He decisively defeated the Ommiad caliph and almost exterminated the family. One Ommiad escaped to Spain, where he founded an independent state in 756, but the rest of the Moslem world accepted Abu'l Abbas as caliph.

Since the Abbasid caliph's primary strength was in Mesopotamia and Persia, he moved his capital to Baghdad, a new city built on the banks of the Tigris. This move symbolized a turning point in the history of civilization. The old unity of the Mediterranean world, shaken by earlier events, was now forever destroyed. The Ommiad caliphs at Damascus had drawn heavily on Greco-Roman civilization, but the Abbasids at Baghdad were increasingly influenced by the ancient traditions of Mesopotamia and Persia. The Moslem world on the southern and eastern shores of the Mediterranean became more and more unlike the Christian world on the northern shores. At the same time, Moslem pressure was forcing Byzantium in on itself and accentuating the peculiarities of the Byzantine way of life.

*Gebel Tarik—Tarik's hill.

A citizen of the Roman Empire had been equally at home in Rome and Constantinople, in Alexandria and Antioch. Now these centers of civilization were drifting apart and becoming more and more strange to one another. By the tenth century a westerner, merely by crossing the Mediterranean, entered a completely different world. Egypt was as strange as China, and even Christian Byzantium seemed remote and Oriental.

Thus the world of the Romans had broken into three fragments of unequal size and wealth. The largest and richest area was held by the Moslems, who also controlled the key trade routes to India and China and all but one of the great cities of the Middle East. Next came the Byzantine Empire, anchored on impregnable Constantinople, rich from its own industry and from the trade that flowed through its lands to the West. Far behind was western Europe, poverty-stricken and ill-governed, no match for the great civilizations centered in Constantinople and Baghdad. For centuries western Europe had depended on the East in trade and industry, in art and religion. It remained to be seen what the Europeans could do now that they were on their own.

NOTES

1. **Morton Borden** et al., *The American Profile* (Lexington, Mass.: D.C. Heath, 1978), pp. 77–80.
2. **Joseph Strayer** and **Hans Gatzke,** *The Mainstream of Civilization* (New York: Harcourt, 1979), pp. 700–703.
3. **Strayer** and **Gatzke,** pp. 167–176.

Fifteen

FIGURATIVE LANGUAGE

A writer uses figurative language to make ideas more vivid and dramatic. Figurative language conveys a different interpretation from the literal meaning or the dictionary definition. For example, when a writer describes a villainous character as "heartless," the word is not meant literally. Heartless is used as a figure of speech. Figurative expressions create images for us by saying one thing in terms of another.

Everyday speech, as well as slang and common clichés, are based on figurative language. You may lose the real meaning of words if you read too literally. A variety of types of figures of speech abound in novels and texts alike. It is important for you to be aware of them as you read.

SIMILE AND METAPHOR

The two most common types of comparisons used in figurative language are the simile and the metaphor. A simile compares two things using the words *like* or *as*. Two examples of similes are:

> **The treetops glistened like silver in the sun.**
> **The old man's face looked like an old leather shoe.**

Metaphors also make comparisons but do not use the words *like* or *as*. Here are two examples of metaphors.

> **The clouds were ribbons tossed about the sky.**
> **The lake was an emerald in the sun.**

Metaphors and similes add a fresh, dynamic touch to familiar ideas. Notice how Stephen Benet uses similes in "The Ballad of William Sycamore."

> *I lost my boyhood and found my wife*
> *A girl like a Salem clipper,*
> *A woman straight as a hunting knife,*
> *With eyes bright as the*
> *Dipper.*[1]

You are able to form a mental picture of the wife. She must be a proud woman, who is sharp and strong yet graceful.

PERSONIFICATION AND HYPERBOLE

Personification attributes human qualities, feelings, or actions to objects or ideas. Frank Marshall Davis's poem "The Four Glimpses of Night" is a classic example of personification.

Night is a curious child, wandering
Between earth and sky, creeping
In windows and doors, daubing
The entire neighborhood
With purple paint.[2]

The poet used three human actions—wandering, creeping, and daubing—to describe night.

Hyperbole is a deliberate exaggeration. The author uses hyperbole to emphasize or intensify some mood or feeling. Hyperbole may be as simple as, "they were packed in the bus like sardines," or as complex as the hyperbole below from Shakespeare's *Macbeth*.

Will all great Neptune's ocean wash this blood
Clean from my hands? No; this hand will rather
The multitudinous seas incarnadine,*
Making the green one red.

*Turn red.

Macbeth is lamenting his involvement in Duncan's death. His guilt is emphasized when he suggests that washing his bloody hands in the ocean would only succeed in turning the entire ocean red—a hyperbolic statement.

You should be alert for these four figures of speech as you read. It is important to take time to understand the message the writer is sending to you, stashed safely away in the cask on the neck of the trusty figure of speech.

ACTIVITY I

The activities on the following pages will give experience identifying and interpreting figures of speech.

Below are some short literary passages. Underline each figure of speech. Indicate the line number as well as the type of figure of speech.

A.

1– A man with a mouth like a mastiff, a brow like a mountain,
2– and eyes like burning anthracite—that was Dan'l Webster in
3– his prime.[3]

(1) _Simile_   ( ) _____   ( ) _____   ( ) _____

B.

1– They waited in the traffic at Fortieth and Sixth
2– Avenue, and three boys walked before the nose of the taxi.
3– Under the globes of light they were cheerful scarecrows,
4– all very thin and all wearing very seedy snappy cut suits
5– and gay neckties.[4]

( ) _____   ( ) _____   ( ) _____

Is the description of the three boys flattering? What word or words support your answer?

_____

_____

C.

> 1– It was the last of autumn and first day of winter
> 2– coming together. All day long the plowmen on their
> 3– prairie farms had moved to and fro in their wide level fields
> 4– through the falling snow, which melted as it fell,
> 5– wetting them to the skin all day, notwithstanding the
> 6– frequent squalls of snow, the dripping, desolate
> 7– clouds, and the muck of the furrows, black and tenacious as tar.[5]

( ) _____   ( ) _____   ( ) _____

How do the figures of speech chosen by the author help create a vivid picture?

( ) _____

( ) _____

( ) _____

ACTIVITY II

Continue to read and analyze the following passages, paying special attention to the figurative language.

D.

> They're mopping when I come out of the dorm, all three of them sulky and hating everything, the time of day, the place they're at here, the people they got to work around. When they hate like this, better if they don't see me. I creep along the wall quiet as dust in my canvas shoes, but they got special sensitive equipment that detects my fear and they all look up, all three at once, eyes glittering out of the black faces like the hard glitter of radio tubes out the back of an old radio.[6]

1. What can you infer about the character telling the story? _____

_____

_____

_____

2. What can you infer from the figurative description of the other characters? _____

_____

_____

_____

E.

> Daring burglaries by armed men, and highway robberies, took place in the capital itself every night; families were publicly cautioned not to go out of town without removing their furniture to upholsterers' warehouses for security. (From *A Tale of Two Cities* by Charles Dickens)

Literally state what Dickens is telling us.

_____

_____

_____

F.

> And then Della leaped up like a little singed cat. Jim had not yet seen his beautiful present. She held it out to him eagerly upon her open palm. The dull precious metal seemed to flash with a reflection of her bright and ardent spirit.[7]

1. How would you describe Della? _____

_____

_____

2. Justify your description by choosing words from the selection. _____

_____

_____

ACTIVITY III

Read the following selections, looking for figurative language. Underline each figurative phrase, indicate the line number, and write a literal interpretation for each.

G.

> 1– The sky was clear, the winds had gone down, and the full moon was setting
> 2– radiantly in the west, when I found myself on the surface of the ocean, in full
> 3– view of the shores of Lofoden, and above the spot where the pool of the Moskoe-
> 4– strom had been. It was the hour of the slack—but the sea still heaved in
> 5– mountainous waves from the effects of the hurricane. I was born violently into
> 6– the 'grounds' of the fishermen. A boat picked me up—exhausted from fatigue—and
> 7– (now that the danger was removed) speechless from the memory of its horror. Those
> 8– who drew me on board were my old mates and daily companions—but they knew me no
> 9– more than they would have known a traveller from the spirit-land. My hair, which
> 10– had been raven black the day before, was as white as you see it now. They say too
> 11– that the whole expression of countenance had changed. I told them my story—

12– they did not believe it. I now tell it to you—and I can scarcely expect you to

13– put more faith in it than did the merry fishermen of Lofoden.[8]

( ) _____

_____

( ) _____

_____

( ) _____

_____

( ) _____

_____

( ) _____

_____

( ) _____

_____

H.

1– The towers of Zenith aspired above the morning mist;

2– austere towers of steel and cement and limestone, sturdy as

3– cliffs and delicate as silver rods. They were neither citadels

4– nor churches, but frankly and beautifully office-buildings.

5– The mist took pity on the fretted structures of earlier

6– generations: the Post Office with its shingle-tortured mansard,

7– the red brick minarets of hulking old houses, factories with

8– stingy and sooted windows, wooden tenements colored like mud.

9– The city was full of such grotesqueries, but the clean towers

10– were thrusting them from the business center, and on the

11– farther hills were shining new houses, homes—they

12– seemed—for laughter and tranquility.[9]

( ) _____

_____

( ) _____

_____

( ) _____

_____

( ) _____

_____

( ) _____

_____

( ) _____

_____

ACTIVITY IV

Analyze the following poems. What types of figures of speech are used to create particular pictures or feelings?

I.

The Lightning is a yellow Fork
From Tables in the sky
By inadvertent fingers dropped.[10]

_____

_____

_____

J.

By the rude bridge that arched the flood,
Their flag to April's breeze unfurled,
Here once the embattled farmers stood
And fired the shot heard round the world.[11]

_____

_____

_____

K.

Be glad of water, but don't forget
The lurking frost in the earth
In the earth beneath
That will steal forth after the sun is set
And show on the water its crystal teeth.[12]

_____

_____

_____

_____

PROJECT

The literary selections on the following pages have been chosen to help you practice finding figurative language. Read each selection and pay particular attention to the lettered sections. Underline the figures of speech. Use this page to jot down these figures of speech and mention whether it is a simile, metaphor, personification, or hyperbole. Note that each selection has been numbered I, II, III, IV. The paragraphs have been lettered A, B, C, or D.

Selection
_____

I A _____

_____

II A _____

_____

III A _____

_____

B _____

_____

C _____

_____

IV A _____

_____

B _____

_____

C _____

_____

D _____

_____

SELECTION I: "SOUNDS"

From *Walden* by Henry David Thoreau

But while we are confined to books, though the most select and classic, and read only particular written languages, which are themselves but dialects and provincial, we are in danger of forgetting the language which all things and events speak without metaphor, which alone is copious and standard. Much is published, but little printed. The rays which stream through the shutter will be no longer remembered when the shutter is wholly removed. No method nor discipline can supersede the necessity of being forever on the alert. What is a course of history or philosophy, or poetry, no matter how well selected, or the best society, or the most admirable routine of life, compared with the discipline of looking always at what is to be seen? Will you be a reader, a student merely, or a seer? Read your fate, see what is before you, and walk on into futurity.

I did not read books the first summer; I hoed beans. Nay, I often did better than this. There were times when I could not afford to sacrifice the bloom of the present moment to any work, whether of the head or hands. I love a broad margin to my life. Sometimes, in a summer morning, having taken my accustomed bath, I sat in my sunny doorway from sunrise till noon, rapt in a revery, amidst the pines and hickories and sumachs, in undisturbed solitude and stillness, while the birds sang around or flitted noiseless through the house, until by the sun falling in at my west window, or the noise of some traveller's wagon on the distant highway, I was reminded of the lapse of time. I grew in those seasons like corn in the night, and they were far better than any work of the hands would have been. They were not time subtracted from my life, but so much over and above my usual allowance. I realized what the Orientals mean by contemplation and the forsaking of works. For the most part, I minded not how the hours went. The day advanced as if to light some work of mine; it was morning, and lo, now it is evening, and nothing memorable is accomplished. Instead of singing like the birds, I silently smiled at my incessant good fortune. As the sparrow had its trill, sitting on the hickory before my door, so had I my chuckle or suppressed warble which he might hear out of my nest. My days were not days of the week, bearing the stamp of any heathen deity, nor were they minced into hours and fretted by the ticking of a clock; for I lived like the Puri Indians, of whom it is said that "for yesterday, to-day, and to-morrow they have only one word, and they express the variety of meaning by pointing backward for yesterday, forward for tomorrow, and overhead for the passing day." This was sheer idleness to my fellow-townsmen, no doubt; but if the birds and flowers had tried me by their standard, I should not have been found wanting. A man must find his occasions in himself, it is true. The natural day is very calm, and will hardly reprove his indolence.

[A] I had this advantage, at least, in my mode of life, over those who were obliged to look abroad for amusement, to society and the theatre, that my life itself was become my amusement and never ceased to be a novel. It was a drama of many scenes and without an end. If we were always, indeed, getting our living, and regulating our lives according to the last and best mode we had learned, we should never be troubled with ennui. Follow your genius closely enough, and it will not fail to show you a fresh prospect every hour. Housework was a pleasant pastime. When my floor was dirty, I rose early, and, setting all my furniture out of doors on the grass, bed and bedstead making but one budget, dashed water on the floor, and sprinkled white sand from the pond on it, and then with a broom scrubbed it clean and white; and by the time the villagers had broken their fast the morning sun had dried my house sufficiently to allow me to move in again, and my meditations were almost uninterrupted. It was pleasant to see my whole household effects out on the grass, making a little pile like a gypsy's pack, and my three-legged table, from which I did not remove the books and pen and ink, standing amid the pines and hickories. They seemed glad to get out themselves, and as if unwilling to be brought in. I was sometimes tempted to stretch an awning over them and take my seat there. It was worth the while to see the sun shine on these things, and hear the free wind blow on them; so much more interesting most familiar objects look out of doors than in the house. A bird sits on the next bough, life-everlasting grows under the table, and blackberry vines run round its legs; pine cones, chestnut burs, and strawberry leaves are strewn about. It looked as if this was the way these forms came to be transferred to our furniture, to tables, chairs, and bedsteads,—because they once stood in their midst.

SELECTION II: "THE TIDE RISES, THE TIDE FALLS"

Henry Wadsworth Longfellow

The tide rises, the tide falls,
The twilight darkens, the curlew calls;
Along the sea-sands damp and brown
The traveller hastens toward the town,
   And the tide rises, the tide falls.

[A] Darkness settles on roofs and walls,
But the sea, the sea in the darkness calls;
The little waves, with their soft, white hands,
Efface the footprints in the sands,
   And the tide rises, the tide falls.   10

The morning breaks; the steeds in their stalls
Stamp and neigh, as the hostler calls;
The day returns, but nevermore
Returns the traveller to the shore,
   And the tide rises, the tide falls.
1879   1880

SELECTION III: "THE LAST LEAF"*

Oliver Wendell Holmes

I saw him once before,
As he passed by the door,
  And again
The pavement stones resound,
As he totters o'er the ground
  With his cane.

They say that in his prime,
Ere the pruning-knife of Time
  Cut him down,
Not a better man was found   10
By the Crier on his round
  Through the town.

But now he walks the streets,
And he looks at all he meets
  Sad and wan,
And he shakes his feeble head,
That it seems as if he said,
  "They are gone."

The mossy marbles rest
On the lips that he has prest   20
  In their bloom,
And the names he loved to hear
Have been carved for many a year
On the tomb.

[A] My grandmamma has said—
Poor old lady, she is dead
  Long ago—
That he had a Roman nose,
And his cheek was like a rose
  In the snow;   30

[B] But now his nose is thin,
And it rests upon his chin
  Like a staff,
And a crook is in his back,
And a melancholy crack
  In his laugh.

I know it is a sin
For me to sit and grin
  At him here;
But the old three-cornered hat,   40
And the breeches, and all that,
  Are so queer!

---

*"This poem was suggested by the appearance in one of our streets of a venerable relic of the Revolution, said to be one of the party who threw the tea overboard in Boston Harbor. He was a fine monumental specimen in his cocked hat and knee breeches, with his buckled shoes and his sturdy cane. . . . an honoured fellow-citizen whose costume was out of date, but whose patriotism never changed with years." Holmes's note. The subject of the poem was Major Thomas Melville, Herman Melville's grandfather.

[C] *And if I should live to be*
The last leaf upon the tree
  In the spring,
Let them smile, as I do now,
At the old forsaken bough
  Where I cling.

SELECTION IV: "THE TELL-TALE HEART"

Edgar Allan Poe

TRUE!—nervous—very, very dreadfully nervous I had been and am; but why *will* you say that I am mad? The disease had sharpened my senses—not destroyed—not dulled them. Above all was the sense of hearing acute. I heard all things in the heaven and in the earth.[1] I heard many things in hell. How, then, am I mad? Hearken! and observe how healthily—how calmly I can tell you the whole story.

It is impossible to say how first the idea entered my brain; but, once conceived, it haunted me day and night. Object there was none. Passion there was none. I loved the old man. He had never wronged me. He had never given me an insult. For his gold I had no desire. I think it was his eye! yes, it was this! One of his eyes resembled that of a vulture—a pale blue eye, with a film over it. Whenever it fell upon me, my blood ran cold; and so by degrees—very gradually—I made up my mind to take the life of the old man, and thus rid myself of the eye forever.

Now this is the point. You fancy me mad. Madmen know nothing. But you should have seen how wisely I proceeded—with what caution—with what foresight—with what dissimulation I went to work! I was never kinder to the old man than during the whole week before I killed him. And every night, about midnight, I turned the latch of his door and opened it—oh, so gently! And then, when I had made an opening sufficient for my head, I put in a dark lantern, all closed, closed, so that no light shone out, and then I thrust in my head. Oh, you would have laughed to see how cunningly I thrust it in! I moved it slowly—very, very slowly, so that I might not disturb the old man's sleep. It took me an hour to place my whole head within the opening so far that I could see him as he lay upon his bed. Ha!—would a madman have been so wise as this? And then, when my head was well in the room, I undid the lantern cautiously—oh, so cautiously—cautiously (for the hinges creaked)—I undid it just so much that a single thin ray fell upon the vulture eye. And this I did for seven long nights—every night just at midnight—but I found the eye always closed; and so it was impossible to do the work; for it was not the old man who vexed me, but his Evil Eye. And every morning, when the day broke, I went boldly into the chamber, and spoke courageously to him, calling him by name in a hearty tone, and inquiring how he had passed the night. So you see he would have been a very profound old man, indeed, to suspect that every night, just at twelve, I looked in upon him while he slept.

Upon the eighth night I was more than usually cautious in opening the door. A watch's minute hand moves more quickly than did mine. Never, before that night, had I *felt* the extent of my own powers—of my sagacity. I could scarcely contain my feelings of triumph. To think that there I was, opening the door, little by little, and he not even to dream of my secret deeds or thoughts. I fairly chuckled at the idea; and perhaps he heard me; for he moved on the bed suddenly, as if startled. Now you may think that I drew back—but no. His room was as black as pitch with the thick darkness, (for the shutters were close fastened, through fear of robbers,) and so I knew that he could not see the opening of the door, and I kept pushing it on steadily, steadily.

I had my head in, and was about to open the lantern, when my thumb slipped

[1] Philippians 2:10, "That at the name of Jesus every knee should bow, of things in heaven, and things in earth, and things under the earth."

upon the tin fastening, and the old man sprang up in the bed, crying out—"Who's there?"

I kept quite still and said nothing. For a whole hour I did not move a muscle, and in the meantime I did not hear him lie down. He was still sitting up in the bed, listening;—just as I have done, night after night, hearkening to the deathwatches in the wall.[2]

Presently I heard a slight groan, and I knew it was the groan of mortal terror. It was not a groan of pain or of grief—oh, no!—it was the low stifled sound that arises from the bottom of the soul when overcharged with awe. I knew the sound well. Many a night, just at midnight, when all the world slept, it has welled up from my own bosom, deepening, with its dreadful echo, the terrors that distracted me. I say I knew it well. I knew what the old man felt, and pitied him, although I chuckled at heart. I knew that he had been lying awake ever since the first slight noise, when he had turned in the bed. His fears had been ever since growing upon him. He had been trying to fancy them causeless, but could not. He had been saying to himself—"It is nothing but the wind in the chimney—it is only a mouse crossing the floor," or "it is merely a cricket which has made a single chirp." Yes, he has been trying to comfort himself with these suppositions: but he had found all in vain. *All in vain;* because Death, in approaching him, had stalked with his black shadow before him, and enveloped the victim. And it was the mournful influence of the unperceived shadow that caused him to feel—although he neither saw nor heard—to *feel* the presence of my head within the room.

[A] When I had waited a long time, very patiently, without hearing him lie down, I resolved to open a little—a very, very little crevice in the lantern. So I opened it—you cannot imagine how stealthily, stealthily—until, at length, a single dim ray, like the thread of the spider, shot from out the crevice and fell upon the vulture eye.

It was open—wide, wide open—and I grew furious as I gazed upon it. I saw it with perfect distinctness—all a dull blue, with a hideous veil over it that chilled the very marrow in my bones; but I could see nothing else of the old man's face or person: for I had directed the ray as if by instinct, precisely upon the damned spot.

[B] And now—have I not told you that what you mistake for madness is but over acuteness of the senses?—now, I say, there came to my ears a low, dull, quick sound, such as a watch makes when enveloped in cotton. I knew *that* sound well, too. It was the beating of the old man's heart. It increased my fury, as the beating of a drum stimulates the soldier into courage.

[C] But even yet I refrained and kept still. I scarcely breathed. I held the lantern motionless. I tried how steadily I could maintain the ray upon the eye. Meantime the hellish tatoo of the heart increased. It grew quicker and quicker, and louder and louder every instant. The old man's terror *must* have been extreme! It grew louder, I say, louder every moment!—do you mark me well? I have told you that I am nervous: so I am. And now at the dead hour of the night, amid the dreadful silence of that old house, so strange a noise as this excited me to uncontrollable terror. Yet, for some minutes longer I refrained and stood still. But the beating grew louder, louder! I thought the heart must burst. And now a new anxiety seized me—the sound would be heard by a neighbor! The old man's hour had come! With a loud yell, I threw open the lantern and leaped into the room. He shrieked once—once only. In an instant I dragged him to the floor, and pulled the heavy bed over him. I then smiled gaily, to find the deed so far done. But, for many minutes, the heart beat on with a muffled sound. This,

---

[2]A reference to "death-watch beetles," insects that make a hollow clicking sound by striking their heads against the wood into which they have burrowed.

however, did not vex me; it would not be heard through the wall. At length it ceased. The old man was dead. I removed the bed and examined the corpse. Yes, he was stone, stone dead. I placed my hand upon the heart and held it there many minutes. There was no pulsation. He was stone dead. His eye would trouble me no more.

If still you think me mad, you will think so no longer when I describe the wise precautions I took for the concealment of the body. The night waned, and I worked hastily, but in silence. First of all I dismembered the corpse. I cut off the head and the arms and the legs.

I then took up three planks from the flooring of the chamber, and deposited all between the scantlings.[3] I then replaced the boards so cleverly, so cunningly, that no human eye—not even *his*—could have detected anything wrong. There was nothing to wash out—no stain of any kind—no blood-spot whatever. I had been too wary for that. A tub had caught all—ha! ha!

When I had made an end of these labors, it was four o'clock—still dark as midnight. As the bell sounded the hour, there came a knocking at the street door. I went down to open it with a light heart,—for what had I *now* to fear? There entered three men, who introduced themselves, with perfect suavity, as officers of the police. A shriek had been heard by a neighbor during the night; suspicion of foul play had been aroused; information had been lodged at the police office, and they (the officers) had been deputed to search the premises.

I smiled,—for *what* had I to fear? I bade the gentlemen welcome. The shriek, I said, was my own in a dream. The old man, I mentioned, was absent in the country. I took my visitors all over the house. I bade them search—search *well*. I led them, at length, to *his* chamber. I showed them his treasures, secure, undisturbed. In the enthusiasm of my confidence, I brought chairs into the room, and desired them *here* to rest from their fatigues, while I myself, in the wild audacity of my perfect triumph, placed my own seat upon the very spot beneath which reposed the corpse of the victim.

The officers were satisfied. My *manner* had convinced them. I was singularly at ease. They sat, and while I answered cheerily, they chattered of familiar things. But, ere long, I felt myself getting pale and wished them gone. My head ached, and I fancied a ringing in my ears: but still they sat and still chattered. The ringing became more distinct:—it continued and became more distinct: I talked more freely to get rid of the feeling: but it continued and gained definitiveness—until, at length, I found out that the noise was *not* within my ears.

[D] No doubt I now grew *very* pale;—but I talked more fluently, and with a heightened voice. Yet the sound increased—and what could I do? It was *a low, dull, quick sound—much such a sound as a watch makes when enveloped in cotton*. I gasped for breath—and yet the officers heard it not. I talked more quickly—more vehemently; but the noise steadily increased. I arose and argued about trifles, in a high key and with violent gesticulations; but the noise steadily increased. Why *would* they not be gone? I paced the floor to and fro with heavy strides, as if excited to fury by the observations of the men—but the noise steadily increased. Oh God! what *could* I do? I foamed—I raved—I swore! I swung the chair upon which I had been sitting, and grated it upon the boards, but the noise arose over all and continually increased. It grew louder—louder—*louder!* And still the men chatted pleasantly, and smiled. Was it possible they heard not? Almighty God!—no, no! They heard!—they suspected!—they *knew!*—they were making a mockery of my horror!—this I thought, and this I think. But anything was better than this agony! Anything was more tolerable

[3]Timbers that support floor boards.

than this derision! I could bear those hypocritical smiles no longer! I felt that I must scream or die!—and now—again!—hark! louder! louder! louder! *louder!*—

"Villains," I shrieked, "dissemble no more! I admit the deed!—tear up the planks!—here, here!—it is the beating of his hideous heart!"

NOTES

1. **Stephen Vincent Benet,** "The Ballad of William Sycamore" from *Ballads and Poems* (New York: Holt, Rinehart & Winston, 1959)
2. **Frank Marshall Davis,** "The Four Glimpses of Night."
3. **Stephen Vincent Benet,** "The Devil and Daniel Webster," from *The Selected Works of Stephen Vincent Benet* (New York: Curtis, 1936).
4. **Katherine Anne Porter,** "Theft," from *Collected Stories of Katherine Anne Porter* (New York: Harcourt, 1965), pp. 60–61.
5. **Hamlin Garland,** "Under the Lion's Paw."
6. **Ken Kesey,** *One Flew Over the Cuckoo's Nest* (New York: Viking, 1962), p. 2.
7. **O'Henry,** "Gift of the Magi."
8. **Edgar Allan Poe,** "The Maelstrom."
9. **Sinclair Lewis,** *Babbitt* (New York: Harcourt, 1922), p. 1.
10. **Emily Dickinson,** "The Lightning Is a Yellow Fork," in *The Poems of Emily Dickinson* (Cambridge, Harvard University Press, 1979).
11. **Ralph Waldo Emerson,** "Concord Hymn."
12. **Robert Frost,** "Two Tramps in Mud-Time," from *The Poetry of Robert Frost*, edited by Edward Connery-Lathem (New York: Holt, Rinehart and Winston, 1969).

Sixteen

READING CRITICALLY: DEDUCTIVE REASONING

It can be difficult to determine whether a conclusion is true or false. It is easier to determine whether or not a conclusion has been arrived at in a logical or "valid" way. The art of arriving at valid conclusions is called deductive reasoning.

A conclusion is *valid* if it follows logically from either true or false premises. A conclusion is *true* if it is arrived at validly from true premises.

Let's take a second to consider validity and truth. When we say that a conclusion is valid, we mean that the conclusion has been arrived at using a valid reasoning technique. When we say that a conclusion is true, we mean that the conclusion is valid and that the facts or premises which lead to the conclusion are true.

The real difficulty comes when we consider statements which are valid but not true. Consider this statement.

All horses have three legs.
Bugs Bunny is a horse so Bugs Bunny must have three legs.

It turns out that this conclusion (Bugs Bunny has three legs) is valid. That is, it follows logically from the information given. However, the information upon which the conclusion is based is clearly false. So, we have a valid but false conclusion.

Consider another valid but false conclusion.

Assassins are loners.
John Wilkes Booth assassinated Abraham Lincoln.
John Wilkes Booth had no accomplices.

Again the conclusion (John Wilkes Booth had no accomplices) is valid, and one of the pieces of information supporting the conclusion is true. However, the general statement that "assassins are loners" is false and so the conclusion is false.

Let me summarize this again. A valid conclusion is one that is arrived at in a logical way from the information given. Just because a conclusion is valid does not mean that it is true. For a valid conclusion to be true, the information used to reach the conclusion must be true. As a critical reader, you should examine conclusions to be sure that:

1. The premises used as the basis of the conclusion are true.
2. The conclusion has been arrived at in a valid way.

Each deductive reasoning situation has at least one major premise, at least one minor premise, and one conclusion.

1. *Major premise* (establishes a relationship): All horses have four legs.
2. *Minor premise* (a statement related to the major premise): Black Beauty is a horse.
3. *Conclusion:* Black Beauty has four legs.

There are many forms of valid deductive reasoning. The three shown below are the most common. For the moment, we will not be concerned with whether the conclusions are true or false.

1. *Major premise:* All water is wet.
2. *Minor premise:* The stuff in my glass is water.
3. *Conclusion:* The stuff in my glass is wet.

1. *Major premise:* All bikes have wheels.
2. *Minor premise:* A pogo stick has no wheels.
3. *Conclusion:* A pogo stick is not a bike.

1. *Major premise:* It rains more in Georgia than in Wyoming.
2. *Minor premise:* It rains more in Wyoming than in Nevada.
3. *Conclusion:* It rains more in Georgia than in Nevada.

EXERCISE I

In the space below, write three more examples of each form of reasoning.

Major premise: _____ _____

_____ _____

Minor premise: _____ _____

_____ _____

Conclusion: _____ _____

_____ _____

Major premise: _____ _____

_____ _____

Minor premise: _____ _____

_____ _____

Conclusion: _____ _____

_____ _____

Major premise: _____ _____

_____ _____

Minor premise: _____ _____

_____ _____

Conclusion: _____   _____

_____   _____

INVALID REASONING

We must be constantly on guard for patterns of deductive reasoning which lead us to invalid or untrue conclusions.

Using the Inverse

1. *Major premise:* Everyone who got an A got over 90 on the exam.
2. *Minor premise:* Bob did not get an A.
3. *Conclusion:* Bob did not get over 90 on the exam. *Invalid.*

Our premise says that getting an A means you got over 90, not that no A means you got less than 90. There could be some students who did not get As but who still had scores over 90. This invalid conclusion assumes that the inverse of the major premise is true.

Using the Converse

1. *Major premise:* All birds have wings.
2. *Minor premise:* An animal with wings just went by.
3. *Conclusion:* That animal was a bird. *Invalid.*

Our premise does NOT say that everything with wings is a bird. Bats have wings but they are mammals, not birds. This invalid conclusion assumes the converse of the major premise.

Non Sequitur

1. *Major premise:* Polluted lakes can poison fish.
2. *Minor premise:* Lake Cherokee is polluted.
3. *Conclusion:* Motorboats should be banned from Lake Cherokee. *Invalid.*

This conclusion certainly does not follow from the premises. *Non sequitur* means "does not follow." The conclusion may or may not be true, but it certainly cannot be reached from these premises.

Unreasonable, Unclear, or False Premises

1. *Major premise:* Ocean liners will eventually kill all the whales.
2. *Major premise:* Research shows that tall men eat a lot of bananas.
3. *Major premise:* Either I will go to the dance or my life is ruined.
4. *Major premise:* The sun is not a star.

Major premise 1 is clearly unreasonable. We would probably never be able to prove it true or false. Major premise 2 leaves too many things unclear. What does "tall" mean and what is "a lot" of bananas? Major premise 3 sets up an unreasonable either-or situation. Major premise 4 is false.

EXERCISE II

Lewis Carroll (C. L. Dodgson),[1] the author of *Alice in Wonderland*, delighted in publishing puzzles in deductive logic. The examples on this page are from a book originally published in 1897. You may find some of these examples challenging. Find the conclusion. If there is no conclusion, write "no conclusion."

1. John is in the house.
   Everybody in the house is ill.

Conclusion: _____

2. Some holidays are rainy.
   Rainy days are tiresome.

Conclusion: _____

3. All pale people are phlegmatic.
   No one looks poetical unless he is pale.

Conclusion: _____

4. I never neglect important business.
   Your business is unimportant.

Conclusion: _____

5. Some lessons are difficult.
   What is difficult needs attention.

Conclusion: _____

6. John is industrious.
   No industrious people are unhappy.

Conclusion: _____

7. Nothing intelligible ever puzzles me.
   Logic puzzles me.

Conclusion: _____

8. Bores are terrible.
   You are a bore.

Conclusion: _____

9. When a man knows what he's about, he can detect a sharper.
   You and I know what we're about.

Conclusion: _____

10. Sandwiches are satisfying.
    Nothing in this dish is unsatisfying.

Conclusion: _____

11. No experienced person is incompetent.
    Jenkins is always blundering.
    No competent person is always blundering.

Conclusion: _____

12. No name in this list is unsuitable for the hero of a romance.
    Names beginning with a vowel are always melodious.
    No name is suitable for the hero of a romance if it begins with a consonant.

Conclusion: _____

PROJECT

Some arguments are presented below in paragraph form.

1. Underline each premise that leads to the conclusion.
2. Circle the conclusion.
3. Label each paragraph V for valid or NV for invalid.
4. Label each paragraph T for true or NT for not true.

A.   Scientists believe that flatworms cannot live in temperatures lower than 4° C. It has long been known that flatworms live on the surface of rocks in warmer climates. In fact, some scientists think that they only live on particular types of rocks. It has long been known that the geesi worms die when the temperature falls below 4° C. Scientists long ago identified the flatworm as a member of the geesi worm family. This research on the flatworms and geesi worms may well open up new horizons in the study of climatic temperature change.

_____

B.   Air and water pollution are problems we must all be concerned with. In fact, these may be our biggest problems. Any animal swimming in a lake or pond pollutes the water. We spend many hours swimming in lakes and ponds. We spend many hours polluting lakes and ponds.

_____

C. During the past decade, the population of New York has grown at a slower rate than the population of California. Most observers agree that the warmer climate in California accounts for this difference in growth rate. The population of Maine has also grown at a slower rate than the population of California. It is clear from this information that the population of New York has grown at a faster rate than the population of Maine.

D. As the temperature drops, molecules of air move more slowly. To study the movement of molecules of air, we established a weather observatory in a field. For a while the temperature dropped and then leveled off. When the temperature stopped dropping, the speed of the molecules of air stopped decreasing. We plan to report fully on our findings in a report to be issued later this year.

E. Transportation is a vital part of our nation's economy. In fact, one can trace the economy of this country through the history of transportation. As transportation has improved, our nation's economy has prospered. Our transportation system has continued to improve. We should spend more money to improve this system to help preserve the economy.

NOTES

1. **C. L. Dodgson,** *The Game of Logic* (New York: Dover, 1897), pp. 112–114.

Seventeen

READING CRITICALLY: INDUCTIVE REASONING

We are seldom presented with a conclusion or viewpoint that is supported by a true and valid logical argument. Writers often try to convince us that a particular outlook, point of view, or fact is true without having a tight deductive argument. In fact, deductive arguments are the exception.

Writers are more likely to present inductive arguments. An inductive argument usually asks the reader to accept a conclusion as a generalization of specific cases. That is, an inductive argument takes what is known about a relatively few cases and asks us to believe that what we know about these cases applies to all similar cases.

For example, an author may be writing about foreign sports cars. The author may check on the prices of five out of eight models and find that the price of each one is over $10,000. The author might ask us to accept the conclusion that all foreign sports cars cost over $10,000. Of course, this inductive conclusion might be false. We have no way of knowing without more information.

In another example, a business writer may survey 20 businesses that went bankrupt. Of these twenty bankruptcies, the writer may find that eight were caused by poor investment planning. The writer might then ask us to accept the conclusion that 40 per cent of all businesses that go bankrupt do so because of poor investment planning. Again, we cannot be certain of this conclusion.

When reading, we should be aware when inductive arguments are being made to support a conclusion, view, or "fact." We should realize that we cannot absolutely count on conclusions reached in this manner and, indeed, that the conclusions may be highly suspect.

However, we cannot reject all inductive arguments. The vast majority of the choices we make and conclusions we reach are arrived at inductively rather than deductively. It is only natural that this state of affairs will be reflected in the material we read.

All conclusions based on statistics are actually arrived at inductively. Certain sampling techniques and other statistical methods, when properly used, increase the likelihood that a conclusion based on statistical methods will be correct. When reading material which reports research, you may notice an entry such as $(p < .05)$. This entry tells the likelihood that the conclusion is incorrect. In this case the entry tells us the likelihood that the conclusion is incorrect is less than 5 per cent.

So when we read, we should be aware when an inductive argument is being made and about the inherent weaknesses in this type of argument. There are other things we should look for even more carefully. The very nature of inductive arguments makes it fairly easy to twist an inductive argument into a fallacious inductive argument. We should be particularly alert for these fallacies as we read.

259

FALLACIOUS INDUCTIVE ARGUMENTS

The following fallacies result when a writer contrives to *present only one side of an argument* or position.

False Analogy

Argument: Learning to read is like learning to fly a supersonic jet plane. One little mistake and it can be all over. So when you read, be careful not to make any mistakes or you may not get another chance.

Fallacious argument! This fallacious argument presents a conclusion which is based on a clearly preposterous analogy.

Hasty Generalization

Argument: In a West Coast study, fifteen rats were injected with pancake syrup. One of the rats developed cancer, proving that pancake syrup causes cancer.

Fallacious argument! This argument makes too hasty and sweeping a generalization for the information available.

Bandwagon

Argument: Most people voted for Lucklaw for president, showing that Lucklaw was the best person for the presidency.

Fallacious argument! Just because most people voted for Lucklaw doesn't mean that she is the best—just the biggest vote getter. The writer is trying to get us on the bandwagon.

Stereotyping

Argument: During the westward expansion of the United States, the Indians became drunkards. That's why the Indians were defeated.

Fallacious argument! This argument bases a conclusion on an obvious and blatant stereotype.

In the following fallacies, the writer tries to *sidestep the issue* and present an unrelated argument to convince you.

Begging the Question

Argument: My years of research have revealed that there are colonies of invisible sea creatures living in the Atlantic Ocean. It is easy to criticize my work, but so far no one has proven me wrong.

Fallacious argument! The writer assumes that the assumption is true and then challenges others to prove that the assumption is false.

Guilt by Association

Argument: Leslie cannot be linked directly to the crime. However, since her father and sister were convicted of similar crimes, she is the primary suspect.

Fallacious argument! If the only link between Leslie and the crime is her relationship with her father and sister, then we are making Leslie guilty by association.

Straw Man

Argument: Does the United Nations aid the cause of world peace? In my view, we are fortunate to have the United Nations and even more fortunate to have it located in the United States. After all, where would we be without this organization?

Fallacious argument! Instead of dealing directly with the question of the U.N. and world peace, the writer has responded in a more general way about the U.N. The writer wants us to believe that he has demonstrated that the U.N. aids world peace. However, as difficult as the statement is to disagree with, the issue has not been addressed.

You Too

Argument: Our candidate may have conducted some dirty tricks in the recent campaign. However, our reports show that the other candidates were doing the same thing.

Fallacious argument! The writer sought to justify the candidate's actions by saying "you too" to the opposition candidates. It may or may not be true of the other candidates, but this argument does not respond to what the writer's candidate has done.

EXERCISE I

Read each argument. Underline the conclusion. Write the fallacy that leads to the conclusion.

1. In Velman's murder trial, the psychiatrist testified that Velman was insane. This proves that she is innocent by reason of insanity.

_____

_____

2. Let me say a few words about whether or not taking vitamins slows down aging. Not one study has shown that taking vitamins speeds up aging. Vitamins are not harmful and have been proven very useful. A few vitamins won't hurt anyone.

_____

_____

3. Car junkyards are not appropriate in a modern society. We certainly would not take a person who was only 10 or 15 years old and throw him on the junk pile.

_____

_____

4. Your honor, I don't think this speeding ticket is fair. On the way over here, I saw others speeding and they didn't get tickets. When the policeman stopped me, there was someone going as fast in the other lane.

_____

_____

5. On the night when Abraham Lincoln was shot, several other assassinations were attempted. Secretary of War Stanton may have been the leader of this conspiracy. Over the years, no one has been able to establish his innocence.

_____

_____

6. Many adolescents who live in the juvenile rehabilitation center commit crimes in the neighborhood. A local home was burglarized and Raoul, who lives at the center, was one of ten people seen in the neighborhood. He is the chief suspect.

_____

_____

7. We tested our soup with over 30,000 people nationwide. These people came from every region and walk of life. Over 80 per cent of the people tested liked our soup, and so we know that you will like it too.

_____

_____

8. American-made cars are notorious gas guzzlers. Jim bought an American car, and so you just know that his gas mileage is terrible.

_____

_____

PROJECT

Consider yourself in this position. You are writing a book and you believe that children who watch "a lot" of television do more poorly in school than those who do not watch "a lot" of television. You really don't have any facts to support your point of view. However, you want to present this idea forcefully in your book.

Under these circumstances, you might consider using a fallacious argument to support your point of view. In the space provided below, write your own example of how each form of fallacious reasoning could be used to support your point of view. Of course you would not use these arguments in actual practice.

False analogy _____

_____

_____

_____

_____

_____

_____

Hasty generalization _____

_____

_____

_____

_____

_____

_____

Bandwagon _____

_____

_____

_____

_____

_____

_____

Stereotyping _____

_____

_____

_____

_____

_____

_____

Begging the question _____

_____

_____

_____

_____

_____

_____

Guilt by association _____

_____

_____

_____

_____

_____

_____

Straw man _____

_____

_____

_____

_____

_____

_____

_____

Eighteen

READING CRITICALLY: PROPAGANDA

Propaganda is any attempt to convince people to accept particular ideas, doctrines, or practices. Propaganda may contain sound arguments or be filled with faulty ones. Propaganda may contain lies or tell the truth. It is not lies or faulty arguments that mark writing as propaganda. It is the writing's attempt to convince or persuade.

We must be most carefully on guard against propaganda which contains lies and/or faulty arguments. However, we must realize that almost every book, including this one, contains propaganda.

We must examine all propaganda critically, particularly when we are susceptible to accepting a fallacious argument. If we believe in a cause or point of view, we are likely to accept supporting propaganda rather uncritically. At the same time, we are likely to reject, without thought, propaganda for a point of view in which we do not believe.

Propaganda is not limited to causes or very controversial issues. Say that a textbook informs you that the world is round, giving certain facts and conclusions based on these facts. This is propaganda! After critically examining the propaganda, you may choose to accept it as the truth.

Just remember that there was a time when all the propaganda said that the world was flat—and at the center of the universe, no less. Just about everyone accepted that propaganda as the truth. Of course, we now know that all the propaganda about the earth being round was false also. The earth is an oblate spheroid.

You should read everything critically, as though it were propaganda. Initially, this will require some effort. After a while, a critical approach to reading will come more naturally. This does not mean that you cannot believe anything that you read. None of us is in a position to independently verify every fact and conclusion. Many writers are quite scrupulous and make every effort to present material in a clear, honest, and even-handed way.

It does mean that propaganda abounds and that we should be constantly on the alert for propaganda and examine critically what we read. The steps that follow will help you structure your approach to critical reading.

Following these steps when reading.

1. Decide if you are susceptible to accepting a lie or a fallacious argument because:
    a. You already believe that the conclusion is correct or true.
    b. You can't check the facts.
    c. You trust the writer.
    d. The propaganda appeals to an emotional issue or to an urgent hope or desire.

(Use steps 2–6 with particular care if any of the above applies.)

2. Identify the main propaganda message.
3. Examine the passage for any lies or misstatements.
4. Examine the passage for any fallacious inductive arguments.
5. Examine the passage for any fallacious deductive arguments.
6. Prepare counterpropaganda or a counterargument. Compare the counterpropaganda with the propaganda.

Consider these steps one at a time. As with all techniques, you will have to use the steps several times before the process becomes a natural part of your reading. With a little use, though, the steps will blend naturally, and unnoticed, with your other reading skills.

Decide if you are susceptible to accepting a lie or a fallacious argument. This is a most crucial step in critical reading. If you are susceptible to accepting facts or arguments uncritically for any of the reasons given, you should read the material with particular care.

You may already believe that the conclusion or premise presented by the writer is true or correct. Often, a writer will present a point of view which the writer feels will gain wide acceptance by the readers. After gaining the reader's agreement and lowering the reader's resistance, the writer may present other ideas or conclusions which are not truly linked to the original premise or conclusion. Yet these ideas or conclusions may be accepted by readers because they fall in the proximity of an idea or conclusion they support.

You may not be able to check the facts or you may trust the writer. This will almost certainly be the case in most college textbooks that you read. While it is not possible to check even a small portion of the facts we read, we must realize that not being able to check facts makes us vulnerable to uncritically accepting propaganda. Similarly, if we trust the writer, or a source, we are vulnerable to accepting propaganda uncritically. If we cannot check the facts or if we trust the writer, we must read with particular care.

The propaganda may appeal to an emotional issue or to an urgent hope or desire. Lynchings have been justified and caused by writers who appealed to their readers' emotions. Much has been justified in literature by "wrapping it in the flag," associating it with motherhood, or putting it on the same plate with apple pie. If we find ourselves emotionally involved, we must read all the more critically.

Perhaps we are most vulnerable to accepting propaganda when it appeals to an urgent hope or desire. On one level, a youngster who reads a description of the seven-in-one decoder on a cereal box and then sends in the dollar may well be the victim of propaganda. If you recall your youth, these things were never as good as they sounded. On another level, reading about a potential cure for an afflicted loved one makes us vulnerable to accepting propaganda. The cure may well exist and we should pursue it, but we must keep our vulnerability clearly in mind.

Identify the main propaganda message. As you are reading, try to identify the main propaganda message being presented by the writer. This process is similar to identifying the main idea. However, we may find that the propaganda message is never clearly stated and indeed may be cleverly hidden among more clearly stated premises and conclusions. In many respects, it is easier to evaluate a clearly stated propaganda message than a subtle, indirect propaganda message.

Examine the passage for any lies or misstatements. It is amazing how many times simply being on guard for clear lies or misstatements can extract us from the propaganda trap. Many times a writer will deluge us with facts and include only one questionable but crucial fact. We are so caught up with the obvious truth of 99 per cent of the facts that we often overlook or dismiss the obvious lie or misstatement. Be particularly alert for statements that should be labeled as estimates or guesses by the writer but are, instead, presented as facts.

Examine the passage for any fallacious deductive or inductive arguments. Steps for identifying fallacious inductive and deductive arguments are given in Chapters 16 and 17. Please refer to these chapters. Fallacious deductive and inductive arguments may be difficult to spot. However, once you have found a fallacious argument, you know that the conclusion does not follow from the premises.

Prepare counterpropaganda and compare it with the propaganda. This is a good last step to employ when deciding whether or not to accept the propaganda. Devise the strongest, best-constructed counterargument or counterpropaganda you can. Then compare your counterpropaganda with the propaganda. Your considered choice between the two will usually be a good guide when deciding whether or not to accept the writer's view.

Uncle Tom's Cabin by Harriet Beecher Stowe has been called the most effective propaganda novel in history. Some have said that this book was a major cause of the Civil War. Most would consider this book "good propaganda." That is, *Uncle Tom's Cabin* was an attempt to convince people of the truth. Nonetheless, it is propaganda.

ACTIVITY I

Read the following excerpt from *Uncle Tom's Cabin*. Keep in mind the steps outlined on the preceding pages. After reading, respond to the questions at the end.

Eliza, a runaway slave, made her desperate retreat across the river just in the dusk of twilight. The gray mist of evening, rising slowly from the river, enveloped her as she disappeared up the bank, and the swollen current and floundering masses of ice presented a hopeless barrier between her and her pursuer. Haley, the pursuer, therefore slowly and discontentedly returned to the little tavern, to ponder further what was to be done. Haley sat him down to meditate on the instability of human hopes and happiness in general.

"What did I want with the little cuss, now," he said to himself, "that I should have got myself treed like a coon, as I am, this yer say?"

He was startled by the loud and dissonant voice of a man who was apparently dismounting at the door. He hurried to the window.

"By the land! if this yer an't the nearest, now, to what I've heard folks call Providence," said Haley. "I do b'lieve that ar's Tom Loker."

Haley hastened out. Standing by the bar, in the corner of the room, was a brawny, muscular man, full six feet in height and broad in proportion. In the head and face every organ and lineament expressive of brutal and unhesitating violence was in a state of the highest possible development. Indeed, could our readers fancy a bull-dog come into man's estate, and walking about in a hat and coat, they would have no unapt idea of the general style and effect of his physique. He was accompanied by a travelling companion, in many respects an exact contrast to himself. The great big man poured out a big tumbler half full of raw spirits, and gulped it down without a word. The little man stood tiptoe, and putting his head first to one side and then to the other, and snuffing considerately in the directions of the various bottles, ordered at last a mint julep, in a thin and quivering voice, and with an air of great circumspection. . . .

"Wall, now, who'd a thought this yer luck 'ad come to me? Why, Loker, how are ye?" said Haley, coming forward, and extending his hand to the big man.

"The devil" was the civil reply. "What brought you here, Haley?"

The mousing man, who bore the name of Marks, instantly stopped his sipping. . . .

"I say, Tom, this yer's the luckiest thing in the world. I'm in a devil of a hobble, and you must help me out."

"Ugh? aw! like enough!" grunted his complacent acquaintance. "A body may be pretty sure of that, when you're glad to see 'em. What's the blow now?"

"You've got a friend here?" said Haley, looking doubtfully at Marks; "partner, perhaps?"

"Yes, I have. Here, Marks! here's that ar feller that I was in with in Natchez."

"Shall be pleased with his acquaintance," said Marks, thrusting out a long, thin hand. "Mr. Haley, I believe?"

"The same, sir," said Haley. "And now, gentlemen, seeing as we've met so happily, I think I'll stand up to a small matter of a treat in this here parlor. So now old coon," said he to the man at the bar, "get us hot water, and sugar, and cigars, and plenty of the REAL STUFF, and we'll have a blowout."

Haley began a pathetic recital of his peculiar troubles. Loker shut up his mouth, and listened to him with gruff and surly attention.

"This yer young-un business makes lots of trouble in the slave trade," said Haley, dolefully. . . .

"If we could get a breed of gals that didn't care, now, for their young uns," said Marks; "tell ye I think 'twould be 'bout the greatest mod'rn improvement I knows on,"–and Marks patronized his joke by a quiet introductory sniggle.

"Jes' so," said Haley; "I never couldn't see into it; young uns is heaps of trouble to 'em; one would think, now, they'd be glad to get clar on 'em; but they arn't. And the more trouble a young un is, and the more good for nothing, as a gen'l thing, the tighter they stocks to 'em."

"Wal, Mr. Haley," said Marks . . . "you say jest what I feel and allers have. Now, I bought a gal once, when I was in the trade,—a tight, likely wench she was, too, and quite considerable smart,—and she had a young un that was mis'able sickly; it had a crooked back, or something or other; and I jest gin't away to a man that thought he'd take his chance raising on't, being it didn't cost nothin';—never thought, yer know, of the gal's takin' on about it,—but, Lord, yer oughter seen how she went on. Why, re'lly she did seem to me to valley the child more 'cause t'was sickly and cross, and plagued her; and she warn't making b'lieve, neither,—cried about it, she did, and lopped round, as if she'd lost every friend she had. It re'lly was droll to think on't. Lord, there ain't no end to women's notions."

Base your answers on the preceding excerpt from *Uncle Tom's Cabin*.

Are you susceptible to accepting a lie or a fallacious argument because:

———— a. you believe that the conclusion is correct or true?

———— b. you can't check the facts?

———— c. you trust the writer?

———— d. the appeal is to an emotional issue or to an urgent hope or desire?

Write the main propaganda message. ———————————————

————————————————————————————

————————————————————————————

————————————————————————————

Did you detect any lies or misstatements in the passage? If so, what are they? _____

_____

_____

_____

Did you detect any fallacious inductive or deductive arguments in the passage? If so, what are they? _____

_____

_____

_____

Think of counterpropaganda or a counterargument. Briefly outline the counterargument or counterpropaganda below. _____

_____

_____

_____

PROJECT

Find three newspaper or magazine articles or editorials that, in your view, are obvious propaganda. Analyze the articles using the six steps above. Bring each article or editorial and your written analysis to class.

Nineteen

TAKING LECTURE NOTES

Effective lecture notetaking is among the most important college survival skills. Many instructors give tests based entirely, or almost entirely, on class lectures. You must learn how to record the important main ideas and details efficiently during a lecture. The most effective way is to take notes.

What is involved in taking notes? Intense listening for a long period of time, identifying the lecturer's main ideas and supporting details, and recording them in a notebook. This is an active listening and thinking process which you can master with a little practice.

ORGANIZE YOURSELF AND YOUR NOTEBOOK

When you are in class, listen for the instructor's main ideas—the organization, relationship, and hierarchy of ideas. After a few classes, you should have an instructor's lecture technique figured out. But you must pay attention if you expect to take notes.

We recommend that you use the "1/3–2/3" notebook technique described below. You should develop your own personal shorthand and abbreviation systems. Do not write your notes in complete sentences. Use key words, main ideas, and phrases.

SUGGESTED NOTEBOOK FORM

About 1/3 Page Width	About 2/3 Page Width
—Reserve this section for review and a key word outline.	—In this section of the page use simplified or dash outline form. Record numbers and important ideas.
—This section should be used for textbook notes that relate to the lecture.	—Make lists or use diagrams to record ideas.

If the lecturer rambles, put facts and main ideas on the left hand and put examples on the right.

BE AN EFFICIENT LISTENER

ACTIVITY I

Taking lecture notes requires effective listening comprehension. How often do you find yourself engaging in these ten poor listening habits? Take this self-help quiz. (A = always, S = sometimes, N = never).

Set specific goals for becoming a more effective listener. Discuss your goals with the instructor.

YOUR PERSONAL LISTENING PROFILE

	Poor Listening Habit	A	S	N	Specific Goals for Changing Listening Behavior
1.	Calling the subject uninteresting and tuning out dry subjects.				
2.	Criticizing the speaker's delivery or mannerisms and tuning out if delivery is poor.				
3.	Getting over stimulated by something the speaker says—entering into a mental argument.				
4.	Listening primarily for facts.				
5.	Trying to outline everything or taking intensive notes using only one system.				
6.	Faking attention to the speaker.				
7.	Allowing interfering distractions.				
8.	Avoiding difficult material.				
9.	Letting emotion-laden words arouse personal antagonism.				
10.	Wasting the advantage of thought speed (daydreaming) by not mentally reviewing. Tending to daydream with slow speakers.				

ACTIVITY II

Listen to the article "Genes That Move to Fight Diseases" by having a classmate read it to you or by reading it yourself. Complete this sample notebook page.

1/3 Page	**2/3 Page**
Vocabulary	A. Genes' purposes (old view): _____ _____ (new view): _____ _____

Gene _____

_____

Immune System _____

_____

Antibody _____

_____

Main Idea Review

1. _____

_____

_____

2. _____

_____

_____

3. _____

_____

Memory Device

B. Steps in shuffling genes to form antibody genes.
   1. Genes selected from many genes.

   2. Next: _____

   _____

   3. Gene strings

      —Shorten trailing means:_____

      _____

      _____

      —Example _____

      _____

      —Added power example: _____

      _____

C. Scientist predictions

   1. _____

   _____

   _____

   _____

   2. _____

   _____

   _____

   _____

   3. _____

   _____

   _____

GENES THAT MOVE TO FIGHT DISEASE[1]

Genes, scientists once thought, were rather passive things, resting in the cells of the body and reliably passing on identical hereditary information from one generation to the next. But a series of stunning discoveries over the last five years has radically shaken biologists' notions of how genes work. Instead of simply carrying the hereditary code with which the cells are endowed, genes can rearrange themselves in the first few months of life to produce new codes and, therefore, new biological substances. . . .

Scientists still aren't certain why some genes are dynamic or what causes them to rearrange themselves, but researchers do understand what happens during the shuffling. According to the most recent findings, the dynamic genes belong to the immune system, the natural arsenal that protects the body from foreign invaders ranging from polio viruses to 24-hour flu bugs. These genes come in three basic varieties, each making one part of the substances that help repel disease-causing organisms.

To form these substances—called antibodies—three types of genes must link together as freight trains do. First one specific gene is selected from the thousands that could determine which virus the antibody will attack. Next, this gene is coupled to a "joining gene" by deleting the extraneous genetic information. Depending on which virus-specific gene is spliced to which joining gene, and on how they are spliced together, the antibody could be effective against an influenza virus, a hepatitis virus, or any of millions of others. There are apparently endless possible ways to combine two genes, enabling human beings to make countless kinds of antibodies. "It's a neat system," says molecular biologist Philip Leder of the National Institutes of Health. "Nature has evolved a very efficient way to use a finite amount of genetic information in an unlimited way."

For the final step in making the antibody gene, another string of genes adds onto the joining gene—after the extraneous genetic information separating them is again discarded. This step allows the antibody to diversify even further. As the antibody cell develops it can shorten this trailing string of genes, which make the antibody's trunk, much as an engineer might detach cars from a train. Although the antibody can still repel the same foreign invader, it might gain additional powers, such as being able to pass through the placenta from a mother to her embryo.

These dynamic genes are doing more than impressing scientists with their agility; within the next two years, biologists predict, the new knowledge many explain the causes of such rare diseases of the immune system as agammaglobulinemia, which strikes in the first two years of life. Ultimately, understanding how nature manufactures germ-fighting antibodies may allow researchers to imitate the process: by cloning these biological soldiers in the laboratory, scientists will help people who can't make their own antibodies. Even further in the future, scientists may discover cures for diseases such as leukemia in which the genes don't work as they should.

NOTEBOOK PAGES

When the notebook pages of a typical college student like yourself are analyzed, there are usually specific recommendations that can be made to make notetaking more effective. For example, here are some specific problems typical of ineffective notetakers with suggestions for improvement:

Problem	Suggestion
1. Everything is written in paragraph form.	1. Listen only for the main ideas; write in phrases, skip lines, omit small words.
2. All words are written down; there are many gaps of missing ideas.	2. Write only important "idea" words. Develop a personal shorthand. Listen for ideas—not words.
3. The lecturer rambles.	3. Concentrate on organizing information into facts in one column and examples in the other. Organize later on.

Problem	Suggestion
4. Main ideas and details cannot be identified in the outline.	4. Concentrate less on standard outline form and more on ideas and details. Use indenting for hierarchical ideas and details. Limit your outline to regular numbers, capital letters, and dashes.
5. Some ideas don't fit into an outline.	5. Don't outline—use a picture, diagram, or chart.

ACTIVITY III

Read the following lecture notes that have been typed from a student's notebook pages. Label the occurrence of the following techniques with the appropriate letter.

A. The 1/3–2/3 technique.
B. Important terms recorded with definitions and examples.
C. Lists or diagrams used.
D. An abbreviation system used.

As you critique these notes, you will find that some of the effective notetaking techniques are not used. Go back to the list of problems and suggestions given in this chapter. What are some techniques that you would suggest to improve this student's notetaking system?

Suggestions for improvement:

1. _____

2. _____

3. _____

4. _____

5. _____

LECTURE—SOCIOLOGY

STATUS AND ROLE
JANUARY 24

I.   Concepts pertinent to status and role

    1. The essence of any social situation lies in the mutual expectations of the people concerned.
    2. These expectations are governed by norms.
    3. Most situations are defined socially and people know the expectations of the situation.
    4. Some people are ignorant of the social expectations of a social situation—extreme upper and lower classes.
       Some people do not care about the social expectations of a social situation—beatniks, hippies, misanthropes.

II. Definitions

    5. Status—a social position in the institutional structure recognized and supported by the whole society.
    6. Role—the manner in which a person carries out his social position.
    7. One occupies a status and plays a role. My status is a student and my role includes the things I do that are associated with being a student.

III. Relationship between status and role

    8. Prescriptive patterns—the idea a person has in his mind before carrying out an idea. These ideas exist before action occurs.
    9. Performance pattern—actually carrying out an idea and the action that does happen.
    10. In any social situation where status and role are found, there are prestructured and performance patterns of behavior.

IV . Identity in a situation

    11. Identity is essential to any interacting situation.
    12. A person enters most social situations with his identity established.
    13. A person's role and identity can change when his social situation changes—servicemen discharged after wars.
    14. Dress helps form a person's role and reflects role.

PROJECT

The following selection, taken from a popular textbook used in human sexuality classes, discusses various schools of thought on the development of sexuality in human beings. For each school of thought, several well-known psychologists are discussed and their theories explained.

Using the note-taking techniques discussed in this chapter, carefully listen to this selection as your partner reads it. When your partner finishes this, trade places and you read it.

Next, compare notes and critique each other's notes according to the guide. These notes should be written on a separate sheet of paper or in your notebook.

THEORIES OF PSYCHOSEXUAL DEVELOPMENT[3]

There are many theories about the development of sexuality in human beings. The research about psychosexual development is vast. Although it is hardly possible or relevant to discuss them all here, it is still important to be familiar with a few of the major contributions to this particular body of knowledge. There is no single theory or hypothesis that can provide all the answers, but, as a whole, they build a framework within which we can begin to understand the development of sexual expression and sexual identity.

THE PSYCHOANALYTIC SCHOOL

Sigmund Freud (1856–1939) and Eric Erikson (b. 1902), both famous psychoanalysts, developed their theories along epigenetic lines, borrowing from the field of biology or, more specifically, embryology. **Epigenesis** is a way of looking at development in stages. The development of one stage depends on the successful completion of the stage immediately before it. When something goes wrong at one point, the next step will not be complete, and all successive stages will be incomplete or abnormal in some way. This is a relatively modern concept. Until the seventeenth century, embryos were thought to be complete human beings at conception, spending the nine months in the uterus merely getting larger. In terms of psychological development, children were also considered merely small adults waiting to get larger. One need only take a look at art of the eleventh, twelfth, and thirteenth centuries to see that children were perceived to be merely small adults. Therefore, the development, or discovery, of the epigenetic construct was important to the theory of human development, both biologically and psychologically.

Sigmund Freud

Sigmund Freud's psychoanalytic theories of sexuality have profoundly influenced Western thought about human behavior. His ideas have become household words; "Freudian slips" are embarrassingly familiar to all of us. Today we look on Freud's theories of sexuality with much healthy skepticism because so many of them have not held up under laboratory scrutiny. However, to many scholars and practitioners, his notion of the *unconscious* is an enduring and valid contribution to the study of human behavior. It must be remembered that Freud was a male who was influenced by his own cultural, historical, and intellectual milieu. He based his work on his observations of his patients, who, by and large, were a rather homogeneous group from the middle and upper classes (females, mostly). In anticipation of some of the criticisms that were to come his way, he wrote, in the preface to the third edition of his *Three Essays on the Theory of Sexuality* (1914), "I must, however, emphasize that the present work is characterized not only by being completely based upon psycho-analytic research, but also by being deliberately independent of the findings of biology."

In essence, the psychoanalytic school of thought believes that sexual drives or instincts are the motivating force behind much behavior that would not be regarded by the average observer as having any connection with sexuality. These sexual drives or instincts are called the **libido.** *Low libidinal energy* commonly means low sexual interest. Libidinal energy in the infant is not specifically sexual in the way an adult experiences sexual drives. Instead, sexual energy eroticizes the body parts through which the infant gains pleasure as it matures into a fully functioning adult. According to Freud, the first step in this maturation process is the **oral phase,** which chronologically coincides with infancy (roughly up to eighteen months). It is a time when a child wholly depends on the nurturing and feeding of an adult, usually its mother. The mouth and lips are stimulated a great deal and are the principal source of gratification at this time. Between the second and fourth years, the **anal stage** occurs. Bowel and bladder control are usually gained at this time, and the child becomes aware of the pleasure associated with giving and retaining bowel movements. The stereotype of a miserly compulsive person is of one, according to Freud, who is fixated in the anal stage, gaining sexual or erotic pleasure from keeping things in and organizing things in a tidy way. In the **phallic** or **Oedipal stage** (four to five years) the major erotic pleasure is thought to derive from the clitoris in females and the penis in males. It is during this time that most children realize there is a difference between their genitals and those of the opposite gender. When boys first notice this difference, they fear that they, too, may "lose" their penis, a conclusion drawn by noticing the lack of a penis in their female counterparts. Castration fears develop. In females, penis envy develops when a girl notices that her male playmates or siblings have an "extra," a penis. Freud felt that the fear of castration ultimately accounted for the male child's identification with his father.

No discussion of the phallic stage would be complete without an explanation of Freud's key to psychosexual adjustment—that is, a healthy resolution of the Oedipal situation that occurs at this stage. The Oedipal situation, as Freud saw it, was the girl's sexual desire for her father and jealousy of her mother and the boy's sexual desire for his mother and rivalry with his father for possession of his mother. Freud named this situation for the mythical king of Thebes, Oedipus. When Oedipus was born, it was predicted that he would unknowingly kill his father, who therefore, to undo the prophecy, abandoned him on a hillside to die. He was found by a shepherd who raised him to manhood. Oedipus then journeyed to Thebes and on his way unwittingly killed his father in an argument. When he arrived at the gate of Thebes, he encountered a sphinx that was terrorizing the city by killing all who could not solve her riddle. Oedipus answered the riddle of the sphinx and saved the city. Out of gratitude, Jocasta, the queen and his true mother, married him. When it was discovered what had happened, Oedipus blinded himself and Jocasta committed suicide. Freud believed that this myth symbolizes the wish that all men have to possess their mothers and compete with or do away with their fathers. The theme of this myth is found in the folklore of many cultures. Primitive versions of it are found in the myths of Uranus and Kronos; a more sophisticated version can be found in the play *Hamlet* (Lidz, 1968). The construct seems weak when it is applied to the process of how females ultimately identify with their mothers, and it may even be difficult to accept the theory of the male's identification with his father. No matter how it is explained, Freud believed that the process of identification with the parent of the same gender was the major key to psychosexual development.

Latency, according to Freud, is the next stage in psychosexual development. It appears, chronologically speaking, roughly between the ages of six to ten or twelve. At those times, he theorized, the sexual drives are quiet and unexpressed. He believed the cause is either that the biological time clock slows down greatly at that time or that the child is repressing all its sexual feelings as a result of the turmoil created during the Oedipal phase.

The **genital phase,** which occurs during puberty and early adolescence, is the final stage in the psychosexual sequence. During the genital phase, Freud believed that the female shifts her erotic feelings from the clitoris to the vagina and the male reinvests his erotic feelings in his penis. Freud considered getting to this stage the final step in achieving emotional maturity. In Chapter 10, you recall, we saw how the Freudian notion of separate clitoral and vaginal orgasms has been refuted by the research of Masters and Johnson.

Eric Erikson

Eric Erikson, a child psychoanalyst and winner of a Pulitzer Prize for his contribution to the knowledge of child development, added to the psychoanalytic theory a social and cultural perspective that may make Freudian theory more plausible. Erikson took into account the roles that the particular environment and culture play in the stages of development through which each person passes. He also proposed that human development evolves over a lifetime. Dividing life into eight stages, and identifying each stage by the psychological task of that stage, he too developed an epigenetic point of view about psychosexual development.

He proposed that the development of trust is the most important basic task for an infant in its first year: "Mothers create a sense of trust in their children by that kind of administration which in its quality combines sensitive care of the baby's individual needs and a firm sense of personal trustworthiness within the trusted framework of their culture's life style" (Erikson, 1963). He believed that the ability to trust makes it possible to establish an intimate relationship with another human being that is satisfying emotionally and sexually. As Gagnon and Simon (1973) put it, this healthy development provides the "social scripts" to make the "physical acts themselves become possible." If the infant fails to develop trust, then, of course, the opposite emotional climate is developed; mistrust. "Trust vs. Mistrust" (Erikson, 1950) describes the opposing emotional forces to be resolved in this first developmental step.

In the second year, the child's psychological task is to resolve the conflict between "autonomy" and "shame and doubt." The child learns muscle, bowel, and bladder control. By learning self-control, the child gains self-esteem and confidence, whereas without it, the child may have a pervasive sense of shame, self-doubt, and lack of self-confidence, ultimately perhaps leading to problems in interpersonal relationships. In the phallic or third stage (corresponding chronologically to two to five years), the child struggles with "initiative versus guilt." During this time the Oedipal struggle must be resolved and the child must internalize the feminine and masculine prerequisites of its environment. The failure to do so may lead to a "lasting sense of guilt" (Lidz, 1968). During latency, Erikson's fourth stage, the child enters school (six years to puberty). If the child does not develop a sense of "industry," gaining approval, affection, and admiration from achievement, she or he is likely to be left with an enduring sense of "inferiority." With adolescence, Eriksonian theory departs from emphasizing genital sexuality in the Freudian tradition, to focusing on ego integration: "The growing and developing youths, faced with this physiological revolution with them are now primarily concerned with what they appear to be in the eyes of others as compared with what they feel they are, and with the question of how to connect the roles and skills cultivated earlier with the occupational prototypes of the day" (Erikson, 1950). If the adolescent is confused about his or her sexual identity, for example, the result is severe role confusion, perhaps even severe emotional disturbances. As the person moves into early adulthood, having achieved a strong sense of self, a clear ego identity, and a sense of trust and autonomy, he or she is ready to risk intimacy with another human being. The task of early adulthood is "intimacy"; the failure of this developmental stage leads to "isolation":

> Body and ego must now be masters of the organ modes and of the nuclear conflicts, in order to be able to face the fear of ego loss in situations which call for self abandon: in the solidarity of close affiliations, in orgasms and sexual unions,

in close friendships and in physical combat, in experiences of inspiration by teachers and intuition from the recesses of the self. The avoidance of such experiences because of a fear of ego loss may lead to a deep sense of isolation and consequent self-absorption (Erikson, 1950).

Erikson characterized a successful young and middle adulthood as one in which the person has developed to the point where her or his interests lie in "generativity," that is, the capacity for and interest in producing and raising the next generation—not only by actually procreating but also by being generally productive and creative in the world and contributing to society as a whole. The inability to be productive or creative leads to "stagnation" of the human being. Finally, the eighth and last stage of life is characterized, according to Erikson, by "the acceptance of one's one and only life cycle" (Erikson, 1950). In this acceptance, one no longer fears death. The failure of the ego to integrate this acceptance is characterized by the fear of death: "Despair expresses the feeling that the time is now short, too short for the attempt to start another life and to try out alternate roads to integrity" (Erikson, 1950).

While Eriksonian theory of psychological development does emphasize the attachment of the libido and the shifts the libido makes, it does so within the context of environment and culture in a way that Freudian theory neglects. Although Erikson believed in the importance of sexuality or genitality, he felt that:

In order to be of lasting social significance, the utopia of genitality should include:

1. *mutuality of orgasm*
2. *with a loved partner*
3. *of the other sex*
4. *with whom one is able and willing to share mutual trust*
5. *and with whom one is able and willing to regulate the cycles of*
   a. *work*
   b. *procreation*
   c. *recreation*
6. *so as to secure to the offspring, too, all the stages of satisfactory development (Erikson, 1950).*

Although aspects of Eriksonian theory may seem heterosexually and culturally biased, certainly his contributions and observations are interesting and add to the theoretical frameworks of psychosexual development in a cogent way.

LEARNING THEORY

The school of learning theorists maintains that behaviors are primarily a product of **environmental reinforcers.** This learning occurs in various ways. It may be consciously taught, picked up less consciously by imitation or through trial and error, or conditioned. The learning theorists maintain that almost no sexual behavior in humans just happens automatically; it all has a learning component. Some learning, such as "reading, writing and 'rithmetic," does take place actively and consciously; other learning, such as emotional responses and attitudes, are seemingly "picked up" in other ways from those around us. There are four basic ways in which we learn: (1) classical conditioning, (2) instrumental or operant conditioning, (3) multiple-response learning, and (4) insight learning.

Learning is a process by which changes can occur in behavior. These changes can be the result of experience or practice. Psychologists define behavior as any response that the organism makes to its environment. These may be actions, thoughts, emotions, or physiological changes in hormones or glands. Although learning can produce changes in behavior, all changes in behavior are not necessarily the result of learning. Some may be due to physical growth, illness, fatigue, or other outside influences.

Most of us are familiar with the experiments of Ivan Pavlov, a Russian physiologist, who discovered that he could create the natural physiological response of salivation in a dog by ringing a bell. The bell, an artificial stimulus, linked during training with the presentation of food, could eventually produce salivation by itself. From this discovery, Pavlov theorized that all habits, even some complex mental processes, were the result of **conditioning.** Therefore, sexual behavior could also be the result of conditioning. Classical conditioning occurs when a biological, involuntary response is made in the presence of a stimulus that will make that response happen again. Classical conditioning is perhaps the simplest form of learning. Applied to a sexual situation, an example might be this: A small boy happens to have an erection and, at the same time, hears his mother sing a lullaby; if these two events, the erection and the lullaby, occur simultaneously over and over again, eventually the lullaby will elicit an erection in the boy.

B. F. Skinner, a famous American psychologist, proposed in 1938 that even complex, voluntary behaviors respond to reinforcers or rewards of some kind. Behavior that is rewarded or rewarding in some way will be repeated. This is called **instrumental** or **operant conditioning.** An example of how instrumental conditioning might apply to sexual behavior would be as follows: When a small boy experiences pleasurable feelings in his penis while riding a rocking horse, he may then rub his penis with other objects, such as his hand, a blanket, or a tricycle, to try to re-create that pleasurable feeling. The pleasurable feelings are rewarding and serve as reinforcers for that particular behavior.

There are many refinements and additions to these basic learning paradigms. Skinner (1938), Dollard and Miller (1950), and Bandura (1969), to name a few, wrote about the many ways in which voluntary behavior (behavior under a person's control) is learned. From their theories developed many types of treatment methodologies for changing dysfunctional behavior or for developing behaviors that have been absent. These types of therapies can be called **behavior modification therapy.** It is therapy that does not attempt to discover the early causes of behavior; the main goal is only to change the behavior or "symptoms" in some way. As we have seen (in Chapter 12), sexual dysfunction therapy is a kind of behavior modification therapy, although it is often used in conjunction with more traditional psychoanalytic methods.

Multiple-response learning is a type in which we link together a sequence of movement patterns to eventually form complicated behavior patterns. Certain stimuli guide the process. In learning to use a typewriter, for example, we use the letters as a guide and move from typing individual letters, one at a time, to quickly typing a series of sentences without even thinking of each individual letter. Sexual behavior can be learned in this way also. When an adolescent girl and boy manage their first kiss, which might seem like a very complicated maneuver in their fantasies, they are starting a series of multiple learning experiences that might eventually lead to intercourse. Eventually the first kiss will not need to be thought out so carefully beforehand.

The fourth type of learning theory, **insight learning,** is based on the work of the psychologist Wolfgang Kohler, who experimented in the early 1900s with chimpanzees. Rather than through trial and error, one might solve problems through understanding the relationships of various parts of the problem to one another. One might draw the analogy that sex education, for example, enables one to apply knowledge through a series of associations about contraception and venereal disease, for example, to solve the problems that a sexual relationship with another human being will ultimately demand. Trial-and-error learning might lead to undesired pregnancy or venereal disease.

Still another component of learning theory important to consider when looking at psychosexual development is the time frame within which things are learned. The **critical-time theory** hypothesizes that there is a biologically determined time span within which a human being or animal must learn certain behaviors in order to achieve the next step in maturation (Scott, 1962). This idea is another example of an epigenetic theory because it is based on the time when an individual's sensory, motor, and psychological capacities are all primed to be influenced in a particular way. Before that moment, the child cannot learn a particular behavior; after that critical time, learned behavior is difficult to unlearn. Toilet training is a good example. Many young parents have been pressured by eager grandparents into beginning the toilet training of their baby before it is ready biologically and psychologically. After trying for months, the parents give up, only to discover that when the child is around three years old the process is suddenly accomplished almost over night. "Everything just seemed ready," they might say. If, by chance, the child should lose control over bowel or bladder functions at an older age, the child will become upset when the skill of retention is only temporarily forgotten. We would all have a lot of trouble if we had to unlearn toilet training!

Dr. Robert Stoller (1968) hypothesized that there is a critical time within which a child needs to fix his or her sexual identity. He believed that if it is not clearly fixed by the age of three, serious psychological problems might ensue for the child. Furthermore, he felt that it is almost impossible to change that sexual identity once it is fixed. More recent work by Dr. Julianne Imperato-McGinely of Cornell University Medical College has given us reason to believe that this hypothesis may not be entirely true. Furthermore, her work gives weight to the fact that the influence of prenatal hormones is a large factor in the child's future sexual identity. What the environment labels a child may not be as important as what the prenatal hormones and genetic makeup of the child predispose her or him to be (Begley and Carey, 1979). There appears to be a critical period of time when the brain is affected by hormones that can permanently change behavior. A physiologist, Roger Gorski, working at UCLA, noticed that to "influence behavior, hormones probably affect the brain during its critical period! At this stage in development the brain is impressionable, and hormones cause permanent changes in it just as they permanently alter sex organs" (Begley and Carey, 1978).

Learning theorists have long believed that assignation of sexual identity is learned by the human being and internalized from the environment at an early age. However, in 1972, through a rare genetic accident, we have been able to see that the "critical time" theory as far as sexual identity goes may not be as important as we thought. Biological factors seem to play an equally important role in our perception of ourselves as masculine or feminine. In that year, a rare genetic disease was discovered in a small village in the Dominican Republic. Eighteen children had been born who appeared at first to have female genitals. They were reared as girls and identified themselves as females, taking on the female roles appropriate to their environment and culture. At puberty, however, they began to develop all the secondary sex characteristics of males. They became men, and all but two of them gave up living as females with no apparent trauma or difficulty. As adult males, they gave up the sex of their rearing and took up a sexual identity congruent with their biological sex. This new sexual identity allowed them to have females as erotic objects. Testosterone acting on the brain *in utero* and on the body at puberty seemed to allow for the development of male characteristics, male sexual identity, and male gender identity in spite of environmental influences to the contrary for several years (Diamond, 1978; Begley and Carey, 1979).

Milton Diamond, a professor of reproductive biology at the University of Hawaii School of Medicine, has taken the learning theorists' point of view and the biological facts and has developed a theory of psychosexual development that seems to reconcile the long debate about this process: What influences us the most—nature or nurture?

> *An individual is born with a biased predisposition to interact with the world in certain ways. Part of this bias leads to a cognitive frame that provides a preprogrammed standard against which possible behavior choices will be considered. [Diamond, 1978]*

Diamond believes that we have a biological "bias," "an inner biological 'voice,' an 'innate feeling' of being male or female [that] develops quite early." This bias determines "how the individual interacted with the environment." Diamond (1978) calls his idea the "bias-interaction" theory.

NOTES

1. **Sharon Begley** and **Mary Hager,** "Genes That Move to Fight Disease," *Newsweek,* V. XCVI, No. 12. September 22, 1980, p. 90.
2. **William H. Gotwald, Jr.** and **Gale Holtz Golden.** *Sexuality: The Human Experience* (New York: Macmillan, 1981), pp. 428–438.

Twenty

EXAMS!

Your success on an examination depends on how you prepare for it as well as what you do while taking the exam. In order to do your best on an examination, you must study effectively and know how to respond to the different types of examination questions.

Let us dispel one myth immediately. Seldom is your difficulty on an examination caused by the instructor's unfairness. You must accept the responsibility for preparing for taking examinations. You must do the studying required to master the material to be covered on the exam. If you do not do the studying, then you must be prepared to accept the consequences. There is no magical way to prepare for an exam.

There are some useful ways to organize your study time. These are summarized below. Techniques for taking examinations are discussed later in this chapter.

STUDYING

The first eighteen chapters of this book describe a number of reading and studying techniques. If you have learned these, then you are on your way to doing well on examinations. However, you must actually use these techniques for them to do you any good. In fact, you may feel that you would do better on examinations if you just could organize yourself and find time to study. The suggestions below should help.

Calendars

Two types of calendars are helpful for scheduling your exam study time.

Semester calendars are often available at the bookstore or student government office at the beginning of the year. It can be devastating to suddenly realize that three tests and two projects are due during the same week. You can avoid this shock by using a semester calendar to show test dates and due dates for projects and papers.

A semester calendar will be found on p. 294. You may make a copy of this calendar if you wish. Fill in the months and dates for this term. Write in each test, project, and paper on its due date. Be sure to include the material to be covered on each test and the form and content of each project and paper.

Indicate an intense study time for each test and an appropriate "writing and preparation" time for each paper or project. Mark with red pencil those weeks which will require you to budget your time efficiently.

Weekly calendars show the schedule that you will generally adhere to during each week of the term. Use a weekly calendar to show classes and regular study, leisure, and work time. A weekly schedule may seem confining at first, but using it will help you study effectively and enjoy your leisure time.

A weekly calendar is given on. p. 295 and may be copied. Use it to make a weekly schedule of college time. Block out class and laboratory times as well as other weekly commitments. Next write in your study times. You should set aside at least two hours for each class. Perhaps you are overlooking useful study times. Which of the times below could be an additional study hour for you?

1. Early morning, before breakfast.
2. The time you travel in a car, bus, or train.
3. While you are drying your hair.
4. While you are eating lunch.
5. Late afternoon, before supper.

AN INTENSE REVIEW SCHEDULE

You should supplement your regular study schedule with intense reviews before important tests. When midsemester tests or important exams are announced, it is your responsibility to set up your intense review schedule. Your review should occur one to two weeks before the test date. Spread the material to be reviewed over several days of study. Most experts suggest spending the night before the test cramming information already studied and reviewed. Notice that this does *not* mean reviewing only in a single night's cram session.

Use the following tips during your intense review. Check those you already use.

INTENSE REVIEW SCHEDULE TIPS

Distribute your review sessions over a period of one to two weeks before the test date. Know the span of information, topics, and sources of information to be covered on the test. Organize the topics to be covered or the entire course into three to five pages of key-word notes. Include lecture and textbook notes, diagrams and charts, vocabulary and terms. Also include a list of the textbook chapter topics, the topics on the course outline, and handouts from the professor.

Revise and rewrite in a summary your class notes and your notes from the textbook. Constantly work at streamlining and restating the ideas into key words and terms. Organize the information to memorize the information. Restating and rewriting information helps you to remember it.

Anticipate the questions that will be asked on the test. Consider the topics emphasized by the professor in lectures and on the course outline. Compare this to the textbook readings. A "study group" of classmates can help predict questions, clarify ideas, and force you into a review session. Study groups do not help you to learn or memorize information.

Study the quizzes and exams taken during the course. These often show the kinds of questions asked on tests, and they demonstrate the topics important to the course.

Attend all class sessions, particularly those before a scheduled exam. Be alert for comments made by the professor that signal important topics or possible exam questions.

Stay calm. Focus on the things you know. Go back and study, reread, and relearn the things you do not know. Ask the professor to clarify difficult concepts in class before the test.

Use the memory techniques described in Chapter 22 of this book to memorize specific information.

EXAMINATIONS

Short-Answer Questions

Short-answer tests include the following types of questions:

1. Multiple-choice items.
2. Fill in the blank.
3. True or false questions.
4. Matching columns.

When these types of questions are asked, several general suggestions will help to improve your test performance. For example, you should survey the entire test before answering any of the questions. In this way you can budget your time so that you spend more time answering the questions on the sections of the test that are worth the most points.

In all types of tests it is important to read the directions carefully. Answer the questions in the correct manner and make sure your answer is in the form required by the question. You should answer the questions you are sure of first. Then, spend extra time on the questions that require additional attention.

Read and follow these suggestions to improve your performance on short-answer test questions. Check those you already use.

Multiple-Choice Items

1. Anticipate the correct answer to the question as you read it. Be sure to read all choices before marking your answer.
2. In a teacher-made multiple choice test, the first and last choice answers are less likely to be the correct choices.
3. Be alert for key terms in questions like "always," "never," "not," "except." These terms may signal the correct answer or preclude other answers.
4. Do not leave any blank answers. If in doubt, guess the answers unless there is a correction for guessing.
5. Carefully consider each choice. Eliminate choices that are clearly incorrect and compare the remaining choices against each other.
6. Sometimes the information from one section of a test will be helpful for answering questions from another section of the test.

True or False Questions

1. Do not read too much into the questions. Answer the question in the same perspective in which it is being asked.
2. Be alert for key terms like "all," "never," "usually," or "often." These terms can signal false or true answers.
3. If an answer is true, it is true without exception.
4. Guess the answer to questions if you're not sure, especially if there is no deduction for guessing.

Fill-in-the-Blank Questions

1. Use the context to help identify the correct answer. Sometimes test makers signal the answer by preceding a blank with the word *a* or *an*. *A* precedes a word beginning with a consonant. *An* precedes a word beginning with a vowel.
2. Guess an answer to questions you are not sure of. If you are not sure of a specific answer, attempt a more general answer. Do not leave spaces blank.
3. Look at the amount of space provided for answers and the number of blanks given for each answer. Use these cues as an aid for writing your answer.

Matching Columns

1. Clarify with the teacher if items can be used once or more than once.
2. Cross off items that have been used.
3. Answer the items that you are sure of first, then concentrate on the items that remain.

The Essay Question

Answering essay questions requires different techniques from answering short-answer questions. Essay answers should be well organized and well written.

The Answer

Plan the essay answer before writing. Take a minute to really think out the question. In the margin of the essay book or on the back of the question sheet, begin to write key words that will be the parts of your answer. Think back to what you read in the text that is related to the question. Also, remember the lecture material about the question. Go back and organize the key words after you have "brainstormed" this information.

Follow these steps when writing your key-word outline:

Example

Question: What types of erosion affect the earth's surface? Describe how each contributes to changing the earth's surface. Give an example of each.

1. Identify the main point of the question. Break this into several key ideas. Use a key word to present each key idea.

Types of Erosion

Running water	Mechanical	Chemical

2. Next, list several important details under each key idea. Each detail should be noted using an important vocabulary term you memorized.

Types of Erosion

Running water	Mechanical	Chemical
Precipitation	Wind	
Stream erosion	Glaciation	Plant action
	Freezing/thawing	

3. Explain each subtopic in several sentences, using examples, and show the relationships between subtopics.

TYPES OF EROSION—wearing away earth's surface.

Running water	Action of flow of water to break up and move soil and rocks. Also includes tidal action on shore.
Precipitation	Various types—rain, snow, hail. Melting produces running water, which causes erosion.
Stream erosion	Various types of streams—"age of river determines degree of erosive action—young rivers have V-shaped valleys and actively cut away at streambed.
Mechanical erosion	(Also called physical weathering) process where rocks are broken apart.
Wind	Particles of sand are blown against surface and are abrasive to surface rock—may be able to mar surface to produce small pits that catch water. Freezing water causes cracks.
Glaciation	Movement of glaciers pulls, tears, pushes rock and soil. Glacial action relates to running water when glacier melts. Glacial weathering is a gross type of weathering.
Freezing/thawing	Water expands when it freezes and breaks rocks apart. Tree and plant roots help to further break up rock—repeated freezing and thawing promote rock breakup.
Chemical erosion	Plants produce carbon dioxide in photosynthesis/CO_2 combines with water to produce carbonic acid—this eats away at the rock surface. "Acid rain" from pollutants also increases chemical action on earth's surface.

Notice that what started as a brief outline now has become expanded to include many aspects of the topic with examples.

Write the Essay Answer

After you have brainstormed the ideas you want to include in your answer, and have organized your answer into a brief outline, you are ready to begin writing. Your essay answer should have a clear point of view (especially if you need to critique, evaluate, or interpret) and your ideas should be logically organized and supported with examples or details. As is the case with all writing, you should write to clearly communicate ideas.

Follow a clear pattern as you write each paragraph and section of the essay.

1. State the main idea for this paragraph or section in a clear general statement.
2. Explain the idea and describe how it divides into subtopics in several related sentences. Show how these subtopics of the main idea are related to this main idea.
3. Cite specific details and examples to further support your ideas. Include names, dates, places, expert testimony, or examples from lectures and readings.
4. Summarize briefly and write a transition sentence to the next part of the answer.
5. Repeat the pattern for the next part of the answer.

It is very important that essay writing be quality writing. Use introductory and summary paragraphs to logically present and conclude your ideas. Use transition sentences between paragraphs and the specific examples. Use diagrams, outlines, or graphic aids if they will more clearly state your answer.

Clear writing and good handwriting are important. If the reader cannot read the answer, you will not get credit for what you have written.

Exercise

On a separate sheet of paper, write your essay answer to the following question:

What types of erosion affect the earth's surface? Describe how each contributes to changing the earth's surface. Give an example of each.

Analyzing the Essay Question

Often you may have difficulty precisely forming your essay answer because you have not understood what the question asks you to do. Listed below are typical verbs used in asking essay questions.

1. Some require a brief, straight-to-the-point answer.
2. Some require an expanded answer with a logically reasoned argument.
3. Others ask for a graphic aid.

compare: Express similarities between ideas.
contrast: Express differences between ideas.
critique: Analyze the pros and cons of ideas with an evaluative opinion.
define: Give a clear and succinct explanation.
discuss: Analyze and explain with complete specifics and examples.
enumerate: Give an ordered list with succinct explanations.
interpret: Explain your ideas with examples.
list: Give a numbered listing of items with a succinct explanation.
prove: Give evidence to show a conclusion.
state: Give the main ideas in a succinct statement.
summarize: Give the main ideas straight and to the point.
explain: Carefully discuss the information and show relationships between the ideas.
illustrate: Use a picture or diagram to answer the question, with limited narrative explanation.
diagram: Use a picture or graphic aid to answer the question with some narrative explanation.

ACTIVITY I

Sort each of the preceding essay question verbs into the correct category of answers. What different interpretation would you give to the verb definition?

A. Essay question verbs requiring a brief, straight-to-the-point answer.

Verb	Your Interpretation
1. _____	_____
2. _____	_____
3. _____	_____
4. _____	_____
5. _____	_____

6. _____   _____

7. _____   _____

    B. Essay question verbs requiring an expanded, logically reasoned answer.

1. _____   _____

2. _____   _____

3. _____   _____

4. _____   _____

5. _____   _____

6. _____   _____

7. _____   _____

    C. Essay question verbs requiring a graphic aid.

1. _____   _____

2. _____   _____

3. _____   _____

4. _____   _____

5. _____   _____

6. _____   _____

7. _____   _____

SEMESTER CALENDAR

SUNDAY	MONDAY	TUESDAY	WEDNESDAY	THURSDAY	FRIDAY	SATURDAY

WEEKLY CALENDAR

TIME	MONDAY	TUESDAY	WEDNESDAY	THURSDAY	FRIDAY	SATURDAY	SUNDAY
6–7							
7–8							
8–9							
9–10							
10–11							
11–12PM							
12–1							
1–2							
2–3							
3–4							
4–5							
5–6							
6–7							
7–8							
8–9							
9–10							

PROJECT

Read the following selection from a sociology textbook. In the selection is a comprehensive discussion of class in American society. As you read, take notes on the page, and concentrate on organizing the information in the selection.

Next, plan and write the answer to the following essay question:

Consider the classes in American society. Identify five major classes in American society. For each, discuss the characteristics of the social class and compare and contrast how aspects of class membership affect other aspects of social life. Be sure to cite specific examples to support your ideas.

Your answer should be written on a separate sheet of paper or in your notebook. It should be about two sides of a piece of paper and include several paragraphs.

THE AMERICAN CLASS SYSTEM[1]

It is inevitable that there will be some inequalities in any human group, if only because its various members will have different talents, skills, looks, personalities, physical strength, and so on. Inequality becomes a major sociological concern when it is *structured* into society. When this happens, entire categories of the population have unequal access to wealth, power, and prestige, and these inequalities are passed on from one generation to the next. This kind of inequality is deeply entrenched in American society in the form of the class system. But how many classes are there in the United States, and what are the characteristics of the different classes?

Problems of Analysis

Social classes do not exist "out there," any more than inches, gallons, or kilograms do. The concept of class, like the concept of an inch, is something people impose on reality. What exists "out there" is social inequality, but various observers may draw the precise boundaries of class in quite different ways. Just as we could create many ways of measuring off the length of a piece of wood, so we can create many ways of categorizing a population into classes.

A sociologist can use three methods to analyze the class structure of a society. The first is the *reputational method,* in which the researcher asks people what class they believe other people belong to. The second is the *subjective method,* in which the researcher asks people what class they believe they themselves belong to. The third is the *objective method,* in which the researcher fits people into an arbitrary number of classes on the basis of some fixed standard, such as annual income. All three methods have been used in the United States, and they have given a generally similar picture of the class system. The precise details vary, however, depending not only on which method is used but also on the wording of the questions and the kind of community in which the respondents live.

The Reputational Method One of the most influential studies using the reputational method was made by W. Lloyd Warner and Paul Lunt (1941) in the small Massachusetts town of Newburyport. Warner and Lunt conducted in-depth interviews with many residents of this community, which had a population of about 17,000 at the time. In these interviews, they tried to find out how many classes the residents saw in their community and why they believed that specific people belonged to one class rather than another. It was soon clear that this small town was anything but classless. Respondents continually described other people as "old aristocracy," "the folks with the money," "snobs trying to push up," "nobodies," "society," "poor folk but decent," or "poor whites." Using these and other cues, Warner and Lunt divided the community into six social classes: an upper, a middle, and a lower, each containing an internal upper and lower level.

The reputational method is useful in small communities where the residents know one another. In these cases it can provide fascinating insights into people's conceptions of the class system. The method has two main disadvantages, however. First, it is difficult or even impossible to apply it to a large community where people do not know many others well, or to an entire society. Second, the method depends heavily on the personal interpretations of the observer. By analyzing their data differently, Warner and Lunt might have been able to find, say, four or ten classes.

The Subjective Method   The subjective method, in which people are asked to locate themselves in the class system, has been used in several studies—usually at the national rather than local level.

In the late forties a *Fortune* poll found that 80 percent of the respondents claimed to be middle class. The magazine took this finding as evidence that the United States was a truly middle-class society. Richard Centers (1949) objected to this conclusion. He pointed out that the poll had offered the respondents only three choices: "upper class," "middle class," or "lower class." Using a national random sample, Centers added a fourth choice, "working class." Approximately half of his respondents placed themselves in this category—a finding that suggested that the United States was primarily a working-class society. The *Fortune* poll had not shown that the United States was a middle-class society; it had simply reflected the fact that Americans have a distaste for the term "lower class." Low-income people will proudly identify themselves as "working class" but will call themselves "middle class" rather than "lower class" if only these two options are given.

The proportion of Americans identifying themselves as working class has shrunk since Centers did his research. In a 1978 *New York Times*–CBS News survey, 35 percent of a national sample described themselves as "middle class," and 34 percent as "working class." Some 6 percent declared that they belonged to some "other class"—and 25 percent asserted that they did not belong to any class at all. This change presumably reflects alterations in the class structure and in attitudes toward class since the earlier survey.

The subjective method has the advantage that it can be applied to a large population by polling a random sample. But the method also has its disadvantages. First, the results are influenced by the form of the question that is asked. Second, many people may rank themselves higher than their incomes and lifestyles seem to justify.

The Objective Method   This method carries a misleading label, for it implies that the approach is more "scientific" and unbiased than the others. In fact, however, it is a purely arbitrary way of analyzing a class system. The sociologist first sets a standard for determining class membership and then divides the population into a number of classes on this basis.

The objective method was pioneered by Lloyd Warner (1949) in his analysis of the class system of a small community. He constructed an "index of status characteristics," based at first on six main indicators: occupation, type of house, area of residence, source of income, amount of income, and amount of education. All these factors, however, were found to correlate fairly strongly. August Hollingshead (1949) also applied the objective method in his study of Morris, Illinois. Using the criteria of place of residence, occupation, and level of education, he divided the families in the community into five classes. Later investigators have often found it sufficient to use the income of the family breadwinner as the main or even the sole criterion of class membership.

The objective method has the advantage that it gives clear-cut results and usually requires no painstaking collection of data. The relevant statistics are readily available from the Bureau of the Census and other agencies and merely have to be interpreted. The main disadvantage of the method is that it is so arbitrary. Different sociologists may use different criteria for determining class membership and may divide the same population into very different class categories. The method also ignores the beliefs that the people themselves have about the class system. There is some debate about whether a sociologist can validly classify people as, say, "working class" when those people are convinced that they belong to another class.

The Social Classes

What, then, is the structure of the American class system? Most sociologists would probably accept, at least in general outline, the picture drawn by Daniel Rossides (1976). He suggests that there is an upper class consisting of about 1 to 3 percent of the population, an upper middle class of 10 to 15 percent, a lower middle class of 30 to 35 percent, a working class of 40 to 45 percent, and a lower class of 20 to 25 percent. . . . A number of other researchers (for example, Coleman and Neugarten, 1971) have come to fairly similar conclusions. We shall now take a look at the characteristics of these classes in more detail. The portraits presented here are, of course, broad generalizations; there are many individual exceptions to the overall class patterns.

The Upper Class   The *upper class* is a very small one, yet its members own at least a quarter of the nation's wealth, and they are disproportionately represented at the highest levels of political and economic power. This class consists of two main elements. The *upper upper class* consists of the old aristocracy of birth and wealth. To be fully respectable in America, money, like wine, must age a little. One can become a member of the upper upper class only by being born into it. The names of people in this class are familiar ones: the Chryslers, Rockefellers, Fords, Roosevelts, Kennedys, Astors, Vanderbilts. The founding ancestors of many of the present clans were never accepted into the upper upper class because their origins were too humble and their wealth was too recently acquired. Only a generation ago Mrs. David Lion Gardiner, the "empress" of the aristocratic Gardiner family of New York, forbade her grandson to play with the Rockefeller grandchildren on the grounds that "no Gardiner will ever play with the grandchild of a gangster" (Lundberg, 1968). Similarly, the author once heard a dowager of an ancient Boston lineage refer to the newly wealthy Kennedy family, at a time when one of them had become president of the United States, as "those low street-Irish." The members of the upper upper class tend to know one another personally, to attend the same schools, to visit the same resorts, and to intermarry. Their names are included in the *Social Register* or the *Blue Book*—volumes that self-consciously imitate *Debrett's Peerage,* a listing of the British aristocracy.

The *lower upper class* are those who have become very wealthy more recently. They may actually have more money, better houses, and larger automobiles than the upper uppers, but they lack the right "breeding" to win full acceptance into the very highest social circles.

The distinctions between the two upper classes are not generally recognized by the rest of society, and they are of little importance outside the elite circles themselves. As we have seen, the upper class as a whole has great power and prestige, and such influence on both domestic and foreign policy that it affects the lives not only of other classes but also of other nations throughout the world (Domhoff, 1971).

The Middle Class   The *middle class* lacks the cohesion of the upper class but has a distinctive life-style: in fact, the values of the middle class form the dominant morality of the United States. Middle-class attitudes and tastes are respected and endorsed by politicians, media, advertisers, and schools. This class also contains two fairly distinct elements.

The *upper middle class* consists primarily of high-income business and professional families. Like the upper class, this group contains a disproportionate number of people from white, Protestant, Anglo-Saxon backgrounds. Members of the upper middle class are highly "respectable," but they are not "society." They tend to live in comfortable suburban homes, to enjoy a stable family life, and to have a high sense of civic duty. They are very active in political life and dominate community organizations. They are concerned with personal career advancement and have high aspirations for their children, who are expected to receive a college education as a matter of course.

The *lower middle* class share most of the values of the upper middle class, but they lack the educational or economic advantages that would let them enjoy the same life-style. This class consists of people whose diverse jobs do not involve manual labor. It includes small-business operators and sales representatives, teachers and nurses, police officers, and middle-management personnel. The lower middle class is very concerned about "proper" behavior, about decency and the value of hard work. Members of this class, who, in fact, usually have to work hard to achieve and retain what they have, are often politically and economically conservative.

The Lower Class   The *lower class* consists essentially of those whose jobs and educational levels prevent them from enjoying the status and life-style of that "typical" American family portrayed in schoolbooks and the media. Racial and ethnic minority groups are disporportionately represented in this class. The lower class can also be divided into two strata.

The upper lower, or *working class,* consists primarily of blue-collar workers—small tradespeople, service personnel, and semiskilled workers of various kinds. Their jobs typically involve manual labor and have little public prestige. Although certain of these workers earn incomes that are higher than those of some members of the middle class, their jobs typically lack the "fringe benefits" of pensions, insurance, sick leave, paid vacations, and job safety. Most members of the working class have modest incomes, and few of them are able to save money. The members of this class cannot afford to live in desirable residential areas but take great pride in being "respectable," self-image they derive largely from the sense that they work hard—at "real" work done with the hands. They are sharply aware of the differences between themselves and the stratum below, against which they often feel antagonistic, especially when they believe that their taxes are being used to support alleged welfare chiselers.

The *lower lower class* (usually simply called the "lower class" to distinguish it from the working class) consists of the "disreputable poor." This class includes the permanently unemployed, the homeless, the illiterate, the chronic "skid-row" alcoholic, and the impoverished aged. They are virtually worthless on the labor market and so are virtually worthless in terms of power and prestige as well. Members of this class are poorly regarded by other Americans. Their supposed laziness, promiscuity, and reliance on public handouts are contrasted with the "morality" of the middle class. They tend to lack a common consciousness, to be alienated from, and cynical about, society, and to be fatalistic about their own chances in life.

Since a person's class status depends primarily on the income of the family breadwinner—usually the father—it is easy to see why class distinctions tend to be handed down from generation to generation. As William Goode (1964) comments, "The family is the keystone of the stratification system, the social mechanism by which it is maintained." The social class of the family strongly influences the opportunities of the children. A child in a high-status family, for example, has a good opportunity to acquire the values, attitudes, personal contacts, education, and skills that make for success in American life. A child from a low-status family is raised in an atmosphere of poverty, interacts only with low-status peers, and lacks the career ambitions and opportunities that children in other classes take for granted. As a result, most people are likely to remain for a lifetime in their class of origin.

Correlates of Class Membership

One of the many reasons social class is important is that class membership correlates with a variety of other aspects of social life.

Political Behavior   The higher a person's social class, the more likely he or she is to take an interest in political affairs, to register as a voter, and to vote. Party affiliation also correlates with social class. People higher in the social hierarchy are more likely to be Republican; people lower in the hierarchy are more likely to be Democrats. The working class is liberal on many economic issues that affect its own interest, but on most other issues it is more conservative than the other classes. Tolerance in attitudes toward issues of civil liberty tends to increase as social class rises (Alford and Friedland, 1975; Wolfinger and Rosenstone, 1980; Nunn et al., 1978; Hyman and Wright, 1979).

Marital Stability   Divorce is more common at the lower social levels, perhaps because unemployment and economic problems generate friction between partners (Goode, 1965). Traditional sex roles are most entrenched in the lower class, and there is evidence that marital relations at this level are relatively lacking in warmth (Komarovsky, 1962; Rubin, 1976). Female-headed families are found predominantly in the lower class, particularly in the black community.

Religious Affiliation   There is a strong correlation, at least among whites, between Protestantism and high status—perhaps because Protestants were the first to establish themselves in the United States and to gain wealth and political power. Within the Protestant churches there is a fairly close correlation between income and membership in a particular denomination. The upper classes prefer denominations that offer quiet and restrained services, while the lower classes are disproportionately represented in revivalist and fundamentalist sects. The most prestigious Protestant denomination appears to be Episcopalian, followed in rough order by the Congregational, Presbyterian, Methodist, Lutheran, and Baptist denominations (Gockel, 1969; Lauer, 1975; Nelsen, 1976; Newport, 1979).

Educational Achievement   Social-class membership has a strong influence on IQ and on educational achievement: the higher the social class of the parents, the more likely it is that their children will have high IQs and high educational achievement. Since the well-educated usually get the best jobs, existing inequalities tend to be reinforced by education (Sewell and Hauser, 1975; Griffin and Alexander, 1978; Jencks et al., 1979). This discrepancy in achievement is not necessarily related to differences in intellectual ability. Less than 10 percent of students with high incomes and high abilities fail to enter college, but about 25 percent of low-income students with comparable abilities do not manage to get to college (Jencks et al., 1972).

Health   In almost all industrialized countries except the United States, health care is regarded as a social service and is therefore available either free or for a low sum. These countries take it for granted that the quality of one's medical attention should depend on how sick one is, not on how wealthy one is. In the United States people have to pay for their health care themselves, either directly or through some form of health insurance. However, about 24 million Americans are not covered by health insurance of any kind, and fear of possible expenses often makes these people reluctant to seek early treatment of medical problems or even causes them to leave some problems unattended. Rich people are very much healthier than poor people. The incidence of most diseases, including diabetes, heart disease, and cancer, is significantly higher in the lower social classes. The higher one's social status, the longer one is likely to live (Fuchs, 1974; Krause, 1977; Kosa and Zola, 1978; Luft, 1978).

Mental Disorder The incidence of mental disorder, and the treatment received, are closely linked to social class (Dohrenwend, 1970; Fried, 1975; Kessler and Cleary, 1980). One study (Hollingshead and Redlich, 1958) found that hospitalization for schizophrenia was eleven times more common for lower-class than for upper-class persons. The upper-class patients were more likely to be treated with psychotherapy and to be hospitalized for only brief periods. Lower-class patients were more likely to be treated with drugs and electric-shock therapy and to be hospitalized for long periods. Another study in Manhattan (Srole et al., 1962) found that nearly one person in every two in the lowest class was psychologically impaired, although only 1 percent of these people were receiving treatment.

Social Participation The middle and upper classes participate extensively in community activities and organizations—charities, parent-teacher associations, women's groups, civic associations, and the like. (In this context, the upper class tends to play high-prestige roles, such as that of honorary president, and the middle-class members are more likely to take on routine roles.) In the working and lower class, on the other hand, social relationships are more inclined to center around family, kin, and neighbors (Komarovsky, 1962; Bott, 1971).

Values and Attitudes Middle- and upper-class people feel a relatively strong sense of control over, and responsibility for, their lives. They are generally prepared to defer immediate gratification in the hope of greater future rewards. Although their values and attitudes set the general moral standards of the whole society, they are somewhat more tolerant of ambiguity in sexual behavior, religion, and other areas than are members of the working and lower classes. Members of the working and lower classes are less likely to defer gratification, and the working class is inclined to be particularly intolerant of unconventional behavior and attitudes. People in the lowest class tend to have a strongly fatalistic attitude toward life. They often see their chances as being determined primarily by luck and other forces beyond their personal control.

Child-Rearing Practices Middle- and upper-class child-rearing practices are chiefly concerned with teaching principles of behavior and helping children to decide for themselves how to act in accordance with these principles. Working- and lower-class practices tend to focus on teaching children to obey the rules and stay out of trouble. Middle- and upper-class training often uses withdrawal of love as a control device, which may cause anxieties and guilt in children. Working- and lower-class training is more disciplinarian and may involve more physical punishment (M. L. Kohn, 1969, 1977; Walters and Stinnett, 1971). These child-rearing practices inevitably color the later personalities of people in different classes.

Criminal Justice A large number of self-report studies have concluded that almost every American has committed some kind of criminal offense (Doleschal and Klapmuts, 1973). However, lower-class people are more likely to be arrested for criminal offenses, denied bail, found guilty, and given long sentences than are members of other classes. This does not necessarily mean that lower-class people commit more crimes; it means that they are more likely to be caught and less likely to have access to "equal justice." In addition, typical lower-class crimes, such as robbery, larceny, auto theft, and burglary, are regarded as much more serious than typical middle- or upper-class crimes, such as embezzlement, forgery, tax evasion, and fraud.

SOCIAL MOBILITY IN THE UNITED STATES

Abraham Lincoln was born in a log cabin but made it to the White House. Andrew Carnegie, John D. Rockefeller, and J. P. Morgan started life in poverty but became millionaires. These tales are such a treasured part of our folklore that it is easy to overlook the countless would-be millionaires or presidents who remained in poverty or obscurity despite their ambitions and efforts.

In European societies, with their long feudal histories and obvious social divisions, people tend to regard their class systems as rigid. They recognize that *social mobility,* or movement from one status to another, is no easy matter. In the United States, with its deep commitment to the ideal of human equality, the belief that one can get ahead with hard work is a central part of the national ethic. What are the facts?

Research on social mobility since the twenties has shown that the American dream of ambition and hard work as the key to success rarely becomes a reality. In one early study, Pitirim Sorokin (1927) found that most men started their occupational careers at about the same level as their father's and that only a very few made significant advances thereafter. In their study of Muncie, Indiana, Robert and Helen Lynd (1929) found that whatever an ordinary worker's chances of becoming a foreman might be in theory, in practice they were minimal. Ely Chinoy (1955) drew similar conclusions from his study of auto workers. Seymour Martin Lipset and Reinhard Bendix (1959) studied the backgrounds of business executives born between 1770 and 1920 and found that some 70 percent of them had come from the upper class, 20 percent from the middle class, and only 10 percent from the working class. Joseph Kahl (1961) found that only 18 percent of the executive elite in the early fifties came from working-class origins. Another study of professional people in the sixties found that some 40 percent of them were the offspring of professional fathers—nearly five times as many as would be expected in a perfectly open system (Jackson and Crockett, 1964).

The most detailed work on social mobility in the United States was conducted by Peter Blau and Otis Dudley Duncan (1967), who collected data from 20,000 men. By analyzing information on the educational and occupational background of the fathers and of the sons, they were able to show that 37 percent of the men in white-collar jobs had a father who held a blue-collar job. Blau and Duncan also established that a person's own level of education has more influence on social mobility than does the father's occupation or education. A person's educational achievement is related to the social background of the family, of course, but Blau and Duncan found that a well-educated son of a working-class father has much the same chance of upward mobility as the poorly educated son of a middle-class father.

These findings do not mean that there is very little social mobility in the United States. In fact, there is a great deal. But most of this mobility involves relatively minor changes of status, not great leaps from lowly origins to lofty positions. The general pattern in American society is one of moderate upward mobility from one generation to the next.

Blau and Duncan suggest three reasons for this trend. First, the American economy has been expanding steadily throughout this century. As the proportion of white-collar occupations has increased, people from working-class origins have inevitably filled the new middle-class jobs. Second, the higher classes have lower birth rates than the lower classes. The higher classes thus fail to supply the personnel needed to fill new high-status jobs, so people lower down in the social hierarchy are able to move upward. Third, immigration of unskilled workers from other parts of the world and from rural areas within the United States has tended to push existing urban groups into higher occupational statuses. Social rather than individual factors thus account for much of the social mobility in the United States.

What makes one person more likely than another to achieve a higher status? A number of factors have been identified, several of them being characteristics over which individuals have little or no control. They include willingness to postpone marriage, willingness to defer immediate gratification in favor of long-term goals, residence in an urban rather than a rural area, high IQ, level of education, racial or ethnic background, childhood nutrition, physical appearance (especially among women), random factors such as chance introductions to future employers or partners, and, of course, class of origin (Blau and Duncan, 1967; Lipset and Bendix, 1959; J. S. Coleman, 1966; Porter, 1968; Hauser and Featherman, 1978; Jencks et al., 1979).

How does intergenerational mobility in the United States compare with that in other industrialized societies? In a classic study of this question, Seymour Martin Lipset and Reinhard Bendix (1959) compared rates of mobility from blue- to white-collar occupations in several industrial societies. They concluded that there was little difference among them. In the United States the mobility rate from blue- to white-collar occupations was about 34 percent, compared with 32 percent in Sweden, 31 percent in Great Britain, 29 percent in France, and 25 percent in West Germany and Japan. In this regard, at least, the United States does not seem to be a land of especially great opportunity.

There is one respect, however, in which mobility in the United States is higher than that in other industrial societies. Working-class Americans have a significantly greater chance of entering the professional elite than do members of the working class in other societies (S. M. Miller, 1960; Fox and Miller, 1965; Blau and Duncan, 1967). About 10 percent of Americans of working-class origins enter the professional elite, compared with about 7 percent in Japan and the Netherlands, less than 3 percent in Great Britain, less than 2 percent in Denmark, West Germany, and France, and less than 1 percent in Italy. Even so, a working-class American's chances of mobility into the highest strata of society are small.

There is only very limited truth, then, to the belief that this is a country of equal opportunity. The fact is that most people remain at or near the level of the families into which they were born and that many of the factors that determine social mobility are beyond personal control.

NOTES

1. **Ian Robertson,** *Sociology,* 2nd ed. (New York: Worth, 1981), pp. 259–268.

Twenty-one

MEMORY TECHNIQUES

Remembering information is a key to success in college. Developing the ability to remember is a process that takes patient practice and conscientious effort. The more you practice remembering and using memory techniques, the better memory becomes. Experts in memory training and those who teach college students to read and study effectively agree that certain procedures and techniques can enhance your ability to remember.

Here are several techniques for developing your memory and for remembering information for tests. Use these techniques in your remembering routine.

UNDERSTAND WHAT YOU WANT TO REMEMBER

Have you read the information completely and do you clearly understand the ideas? Clearly understand ideas before you try to remember them. Rote memorization, memorization without understanding, is the least effective form of memorization. Read information carefully from texts and rewrite the ideas in your own words in your notebook until you understand. In some cases it may be necessary to reread sections of your notes and the text. Actively listening, reading, and observing are a cinch to improve understanding.

Clarify difficult concepts by rereading the material, asking the professor to explain, or discussing it with classmates. Relate new ideas to information you have already learned or already know about the topic. It is not possible to remember something you do not understand or something you have not read.

MAKE A CONCERTED EFFORT TO REMEMBER

Good students who typically earn high test grades make a concentrated effort to remember the information they read and study. Unless you intend to remember what is learned, it will be forgotten quickly. Remembering requires a positive attitude and a positive mental set. When studying and when reading the textbook, concentrate on imbedding the information in your memory. The more interested you are in the information being studied and the more enthusiastic you are for remembering the information, the better your memory will develop.

Concentration is necessary for memory. Intending to remember and even forcing yourself to remember will have positive results—remembering becomes easier! Remembering does not "just happen."

ACTIVITY I

Listed below are typical barriers to concentration which have been suggested by college students like yourself. Examine each concentration barrier listed, discuss it in class, and write a useful technique or suggestion for overcoming the barrier to concentration. Expand your list of suggestions with ideas from your classmates.

Barrier to Concentration	Suggestion for Overcoming the Barrier
1. Unfamiliarity with the material to be learned and remembered.	
2. Falling asleep during study.	
3. Distractions while studying (noise, music, TV, friends).	
4. Not enough time to study.	
5. Textbook assignments are too long.	
6. Not interested in information to be studied.	
7. Procrastination and avoiding study.	

ORGANIZE INFORMATION TO BE MEMORIZED

Is the information to be remembered organized in a meaningful way to you?

1. Organize the information to be learned into rememberable units. Concentrating on the main ideas for a given set of information helps a great deal.
2. Attach details to the main ideas you have identified and be selective of the facts you need to learn. It is useless to learn unimportant information. Thinking in categories is most helpful. Often breaking a difficult concept into subideas will help with organization.

ACTIVITY II

Look at the terms at the top of p. 307. Have a classmate time you for one minute. Then write the terms (or as many as you remember) in the space following the terms. There are 22 terms. How many did you remember?

Celsius, spasm, catabolic reaction, I.Q., brewer, metallurgy, dial, G.N.P., conceptualizing, arousal, calorie, gastrointestinal specialist, time, steward, synaptic transmission, actuary, systolic pressure, C.E.O., counting, articulation, statistician, biting

_____

_____

_____

_____

_____

Now, carefully review the terms and clarify any that are not understood by you. Take a second timed minute to memorize the terms.
Cover all of the above and list the terms below:

_____

_____

_____

_____

_____

We have said that repetition, distributed practice, and organization of the information aid memorization. Each of the 22 terms fits into one of the following categories. Take a third timed minute to memorize the terms. This time, write the term in the correct category. Did you remember more terms?

Biological/Physiological Processes	Measurement	Job or Profession
_____	_____	_____
_____	_____	_____
_____	_____	_____
_____	_____	_____
_____	_____	_____
_____	_____	_____
_____	_____	_____
_____	_____	_____
_____	_____	_____

MNEMONIC DEVICES

Mnemonic devices are memory words that are effective for remembering specific information. They are important because they develop memory from merely a repetition level to an association level.

Mnemonic devices work like this. A word, phrase, jingle, or acronym is invented to aid in remembering information. Often the first letters of a series of ideas to be memorized are put in a meaningful order with the mnemonic device. For example, the names of the Great Lakes of North America can be remembered by the acronym H O M E S.

List the Great Lakes of North America:

H_____O_____M_____E_____S_____

Another example from science is ROY G. BIV. Roy G. Biv is not a famous scientist. Rather, these letters spell the first letters of the colors of the spectrum in order. List the colors:

R_____O_____Y_____G_____B_____I_____V_____

ACTIVITY III

The ten provinces and two territories of Canada are listed below. Make up your own mnemonic saying to help you remember them.

Northwest Territory	**Ontario**
Yukon Territory	**Quebec**
British Columbia	**Nova Scotia**
Alberta	**Newfoundland**
Saskatchewan	**Prince Edward Island**
Manitoba	**New Brunswick**

Mnemonic saying _____

_____

_____

_____

MEMORY TECHNIQUES—SUMMARY

Remembering what we read and study can be made easier if we consider some basic ideas that affect memory. Consider the following factors that affect memory of ideas usually found in college classes:

1. Clearly understand ideas before the ideas are to be remembered. Reading information carefully from texts and rewriting the ideas in your own words in your notebook are effective methods of completing this.
2. You have to make a concerted effort to remember. Unless you intend to remember what is learned, it will be forgotten. You must have a positive attitude and mental set.
3. Organize the information to be learned into remembered units. Usually concentrating on the main ideas for a given set of information helps a great deal.
4. Attach details to the main ideas and be selective of the facts you need to learn. It is useless to learn unimportant information. Picture ideas in your mind.

5. Clarify difficult concepts by rereading the material, asking the professor to explain it, or discussing it with classmates. Relate new ideas to information you have already learned.

6. Give yourself time to assimilate what is to be learned and set aside time to practice remembering the information. Repetition is necessary, so space your practice study. Test yourself on the information periodically.

7. Mnemonic devices (memory association techniques) are very helpful for remembering ideas. Consider these techniques:

   a. Make up a phrase or jingle to associate important ideas.
   b. Acronyms are words whose letters represent the first letters of words to be remembered. HOMES, for example, helps to identify the Great Lakes of North America.
   c. String or chain important ideas to each other.
   d. Connect words or ideas to a physical action or to parts of your body.
   e. Associate words or ideas with pictures or diagrams.

PROJECT

The following selection from a biology textbook discusses disorders of the respiratory system and alternative respiratory systems.

List the important respiratory disorders and their meanings. Organize a memory association device to memorize the disorder and the part of the respiratory system affected.

Next, memorize alternative respiratory systems, how they work, and the kinds of organisms that have the alternative respiratory system. You will find that a chart or diagram will help with memorizing this information.

Write your memory association device and your chart of alternate respiratory systems in your notebook. After you have written each, study them and have a classmate or the teacher quiz you.

If you increase the amount of time memorizing, or study several times, does your quiz score get better?

SOME DISORDERS OF THE RESPIRATORY SYSTEM[1]

Because the body has no organ that stores oxygen for a long time as the liver and fatty tissues do foods, anything that interferes with the proper functioning of the respiratory system could produce immediate and serious consequences.

Noncommunicable Disorders of the Respiratory System

Suffocation can result from choking on food, drowning, or any other event that prevents the flow of air to the lungs. Occasionally, the epiglottis may fail to cover the larynx during swallowing—as when one is frightened or otherwise surprised during eating. If a large enough piece of food blocks the larynx or trachea, air cannot enter the lungs, and one is in imminent danger of death by suffocation because a fresh supply of oxygen is no longer reaching the alveoli.

Drowning results from the inhalation of water into the lungs. Because water holds less oxygen than air does, insufficient oxygen reaches the lungs to support life. One of the first steps in first aid for a drowning victim is the removal of water from the lungs.

Drugs and poisons that inhibit the functioning of the nerves that stimulate the respiratory muscles may paralyze these muscles and so cause suffocation. The

Botulism is contracted primarily by consuming improperly canned (especially home-canned) beans and meats that contain *Clostridium botulinum*. This bacterium, which thrives in such cans, produces botulin.

toxin **botulin,** which is ingested in food, is a potent nerve poison and paralyzes many muscles of the body, but death usually results from the paralysis of respiratory muscles.

Hay fever and **asthma** are allergies to certain airborne particles, especially pollen. They cause the formation of mucus in the respiratory passageways. At the least this is annoying, but if excessive quantities form, it may interfere with breathing.

Industrial pollutants in the air and substances in cigarette smoke cause some forms of bronchitis, emphysema, and lung cancer. Persons who must work in dusty areas are likely to contract a respiratory disease associated with their particular industry (such as **black lung disease** of miners, **silicosis** of sandblasters, or **asbestosis** of those who work with asbestos).

Communicable Diseases of the Respiratory System

Communicable respiratory diseases are spread primarily through the air. Microorganisms are sneezed or coughed out of the sick person's respiratory system and are carried about by even the gentlest of breezes for quite some time before they settle to the ground. In the meantime they may be inhaled by another person. Many respiratory diseases ensure their transmission from person to person by causing coughing or sneezing. Because of the intercommunication of the digestive and respiratory systems at the pharynx, kissing or the sharing of eating utensils may spread some respiratory diseases.

Among the airborne diseases are tuberculosis, diphtheria, whooping cough, some forms of pneumonia and bronchitis, psittacosis, the common cold, septic sore throat, influenza, smallpox, chicken pox, measles, and mumps.

When **tuberculosis** bacteria (*Myobacterium tuberculosis*) enter the lungs, the body usually contains these bacteria by building a fibrous wall around them. This results in the formation of small tubercles in the lungs. In these tubercles the bacteria may remain alive but harmless for many years. Many persons have at least a few such tubercles without ever having had tuberculosis. If the tubercle walls should break down (or fail to form properly in the first place), the bacteria can multiply and spread throughout the lungs and cause more tubercles to form. As more and more lung tissue is damaged, the surface area through which oxygen is absorbed is reduced. In advanced cases, death may result.

The **diphtheria** bacteria (*Corynebacterium diphtheriae*) live in the respiratory system, but they produce a toxin that travels to other parts of the body in the bloodstream and causes most of the symptoms of the illness. However, the bacteria, together with some blood cells and dead tissue cells of the host, may form a membrane that extends across the trachea and suffocates the patient.

The different types of **pneumonia** have different causes, but they are characterized by the filling of the alveoli with body fluids or blood cells, thus interfering with the passage of oxygen into the blood capillaries. . . .

OTHER RESPIRATORY SYSTEMS

Very small animals have no need for a special respiratory system. Each cell is either at the surface of the animal or not very far from it. Therefore, exchange of gases with the environment occurs through the animal's surface only and it goes on rapidly enough to satisfy the needs of all the tissues.

The need for a respiratory system depends in part on the size of the animal (generally the larger the animal, the greater the need), and in part on other things. For instance, a very small insect living in a dry environment probably is protected from desiccation by an external skeleton that also prevents the absorption of much oxygen through the body surface. Therefore, that animal needs some special, internal respiratory surface that can be kept moist and permeable to oxygen, whereas an aquatic animal of the same size might need no special respiratory surface. The more active an animal is, the more likely it is to need a respiratory system.

Hydra, with its large gastrovascular cavity . . . , is bathed inside and out with the water with which it exchanges gases. A variety of small worms—flatworms, roundworms, and others—have no respiratory systems. Even earthworms, which are larger than most other worms, have no special respiratory systems, but exchange gases with the environment through their body walls.

Earthworms, however, do illustrate a problem that terrestrial animals have with respiration. Air holds more oxygen than water does, and the respiratory surface that absorbs oxygen from air must be exposed to it. Yet the cells that absorb the oxygen must, like other active cells, remain moist to stay alive and functioning. Therefore, respiratory surfaces of terrestrial animals must be exposed to the air yet not be permitted to dry out. Earthworms usually maintain a good balance by staying underground at a depth where the moisture in the soil keeps them damp and the air spaces keep them well supplied with oxygen. When the ground becomes flooded after a heavy rain and the air spaces fill with water, earthworms come to the surface, where, for a while at least, the damp air is suitable. When the rain stops and the air becomes dry, earthworms return to their underground burrows. Any laggards caught unawares on a sidewalk soon dry up. (Sunlight is also damaging to earthworms.)

As an adaptation to terrestrial life, most land animals with respiratory systems have **lungs,** which are pouches extending into the body. The lungs have relatively small openings to the outside. This helps to maintain a high relative humidity inside the lung, so the air at the respiratory surfaces remains moist. Any water lost by diffusion and evaporation through the openings ordinarily can be replaced easily by drinking water.

Aquatic animals with respiratory systems generally have **gills,** which are outgrowths from the body. Because the gills are always bathed in water, there is no problem of drying out as long as the animal stays in its own environment. The few terrestrial animals with gills—some salamanders, for instance—keep to cool, shady, damp places. The few aquatic animals with lungs—such as whales, dolphins, and seals—come to the surface frequently and breathe air.

Some gills are rather simple. Nudibranchs (sea slugs) have gills that look like not much more than fingerlike extensions from their backs (Fig. E32-1.1). They do increase the surface area of the animal, but as gills go, they do not increase it very much. Some gills are very finely divided and look like small, delicate feathers; these greatly increase the respiratory surface of the animal. The feather-duster worms are related to the common earthworm but are marine animals.

Fishes, which are generally quite active animals and require a good deal of oxygen, have a series of finely divided gills crowded into gill chambers between the pharynx and openings on either side of the fish (Fig. E32-1.2). In bony fishes the opening is protected by a covering called an operculum. Fishes often give the appearance of drinking water, but they rarely swallow it. Instead, they direct the water that they take into their mouths into the pharynx and then past the gills and out of the opercular openings. This forces fresh water relatively rich in oxygen past the gills. The gills themselves are finely divided and so present a great deal of surface area to the water. Blood vessels with numerous fine capillaries ramify through the gill tissue. The blood in the capillaries receives oxygen and releases carbon dioxide to the water.

The respiratory system of a grasshopper and that of most other insects consists of a series of tubes called **tracheae** (which may be considered a type of lung). The tracheae open to the outside **spiracles** (grasshoppers have 10 spiracles on each side). Tubes running longitudinally in the animal connect the spiracles

Fig. E32–1.1

Two aquatic animals with gills that increase their respiratory surface area. The gills of the nudibranch contain portions of the digestive system and so also have a digestive function. The gills of the feather-duster worm serve as tentacles as well as respiratory organs. The feather-duster worm can draw its delicate gill tentacles into its tube in times of danger.

Gills

Nudibranch
Hermisenda crassicornis

Gills

Tube

Feather-dust worm

Fig. E32–1.2

Gills of a fish are finely divided into gill filaments that provide a great deal of surface area through which oxygen is absorbed from the water. Blood capillaries run through the gill filaments. The gill rakers filter out particles that might otherwise clog the gills.

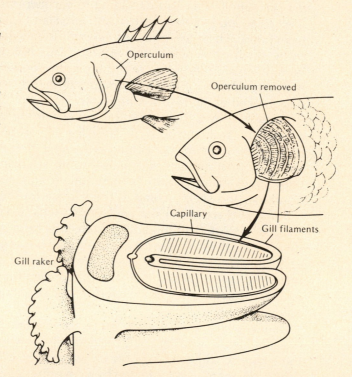

Operculum

Operculum removed

Capillary

Gill filaments

Gill raker

and make them part of one intercommunicating system (Fig. E32-1.3). The tracheae branch repeatedly within the grasshopper. Some dead-end branches are enlarged into **air sacs.** Other fine endings are **tracheoles.**

Tracheoles are filled with fluid, and they abut on active tissues—muscles, for example. Oxygen from the air dissolves in the fluid within the tracheoles and from there moves into the neighboring tissues. Waste carbon dioxide moves in the opposite direction. The fluid-filled tracheoles thus function much like the capillaries of the circulatory system in human beings and many other animals (grasshoppers have no capillaries).

Fig. E32–1.3
(a) Grasshopper respiratory system. (b) The fluid-filled tracheoles exchange gases between the air and muscle cells.

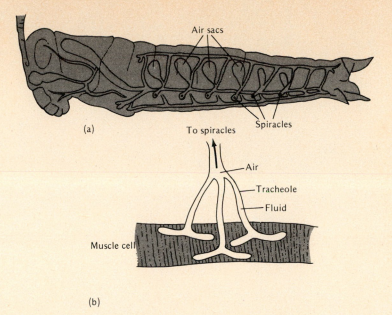

Mere diffusion of gases along the passageways of the tracheae would be too slow for the needs of so active an animal as a grasshopper. Action of muscles alternately constricting and relaxing causes air to be pumped into and out of the tracheae. The more active the animal, the more air is forced through the tracheae. In the grasshopper, the four pairs of spiracles nearest the anterior end of the animal are open while the posterior six pairs are closed and vice versa. This, combined with the action of muscles, allows for one-way movement of air along the major passageways, thus ensuring that fresh air replaces stale air.

NOTES

1. **Joan Elma Rahn,** *Biology,* 2nd ed. (New York: Macmillan, 1980), pp. 416–421.

Twenty-two

AIDS TO READING IN THE LIBRARY

Your library contains many useful reference and research aids. Among these are aids that will help you as you read and study for your courses. The most useful reading and study guides index or summarize information contained in periodicals (magazines), books, and newspapers.

In this chapter we will introduce you to four of the most often used aids:

The Reader's Guide to Periodical Literature
Book Review Digest
Psychological Abstracts
The New York Times Index

This chapter will also list other aids with the same format as those mentioned above. Your librarian will be happy to help you locate these aids in the library.

Most libraries have information stored on microfilm or microfiche. Speak with the librarian to find out what is available in your library. You must use microfilm or microfiche readers to look at this information. Someone in your library will be happy to show you how to operate these machines.

THE READER'S GUIDE TO PERIODICAL LITERATURE

This guide is an alphabetical author and subject index to a wide range of magazines published in the United States. All articles related to a subject or written by an author are indexed under that heading. Each month, the *Reader's Guide* gives a complete index to all the articles published in about 200 magazines. An annual guide is issued at the end of each year. The *Reader's Guide* is probably the best starting source for any reading research assignment.

Examples of the two types of entries found in the *Reader's Guide* are given below. Each entry is followed by a brief statement interpreting the entry.

CAPITAL INVESTMENTS

How to regain our competitive edge. W. Bowen il. Fortune 103:74–8 + March 9, 1981

Under the general heading of CAPITAL INVESTMENTS we see that an illustrated article by W. Bowen titled "How to Regain Our Competitive Edge" appears on pages 74–78 and other pages of the March 9, 1981, edition of *Fortune* magazine.

CARETTO, Ennio
 Renaissance in New York. Il. World press R 28:45 February, 1981

Under the author listing of Ennio CARETTO, we see that he wrote an illustrated article titled "Renaissance in New York," which appears on page 45 of the February, 1981, edition of the *World Press Review*.

Other readers guides with a similar format include:

Business Periodicals Index
Education Index
Social Sciences Index

Refer to these guides for specialized information in the appropriate fields.

ACTIVITY I

Write a brief statement interpreting each entry shown below. You may encounter unfamiliar abbreviations. The abbreviations are explained in each index or guide.

Business Periodicals Index:

DISTRIBUTORS
 Alabama jobber learns about decontrol the hard way NPN 73:105 Mr 81

_____

_____

_____

OIL spills
 AIA: restructuring parts of federal proposals needed. Nat Underw (Prop ed) 85:4+ Mr 20 '81

_____

_____

_____

Social Sciences Index:

Herring, Richard J., and Marston, Richard C.
 On the feasibility of sterilization by more than one country J Pol Econ 88:194–8 F'80

_____

_____

_____

Hindu symbolism
 Female lingarrr. interchangeable symbols and paradoxical associations of Hindu gods and goddesses (with discussion) G. E. Ferro-Luzzi. bibl il Cur Anthrop 21 45–68 F'80

_____

_____

_____

Reader's Guide to Periodical Literature:

> **HOUSTON, University, Houston Tex College of Education**
> **National Teacher Examination: can it predict classroom performance?** [study of preservice teachers] M. K. Piper and P. S. O'Sullivan. Phi Delta Kappan 62:401 Ja '81

_____

_____

_____

> **HOWARD, Michael**
> **Return to the cold war?** For Aff 59:459–73 Sp Issue '81

_____

_____

_____

THE BOOK REVIEW DIGEST

The Book Review Digest summarizes and cites reviews of current fiction and nonfiction books published in the United States and Canada. Government pamphlets, textbooks, and books with an exclusively technical audience are not included. A book must be reviewed several times before it is included.

The *Book Review Digest* has a subject and title index in the rear of each issue. The main body of the digest contains the book summaries and reviews alphabetically by author. If you know the author of a book, refer directly to the body of the *Digest*. If you know the title, or if you are looking for a book on a particular subject, refer to the index.

The *Book Review Digest* is the place to go to decide which book to read for an assignment or to get a summary and reviews of a known book.

ACTIVITY II

A sample entry from the *Digest* is shown below.

_____

> POST, ELIZABETH. The complete book of entertaining from the Emily Post Institute (by) Elizabeth Post, (and) Anthony Stattieri; il. by Lori L. Lambert, 381p $14.95 1981 Harper & Row
> > 642 Entertaining
> > ISBN 0-690-01970-X   LC 80-7879

> This guide to entertaining provides information "on menu planning, party equipment, table settings, decorations, invitations, temporary help, and entertainment. Working count-down timetables are included to help in planning an event from three weeks in advance to party day. Suggestions for seasonal parties, with suitable recipes, are given—New Year's Day Brunch, July 4th Clambake, Labor Day Luau, BYO Halloween Party, Pre-Christmas Open

House, etc.—along with ideas for children's parties. Appendixes contain lists of calendar holidays, freezer tips, herb and spice charts, wine cookery table, ethnic toasts, stain removal charts, and (a) source manual." (Library J) Bibliography. Index.

———

"This manual is for the hostess who takes her entertaining seriously, is willing to spend both time and money, and has the self-discipline to follow the carefully detailed instructions set forth. The authors are well qualified. Elizabeth Post being director of the Emily Post Institute and Stattieri formerly having been East Coast party consultant for one of the world's largest party and catering equipment rental agencies. . . . A Source Manual and Bibliography lists and briefly annotates organizations, books, and pamphlets on related subjects from audio equipment to wines and spirits, with cookbooks, music, and napkin folding in between. Adequately indexed, it admirably supplements The New Emily Post's Etiquette, also by Elizabeth Post, which it frankly duplicates—in part but with emphasis on parties."
Booklist 78:401 N 1 '81 220w
Reviewed by M. A. Wasick
Library J 106:660 Mr 15 '81 110w

Write a brief interpretation of this entry.

_____

_____

_____

_____

_____

_____

_____

_____

_____

_____

PSYCHOLOGICAL ABSTRACTS

Psychological Abstracts contains summaries of worldwide publications in psychology and related disciplines. The abstract includes journal articles, books, chapters of books, and instructional materials.

Each issue has a subject index and an author index in the rear. Each index entry is followed by a number or numbers, which will guide you to the summaries in the main body of the abstract.

The summaries in the main body of the abstract are divided into sixteen categories. These categories are shown in the table of contents found at the front. Within each category, summaries are listed alphabetically by author.

Biological Abstracts and other abstracts that you will find in the library follow essentially the same format as the _Psychological Abstracts_.

ACTIVITY III

An entry from _Psychological Abstracts_ is shown at the top of p. 319.

6744. Vacc. Nicholas A. & Greenleaf, Susan M. (U North Carolina, School of Education, Greensboro) Relaxation training and covert positive reinforcement with elementary school children. *Elementary School Guidance & Counseling*, 1980 (Feb), Vol 14(3), 232-235.— Investigated the effects of deep muscle relaxation (DMR) and covert positive reinforcement (CPR) on maladaptive behavior in the elementary school. 28 emotionally handicapped children, aged 6–12 yrs, were ramdomly selected from among 60 enrollees attending special classes for the behaviorally disturbed. Ss were assigned to 1 of 4 experimental groups: (a) DMR training, (b) DMR training supplemented by CPR, (c) placebo (unrelated unsupervised activities), or (d) no treatment. Groups (a) and (b) received half an hour of training twice a week for 4 wks. Pretest, posttest, and follow-up scores on the Behavior Rating Scale and Taylor Manifest Anxiety Scale were analyzed by 1-way analyses of covariance. Although both treatment groups showed more improvement on these measures than did the 2 control groups, the differences were not significant. Further study of DMR and CPR techniques is warranted. (10 ref.)—*C. B. Barad.*

Write a brief interpretation of this entry.

_____

_____

_____

_____

_____

_____

_____

_____

_____

_____

_____

THE NEW YORK TIMES INDEX

The New York Times Index is a guide to all news stories carried in *The New York Times* from 1851 to present. The index presents subject headings alphabetically for the time period covered by the index. Each entry under a heading summarizes a new story related to the heading.

Each entry is followed by the date, page, and column where the news story can be located in *The New York Times*. For example, Jl 16, 2:3 indicates that the story appeared on July 16, page 2, column 3. Roman numerals identify sections of the Sunday *New York Times*. Thus, F 13, IV, 39:5 indicates that the story appeared on February 13 in section IV, page 39, column 5.

Once you have located a story or stories of interest, you should find them in *The New York Times* or in the microfilm copy of *The New York Times*.

The Wall Street Journal Index can be used in much the same way as *The New York Times Index*. The *Journal* index focuses on business-related stories. The entries in *The Wall Street Journal Index* are coded as follows: 2/4—8:1, which indicates that the story appeared on February 4 on page 8, column 1.

PROJECTS

Go to the library to complete these projects. The librarian will be pleased to help you find the reference books you are looking for.

1. Use the 1980 edition of *The Book Review Digest*. List the authors and titles of the four books about shipwrecks.

   _____

   _____

   _____

   Which book is about the *Andrea Doria*?

   _____

2. Use the July 1980 issue of *Psychological Abstracts*. List the authors and titles for each of the four entries about minority groups.

   _____

   _____

   _____

   Which of the four explores vagabondage?

   _____

3. Use the 1981 *New York Times Index*. List the date, page, and column for a story about Libya lowering its crude oil price to $39.90.

   _____

   Bring a copy of the story to class.
4. Use the 1980 *Wall Street Journal Index*. List the date, page, and column of a story which describes a $700 rebate offered by Fiat.

   _____

   _____

Index

A

Abbreviations
   and note taking, 185, 190
Analytical approach, 61
Arithmetic skills test, 196–197
Attention. *See* concentration

B

Book Review Digest, 315, 317

C

Calendars
   semester, 287, 294
   weekly, 287, 295
Cards for recording science terms, 205
Comprehension of textbooks, 164–165
Concentration
   barriers to, 306
   and listening, 272
   and memory, 305
   and reading, 133–134
Conclusions
   in deductive reasoning, 253–254
   in inductive reasoning, 259
Context clues, 1

D

Deductive reasoning
   forms of valid reasoning, 254
   true and false conclusions, 253–254
   valid and invalid conclusions,
      253–254
   see invalid deductive reasoning
Details, 87
   main idea and, 71
   clues to find, 87–88
   numbering and, 87
   punctuation and, 88
   qualifiers, 87
   in studying history, 219
   in studying science, 206

Dictionary use, 7
Distractions. *See* concentration

E

Examinations, 287–293
   essay questions and answers,
      290–293
   fill in blank, 290
   matching, 290
   memorizing for, 305–309
   multiple choice, 289
   preparing for, 287–289
   question types, 289–292
   short answer, 289–290
   studying for, 287–288
   taking, 289–295
   true-false, 289
   understanding questions, 292
Eye movements, 135

F

Fallacious inductive arguments
   band wagon, 260
   begging the question, 260
   false analogy, 260
   guilt by association, 261
   hasty generalization, 260
   stereotyping, 260
   straw man, 261
   you too, 261
Figurative language, 237
   comparisons and, 237
   definition of, 237
   examples of, 237, 238
Fixations, 135
Flexible reading rates, 107–109,
      134–135

G

Glossary, 163
Graphic aids
   previewing, 17–18

Graphic aids (continued)
 reading, 164, 169
 in science, 205–206

H

Headings
 and previewing, 17, 18
 and textbook study, 164, 168
Highlighting, 165, 185
History, reading, 219–220
 facts, 219
 time line
  example, 220
  making, 219–220
  using, 220
Hyperbole
 definition of, 238
 examples of, 238

I

Indexes
 to periodicals, 315–319
 in textbooks, 163
Inductive reasoning
 description, 259
 examples, 259
 in statistics, 259
 see falacious inductive arguments
Invalid deductive reasoning
 non sequitur, 255
 unreasonable premise, 255
 using the converse, 255
 using the inverse, 255

K

Key word
 and important modifiers, 51–52
 outlines, 185–186
 and sentences, 51

L

Lecture notes
 listening and, 272
 organizing notebooks, 271
Library reading aids
 Book Review Digest, 315, 317
 Business Periodicals Index, 316
 Education Index, 316–317
 New York Times Index, 315, 319
 Psychological Abstracts, 315, 318
 Reader's Guide to Periodical Literature, 315, 317
 Social Sciences Index, 316
Linking words, 53

Listening efficiently, 272
Literal meaning, 237

M

Main idea,
 definition of, 71
 details and, 71
 listening for, 271
 marking in textbooks, 186
 reading for, 133
 stated, 71
 in studying history, 219
 in studying science, 206
 topic sentence and, 71–72
 topic and, 71
 unstated, 72
Marking textbooks
 in science, 205–206
 in text note-taking techniques, 185–186
Mathematics, reading, 195–202
 arithmetic, 196
 equations, how to read, 199–200
 mathematical symbols, 195
 using a calculator, 197
Memory
 techniques for remembering, 305–309
  acronyms, 308
  mnemonic devices, 307–308
  repetition, 309
  summary of, 308–309
Metaphor, 237
 definition of, 237
 examples of, 237
Mnemonics, 307–308

N

New York Times Index, 315, 319
Note taking
 examples of, 186–187, 271, 277
 from lectures, 271–278
 and listening, 272
 marginal notes, 185
 organization of, 271
 and rambling lecturers, 271, 274
 suggestions for, 271, 274–275
 in textbook, 185–186
Note taking and textbook reading, 185–186, 190
Numbering. *See* Details

O

Organization
 and memory, 306
 of notes, 271
 of study time, 287

Outlines
  and essay answers, 290—293
  key word, 185, 190
  in studying science, 207—208

P

Paragraph, 61
  definition of, 61
  details in, 71
  development pattern and, 95
  elements of, 61
  purpose of, 95
  structure of, 95
  See also Paragraphs, patterns and development of, *and* Paragraph, types of
Paragraph, types of
  descriptive, 96
  expository, 96
  integrated, 98
  narrative, 95
  persuasive, 97
Paragraphs, patterns and development of
  cause and effect, 99
  comparison and contrast, 98
  definition, 100
  illustration and example, 100
Personification, 237
  definition of, 237
  examples of, 237, 238
PQRST, 163—165
PQ4R, 163—165
Prefixes, 6
Premises
  in deductive reasoning, 253—254
  major and minor, 254
Previewing
  chapter in a textbook, 17
  definition of, 17
  essay, 22
  importance of, 17
  novel and short story, 25
  play, 26
  poem, 26
  in reading rapidly, 133
  in studying history, 219
  in studying science, 206
  and textbook study, 164
  Print aids
    boldface, 133
    italics, 133
    marginal summaries, 133
  Propaganda
    definition, 265
    examples of, 265
    steps to follow when reading for, 265—266
    susceptibility to, 265

Psychological abstracts, 315, 318
Punctuation, 88

Q

Qualifiers, 87
Questions
  and prereading, 164—165
  and previewing, 17, 21, 25, 27
  See also examinations

R

Reader's Guide to Periodical Literature, 315, 317
Reading
  graphs, charts, tables, 133, 164
  problems with, 136
  rates, 134, 137, 141
  and understanding, 164—165
Remembering. *See* Memory

S

Scanning, 109
  definition of, 107
  effective, 109
Science, reading, 205—208
  charts and diagrams, 205—206
  steps to follow, 206—207
  symbols, 206
  terms, 205—206
Sentence meaning, 51
  key words and, 51—52
  linking words and, 53
  modifiers and, 51—52
  paragraphs and, 51
  relation of subject to, 52
  relation of verb complement to, 52
  thought patterns and, 53
Simile,
  definition of, 237
  examples of, 237
Skimming and reading rapidly
  definition of, 107
  different paragraph types and, 107
Speed reading, 133—134
SQ3R, 163—165
Stated main idea. *See* Main idea
Studying, 287—288
  See also Concentration
Suffixes, 6—7

T

Table of contents, 163
Tests
  See Examinations

Textbook
  marking, 185
  note-taking techniques in, 185–186
  parts of, 163–164
  print aids, 3, 164
  reading rapidly, 133–134, 136
  studying techniques for, 164–165
  understanding, 164–165
Time line
  in studying history, 219–220
Time, scheduling for exams, 287–289
Topic, 61
  analysis of, 62
  definition of, 61, 71
  general, 61
  precise, 61
  specific, 61
  in studying history, 219
  in studying science, 206

Topic sentence. *See* Main idea
Transitional words, 96

U

Unstated main idea. *See* main idea

V

Vocabulary
  and context clues, 1
  and prefixes, 6
  and suffixes, 6–7

W

Word problems. *See* Mathematics